How Close Reading Made Us

How Close Reading Made Us
The Transnational Legacies of New Criticism

Yael Segalovitz

Cover Credit: Rebecca Sevinir, *With In*, 2023.

Published by State University of New York Press, Albany

© 2024 State University of New York

All rights reserved

Printed in the United States of America

No part of this book may be used or reproduced in any manner whatsoever without written permission. No part of this book may be stored in a retrieval system or transmitted in any form or by any means including electronic, electrostatic, magnetic tape, mechanical, photocopying, recording, or otherwise without the prior written permission in writing of the publisher.

Links to third-party websites are provided as a convenience and for informational purposes only. They do not constitute an endorsement or an approval of any of the products, services, or opinions of the organization, companies, or individuals. SUNY Press bears no responsibility for the accuracy, legality, or content of a URL, the external website, or for that of subsequent websites.

For information, contact State University of New York Press, Albany, NY
www.sunypress.edu

Library of Congress Cataloging-in-Publication Data

Name: Segalovitz, Yael, author.
Title: How close reading made us : the transnational legacies of new criticism / Yael Segalovitz.
Description: Albany : State University of New York Press, [2024]. | Includes bibliographical references and index.
Identifiers: LCCN 2023055172 | ISBN 9781438498690 (hardcover : alk. paper) | ISBN 9781438498706 (ebook) | ISBN 9781438498713 (pbk. : alk. paper)
Subjects: LCSH: New Criticism—Influence. | New Criticism—Case studies. | American literature—History and criticism. | Brazilian literature—History and criticism. | Israeli literature—History and criticism. | LCGFT: Literary criticism.
Classification: LCC PN98.N4 S44 2024 | DDC 801/.95—dc23/eng/20240227
LC record available at https://lccn.loc.gov/2023055172

To my parents, Lily and Alex,
who have taught me to listen to the living and to the dead

For though reading seems so simple—a mere matter of knowing the alphabet—it is indeed so difficult that it is doubtful whether anyone knows anything about it.

—Virginia Woolf

Contents

ACKNOWLEDGMENTS — ix

INTRODUCTION
Attention as Unselfing: A Comparative Perspective on
New Critical Close Reading — 1

Part I: The US: The Haunted Reader

CHAPTER ONE
Self-Deadening: Cleanth Brooks and the Living-Dead Reader
of New Critical Theory — 27

CHAPTER TWO
"I Wrote This Book and Learned to Read": Sound, Fury,
and William Faulkner's Negative Audition — 55

Part II: Brazil: The Unsavaged Reader

CHAPTER THREE
Unsavaging: Afrânio Coutinho's *Nova Crítica* and the
Problem of the Brazilian Exact Reader — 85

CHAPTER FOUR
Exact and Exhausted Reading: Clarice Lispector and
Catching the Apple in the Dark — 123

Part III: Israel: The Unlocalized Reader

CHAPTER FIVE
Unlocalizing: The Tel Aviv School and the Israeli Crisis of Social Disintegration   153

CHAPTER SIX
Maximalist Reading Gone Wild: Yehuda Amichai and Creative Unintegration   193

EPILOGUE
New Critical Studies   221

NOTES   229

BIBLIOGRAPHY   275

INDEX   297

Acknowledgments

This book, though signed under one name, is the culmination of a collective effort and an ongoing dialogue. This conversation commenced at Tel Aviv University (TAU), where I earned my BA and MA, evolved throughout my formative graduate years at the University of California, Berkeley (UCB), and continues to flourish in my current position at Ben Gurion University of the Negev (BGU). My acknowledgments serve as a token of gratitude to all those who not only contributed to this project through their dedicated and often uncompensated efforts but also encouraged me to push against the boundaries of my own thought.

At the Department of Literature at TAU, I have had the privilege of working under the nurturing mentorship of Iris Milner and Michael Gluzman, whose keen critical insights have been a guiding force throughout this journey. Also pertinent to this research were the teachings of Michal Ben-Naftali, who ushered me into the intricacies of Derrida's thinking with great generosity.

This study has drawn much of its inspiration from the vibrant academic environment of the Department of Comparative Literature at Berkeley, and from Bay Area life more generally. Chana Kronfeld has consistently propelled my ideas forward, providing meticulous readings and tenderly cultivating my intellectual self-confidence. Dorothy J. Hale's persistent and imaginative engagement with my work has left an indelible mark on my thinking; I carry her voice with me as a constant source of inspiration. Judith Butler, a longtime intellectual beacon, also proved to be an empathetic adviser and a compassionate teacher during intimate discussions and seminars. Marília Librandi welcomed me into the world of Brazilian letters, a realm I once observed from a distance and now feel deeply connected to, thanks to her kindness. I also owe a deep gratitude to other scholars at Berkeley: Robert Alter, who guided me through challenges in and outside translation; Miryam Sas, for whom I wrote my first paper on attention; and Candace Slater, whose seminars left a lasting impact.

Upon joining the Department of Foreign Literatures and Linguistics at BGU, I found an intellectually stimulating home among brilliant colleagues and students who have steered this project in exciting new directions. Among the many who have contributed significantly, I offer special heartfelt thanks to Eitan Bar-Yosef, Yael Ben-zvi, and Zohar Weiman-Kelman, whose guidance has ranged from patient listening to helping navigate the obstacles of publication.

Various others have aided in bringing this project to life. The Helen Diller Family Fund in Jewish and Israel Studies, the Regents Intern Fellowship, and the Irving and Helen Betz Foundation Fellowship granted me the peace of mind necessary for intense academic work. The Center for Jewish Studies at Berkeley, the Townsend Center for the Humanities Dissertation Fellowship, and the Posen Doctoral Fellowship assisted me throughout my research.

At the State University of New York Press (SUNY), I have found a true companion in Rebecca Colesworthy, whose unwavering support, patience, and astute guidance were indispensable for the making of this book. More generally, I thank the dedicated team at SUNY Press, whose collective efforts have brought this project to fruition. I would also like to acknowledge the valuable feedback provided by Laura Heffernan and Adriana X. Jacobs during the revision process. Their observations revealed growth opportunities that I was no longer able to see after numerous readings.

I would also like to thank Schocken Publishing House and Hana Sokolov-Amichai for their collaboration and permission to incorporate Yehuda Amichai's poignant poems into this work. With their consent, the following poems by Amichai are included:

- "אבי" ("Avi"), from *Poems 1948–1962*, 1977, Schocken Publishing House.

- "גשם בשדה קרב" ("Geshem bi-sde krav"), from *Poems 1948–1962*, 1977, Schocken Publishing House.

This project also greatly benefited from the thorough reviews and encouragement I received from venues that previously published sections of this work. Chapter 1, in an earlier version, appeared in *Arizona Quarterly* 75, no. 1 (2019): 49–83 as "William Faulkner, Cleanth Brooks, and the Living-Dead Reader of New Critical Theory" (© 2019 Arizona Board of Regents, University of Arizona) and chapter 2 was originally published in *MFS Modern Fiction Studies* 69, no. 3 (Fall 2023): 417–43 as "The Music of the Prose Takes Place in Silence: Sound, Fury, and Faulkner's Negative Audition" (© 2023 Purdue Research Foundation by Johns Hopkins University Press).

In addition, I extend my sincere appreciation to Rebecca Sevinir for generously contributing her talents to creating the book's remarkable cover art. I was both moved and struck by her ability to visually articulate the full complexity of this project.

A special thanks goes to Eden Ashkenazi and Sagi Felendler, my exceptional research assistants, who treated every word in this book with profound care and (unselfing?) attention. In addition, I could not have accomplished this book without Kali Handelman, my developmental editor, who supported me from shaping initial ideas to enhancing the overarching narrative with her unique calm and compassion.

And what would I have done without my extraordinary friends and colleagues who relentlessly lifted my spirits and offered intellectual and emotional support during this book's long writing process? I express my deepest appreciation to Shir Alon, Nana Ariel, Ron Ben-Tovim, Ashley Brock, Alex Brostoff, Krista Brune, Alex Catchings, Katrina Dodson, Nimrod Dori, Ayelet Even-Nur, Sheer Ganor, Iris Idelson-Shein, Marianne Kaletzky, Danny Luzon, Anneleen Masschelein, Ramsey McGlazer, Jamille Pinheiro Dias, Naomi Seidman, Gilad Sharvit, Simone Stirner, Monica VanBladel, Cindy A. Weinstein, Sarah Weinstein, and Rosetta Young. Taylor Johnston-Levy and Eyal Bassan hold a truly unique place in this Acknowledgments. They have been with me from the inception of this work to its completion, providing care, rereading revisions, and offering both humor and an embrace when needed.

Finally, this book owes its very existence to my beloved parents, Lily and Alexander, and to my dauntless big brothers, Yair and Erez, who have placed their faith in my unconventional intellectual journey. And, above all, the deepest and most profound thanks go to my very own Noam, Eitan, Doron, and Yiftach; without them I would have simply been lost.

Introduction

Attention as Unselfing:
A Comparative Perspective on New Critical Close Reading

> I must confess that I am much more interested in problems about techniques of the self and things like that rather than sex . . . [and in] the role of reading and writing in constituting the self.
>
> —Michel Foucault

Close reading refuses to disappear. It has withstood countless attempts to declare it obsolete, irrelevant, and even harmful; nothing about it remains uncontested from its place and time of inception through its practical instructions to its political agenda. This book explains close reading's endurance by exploring its function as a technique of the self that makes its own practitioners, namely, *us*. By following the transnational distribution of the New Criticism, *How Close Reading Makes Us* portrays this foundational practice as producing attentive subjects through a self-inflicted process I term *unselfing*.

However, in contrast with the expectations I frequently encounter in presenting this project, this book is neither a defense of the New Criticism against well-known objections to its ostensibly conservatist ideology and ahistorical thinking, nor a rejection of the New Critical theory and its accompanying practice in order to unseat them from their still central position in the discipline of literature and in the humanities writ large. Instead, the book sketches an intellectual and literary history that proves to be much too disorderly, intricate, and variegated to fit any stable value-laden binary. As Edward Said observed in his conceptualizations of "traveling theory," "what we also need . . . is the critical recognition that there is no theory capable of covering, closing off, predicting all the situations in which it might be useful."[1] That is, as theories, ideas, and praxes of reading move from person to person, from place to place, from situation to situation, and from one language or period to another, they acquire different political valences, become immersed in specific local and contemporaneous cultural debates, and are leveraged for various agendas; they shift, turn, and mutate away from any model of "one" theory or practice to be judged as wholesale "good" or "bad." In this regard, I hope to intervene through this book in the current debate dubbed "the method wars," which centers on close reading, and which, as critics like David Kurnick point out, frequently tends toward binary thinking (close vs. distant reading, critique vs. postcritique, paranoid vs. reparative reading) in an attempt to veer the discussion into a different direction.[2]

Instead, I want to follow the unexpected journeys of close reading away from the anglophone center. Through these travels, I aim to expose this method's internal contradictions and surprising potentialities, its acquisition of politically and culturally charged local meanings and uses, and to demonstrate this practice's deep interaction with the transnational modernist production of its time. In this context, close reading appears not only as designed to fit modernist aesthetics, as has been previously and convincingly shown, but as a method that instigated modernists to respond in their writing to the imperative to close read in its local iterations, as well as a practice whose implicit theory of the reader's subjectivity relied on modernist depictions of reading scenes and underlying instructions on how to read.

The method of and theory behind close reading was first developed in mid-century North America but has its roots at Cambridge University of the 1920s UK. The American scholars who later adopted the title "New Critics" started working together in the Southern United States, at Vanderbilt University in Tennessee. There, they set out to develop a theory of literature and an accompanying formalist method of reading that would involve acute concentration and patience, as an explicit reaction against what they took to be the destruction of culture taking place in the North as a consequence of expediated processes of industrialization. The mode of reading they advanced—namely, close reading—was then canonized up north at Yale (where several of these scholars later found positions) and went on to become the central method of engagement with literature that reigned over the North American scene until the 1970s. Although the theory behind this reading mode has long since been declared "dead," close reading remains the prevailing operative method taught in a majority of undergraduate courses on critical reading and writing in the US and abroad, while also setting the tone for most MFA programs.[3]

Attesting to its persistent centrality is the intense scholarly interest sparked by the New Critical practice in the last two decades. First, as I noted, there has been an attempt to replace it with alternative modes of reading, such as "distant reading," "surface reading," "reparative reading," and "descriptive reading."[4] Second, we have witnessed a New Formalist rethinking of the method as a contemporary response to emerging digital tendencies in the humanities.[5] Third, there have been much-needed endeavors to revisit the history and pedagogy of the New Criticism, as seen in works by Joshua Gang, Joseph North, Helen Thaventhiran, Rachel Sagner Buurma, Laura Heffernan, and Andy Hines.[6] However, what I find sorely missing from contemporary attempts to examine what it is that we do when we close read is precisely what I hope to bring to the table: a transnational, decentralizing perspective. By and large, these interventions take as their basic assumption that the New Criticism with its method of close reading was strictly an Anglo-American phenomenon. This is so much the case that while scholars of close reading ardently debate the affinity (or lack thereof) between the British predecessors of the New Criticism and the school's American members, they rarely ask what occurred beyond the anglophone orbit. In truth, the New Criticism had a wide transnational circulation. This global history has been recently recognized in Peter Button's, David M. Stewart's and Paul Nadal's important essays on the New Criticism in China, Taiwan, and the Philippines, respectively, but a comparative exploration of close reading's international metamorphoses remains outstanding.[7]

This book follows the New Criticism as it travels to Brazil and Israel. This journey testifies to the active role the so-called periphery of world literature played in originally and unexpectedly modifying the never-singular American "source" in accordance with the local languages, geographies, traditions of interpretation, and sociopolitical realities. This is in line with Marta Puxan-Oliva and Annalisa Mirizio's call to "consider contexts in World Literature Studies as places from where we think critically, rather than places that participate in World Literature from an auto-ethnographic standpoint."[8] And indeed, "thinking critically" about the New Criticism through its reception in Brazil and Israel radically challenges ossified assumptions about the North American version of close reading that have been taken for granted for almost a century.

Brazil and Israel are in no way a random sample: the role the New Criticism played in the Brazilian and Israeli intellectual, institutional, and literary history is remarkable. To illustrate, while the Portuguese terms for close reading (*leitura de perto*) and New Criticism (*nova crítica*) have been an inseparable part of the Brazilian humanist lexicon from the 1950s onward, one cannot find a Hispanic equivalent for the school's name (it is usually referred to simply as "New Criticism"), and the Spanish "*lectura de cerca*" has only a modest circulation in the countries bordering Brazil. In Israel, a local term for close reading (*kri'a tzmuda*, literally, *attached reading*) won similar popularity. In addition, the first theoretical book published by the Tel Aviv School, the main mediator of the New Criticism into the Israeli scene, had been translated soon after publication into one language only—Brazilian Portuguese—still the only translation of the book to this day; a translation accompanied by an introduction that indicates how intellectuals in both locales bonded over their unique interest in the New Critical creed and neighboring formalist thought.[9] The unexpected comparison between American, Brazilian, and Israeli literary systems holds the potential to push all three out of their hermeneutic comfort zones and thus widen our scope on the workings of close reading.

The tight Israeli and Brazilian intellectual affinity with the North American literary theory resulted, among other factors, from the personal border-crossing of two prominent local intellectuals: the Brazilian Afrânio Coutinho and the Israeli Benjamin Harshav (formerly, Hrushovski). Both thinkers traveled to the US during the 1940s and 1950s, respectively, studied under the guidance of New Critics, and in bringing this theory home, triggered nothing less than an institutional and cultural revolution. Coutinho ardently promoted his version of the American theory, the *nova crítica*, and in its spirit founded the first autonomous literature department in Brazil at the Universidade Federal do Rio de Janeiro (1967). In Israel, after returning from his Yale graduate studies under René Wellek, Harshav founded the first theory-oriented department of literature (the Department of General Literary Theory at Tel Aviv University), and within it, the Tel Aviv School of Poetics and Semiotics, which was deeply engaged with the American New Criticism. This is not to say that the New Criticism was received intact in these two locations; in fact, it went through significant alterations, aligned much more closely with Positivism in Brazil, and put in intense dialogue with Structuralism and Formalism in Israel. As David Damrosch notes in quoting Vilashini Cooppan, "A full appreciation of world literature requires us to see it as at once 'locally inflected and translocally mobile.'" The same, I would stress, goes for "world theory," or "global theory" in Cooppan's terms.[10]

What is more, in both Brazil and Israel, the forceful entry of New Critical ideas into the cultural mainstream had a far-reaching influence on local literary production. The practice of close reading provoked exciting literary experiments that laid the groundwork for, played around with, and tested the limits of the assumptions underlying this readerly practice. Several of these bold Brazilian and Israeli works went as far as to dramatize and theorize sophisticated alternatives to close reading, long before "distant" or "surface" reading were in sight, a discovery that sheds light on the link between the New Criticism and literary trends in North America as well. The transnational travels of close reading, then, offer us a new take on the genealogy of global modernism, and introduce a new literary archive conjoined with the New Critical creed, which includes the work of the American William Faulkner, the Brazilian João Guimarães Rosa and Clarice Lispector, and the Israeli A. B. Yehoshua and Yehuda Amichai. This archive reminds us that we should "theorize from, rather than into, the works we deem important," to ventriloquize Chana Kronfeld's paraphrase of Barbara Christian.[11]

Attention as Unselfing: A Technique of the Self

The Brazilian and Israeli versions of close reading—Brazilian "exact reading" (*leitura exata*, to later circulate as *leitura de perto*) and Israeli "maximalist reading" (*kri'a maximalit*, also called *kri'a tzmuda*)—destabilize two deeply engrained assumptions about the American New Criticism. First, the US school viewed the literary text as independent of its consumer and was thus uninterested in the reader and her mind.[12] This stance is paradigmatically articulated by Terry Eagleton, who claims that "if the poem was really to become an object in itself, New Criticism had to sever it from both author and reader."[13] This standpoint indeed comports with paradigmatic New Critical declarations, such as John Crowe Ransom's, that the "first law to be prescribed to criticism . . . is that it shall be objective, shall cite the nature of the object rather than its effects upon the subject."[14] Consequently, we have come to think of the New Criticism as lacking in theorization of the reader's mind and reactions, and consider such schools as Reader Response as reactions against, rather than an expansion of, New Critical ideas.[15]

Another widely held assumption is that close reading is either apolitical or rigidly conservative. This bifurcated assumption presents the other side of the same coin: the New Critics' presentation of the literary work as a pseudoreligious autonomous object (a "verbal icon") that should thus be read apolitically (without "extrinsic" information like historical or cultural background) is conceived as revealing these theorists' conservative ideology, their "wish for a social and intellectual world and a literature that expresses belief in . . . the ultimate union of warring dualism in the Word of God and the metaphor of poetry."[16] In the same spirit, Karen O'Kane argues that "the formalist precepts of the New Criticism" served as "a cover for their [the Nashville Group] Agrarianism's proto-fascism"; Daniel Green, on the other hand, presents the New Criticism as apolitical: "the New Critics would find it distressing in the extreme to witness the return of the politicized mode of criticism they thought they had successfully taught us to repress."[17]

The Brazilian and Israeli interpretations of the American theory and practice call for a drastic qualification of these two assumptions. They do so by exposing the import of a central concept in the New Critical body of work that has largely passed under the scholarly radar: the concept of "attention."[18] While it is true that the New Critics in the US described the poem as a unified object, containing an immanent and stable meaning, they tacitly conceptualized the poem's "independent" status as, paradoxically, utterly dependent on the reader's active participation in its creation as such.[19] The New Critics urged the reader to engage in a process that I term *unselfing*, which involved the deliberate suspension of subjectivity (a loaded concept as we will see) through the intense activation of the faculty of attention. In the words of Wimsatt and Beardsley, reading requires the suspension of the "personal"—bodily sensations, "private" memories, "idiosyncratic" associations—for the sake of investing all readerly "analytical" faculties in identifying the internal cohesion of the text, thus reinforcing the illusion that the literary work is indeed a "self-sufficient whole."[20] Readerly attention as unselfing, then, was taken to function as a precondition for the emergence of the poem as autonomous. Achieving this unselfing attention was no small feat, which is why the New Critics were deeply concerned with training and disciplining their readers' mental interaction with the literary text.

Importantly, the Brazilian and Israeli intellectuals affiliated with the New Criticism perceptively identified this latent yet steadfast pedagogical impulse. Accordingly, they conceptualized close reading as a tool for subject formation contingent on attention, and selected those aspects of subjectivity that require "unselfing" in accordance with local political pressures, historical circumstances, and traditions of reading and exegesis. Thus, the Brazilian Afrânio Coutinho referred to I. A. Richards's didactic title *How to Read a Page* as best expressing the New Critical overall project (viewing the American theory as inseparable from its British roots), and linked close reading with the unselfing of what he took to be a Brazilian internal tendency for distraction.[21] The Israeli Tel Aviv School went as far as insisting that there is no inherent contradiction between the New Critical creed and Reader Response theories, and conceptualized the attention inherent to close reading as linked to the suspension or unselfing of national affiliations. Over and above their differences, the New Critics in all three locations shared a unique vision of the close reader as a receptacle, capable of extracting certain elements of subjectivity from within during the reading process—that is, to unself—in order to better her engagement with the literary work. In the following pages, I will shift between "unselfing" to such terms as "self-depletion," "self-suspension," "self-deadening," "unsavaging," and "unlocalizing" in order to sketch a semantic field around this complex process with the varied meanings and connotations it has accrued in different cultural contexts.

One may rightly wonder what distinguishes T. S. Eliot's famous concept of "impersonality," which has become so deeply associated with modernist aesthetics as well as with close reading, and my concept of unselfing. Few of Eliot's statements are more quoted than "poetry is not a turning loose of emotion, but an escape from emotion; it is not the expression of personality, but an escape from personality."[22] As he explains earlier in "Tradition and the Individual Talent," the poet's personality—namely, her feelings and experiences—are an obstacle for the creation of "good" poetry, since the poet should function as a synthesizing "receptacle" for previous voices ("tradition") and circulating cultural images, phrases, and tropes.[23] Eliot has the poet in mind, while this book centers on the reader. And yet, it seems that the process of self-suspension that I discuss in the context of close reading already has a term. However, as Christina Walter deftly points out, Eliot's modernist imperative has come to be mistakenly taken as a disinterest in subjectivity writ large and in bodily processes: "Scholars have read the modernist rejection of Romantic expressivity . . . as both a complete evacuation of a writer's subjectivity and a denial of embodied specificity. . . . However, modernists didn't actually treat impersonality as a simple negation of personality. Instead, they took up the more fundamental question of what a personality is, as well as what more there is to the human subject than the person."[24] Walter challenges the disembodiment presumption by following the link modernist writers made between impersonality and vision, while I focus on the affinity between the bodily-cognitive effort of attention and the readerly process of self-suspension.

Even more importantly, I take the term *unselfing* to stand for the pluralization of "impersonality." As mentioned above and as I will go on to demonstrate, what the local New Critics meant by the "self" that should be excluded during the reading process, and that indeed surpasses any limited understanding of "personality," varied drastically from place to place. One can see this specificity in Eliot's own articulation of "impersonality." After all, "Tradition and the Individual Talent" is deeply morbid in tone and language, saturated with what Kazuki Inoue calls, in adopting Ezra Pound's words, "ghost psychology."[25] Eliot imagines poets as spiritual mediums who suspend themselves for the sake of allowing dead poets to speak through them. As we shall see in the first and second chapters, the understanding of the reader's attentive self-suspension as involving interaction with living-dead entities is unique to the US New Critics and the modernist writers they promoted, and is informed by the specific violent histories of the American South. Unselfing, then, denotes a labor performed by the reader, contingent on the work of attention, and inherently local and hence plural. Among other aims, then, this book sets out to specify and historicize Eliot's and the New Critics' purported universal and ahistorical "impersonality" through the reception histories of the New Criticism in Israel and Brazil.

These shrewd global interpretations of the New Criticism, facilitated by the Israelis' and Brazilians' command of both hegemonic and non-Western bodies of knowledge, disclose the North American scholars as being highly invested in exploring the reader's mind, thus unsettling the first assumption mentioned above. In addition, this pedagogical preoccupation acquired a deep political valence in the Israeli and Brazilian contexts, which in turn prompts us to reconsider the politics of close reading within the American context. It is well known that the founders of the US New Criticism—John Crowe Ransom, Allen Tate, and Robert Penn Warren—affiliated themselves early on with the politically conservative movement of Agrarianism. And, as Andy Hines has recently showed, there exists a rich history of midcentury Black interpretive praxes developed in direct opposition to the New Critical creed.[26] However, to quote Edward Pickering, "Merely to say that New Criticism was shaped by Southern Agrarianism is a generality that levels complexity as much as it illuminates. Precisely how great an influence Agrarianism had on New Criticism remains a vexed question."[27] Indeed, a narrow approach that would inspect the politics of close reading only through reference to the explicit ideology of the New Critics is at risk of missing the more complex politics that arise from their critical writings themselves, possibly even transcending the writers' stated intentions.[28] The New Critics' implicit theory of mind indicates that they perceived the reader's cognition as a vehicle for political change, one much more nuanced—at times bluntly leftist—than their biographical affiliation with Agrarianism might suggest.[29]

The American New Critics, and their Brazilian and Israeli counterparts, understood cognition as a political space: since the subject's mind plays a central role in organizing and designing reactions to the social reality around her, intervening in the reader's psyche constitutes a political intervention. In that spirit, the abovementioned Allen Tate, a central figure in the initial Vanderbilt core group of New Critics, sees no obstacle in drawing a direct link between the mental and the political realms in his depiction of the malaise of modernity, which, he claims, is "an intolerable *psychic* crisis expressing itself as a *political* crisis [emphasis in original]."[30] It follows, then, that modifying the singular mind might alter the political. For Tate, the mind is not an enclosed domain of bourgeois individualism. On the contrary, it is an open sphere that is constantly affecting and affected by the social: "What happens in one mind may happen as influence or coincidence, in another; when the same idea spreads to two or more minds of considerable power, it may eventually explode, through chain reaction, in a whole society; it may dominate a period or an entire epoch."[31] Tate's comment—as a paradigmatic example of a pervasive New Critical assumption—qualifies John Fekete's claim that during the latter part of the 1930s, the New Critics renounced "all sanction for the possibilities of reshaping the exterior world."[32] For the New Critics, the mind, and specifically the capacity to self-divest via attention, became the vehicle for such social and political intervention.

The politics that emerge from such a conceptualization of the reading process is necessarily general in nature. It does not advance highly specified political modifications, but tries to intervene in the more comprehensive social and cultural crises that the local New Critics believed surrounded their readers. Indeed, the New Critics in all three locations shaped their theory of mind in light of what they understood to be the most urgent political, and especially national, crises. This is particularly salient in the Brazilian case, where *leitura exata* is explicitly presented as a mental "cure" to a national "disease." Coutinho and his followers internalized the demeaning colonialist view of the Brazilian as a "savage" incapable of analytic thinking, and—inspired by New Critical vocabulary—framed this national problem in terms of "attention" and "distraction." These scholars perceived the practice of close reading, which enhances "attention," as a tool for extracting from within the Brazilian an "innate" tendency for distracted thought, in the hope that this training would later shape the reader's interactions with the social world more generally. In the Israeli context, the political aspect of close reading remained more implicit since the local intellectuals who borrowed from the New Criticism presented their methods as apolitical. In fact, they demanded that the reader detach herself from the prevailing ideological Zionist narrative while engaging with literature, in order to combat what they found to be an overbearing tendency in Hebrew literary criticism to interpret texts as national allegories. However, these scholars' insistence on "integration" as the key operation of close reading points to their covert preoccupation with the crisis of sociopolitical *dis*integration, which they feared hovered over Israeli society of the 1960s and 1970s. In that sense, the Brazilian and Israeli cases are emblematic of the multifaceted political dynamics that accompanied the understanding of close reading as a tool for subject formation; while close reading deepened racial stereotypes in Brazil, it also generated a striking revival in the field of Brazilian literary studies and literary production. And while the Israeli New Critical method expressed the anxieties of a social elite that was losing its power, it forced the local intellectual sphere out of politically and formally limiting forms of reading and opened it up to exciting new theoretical, methodological, and creative horizons.

It is the understanding of close reading as a tool of self-formation, one which works through laborious cognitive self-negation (i.e., unselfing through attention), that brought me to Michel Foucault's concept of "technology of the self," with which I opened this introduction. Toward the end of his life, Foucault commenced a project that he hoped would include "different papers about the self . . . about the role of reading and writing in constituting the self."[33] Foucault presented his initial ideas in 1982, at a faculty seminar on "Technologies of the Self" held at the University of Vermont, where he introduced an additional form of technology to compliment his previously conceptualized "technologies of production," "technologies of sign systems," and "technologies of power."[34] This fourth type is one manipulated by the subject in order to constitute herself: "technologies of the self . . . permit individuals to effect by their own means or with the help of others a certain number of operations on their own bodies and souls, thoughts, conduct, and way of being, so as to transform themselves in order to attain a certain state of happiness, purity, wisdom, perfection, or immortality."[35] Foucault specifies reading and writing as key technologies of this kind, an understanding, I claim, that is surprisingly shared by the New Critics discussed in this book.

What I find especially important in Foucault's formulation is that his view of reading as a technique of the self is devoid of value judgment. The reader's use of this technique points neither to her complete passivity nor to the technique's necessary malevolence.[36] It is the combination of the subject's agency, the techniques that are proposed and available to her, and political and historical pressures that comprise any singular use of such a technology. What Foucault also reminds us of in this context is that praxes of reading are slowly learned and deeply engrained so as to become part of one's form of being, rather than methods to be easily exchanged. In Mark Kelly's words, "The notion of techniques and practices of the self imply that we have to learn how to constitute ourselves in certain ways in order to do so. . . . We acquire our practices, and so they are habitual."[37] The New Critics were astute in their conception of reading as a labor that requires instruction and practice, that involves the active participation of the reader, and that has the potential to achieve a change in the self, and consequently, in the world. The readers and writers that this book follows at times surrendered themselves to this suggested technique, and at times played with it in ways that permitted other forms of reading and of subjectivity to rise to the surface.

When I ask in the title of this book, then, how close reading made us, I have three meanings in mind. This question first points to the ways the New Criticism constructed the discipline of literature—its institutions, curriculums, trajectories of development, and even its surrounding literary production. This question is asked with an emphasis on the intercultural, transnational, and multilingual nature of this discipline with which, I assume, we—the readers of this book—find ourselves affiliated, one way or another. Second, I wish to consider what the "close" in close reading stands for; that is, how "close" does reading in a New Critical manner turn one and what is the object of this practice's proximity. The close reader is not, I suggest, close to herself. Instead, she is urged to come nearer to the literary work as an alterity that resists domination or control, as

I will discuss in the following section. Third, and most emphatically, my title intends to open a conversation about the ways in which methods of reading *make* subjectivity, a question that I believe preoccupied the New Critics themselves. Put differently, this book sets out to examine how close reading has shaped us, its practitioners.

To do so, I examine, in the six chapters to follow, the complex relations between four parameters: (1) the local adaptation of close reading and the definition of "attention" it implied, under the overarching understanding of this mental state as an act of unselfing; (2) the political and cultural conditions that gave rise to the specific understanding of readerly attention, as well as the political role this mental state was thought to serve; (3) the aesthetic criteria that emanated from the encounter between the definition of attention and the local literary production; and (4) the cultural responses to the figure of the attentive reader in the form of translation projects and literary production, which were geared toward promoting close reading or inciting counterattention.

This investigation stretches over three parts, each dedicated to the trajectory of New Critical close reading in a specific geocultural site. These sections are organized chronologically, starting with midcentury US, then moving to Brazil of the 1950s and 1960s, and concluding with Israel of the long 1970s (1967–1984). Each part includes two chapters: the first chapter is dedicated to the local intellectual history of close reading, the political and ethical needs close reading was imagined to fulfill via its enhancement of attention and the practice of unselfing, and the literary styles the local thinkers canonized or viewed as a model for close reading. The second chapter looks carefully at the literature itself to examine how specific authors manipulated literary form to amplify unselfing, what literary avenues other works took to push against the imperative to attend, and which concepts of the reading process emerged from each of these strains. In the following three sections of this introduction, I lay the foundation for this exploration and provide a more detailed overview of the chapters' content. I first introduce the ethics of close reading, then launch the discussion on modernist reactions to the New Critical readerly model, and I end by asking whether attention has always been requisite for reading "well."

The Ethics of "Loving Attention": North American Roots

That the affinity between close reading and attention has so far gone unexamined is especially surprising given the frequency of this association. The two are presented together not only in the writings of the New Critics, but also, and more explicitly so, in more recent depictions of this reading practice, from a variety of undergraduate guides to critical reading and writings to sophisticated accounts of literary theory. In all these manifestations, however, "attention" appears undefined, and the source of the association between this readerly method and the mental state it requires goes unquestioned. Thus, the undergraduate guide *Falling in Love with Close Reading* instructs its readers that "the more carefully we pay attention, the closer we read, the more that can be revealed";[38] Paul de Man, the guru of deconstruction, echoes this terminology when he defines close reading as a method in which "delicate attention is paid to the reading of forms"; Jane Gallop states that "[c]lose reading pays attention to elements in the text . . . which textually call attention to themselves"; and Terry Eagleton claims that "paying due attention to the text" is the core of the New Critics' technique.[39] Finally, in *Close Reading: The Reader*, Andrew DuBois goes as far as to establish attention as the condition of possibility for the practice: "Paying attention: almost anyone can do it; and it's not requisite for reading, but for reading well? . . . As a term, *close reading* hardly seems to leave the realm of so-called common sense, where it would appear to mean something understandable and vague like 'reading with special attention.' "[40] The truth of the matter is that attention is indeed requisite for close reading, but there is nothing simply understandable or commonsensical about the New Critical subtle definition of this "special" mental state.

I would, therefore, like to delve momentarily into the North American roots of this affinity, to lay the grounds for the transnationally oriented discussion to follow. Attention is a central concept that can be traced throughout the writings of key North American New Critics and their British precursors, from I. A. Richards and William Empson to John Crowe Ransom, Allen Tate, Cleanth Brooks, René Wellek, Austin Warren, William Wimsatt, and Monroe C. Beardsley. In the works of these and other New Critics, attention is made to explicitly signify a mental labor that allows the subject to distinguish between "relevant" and "irrelevant" textual meanings. The former are defined as meanings that independently arise from the text, and the latter as meanings rooted in the private and "irrelevant" experience of the reader. One of the clearest iterations of this stance is Wimsatt and Beardsley's 1946 "The Intentional Fallacy," frequently anthologized as the archetypical New Critical essay: "Judging a poem is like judging a pudding or a machine. . . . Poetry succeeds because all or most of what is said or implied is relevant; what is irrelevant has been excluded, like lumps from pudding and 'bugs' from the machinery."[41] Wimsatt and Beardsley present "irrelevant" meanings as already absent when the reader encounters the text, excluded earlier on either by the writer or by the very nature of poetry ("what is irrelevant *has been* excluded"). This view, however, is constantly undermined by the New Critics themselves, who imply that this process of differentiation in fact comes about through the reader's active and learned ability to mentally put her subjectivity on hold while engaging with the literary text, what I suggested we call unselfing. In that vein, Wimsatt and Beardsley go on to add: "For all the objects of our manifold experience, for every unity, there is an action of the mind which cuts off roots, melts away context."[42] This "action of the mind" is attention, namely, the ability of the reader to "melt away" her individual presence—the "context" of reception—in order to become an empty space in which the work can reverberate.

A few years prior to "The Intentional Fallacy," René Wellek and Austin Warren refer to this process as "loving attention."

> [The aesthetic experience] is connected with feeling . . . but it objectifies and articulates feeling—the feeling finds, in the work of art, an "objective correlative," and it is distanced from sensation and conation by its object's frame of fictionality. . . . The aesthetic object is that which interests me for its own qualities, which I do not endeavor to reform or turn into a part of myself, appropriate, or consume. The aesthetic experience is a form of contemplation, a loving attention to qualities and qualitative structures.[43]

As Wellek and Warren's terminology evinces, and as we shall see in the coming chapters, the New Critical process of training attention is dialectical, simultaneously driven by a disciplining Foucauldian thrust and a countervailing ethical impulse. The reader is taught to actively make her individual presence invisible ("an action of the mind which *cuts off roots*"; "[The aesthetic experience] is *detached* from sensation and conation"), but this self-erasure is also understood as a form of ethical interaction with the literary text as an alterity that deserves its own autonomy within the reading subject. The literary work is thus an aesthetic object that "I do not endeavor to reform or turn into a part of myself, appropriate, or consume." In that respect, Wellek and Warren's emotional terminology might seem perplexing, presenting the aesthetic experience as connected with the reader's "feeling"; but the task of "attention" is precisely to put off the subject's senses. The reader lends herself to the work of art that "objectifies" her feelings and cognizes the aesthetic experience into a "form of contemplation" rather than feeling. The "loving" attribute associated with attention, then, refers less to the subject's love as desire and more to the willingness to surrender oneself to the text as an alterity at the price of momentary self-erasure, an ethical dimension that runs through the different iterations of close reading in and outside the anglophone world.

On the side of literature, the New Critics depict worthy works as those that facilitate the reader's work of attention. Allen Tate already phrases this idea, in a talk given at Vanderbilt in 1950, as a question: "Is the purpose of teaching imaginative works to provide materials upon which the critical faculty may exercise itself in its drive towards the making of critical systems, which then perpetuate themselves without much reference to literature?"[44] The "critical faculty" Tate has in mind is closely linked with the process of unselfing: "[T]he critic will need all the humility that human nature is capable of, almost the self-abnegation of the saint. Is the critic willing to test his epistemology against a selfless reading of *The Rape of the Lock*, *War and Peace*, or a lyric by Thomas Nashe?"[45] Tate advocates for "self-abnegation" and a "selfless reading," even while he is aware of the acute "epistemological" effort such a move would require ("what critic has ever done this?" he writes in concluding his discussion).[46] This advocation for selflessness, Tate makes clear, is not only driven by a will to guard the text from the reader's subjectivity, but it is also an attempt to sketch a more general ethical alternative for interacting with literature as alterity, a capacity that might then "perpetuate . . . without much reference to literature."[47] Likewise, Cleanth Brooks, who thought of Tate as his mentor, delineates self-suspension as an almost unachievable ideal that nevertheless should mark the critical horizon of expectation.[48] He asks, "Should all criticism, then, be self-effacing and analytic?" and answers, "Of course not," since "in practice, the critic's job is rarely a purely critical one."[49] However, above and beyond practicality, "it will do the critic no harm to have a clear idea of what his specific job as a critic is."[50] That is, in its purity, "the specific job" of the critic indeed involves an endeavor of "self-effacing." That these critics are aware of the distinction between an ideal critic-as-reader and the actual perceiver of literature does not turn their project less pedagogical; they are presenting the reader with self-negation via attention as a goal one can aspire to, even if it ultimately remains beyond reach.[51]

As we will see in chapters 1 and 2, I believe that the North American New Critics' drive to mold a reader who is mentally "open to the other" unexpectedly foreshadows Jacques Derrida's deconstructionist "ethics of alterity" and concept of "hauntology" (his portmanteau of "haunting" and "ontology"). More broadly, my understanding of ethics, throughout the book, derives from Derrida's hauntological conceptualization of the subject's (in)capability to approach that which is other to her.[52] In destabilizing the Freudian preference for "mourning" over "melancholia," Derrida suggests that a melancholic approach to the Other holds an ethical valence. While in "mourning," the lost other is fully integrated into the self (decataxis), in the melancholic state the Other occupies the subject as an internal "foreign enclave," at the price of self-depletion; that is, the hauntological Other acts as an autonomous entity within the subject, a position that leaves "the other [its] alterity." For the New Critics, the literary text functions not unlike Derrida's Other. This is already evident in Wellek and Warren's definition of the aesthetic experience as an encounter with literature devoid of the "endeavor to reform or turn [it] into a part of myself, appropriate, or consume," and in Tate's petition for "selfless reading."[53] Namely, close reading, as the very bedrock of the discipline of literature, has much more in common with deconstruction's "ethics of alterity" than with either humanism or Kantian idealism, as is usually assumed.[54]

A Modernist Aesthetics of Attention

On the whole, close reading is taught today as a practice fit for any literary text, regardless of genre classification or period and region of publication. This pedagogical convention is a result of the neutralization of the method from its underlying theory, making it even more universal and ahistorical than the New Critics sought to present it.[55] However, as Chana Kronfeld and David James deftly note with regard to Israeli and anglophone modernisms, respectively, close reading must be examined in relation to its contemporaneous literary trends, since it was developed to fit and promote these models.[56] This corrective was pointed out self-consciously by John Crowe Ransom, who wrote: "The poetry which deals with things [Imagism] was much in favour a few years ago with the resolute body of critics [the New Critics]. And the critics affected the poets. If necessary, they became the poets, and triumphantly illustrated the new mode."[57] When investigating the fundamentals of close reading, then, one must take into account the literary production ("the new mode") that surrounded the New Critics globally, the writers and literary trends they were "in favor" of, and the works they deemed less worthy of inquiry or even, as Ransom writes, of imitation. In the rare cases in which this affinity is discussed (almost exclusively in the context of Anglo-American literature), it is repeatedly assumed to be one-directional; the New Critics are accused (or, on occasion, praised) for forcing their aesthetic and ideological criteria on the body of literature they encountered. John Guillory is paradigmatic in this regard, asserting that the canon which first "emerged in T.S. Eliot's earlier criticism, was presented as canon by Cleanth Brooks in *The Well Wrought Urn*, and has since become institutionalized to a greater or lesser degree in the curricula of university English departments."[58] According to Guillory, the ideology of the New Criticism neutralized the reason for which "*some* literature" is seen as "worth preserving" and "*innately superior*" (emphasis inoriginal).[59] As prominent cultural figures, the New Critics clearly had an impact on processes of canonization worldwide, but the relationship between literary theory and literary production, and specifically between the New Criticism and High Modernism, is much more layered and reciprocal in nature, informed as well by complex processes of translation, international affiliations, and disciplinary institutionalization.

The New Critics not only affected canonization, and were informed by existing literary trends, but their model of readerly subjectivity inspired creative literary attempts to rethink—at times fundamentally challenge—the notion of attentive reading.[60] To illustrate the dialogue between close reading and modernist experiments, I turn in chapter 3 to the short story "The Mirror" (*O espelho*) by the Brazilian João Guimarães Rosa as a parody of the unselfing "exact" reader. Rosa sardonically undermines the assumption that the "savage" properties of the Brazilian reader indeed hinder analytic thinking. Other works, as I note above, not only questioned close reading but also astutely theorized alternatives to close reading and strove to provoke in the reader counterattentive states of mind; such is the case with Clarice Lispector's "exhausted reading" and Yehuda Amichai's "unintegrating reading," to be discussed in chapters 4 and 6, respectively. To clarify, I do not argue that these writers set out to deliberately carve a literary response to the New Criticism. But the figure of the close reader had such a strong presence in the culture of their time that it, perhaps unwittingly, entered and shaped their oeuvre in significant ways. In addition, texts that were written in tandem with, or shortly before, the rise of the New Criticism were in turn adopted by proponents of the New Criticism as perfect examples for an aesthetics that promotes attention, a perception that drastically and indefinitely changed these works' reception. This is the case with the work of the Israeli A. B. Yehoshua (discussed in chapter 5) and William Faulkner (examined in chapters 1 and 2), whose endorsement by the New Critics is usually—and mistakenly, in my view—taken to be independent of their aesthetic theory and practice.

My investigation focuses on prose-fiction, a decision that might seem imprudent given that the New Critics were globally more invested in poetry.[61] But I have consistently found that New Critical engagements with prose-fiction, albeit infrequent, push the method's boundaries to their limits and consequentially bring to the fore the basic contours of close reading. This is quite visible, for example, in the Israeli case, where Yehuda Amichai's poetry was celebrated by critics affiliated with the New Criticism, since they believed it incited readerly attention in its local iteration. On the other hand, Amichai's prose-fiction, which was published alongside his verse, was received with resounding silence by the same theorists. The reason is that in Amichai's prose, the distracting thrust of his famous metaphoric constructions comes fully into view. Amichai's oeuvre, then, provides us with a sort of Israeli attention-scale, demonstrating where literary form became too "wild" or "loquacious" to fit close reading in the eyes of the local critics.

As in the case of Amichai, the concept of "attention" figures prominently in both the positive and negative transnational New Critical evaluations of the literary works this book looks at. That is, works admired by the North American New Critics and their international affiliates are often presented as enhancing attention and unselfing, while the works found lacking are charged with provoking "distraction." However, this conceptualization is unstable in the New Critical body of work, especially within the US, leaving ambiguous the agency of the reader in relation to attention. At times, valuable literature is defined as a type of literature whose form elicits attention in the reader as a passive recipient. In other instances, attention is presented as a readerly skill that can be actively applied to any literary text whatsoever. And every so often, works will be presented as holding universal value, utterly independent of the reader's mental response.

This internal tension is evident, for example, in the writings of Ransom, who refers to T. S. Eliot's objection to romanticism as exemplary of the formalist criticism he tries to advance: "romantic literature is imperfect in objectivity, or 'aesthetic distance,' and . . . out of this imperfection comes its weakness of structure."[62] In this iteration, the value of the work appears universal, and the critic-as-reader identifies its inherent "weak[ness]" of "structure," notwithstanding its capacity to provoke attention. On the other hand, in his *New Criticism*, Ransom discusses the intensity of the reader's psychological reaction of attention as a measure of the poem's worth: "A completely unexpected situation, if it is strong enough, will compel attention, and so will the opening image of the poem. . . . [In the case of] an aimless succession of experiences . . . fatigue sets in and the pitch of our attention is quickly lowered. This is what must not happen in the poem."[63] In this formulation, the reader's attentive reaction is of the utmost importance; it is the reader's central indication of the work's worth.

Later on, Ransom identifies "suspense" as the specific aesthetic quality he believes "compels" attention.[64] Indeed, in all three New Critical iterations to be discussed, "suspense" is considered an attribute advantageous to attention and unselfing. As Ransom elucidates, the New Critics took a "suspenseful" work to mean one that presents the reader with a small enough amount of information to make her strain her mind in probing the "items," while finally leading her to an encompassing "context": "we must feel constantly that we are coming to it [the structure], and finally that we have got it; otherwise attention is not proceeding normally, and we leave it off, or else, if we continue it, we feel finally that we have been cheated."[65]

Interestingly, the writers who were trying to conform with or push against the imperative to read attentively frequently turned to "suspenseful" genres. In that spirit, the Brazilian Lispector, to whom I turn in chapter 4, manipulates the genre conventions of the crime novel in order to cause attention to "proceed [ab]normally" and thus challenge exact reading (*leitura exata*). She constructs her 400-page-long novel, *The Apple in the Dark* (*A maçã no escuro*), as a readerly ruse, devising the first chapter to raise the expectation that the novel will revolve around a murder mystery, only to then abandon this mystery altogether. This deceit provokes the reader to "look at them [the details] harder in order to have the right values ready when they can be used," until she indeed feels that she has "been cheated." But by that time, Lispector has made sure that the reader is tired enough to surrender to an alternative "exhausted" rhythm of engagement with the text.

The question remains, nevertheless, whether readerly attention was seen by the New Critics as provoked by the text or as actively inflicted on it. The answer, I suggest, lies in between. This is best expressed by

Wellek and Warren, who present close reading as the encounter between a reader sufficiently trained in attention-as-self-suspension and a literary text whose aesthetics reinforce that kind of attention: "Is [the locus of aesthetic values] the poem, or the reader of the poem, or the relation between the two? . . . The values exist potentially in the literary structures: they are realized, actually valued, only as they are contemplated by readers who meet the requisite conditions."[66] As Ransom offered above, the aesthetic value of literature lies in its "literary structure"; yet Wellek and Warren make clear that this formal quality exists only "potentially" and must be "realized" by a reader. The poem can assert its control only over a reader who meets "the requisite conditions," which, I suggest, center on the disposition to attend.

In sum, then, an interdependent triangulation is necessary: an attentive reader must engage with a text whose (suspenseful) structure then exerts its control over her realization of its "literary structures" in order for close reading to come about. For the New Critics, there is no such thing as close reading without an attentive reader, and no close reader without an attention-provoking literary work.

Has Reading Always Been Attentive?

If we accept that New Critical close reading has indeed been intertwined with the labor of attention from its inception, it remains to be asked if this affinity is in any way exceptional. The New Critical conception of readerly attention as entailing a form of unselfing and as oriented toward subject formation might be specific to this school of thought, but has reading not always been associated with acute concentration or intense cognitive labor? Two quick examples from the traditions discussed in this book suggest that this is not the case and vividly demonstrate just how diverse the history of reading praxes is, along with the range of mental states they were expected to invoke.

Benjamin Harshav—who, as I noted, was key in the importation of close reading into the Israeli scene—opens his 1974 book, written with his student-turned-colleague, Ziva Ben-Porat, with a reference to the Jewish exegetical tradition.[67] Ben-Porat and Harshav present "Traditional Jewish Poetics" as the foundation for the Tel Aviv School's mode of engagement with literature, which, as I show in chapter 5, relied heavily on the New Critical method: "The rigorous interpretation of texts, with reference to subtleties of language, contextual meaning and formal traits, such as repetition, is an old and entrenched tradition in Hebrew writings, going back to the time of the Bible's canonization."[68] Indeed, the practice of the *midrash*, the basic interpretation method of the Talmud and rabbinical literature, shows similarities with close reading: it involves the careful unpacking of the Hebrew Bible in an attempt to make sense of its various linguistic levels. However, the act of *drash* (the verbal root from which *midrash* is derived) is only one particular form of reading from an array of reading modes suggested by the Hebrew Bible and later advocated by rabbinic literature.[69] In most of these modes, reading signifies a practice very different from the New Critical one, a speech-act that is oral, social, and collective. Reading in the traditional Jewish context stands, by and large, for a demand that the reader fulfill the obligation to follow the document aloud in a communal, ritual setting; in Daniel Boyarin's words, " 'Reading' is a proclamation, a declaration, and a summons."[70] Even in the specific case of *drash*, Boyarin adds, "the project is undertaken always as part of a dialogical encounter. Thus, a typical situation involves a claim made by a given Rabbi, which is challenged by his fellows, and to which he answers, 'I am reading [*doresh*] a verse from the Torah.' "[71] In the context of our discussion, then, Boyarin's explication indicates that the figure of the solitary reader, who concentrates on the text at the expense of other stimuli, is foreign to the Jewish tradition of reading. Instead, this tradition emphasizes recitation within a lively social setting, where various stimuli must be considered simultaneously.

A striking example for rabbinic literature's explicit discussion of reading modes can be found in the Talmudic tractate *Megillah*. The title "Megillah," "scroll" in Hebrew, stands for the central text this tractate explores—the Book or Scroll of Esther. However, the major concern of the tractate is not the exegesis of this scroll but its accurate performance. Since the public reading of the Book of Esther is a required practice during the Festival of Purim, the Talmud dedicates a complex discussion to the "modalities of its reading," in Harold Fisch's words, which are altogether outside the New Critical scope.[72] The tractate states, for example, "If one reads the *Megillah* backwards, he has not performed his obligation. . . . If one reads it with breaks or while half-asleep, he has performed his obligation."[73] Namely, reading in a lethargic state is considered valid, while skipping parts of the text or reciting them in the wrong order is scorned, since the value of reading lies not in the reader's mind, in contrast with the assumption underlying the New Critical creed.

In the Brazilian case, the readerly model which preceded that of the *nova crítica* will be discussed in detail in chapter 3. As I show, the romantic novelist, José de Alencar, presents this model at the opening of his nineteenth-century masterpiece, *Iracema: A Legend of Ceará* (*Iracema: lenda do Ceará*). The novel begins with a note to the reader that includes reading instructions: "This book will naturally find you . . . cradled in [your] hammock, soft and snug . . . I wrote [the novel] to be read there, on the porch of a rustic cabin or in the garden's fresh shade, in the sweet rocking movement of the hammock."[74] In chapter 3, I place the discussion of this paragraph in the larger context of the hammock's role in the Brazilian cultural imaginary, but for now suffice it to say that Alencar does not expect his reader to pay intense attention to the words on the page. Instead, he anticipates a much more relaxed reading experience, which takes its cue from the back-and-forth movements of the hammock, and which involves a state of mind resembling that of near-falling asleep.

The figure of the relaxed, rocking reader perseveres in Brazilian culture into the twentieth century, alongside the rise of the *nova crítica*'s model of the attentive reader. This is visible, for example, in the short story, "Covert Joy" ("Felicidade clandestina"), published in 1964 by Clarice Lispector.[75] At the center of Lispector's story is a girl who yearns for a book owned by a classmate, but which she cannot afford. The classmate tortures her with endless waiting, until the book finally reaches its destination. But instead of immediately consuming the book, the girl postpones her pleasure: "sometimes, I'd sit in the hammock, swinging with the book open on my lap, not touching it, in the purest ecstasy."[76] In reading this scene, Hélène Cixous, one of Lispector's most ardent readers, writes, "At the moment where one could expect a final immobility . . . movement radiates erotically through this kind of marvelous balancing of the hammock."[77] Cixous arrives at the conclusion that the story "is a lesson of reading. To know how to read is to take infinite time to read . . . One reads while eating bread and butter, while walking, while opening and closing with the book the whole space of a lifetime."[78] Cixous undoubtedly has a point. After all, Lispector's publisher chose to place on the book's very cover an image of a girl reading in a hammock (see figure I.1).[79] For Lispector and Cixous, then, who enter into dialogue with earlier Brazilian traditions of reading, engaging with literature entails movement, postponement, and erotic pleasure, traits very different from those the New Critics had associated with the labor of attention and with valuable reading.

Figure I.1. Book cover, Clarice Lispector's *Felicidade clandestina* (Rio de Janeiro: Editora Nova Fronteira, 1981).

In contrast, then, with such paradigmatic statements as Steven Connor's, who contends that "fiction has always subsisted upon the larger ideological fiction of the reader's continuous and uninterrupted attention," attention has not been either universality or transhistorically associated with the reading of literature, or reading per se.[80] Instead, the prevalent assumption that engaging texts necessitate this specific mental state testifies to the intense modern historical-cultural process of linking these two together, a process in which the New Critics played a central role, transnationally. It is the story of this process that I hope to let unfold in the following pages.

And so, whether you read this book in the hammock, among friends, or in attentive quietude, I hope it answers for you, how close reading made us.

Part I
The US: The Haunted Reader

Chapter One

Self-Deadening

Cleanth Brooks and the Living-Dead Reader of New Critical Theory

The urn to which we are summoned . . . is the poem itself.

—Cleanth Brooks

The self: a cemetery guard. The crypt is enclosed within the self, but as a foreign place, prohibited, excluded. The self is not the proprietor of what he is guarding.

—Jacques Derrida

In 1940, just a year before John Crowe Ransom's *The New Criticism* formalized the school's title, Allen Tate—the school's key member who was also the editor of the *Sewanee Review*, and a poet in his own right—published an article carrying a peculiar title, "Miss Emily and the Bibliographer."[1] Its central claim would ring familiar to anyone acquainted with the New Critical creed: historical analysis of a literary work is insufficient to understanding its singularity, which could be grasped only through an exploration of "the concrete form of the play, the poem, the novel," the "coherence of image and metaphor, control of tone and rhythm, the union of these features."[2] After all, the paradigmatic practice advanced by the New Critics, namely, close reading, focuses on the suspension of historical analysis for the sake of an exploration of irony and paradox—the formal ways in which the literary work brings into "coherence" and "union" images or ideas that seem contradictory. And yet the central metaphor that Tate selects to carry forth his argument does not fall easily into any established image of the New Critics and their theory.

Tate opens his article with an analogy based on an intertextual dialogue. The interaction between the historian (or "bibliographer" in Tate's terms) and the literary work is compared to the relationship between Miss Emily of William Faulkner's "A Rose for Emily" and none other than the corpse of her dead lover. "You will remember," Tate writes, that Emily is "a curious spinster [who] conceals the dead body of her lover in an upstairs bedroom until concealment is no longer possible."[3] The historian, Tate charges, is even worse than Emily. He not only wants his literary "corpus" dead, but wishes to bury it altogether so that "he would never afterwards have to be reminded what he was doing the bibliography of."[4]

As a counter, Tate takes Emily's side and declares that it "is better to pretend with Miss Emily that something dead is living than to pretend with the bibliographer that something living is dead."[5] In this analogy, that "something dead" considered living is the literature of the past. While the historian examines past literature as a static, "dead" entity, the reader Tate has in mind, and whom the New Critic tries to emulate, is able to revive that seemingly lifeless text through a "living imagination": "[T]he tradition that we are interested in is almost always seen as a traditional 'body' of literature, not operative today—not living, as the very word body implies," but for Tate we may, and should, "keep [the past] alive by being alive ourselves."[6] Put differently, while the bibliographer judges "a work of past from a high and disinterested position," the reader Tate advances is aware "that the literature of the past can be kept alive only by seeing it as the literature of the present."[7]

Though very powerful and doubtlessly unconventional, Tate's analogy is not altogether stable. On the one hand, he claims that it is within the reader's power to keep the literature of the past alive; on the other, he hints that this textual death is irreversible: the reader is only "pretend[ing]" with Miss Emily that "something dead is living." The literary text in Tate's article, then, teeters uneasily between life and death, an understanding that, as I will go on to show, runs throughout the US version of the New Criticism. But before diving into the internal logic of this liminality, I would like to point out that Tate's discussion of Emily and the literary historian calls into question two ossified assumptions about the New Criticism, which this chapter and the following ones will continue to challenge.

The New Critics, we are constantly told, were uninterested in the reader, her reactions, or her mind, since they insisted that the literary work is a self-contained entity independent of its producer and consumer. The reader can only contemplate the autonomous literary object rather than actively participate in its meaning-making.[8] Consequently, the reader the New Critics allegedly supposed in their writing, and the attitude they consequently adopted as model readers themselves, is uninvolved, serene, and technical, a position that implies that the reader's reactions indeed deserve no special investigation. As John Paul Russo paradigmatically puts it, "New Criticism fostered the straightforward, roll-up-your-sleeves attitude to criticism that mirrored technocratic expertise, objective neutrality, teamwork, bureaucratized efficiency, and anonymity."[9] The word scholars most commonly use in this context is *disinterest*, linking the New Critics and their close reader to Kantian idealism.[10]

This standpoint indeed jibes with several of the New Critics' articulated views, as illustrated by Ransom's quote, mentioned in the Introduction: "[T]he first law to be prescribed to criticism . . . is that it shall be objective, shall cite the nature of the object rather than its effects upon the subject."[11] However, Tate's article, which as we will soon see is exemplary, suggests that the New Critics were in fact very much concerned with the reader's active role in the reading process—after all, the reader is responsible for bringing the text to life. Against this backdrop, the New Critic's reader arises as anything but disinterested; she is encouraged to bequeath her very life force to the literary work, an understanding that can account for Tate's morbid vocabulary and emotionally invested tone. Notably, Tate describes the "bibliographer" rather than the close reader as working from a "high and disinterested position," and marshals his form of engagement with literature as an antithesis.

Tate's article also troubles the assumption that the New Critics' long-standing fascination with William Faulkner's oeuvre was fueled solely by regional comradery. That is, the New Critics' investment in Faulkner's work is usually taken to be unrelated to their aesthetic theory and project. Instead, Tate relies on Faulkner's gothic imaginary to design the very image of his theory's protagonist, namely, the close reader—an affinity between the New Critics and Faulkner's modernism that, I will show, goes beyond this specific essay.

This chapter will explore the North American New Critical conceptualization of the reading process and its reliance on the figure of the living-dead through the work of the self-proclaimed "typical New Critic,"

Cleanth Brooks. As I propose in the Introduction and will demonstrate throughout the book, the New Critics globally positioned at the center of their reading method the praxis of unselfing, the reader's momentary suspension of subjectivity during her engagement with the literary text, carried out through the effort of attention, a cognitive labor the New Critics took to involve an immersion in the literary work intense enough as to help pull the reader outside of herself. However, the meaning of "subjectivity"—that which requires extraction during the reading process—varies widely between the different locations in which the New Criticism finds its footing, in accordance with local historical, political, and social pressures. In the case of the US, as Tate's article hints and Brooks's work corroborates, what the reader is asked to suspend during the reading process is her vitality, which she is encouraged to bestow on the literary text as a living-dead entity. This morbid, haunted theorization is charged with the memory of the US's Civil War and violent history of slavery, both leaving an indelible mark on the South from which the New Critics emerge.

At the center of this chapter will stand Brooks's tour de force of close reading, *The Well Wrought Urn: Studies in the Structure of Poetry*, and his seminal interpretations of Faulkner, rarely examined in the context of the New Critic's aesthetic theory.[12] Though the New Critics were famously interested in poetry rather than prose, as I note in the Introduction, it is precisely their critical explorations outside their comfort zone that I believe throw into relief their implicit assumptions about close reading and its imagined practitioner. Indeed, when *The Well Wrought Urn* and Brooks's analyses of Faulkner are read in unison, these two ostensibly removed works of criticism expose a consistent model of reading underlying Brooks's thought, one that echoes Tate's conceptualization, and brings together the New Critical imagined process of unselfing, the labor of attention, and the US' haunting past.

In these works, one finds that Brooks labors to cultivate in his reader an attentiveness so profound as to lead to self-deadening. The close reader is instructed by Brooks to turn herself into an empty hall in which the literary work could fully play itself out. This readerly unselfing is continually associated, for Brooks, with death, mourning, and loss. However, as in Tate's case, Brooks does not present this process as solely negative. Similar to the logic leading Tate's argument, the cognitive effort of self-draining, which for Brooks resembles a state of momentary death, allows the reader to grant her vitality to the literary work and to thus miraculously bring to life the text as a complex unity in which the like and the unlike harmoniously reside. Put differently, through self-deadening, the reader generates life, and—through this forceful experience—paradoxically gains, as Brooks terms it in paraphrasing Donne, "a more intense life." In that sense, Brooks theorizes a nuanced reading process, which concurrently involves a sense of loss and an experience of intense liveliness, very much at odds with the conventional view of the ideal close reader as uninvolved or "technocratic."

Brooks's morbid theory also holds an ethical dimension. In his model of the reading process, the text figures as an Other that deserves autonomy, and thus should be incorporated into an emptied self, where it would be left to make its literary voice heard without the intervention of what he considered the reader's "animated" subjectivity. Against this backdrop, the figure of the "urn," which came to represent not only Brooks's aesthetics but the New Criticism more generally (and to which I will return in the following chapter), is revealed to have a meaning markedly different from traditional views. Usually, Brooks's "urn" is understood to metaphorically represent the more general New Critical view of the literary text as an "enduring thing," to quote Douglas Mao—that is, an autonomous and self-enclosed object of study independent of both writer and reader.[13] Yet Brooks's theory of reading as self-deadening exposes a different, and almost obvious, facet of this figure: the urn as a burial vessel, a "final memorial for one's ashes," in the New Critic's words.[14]

The urn plays a doubly figurative role in Brooks's model: the poem itself is imagined to be a tombstone, a marker of a lifeless form waiting to be animated by the reader. And the reader, through her process of attention, is instructed to turn herself into an urn, into an empty chamber in which the dead (the poem) could reside—a mental process, as noted, that holds both negative and positive connotations, simultaneously. This model of readerly attention is further elaborated on from a different perspective in Brooks's *William Faulkner: The Yoknapatawpha Country*, where stories of the past take the place of the poem as alterity, and where the metaphor of readerly-death-turned-"intense life," which remains implied in *The Urn*, is clarified. Nevertheless, in both critical works, Brooks's theory of reading as an encounter with Otherness is performed rather than explicitly stated.

Surprisingly, the New Critic's ethical stance is usefully elucidated in the work of none other than Jacques Derrida, whose reflections on death and alterity echo Brooks's ideas, notwithstanding the traditional view that Deconstruction was a backlash against the New Criticism.[15] This is not to say that Derrida is reading Brooks or vice versa, but that the French thinker's theory helps to explain the association Brooks makes between death, loss, and the reader's capacity for animating otherness.

As I mention in the Introduction, Derrida outlines his "ethics of alterity," among other places, in his reflections on melancholia, and in his discussions of hauntology.[16] Thinking through the mental state of melancholia and the ontological positioning it implies, he enters into dialogue with Freud's theorization of mourning. The psychoanalyst, as presented by Derrida, sees the healthy mourning process as involving a renewed integration of the energy formerly invested in the lost object (decathexis), and views melancholia as the pathological mirror image. In melancholia, libido is never regained since the subject is unable to detach herself from the lost object, who continues to haunt her as a foreign body within the self. Derrida concurs with Freud as to the suffering that inevitably accompanies the melancholic state, but insists on depathologizing this position. For the French thinker, allowing the dead to remain an autonomous "cryptic enclave" within the self at the price of self-depletion (losing libido without ever recapturing it) is an ethical stance toward the Other.[17] He writes,

> What is impossible mourning? What does it tell us, this impossible mourning, about an essence of memory? And as concerns the other in us . . . where is the most unjust betrayal? Is the most distressing, or even the most deadly infidelity that of a *possible mourning* which would interiorize within us the image, idol, or ideal of the other who is dead and lives only in us? Or is it the impossible mourning, which, leaving the other [the other's] alterity, respecting thus [the other's] infinite remove, either refuses to take or is incapable of taking the other within oneself, as in a tomb or the vault of some narcissism?[18]

The "normal" mourning process in Freud's terms is referred to by Derrida as "possible mourning," which he perceives as a "betrayal" of, or "infidelity" toward, the dead. In this process, he claims, the lost object is interiorized into the self as an "idol" or "ideal," becoming an integral part of the subject, who is now enlarged at the expense of the Other's autonomy.

Melancholia, on the other hand, becomes in Derrida's terms "impossible mourning," a never-ending process of incorporation (versus interiorization), in which the subject refuses to take "the other within oneself" in a narcissistic process of self-recuperation, and instead allows the Other to remain an internal alterity; it is the melancholic position, Derrida claims, that most respects the Other's "infinite remove." In other words, rather than assimilating the dead into the living self and thus erasing their Otherness, Derrida posits a radical alternative: to internally "keep the dead alive" at a cost of a partial self-death.[19] For this reason, the melancholic subject, per Derrida, is hauntological: she occupies a liminal space between death and life.

It is a similar preoccupation with the incorporation of the dead, and an analogous combination of suffering and a positive ethical potentiality that we find in Brooks's model of close reading, where works of literature are imagined as lifeless entities to be revived, and the reader's self-deadening figures as "a more intense life." In Derrida's terms, Brooks offers us an ethical take on the reading process. In order to respect the poems' "infinite remove," the reader must deaden herself, that is, momentarily subdue her liveliness through attention, so that the dead can be enlivened within her vacated self. This process of unselfing—melancholic as it may be—carries for Brooks, I would like to propose, a positive and even utopian potentiality.[20]

The Death of the Reader

Readers might still be thinking that no one could seem further removed from the gothic enterprise of "deadening" the reader than Cleanth Brooks, the New Critic whose "very claim upon our admiration," as John Guillory puts it, is his "detachment" and the New Critical purported signature-trait of "disinterestedness."[21] These characteristics are especially salient in *The Urn*, where he is said to strike a tone of "balance and ease," to quote Robert Heilman.[22] Brooks's close readings and their harmonious quality came to be considered the quintessential example of the New Critical method, that is, "close reading at its best."[23] In fact, according to Daniel Green, *The Urn*, along with the work of W. K. Wimsatt, was "responsible for bringing final academic respectability to New Criticism."[24]

That Brooks became a representative of close reading is not surprising. A student of the abovementioned Allen Tate along with John Crowe Ransom, the coauthor of *Understanding Poetry* with Robert Penn Warren and of *Literary Criticism: A Short History* with William Wimsatt, and the cofounder of the *Southern Review*, Brooks played a principal role in the social network and intellectual formation of the North American New

Criticism. The archetypical status of his critical work might explain why arrows of criticism directed at the method of close reading are frequently sent his way: "'Brooks is dead (or ought to be)."[25] Yet pulling on *The Urn*'s threads of attention and death, one reveals a text not quite as serene and harmonious as expected.

To begin with, Brooks's concern with readerly attention is related to his more general anxiety about the effects of modernity on the reading process. In *The Urn*, he detects a cognitive problem in the modern reader and presents his project as a possible solution. For Brooks, throughout his work, "good literature" is defined as possessing a "coherence" of a specific sort, namely, "the hanging together" of "the like with the unlike," a structure of meaning he famously refers to as "paradox," as do the New Critics writ large.[26] Subsequently, "reading well" is understood by Brooks as predicated on the ability to identify that complex unity. On that account, he assures his readers that if they are able to recognize harmony or synthesis where contradiction or disorder seem to be, they are on the right track: "If we see how the passages [in *Macbeth*] are related to these symbols, and they to the tragedy as a whole, the main matter is achieved"; elsewhere he warns the "dull or lazy reader" of Keats against "insisting very much on the statement in isolation . . . the relation of the final statement in the poem to the total context is all-important."[27]

The problem, however, is that "modern man, habituated as he is to an easy yes or no" can hardly grasp this complexity, according to Brooks: "[W]e are disciplined in the tradition of either-or, and lack the mental agility . . . which would allow us to indulge in the finer distinctions and the more subtle reservations permitted by the tradition of both-and."[28] As a consequence, Brooks sets out on a mission to reeducate his readers' minds out of "conventional reading habits" and into ones that would allow them to see structures of "both-and," that is, paradoxes.[29]

The "mental agility" that the modern reader lacks, Brooks believes, is inextricably linked with the capacity to "attend," and the cure for this cognitive deficiency is the activating power of paradox. Valuable literature, characterized by coupling "the like with the unlike," facilitates attention, a state of mind that in its turn allows the reader to identify paradoxical structures. This claim is outlined in the book's first chapter, where Brooks states that the very raison d'être of the poetic use of paradoxes is the instigation of attention.[30] Reading Wordsworth's "Composed upon Westminster Bridge," he quotes Coleridge and then moves on to draw his own conclusions.

Coleridge was to ... make even more evident Wordsworth's exploitation of the paradoxical: "Mr. Wordsworth ... was ... to give the charm of novelty to things of every day, and to excite a feeling analogous to the supernatural, by awakening the mind's attention from the lethargy of custom, and directing it to the loveliness and the wonders of the world before us" ... "awakening the mind" suggest[s] the romantic preoccupation with wonder—the surprise, the revelation which puts the tarnished world in a new light. This may well be the *raison d'être* of most Romantic paradoxes: and yet the neo-classic poets use paradox for much the same reason.[31]

Brooks links the Romantic fascination with "wonder" to Coleridge's and Wordsworth's self-confessed attempt to awaken "the mind's attention from the lethargy of custom." This romantic tendency is generalized by the New Critic to the metaphysical poetry he famously admired, and later on in the text to drama and prose fiction as well. According to this logic, the writer's mission is to compose paradoxical structures that will "awaken" the reader's attention and thereby allow her to grasp the "wonders of the world." But the importance of paradox, for Brooks, does not lie in its ability to aid the reader in overcoming familiarity with the world outside the text, which differentiated his position from that of the Russian Formalists, for example. For Brooks, the good reader dwells with the text, which, he believes, holds a dormant agency and a potentially autonomous life.

Consequently, Brooks conceptualizes paradox and attention as first and foremost converting the subject into a better reader of the poem itself: the structure of paradox invites attention, which then enables the reader to recognize and appreciate structures of paradox. This is not a one-sided process; the reader's attention is activated by the paradox as much as her practice of attention permits her to see the paradox to begin with. That this is the case is already evident in Brooks's quoted statement. Attention, elicited by the text, grants the reader the ability to see the "wonders" of the world. But the word *wonder* also stands, throughout *The Urn*, for one of the two basic types of literary paradoxes Brooks identifies: those that "insist on irony" and those that beget "wonder."[32] Brooks hints, then, that Coleridge's and Wordsworth's poetic structures "awaken" the reader's mind to the text (to wonder-paradoxes). This very same logic appears in Brooks's discussion of Shakespeare in relation to John Donne. There he argues, "since *Songs and Sonnets* of Donne ... requires a 'perpetual activity of attention' . . . the discipline gained from reading Donne may allow us to see more clearly the structure of paradox in Shakespeare."[33] In other words, the paradox in Donne brings about attention, which permits the reader to see Shakespeare's paradox.[34]

This theoretical construction seems to suggest that both the text and the reader are active agents in the reading process: the text *begets* attention and the reader, in response, *perceives* paradoxes via mental capacities. But this simple understanding of both participants as animated, or, in Brooks's terms, as "living" entities is complicated later on in *The Urn*. The Coleridge quotation depicts the state of being "attentive" as associated with being "awake," which also insinuates certain "aliveness": paradox works "by awakening the mind." And indeed, in various places in *The Urn*, Brooks characterizes the attentive reader, who recognizes the paradoxical unity of the text, as one who is "alive" to it: "Even the most direct and simple poet is forced into paradoxes far more often than we think, if we are sufficiently *alive* to what he is doing" (emphasis mine).[35]

However, in the paragraphs preceding and leading to the discussion of Coleridge, Wordsworth, attention, and life, Brooks is preoccupied with the proximity between paradox and death, rather than life. While discussing the paradox embedded in Wordsworth's line, "Dear God! The very houses seem asleep," he comments that the poet "has been in the habit of counting them [the houses] dead—as just mechanical and inanimate; to say they are 'asleep' is to say that they are alive."[36] The paradox of death that is in fact life—"It is only when the poet sees the city under the semblance of death that he can see it as actually alive"—is strangely what leads Brooks to think about Coleridge's idea of "awakening the mind."[37] This associative link between poet and reader, between the inanimate city and the text, and between death and life suggests that Brooks is diagnosing not just a cognitive condition of the modern reader, but an enduring ethical condition. The New Critic understands attention itself to function in a paradoxical fashion, in the gray zone between death and life: in order for the reader to be "alive" to the text, she must deaden herself, and the poem, though activating attention, is predominantly lifeless, as *The Urn* will go on to insinuate.[38]

It is evident throughout *The Urn* that Brooks, like Tate, imagines literature as a revivable "dead." Keats's "Ode on a Grecian Urn" is presented as "a poem in stone," which, in the context of the poem, evokes not just any static form but a gravestone specifically;[39] Pope's "The Rape of the Lock" is "the cries of those who die 'in *Metaphor*, and . . . in

Song";[40] and Thomas Gray's "Elegy Written in a Country Churchyard" is an "epitaph" engraved on a tombstone, which we, as "kindred spirit[s]," are invited to read (more generally, it is surprising to realize how many poems centered on death are collected in Brooks's archive of ostensible "balance and ease").[41]

Yet the ontology of these inanimate stone-poems is not clear-cut; Brooks depicts the literary work as always carrying a potentiality for life. In that spirit, Wordsworth's "houses" quoted above lend themselves to the observation of the speaker (to his "reading") as "mechanical and inanimate," but only until they are given life in the form of "sleep." Similarly, Brooks depicts Robert Herrick's "Corinna's Gone a-Maying" as a lifeless "object," but in that very sentence suggests that it can become a lived "experience" if "we," his close readers, will mentally participate in the reading process: "If we are willing to use imaginative understanding, we can come to know the poem as an object—we can share in the experience."[42] This idea is further stressed in Brooks's interpretation of Keats's "Ode," where the New Critic writes: "If we have been alive to the paradoxes which work throughout the poem, perhaps then, we shall be prepared for the enigmatic, final paradox which the 'silent form' utters."[43] The ability to animate Keats's poem as gravestone, to make the "silent form" speak, depends on the reader's efforts, her being "alive"—that is, attentive—to the work as a dynamic unity.

In this interpretation of Keats, Brooks repeats his depiction of the attentive reader as being "alive." However, as his analysis of Yeats's "Among School Children" demonstrates, this liveliness is in fact predicated on self-disintegration, or what I call "unselfing." Reading Yeats, Brooks writes: "The mature man can see the harmony, the unity of being, possessed by the tree or the lamb or the child; but the price of being able to see it is not to possess it in one's self. . . . Or to state the matter in Yeats's own terms: 'For wisdom is the property of the dead, a something incompatible with life.' "[44] Brooks discusses here the poet (Yeats) not as a producer of art but as a perceiver of "the unity of being." In that sense, Brooks is preoccupied in this segment with the consumption of art rather than with its production. According to this statement, the ability to discern "the unity of being" is dependent on the nonunity of the observing self.

If we were to translate this statement into Brooks's theoretical terms presented above, it would appear that in order to recognize via attention the paradoxical coherence of a text, in order to hear that poem "utter," the reader must pay the price of self-undoing. This discussion is concluded with a quote from Yeats, which further complicates affairs: "to state the matter in Yeats's own terms: 'For wisdom is the property of the dead, / A something incompatible with life.' "[45] If the ability to "see" unity, which we know is predicated on attention, is parallel to "wisdom," then the capacity to attend appears to be the sole "property of the dead." Brooks's reader, then, who wishes to engage well with the text, to animate its paradoxes, must make herself "incompatible with life"; being "alive" to a text is contingent on self-deadening.

As we can clearly see at this point, Brooks's hauntological model of the reading process fits perfectly with his choice of the urn as a central figure. After all, he understands both reader and text to be partially dead. Yet Brooks's metaphor works on an even deeper level, as shown by his discussion of Donne's "Canonization." The urn, as is well known, is this poem's thematic core, but Brooks goes on to claim that "Canonization" also becomes the concretization of the object it depicts.

> The poet is saying: "Our death is really a more intense life." . . . The poem is an instance of the doctrine it asserts; it is both the assertion and the realization of the assertion. . . . The poem itself is a well-wrought urn. . . . Having pre-empted the poem for our own purposes, it may not be too outrageous to go on to make one further observation. The urn to which we are summoned . . . is the poem itself.[46]

"Canonization," Brooks states, does not only delineate an urn, but is also a "well-wrought urn" itself, an object whose morbid connotations are made to stand out by Brooks's paraphrase: "Our death is really a more intense life." This is a reiteration of Brooks's continuous conceptualization of the literary work as a lifeless entity deeply associated with death, as we've seen with Keats's "Ode" as gravestone, and Gray's "Elegy" as an "epitaph." When Brooks names his project, then, "The Well Wrought Urn," he insinuates that not only "Canonization," but poems more generally, are urns of sorts, markers of death.

Yet, to follow Brooks's logic, "death is really a more intense life." That is, as I demonstrated before, Brooks views poems as tombstones that hold the potentiality for revival; they can "utter" paradoxes if only paid enough attention. These basic premises allow Brooks to venture on his final "outrageous" claim: "The urn to which we are summoned . . . is the poem itself." The "we" who are "summoned" into the poem as an "urn" are, of course, Brooks's close readers. This indicates that the reading process of "Canonization," as a paradigmatic example, requires the reader too to be in contact with the urn, to enter its space, where the dead lie. This rare "experience" will grant her, as it does the poem-as-urn, a "more intense life." Although the "urn" then stands for both reader and text, the bondage with death in both cases is never stable. The dead urn, as Gray's "Elegy" suggests, can be potentially animated: "Can storied urn or animated bust / Back to its mansion call the fleeting breath?"[47]

Facing the ghostly reading model that arises from Brooks's supposed work of "balance and ease," several pertinent questions arise: What does it practically mean to deaden oneself via attention? What is the ethical or political significance of this readerly labor, which finally grants the consumer of literature "a more intense life"? And why does Brooks turn to such gothic vocabulary to depict the animation of poetic form? An important path for understanding Brooks's melancholic vocabulary suggests itself in the critic's two-volume tome dedicated to William Faulkner, the master of Southern Gothic. More specifically, *The Yoknapatawpha Country* reveals that Brooks finds in Quentin, the suicidal protagonist of *Absalom, Absalom!*, a paradigm for the close reader. It also offers insight into Brooks's morbid configuration of the reader as a container of ashes in *The Urn*. In *The Yoknapatawpha Country*, Brooks demonstrates his understanding of the readerly process of self-deadening as a form of self-depletion. According to Brooks, the readers' attentive effort can transform them into an empty chamber that resonates with the voices of the now-enlivened literary text.

Brooks's readings of Faulkner also propose an ethical bearing to the New Critic's gothic construction. The poetic text in *The Yoknapatawpha Country* appears not only as a dead entity to be awakened, but as an alterity that deserves autonomy within the reading self. Finally, interacting with Faulkner's work, Brooks turns from the poem as literary text to the socially grounded stories of the past, thus exposing the Southern racial history that informs his notion of the reader as a subject willing to surrender her powers of life to the animation of others. For the New Critic, the literary text and history—the traumatic one as a limit case—hold a similarity: they are both paradoxical unities that the self can only approximate yet can never possess or fully comprehend. An intimate interaction with them, then, which includes bringing them to life, demands a form of ethical unselfing.

In the context of Faulkner's work, this process is translated into historical terms: the white guilt-ridden Quentin erases his subjectivity as the reader of his family's past in order to bring the very novel and the brutal history it depicts into being. In *The Urn*, the close reader is not driven by Quentin's melancholic historically contingent affect, but is similarly trying to animate the poem as a complex unity, this time through the cognitive labor of attention. Over and above these differences, Quentin and the close reader are alike for Brooks: at the price of self-loss, they are granted singular powers of creation.

When the Dead Tongue Speaks

In 2009, the acclaimed *Oxford American: A Magazine of the South* asked 134 scholars and writers to select the best Southern novel of all time; Faulkner's *Absalom, Absalom!* was chosen almost unanimously.[48] But this is hardly indicative of the novel's status at the time of its publication. Academic and popular reviews jointly labeled the work "gothic" and reprimanded it for wallowing "in morbidity," practicing "demonology," and presenting its audience with "psychopathic ghosts."[49] Even Malcolm Cowley, the editor of *The Portable Faulkner*, suggested in a disapproving tone—aligning himself with the negative evaluation of the gothic novel, typical of his time—that *Absalom, Absalom!* should be read within the Poe tradition.[50]

The traditional narrative of Faulkner's reception history, and that of *Absalom, Absalom!* specifically, depicts the New Critics (along with the New York intellectuals) as forcing Faulkner's work out from under the umbrella of gothic literature and repositioning it in the category of modernism.[51] In that spirit, Brooks memorably remarked that Faulkner's work should be read as "more than a bottle of Gothic sauce."[52] Nevertheless, Brooks's recurrent fascination with Faulkner's characters who are haunted by death insinuates that the New Critic was drawn to and found a positive potential in the writer's gothic sensibility. Importantly, this might explain Brooks's aesthetic preferences and illuminate Brooks's choice of *Absalom, Absalom!* as "the most brilliantly written of all Faulkner's novels," a text whose narrative is told and produced by a living-dead "ghost," and in which death in life propels the narration.[53]

Absalom, Absalom! is a "racial tragedy," to quote Sheldon Brivic, one that centers around the Civil War story of a white man, Thomas Sutpen and his grand, though failed, "design" to rise up from his position as a "cattle"-like poor white by establishing a monstrous hundred-square-mile plantation, and begetting a "purely white" dynasty.[54] But this novel, as has been repeatedly established, is first and foremost the story of guilt-ridden Quentin Compson, or, more precisely, the story of Quentin being told (by Miss Rosa and Mr. Compson) and then telling (Shreve) the racially provocative narrative of the Sutpen family.

Due to this unique role, several scholars, including Brooks, singled Quentin out as the surrogate of the reader in the diegetic world, as I will go on to discuss. And indeed, especially in the first half of the novel, Quentin is primarily an absorber of stories, "a Special Listener," in George Marrion O'Donnell's words.[55] By virtue of this trait, both old Rosa Coldfield and his father choose him as a vessel (an auditory "urn," as we will see in chapter 2) for the stories of the long-dead Thomas, Allen, Henry, Judith, and Charles, and the larger racialized American history they represent. Rosa and Mr. Compson do not expect Quentin to intervene in the narrative he receives, but rather to incorporate it and thus give it presence in the world. In that vein, Miss Rosa claims she tells Quentin her story for it to be written down—an expectation that would emphasize his active participation—but the young student quickly realizes that his interlocutor in fact only wants her story read; his role, as she sees it, is to act as a reader rather than a writer, a mediator rather than a producer ("and maybe you will remember this and write about it . . . *only she dont* [sic] *mean that*, he thought. *It's because she wants it told . . . so that people . . . will read it*").[56]

The third-person narrator of Faulkner's novel informs us that the role of channeling other people's voices is anything but new to Quentin, and in many ways can be said to function as the defining feature of his being.

> It was a part of his twenty years' heritage of breathing the same air and hearing his father talk about the man; a part of the town's—Jefferson's—eighty years' heritage of the same air which the man himself had breathed between this September afternoon in 1909 and that Sunday morning in June in 1833. . . . Quentin had grown up with that; the mere names were interchangeable and almost myriad. His childhood was full of them; his very body was an empty hall echoing with sonorous defeated names; he was not a being, an entity, he was a commonwealth. He was a barracks filled with stubborn back-looking ghosts.[57]

What allows Quentin to function as the "reader" of the Sutpen family is his morbid ontology. The protagonist carries in his body the voices of the antebellum dead—those who were "defeated" by their "sin of slavery," and those who were their victims—without integrating them into his sense of self. What can be thought of as his subjectivity shrivels up in order to form an "empty hall" for the dead to make their presence felt. For that reason, Quentin is depicted as a "commonwealth": he is not a unified subject enclosed within clear boundaries of self, but a collective and historical echo-chamber that encompasses the whole of the community and serves as its unifying space.[58] In that sense, and over and above the numerous differences that pull them apart, Quentin conforms to Derrida's melancholic subject presented earlier. Like Derrida's mourner, who resists the introjection of the dead as an "image" or "idol" into a now augmented self, Quentin engages in "impossible mourning." He takes in but does not "interiorize" the dead, thereby remaining loyal to the Other's "infinite remove," in Derrida's terms, at the price of immense pain.

Yet we must remember that Quentin does not *choose* his ethical melancholic stance in the simple meaning of the term, which assumes complete agency. The familial and cultural context in which he is raised—saturated with unspoken acts of violence, tormenting secrets, and the daunting, all-consuming, presence of slavery as an unrepentable sin—molds him affectively into an "empty hall" for the dead. In the place of "choice," then, Derrida proposes "refusal" as the act that characterizes the ethical melancholic subject, a resistance to the assimilation of the complex Other at the expense of its autonomy.

> The cryptic enclave as an extraneous or foreign area of incorporation . . . According to Freud's *Mourning and Melancholy* . . . the self recuperates its previous cathectic investment from the lost object, while waiting for a libidinal reorganization. Sealing the loss of the object, but also marking a refusal to mourn, such a maneuver is foreign and actually opposed to the process of introjection. I pretend to keep the dead alive, intact, safe (save) inside me, but it is only in order to refuse, in a necessarily equivocal way, to love the dead as a living part of me, dead save in me, through the process of introjection, as happens in so-called normal mourning.[59]

The melancholic subject "refuses to mourn" a "so-called normal mourning" by forming the lost Other into a part of the living self. Instead, like

Quentin, the "impossible" mourner gestures toward the unattainable goal of keeping the dead alive within a diminished self, who shrivels to allow for a "cryptic enclave as an extraneous or foreign area of incorporation" to act within her. In other words, in order to allow for the "defeated names" to echo, Quentin deadens himself, becoming a nonbeing.

Paradoxically, it is this melancholic positioning that places Quentin in the privileged position of the narratee within the fictional world. His historically determined disposition to "listen," in O'Donnell's terms, provides him access to knowledge from his surroundings which would otherwise be unavailable, and allows him to cultivate the narrative of *Absalom, Absalom!* within him. With the backdrop of *The Urn*'s theory of attention, we can already sense a similarity between *The Urn*'s close reader and Quentin: both deaden themselves in order to animate a complex unity, poetry and history respectively, unexpectedly gaining in this manner "a more intense life." Or, put differently, they are both instructed, Quentin by his social milieu and the close reader by Brooks, to animate a lifeless entity within them, either a "storied urn" or "stubborn back-looking ghosts," thus coming into intimate contact with alterity. An important difference between the two models is found in the reader's motivation: Quentin is driven by affect, while the close reader deadens herself via cognitive effort, as we will discuss in detail later on. Yet their similarities suggest that when *The Urn*'s close reader is requested to deaden herself via attention, she is in fact instructed, like Quentin, to momentarily become an "empty hall echoing with sonorous defeated names." That would explain, of course, Brooks's selection of "the urn" as an apt metaphor for the close reader who, he hopes, will become an empty container filled with the dead.

Brooks turns to *Absalom, Absalom!* in order to think through his readerly model, since this novel forces to the fore the New Critic's notion of the good reader as a living-dead vessel capable of animating a lifeless alterity. This is especially evident in *Absalom, Absalom!*'s famous scene centering on Judith's love letter from Charles Bon. The scene follows one in which Henry murders Bon after realizing that he is none other than Judith's half-brother, or, as the novel puts it, Sutpen's "sixteenth part negro son" from his prior Haitian "eighth part negro mistress," whom Sutpen abruptly abandons upon realizing she does not fit his racialized "design."[60]

Judith, then, approaches Quentin's grandmother, a foreign acquaintance who she conceives of as a "stranger," in order to bequeath her Bon's final letter, "the only one she ever showed."[61] But the goal of Judith's transaction, we find, is not historical preservation in the traditional sense, that is, making sure that her love story with Bon and its violent resolution will persist in the public sphere through the continuous reading of the letter. As befits a novel that explicitly takes on an investigation of what history means, Judith's reasoning for her actions is far more complex. She instructs Quentin's grandmother: "Destroy it. As you like. Read it if you like or dont [sic] read it if you like."[62] The point, for Judith, in passing her "scrap of paper" from "one hand to another, one mind to another," is not the conservation of life, but an attempt to "scratch" the utterly sealed surface of death.

> You get born and you try this and you dont [sic] know why only you keep on trying . . . and then all of a sudden it's all over and all you have left is a block of stone with scratches on it provided there was someone to remember to have the marble scratched . . . and so maybe if you could go to someone, the stranger the better, and give them something--a scrap of paper . . . it would be at least a scratch, something, something that might make a mark on something that *was* once for the reason that it can die someday, while the block of stone cant [sic] be *is* because it never can become *was* because it cant [sic] ever die or perish.[63]

The grave, the "block of stone," which is the memorial, the urn, cannot be *is*, cannot portray a life, because it is imperishable, unchangeable. The telling of history, on the other hand, requires modification. For a story to unfold, one must scratch or make a mark on that lost life, forcing it to speak, to change, to animate.

These exact same concepts, as we have seen, are at the center of Brook's *Urn*, where the attentive reader is the one who is capable of making the memorial—the "poem in stone"—speak or "utter" its paradoxes.[64] But the resemblance does not end there; in his novel, Faulkner also goes on to present two models of readers who encounter the letter, and like Brooks, he prefers the readers who are able to revive the dead letter over those who are restricted to perceiving its lifelessness. The latter model is embodied by Mr. Compson, who depicts his reading of the letter in a fashion characteristic of his didactic rhetoric, generalizing it into a statement about the essence of history.

> We exhume from old trunks and boxes and drawers letters without salutation or signature, in which men and women who once lived and breathed are now merely initials or nick-

> names. . . . They are there, yet something is missing . . . the paper old and faded and falling to pieces, the writing faded, almost indecipherable, yet meaningful . . . but nothing happens . . . you re-read, tedious and intent, poring, making sure that you have forgotten nothing, made no miscalculation; you bring them together again and again and nothing happens: just the words, the symbols, the shapes themselves, shadowy inscrutable and serene, against the turgid background of a horrible and bloody mischancing of human affairs.[65]

That "something," small as it might be, that Judith hopes would occur when the letter passes from "one mind to another" is precisely what refuses to happen in Mr. Compson's case. He rereads, "tedious and intent," making sure nothing is forgotten, but "*nothing*" rather than "something" happens, and the letter remains a stone: "[J]ust the words, the symbols, the shapes themselves."

On the other hand, Quentin's interaction with the letter, especially when juxtaposed with his father's, appears altogether different.

> Quentin took the letter from him [Mr. Compson] and beneath that dim bug-fouled globe opened it, carefully, as though the sheet . . . were not the paper but the intact ash of its former shadow and substance . . . he read the faint spidery script not like something impressed upon a letter by a once-living hand but like a shadow cast upon it which has resolved on the paper the instant before he looked at it and which might fade, vanish at any instant while he still read: the dead tongue speaking after the four years and then after almost fifty more.[66]

For Quentin, a nonentity that hosts the Southern dead, Judith's letter is not a tombstone, a "scrap of paper," but the very ashes "of its former shadow and substance" that now echo within the reader as an urn. The protagonist does not read the letter as if it is a remnant of the past, of people "who once lived and breathed" and are "now merely initials or nicknames," in his father's terms. For him, the letter is composed in the present, written by the dead hand just an "instant before he looked at it," to the extent that he can hear "the dead tongue" speak while he reads.

No doubt, Quentin is the reader Judith—and the novel more generally—imagines for the torturous history of the American South, one who would scratch the surface of the enclosed tombstone by making the dead tongue speak again. But, interestingly, Quentin also represents the readerly model that Brooks embraces.

"Follow Quentin's Example"

The traditional view of the New Critical close reader that I mentioned earlier might lead one to assume that it would be the rational reading process that Mr. Compson conducts—one that involves "re-reading," "no miscalculation," and "making sure that you have forgotten nothing"—which would stand in the eyes of Brooks for the close reader within Faulkner's imaginary universe. But this is not the case; Brooks consistently finds Quentin's liminal ontology to be his favorite and theorizes close reading via the ghostly character. The originality of this position is underscored when taking into consideration the conventional scholarly conception of Quentin as the surrogate of the reader within the novel.

Much of the criticism that came after Brooks views Quentin as going through a radical shift halfway through the novel: while the first half portrays the protagonist as a receptor, many critics believe him to transform into an active creator of the narrative in the latter part of the text.[67] In his dorm at Harvard, Quentin relates the tragedy of the Sutpen family to Shreve, his Canadian roommate, and together they inject their own speculations into the story and fill in its most salient gaps. This process marks, the critical convention goes, Quentin's shift from a passive narratee to a narrator. As Richard Godden succinctly puts it, "The critical tradition has garnered their [Quentin and Shreve's] achievements largely from chapters eight and nine under some variant of the generic title 'creative history.' "[68] In this context, "creative" signifies the ability to invent the text from one's own imagination, to act as a free agent within the realm of the narrative.[69]

Brooks presents a position radically different from this critical consensus and surprisingly more in line with Derrida's hauntological deconstruction of the liberal subject. The New Critic points out the interpretive significance of the intratextual dialogue between Faulkner's different novels. Given Quentin's tragic death in *The Sound and the Fury*, Brooks concludes that Quentin never finds his place among the living, not in the second part of the novel and not at all. In his mind, "Quentin is really, as his sister knows, in love with death itself."[70] This obsession brings agony to the student but also carries a positive potential, according to Brooks, since Quentin's fascination with death functions as the fuel that keeps the novel, and its reader, going: "For the novel *Absalom, Absalom!* does not merely tell the story of Thomas Sutpen, but dramatizes the process by which two young men of the twentieth-century construct the character of Thomas Sutpen.... The second half of the book may be called an attempt at interpretation."[71] In line with the critical tradition discussed above, Brooks too identifies a line of demarcation between the two halves of the novel, but for him Quentin's process of "inference," "conjuncture," and "guesswork" is not a bright one. Shreve, on the other hand, is a different story.

The New Critic distinguishes the narration conducted by Quentin from that of his roommate. While the novel indicates that "it might have been . . . in a sense both" roommates that conjure Sutpen's story, Brooks insists that it is Shreve, the Canadian "outsider," who "does most of the imaginative reconstruction."[72] This initially counterintuitive claim by Brooks follows a compelling logic; one might indeed say that Quentin does not understand himself to be "imagining" at all. Both students envision the missing scenes from Sutpen's narrative together, but of the two, Shreve is the one who self-consciously refers to it as the work of the imagination. He makes sure to announce the beginning of the creative process by using markers such as, "Let me play a while now" or "all right, don't bother to say he stopped talking now; just go on."[73] In this sense, Shreve differentiates between knowledge emanating from others and fiction he himself creates.

Quentin, on the other hand, does not recognize the boundaries between others' stories and his own, and rarely takes ownership of information he imagines or even discovers.[74] He also moves in his speech between details supported by the outside and those emerging from his inside, but does not acknowledge these shifts.[75] He never announces, as Shreve does, that he is at a certain moment engaged in the "play" of imagination and thus sheds doubt on his own acceptance of these narratives as fictional.

Thus, when Brooks contends that it is Shreve who does "most of the imaginative reconstruction," he makes a valid point. For Quentin, stories arising from the inside are just as foreign as those coming from external sources. Quentin, we remember, is a listener/reader adroit at hearing the stories of the past within him ("his very body was an empty hall echoing with sonorous defeated names"). At times, he is even able to sense these stories without the need for linguistic articulation ("but you were not listening because you knew it already . . . absorbed it already without the medium of speech").[76] What Shreve, then, conceives as the "play" of imagination could very well be for Quentin an act of listening to foreign voices that he takes in.

It is highly significant, then, that although Brooks flags Shreve as performing much of the "imaginative" work, he advises Faulkner's readers to model themselves on Quentin.

> The story embodied the problem of evil and the irrational. . . . Had Henry cared less for Bon, or else much less for Judith, he might have promoted the happiness of one without feeling that he was sacrificing that of the other. Or, had he cared much less for either and much more for himself, he might have won a cool and rational detachment. . . . Had Henry been not necessarily wiser but simply more cynical or more gross or more selfish, there would have been no tragedy. To say that Quentin was peculiarly susceptible to this meaning of Henry's story is not to make of Shreve a monster of inhumanely cool irrationality [sic]. But Shreve is measurably closer to the skepticism and detachment that allow modern man to dismiss the irrational claims from which Quentin cannot free himself and which he honors to his own cost. The reader of *Absalom, Absalom!* might well follow Quentin's example. . . . The aspect of the story to stress is not the downfall of Thomas Sutpen, a man who is finally optimistic, rationalistic, and afflicted with elephantiasis of the will. Instead, he ought to attend to the story of Sutpen's children.[77]

Brooks implicitly identifies Quentin and Shreve as two models of readers embedded within *Absalom, Absalom!*'s diegetic world—in a manner similar to the juxtaposition between Quentin and Mr. Compson that we have seen before—and favors the former over the latter. The close reader is asked to join Quentin's group, which includes Henry and Judith as well. These three are clustered together since they are associated with "irrationality" and "attachment," which, we learn, are valuable readerly qualities for Brooks.

Not only does Brooks opt for a reader that "cannot free himself" from "irrational claims," but he also urges any reader to follow Quentin's example and focus, in the text, on characters like Henry and Judith, who exhibit similar traits. Henry, after all, is so "attached" to and so "cares" for Bon and Judith (and so unattached and careless when it comes to himself) that he is described as the very opposite of "rational detachment."[78] Brooks's close reader, then, is asked to imitate not Shreve and Sutpen, associated with "optimism" and "rationalism," but Quentin, Henry, and Judith, who are unselfish, notwithstanding the "tragedy" this subject position implies. To push this claim even further, one might say that in order to read like Quentin, who is a "notpeople," or like Henry who pays the price of death for his limitless "care," Brooks's close reader need not be unselfish but, at least momentarily, selfless.[79]

However, *The Urn*'s close reader is never instructed to "care" or emotionally "attach" herself to the text. She is not made to be haunted by "irrational claims" from which she "cannot free" herself, like Quentin. This is where attention as "mental agility," in Brooks's terms, comes into play. Given that not all readers are motivated into a melancholic stance by historical circumstances, affect, or "attachment," the New Critic systemizes his ethical model into a cognitive one in *The Urn*. He teaches his reader how to utilize attention to forgo her integral self and animate the poem as an Other.

In that vein, when Brooks shifts from his description of Quentin as "irrational" to his instructions for the reader in the paragraph above, he substitutes "attachment" with "attention" and insists that in order to read like Quentin, the reader "ought to *attend*." The "tragedy" and "sacrifice" that motivate Quentin's compulsion to evacuate himself are replaced, in the case of the close reader, with an active and disciplined cognitive effort of attention. This might explain why the word *irrationality* proves to be unstable for Brooks. The New Critic begins by associating "rationality" with Shreve and Sutpen's "cool . . . detachment," but goes on to describe Shreve as "a monster of inhumanely cool irrationality." In fact, logic and reason belong to both readerly models Brooks identifies in *Absalom, Absalom!*: Shreve is "rational" in his "skepticism" and "detachment," while the close reader, who pertains to Quentin's group, is required, via "rational" cognitive labor, to transform herself into a selfless "empty hall."

That Quentin's mode of reading history and the close reader's efforts of attention in *The Urn* are aligned for Brooks is evident in the New Critic's further differentiation between Shreve and Quentin. Faulkner's work, he writes, requires "the heightening, special focus" that all good fiction "demands and justifies," a "focus" that echoes *The Urn*'s "attention."[80] Yet in the context of *Absalom, Absalom!* and the reading of history, the labor of "focus" or "attention" is replaced with the work of "projection": "*Absalom, Absalom!* is a persuasive commentary upon the thesis that much of 'history' is really a kind of imaginative reconstruction. The past always remains a mystery, but if we are to hope to understand it in any wise, we must enter into it and project ourselves imaginatively into the attitudes and emotions of the historical figures."[81] History, like *The Urn*'s poems, is a "mystery" not easily accessible. To come into contact with it "in any wise," one must make a special effort and project oneself "into the attitudes and emotions of . . . figures."

The argument that history involves a "projection" of the self into an Other might seem banal, but the term Brooks chooses here makes it anything but hackneyed. A more conventional term would have been *identification*, which traditionally implies an imagining of the self as similar to an Other, a process in which the integrity of the self is maintained. Projection, on the other hand, from the Latin *proicere*, "stretch out, throw forth," means in Brooks's work an ejection, a forcing out of parts of the self. This would explain why he writes that "we," the readers of Faulkner and of history, must "project ourselves imaginatively *into*" rather than *onto*, "the historical figures." The process of projection denotes, in the context of Brooks's critical writings, a literal movement between entities: giving up parts of the self in order to take in parts of the Other.

A similar movement is generated via attention as conceptualized in *The Urn*; the reader's cognitive labor allows her to remove parts of the self and incorporate the poem while keeping it external, that is, a not fully integrated entity. What does seem to destabilize Brooks's idea of reading as leaving the Other its agency is the critic's assertion above that the interaction with history requires "imagination," a term which implies that agency fully remains on the side of the reader. But this apparent tension is resolved when Brooks discusses the different kinds of "projection" performed by Shreve and Quentin as "readers" of Sutpen's history.

> Both of the boys make this sort of projection. . . . He [Shreve] finds it, in his lack of any serious emotional commitment, a fascinating game. . . . Quentin on the other hand is too much involved—too fully committed to the problems and the issue—actually to enjoy the reconstruction. He feels a compulsion to do so, of course, the same compulsion that had caused him, against his better judgment, to go up into the bedroom at Sutpen's Hundred and look upon the wasted face of Henry Sutpen. . . . One of the most important devices used in the novel is the placing of Shreve in it as a kind of sounding board and mouthpiece. By doing so, Faulkner has in effect acknowledged the attitude of the modern "liberal," twentieth-century reader,

who is basically rational, skeptical, without any special concern for history, and pretty well emancipated from the ties of family, race, or section. In fact, Shreve sounds very much like certain literary critics who have written on Faulkner.[82]

While Shreve stands for the "twentieth-century reader . . . rational, skeptical" of whom Brooks disapproves, as his sarcastic tone indicates, Quentin embodies the "too fully committed" alternative who projects himself, that is, throws himself into, the "stubborn back-looking ghosts" of the past.

The process of projective imagination that Brooks has in mind is not one of inventing something new ("a fascinating game"), but of committing to alterity at the price of self-disintegration. Whether that Other is the traumatic racial history of the American South (as in the case of Quentin), or the paradoxical "unity" of the text (as in *The Urn*), Brooks's close reader is urged to "follow Quentin's example" in the sense of becoming "an empty hall echoing" with the voices of alterity, hence being allowed an intimate contact, partial as it may be, with its "mystery." If we accept my suggestion, then, that unselfing as a praxis of self-extraction runs through close reading in its various global iterations, then in the case of the US, it is her very sense of life that the reader is asked to postpone while engaging with literature. This "technology of the self," in Foucauldian terms, is charged with local politico-historical valence and is construed in such a way to invoke self-harm and self-control but to simultaneously hold ethical potentiality.

∼

As I note in the Introduction, the theory and practice of the New Criticism have recently been subject to binary thinking. This polarity often arises in discussions of the affinity between the politically liberal British scholars, such as I. A. Richards and William Empson, considered the forefathers of the New Criticism, and the US New Critics, who were aligned with highly conservative ideologies. The problem is that this biographical-political starting point is at times extended to interpretive aspects of the theories themselves. The danger lies in the tendency to assume that the theories' manifestations on the page must perfectly chime with the explicit ideological stances of their respective writers.

Thus, for example, Joseph North, in his recent *Literary Criticism: A Concise Political History*, claims that the "left-liberal . . . internationalist . . . and secularist" Cambridge scholars "advanced a utilitarian model of aesthetic and practical education."[83] On the other hand, the "Southern U.S. Christian" New Critics institutionalized the method of close reading "as a thoroughly idealist practice, based in a neo-Kantian aesthetics of disinterest and transcendent value," which translated into "the famously radical New Critical attempt to secure the autonomy and self-sufficiency of the aesthetic object."[84] Yet Brooks's theory of mind presented in this chapter significantly qualifies North's paradigmatic view.

The New Critic's readerly protocol, implicitly presented and carefully developed in both *The Urn* and *The Yoknapatawpha Country*, is not a "thoroughly idealist practice" and promotes something very different from an "aesthetics of disinterest." *The Urn*, saturated with graveyards, "half acre tombs," "daggers," "ashes," "mortal wounds," and "melancholy," emerges as no less gothic than Faulkner's universe.[85] At the heart of this melancholia is Brooks's close reader, who is diligently taught how to deaden herself during the reading process. That is, the "autonomy" of the literary text is indeed central to Brooks's thinking, but it is not an "idealist" autonomy that assumes textual "self-sufficiency." Instead, it is an autonomy that paradoxically can only come into play during an interaction with a reader who is willing to make an active cognitive effort for the poem to make its singular voice heard.

The close reader is not "detached" or "disinterested"; rather, she empties herself of subjectivity to internally engage with the poem as alterity. This readerly melancholic effort not only leaves "the other its otherness," as Derrida puts it, but is also utilitarian in nature. It educates the reader in approaching a "more intense life" beyond the confines of literature through intimate and nonintrusive encounters with alterity. In this light, New Critical close reading, the foundation of literary discipline, appears to be rooted in a utilitarian model of aesthetic and practical education, in contrast with North's assertion. If we are sufficiently "dead" to the New Critical creed, then, perhaps we will be able to hear the provocative reading practice it "utters."

In the next chapter, we will delve deeper into the readerly model underlying the New Critical creed by turning our attention to Faulkner's renowned novel, *The Sound and the Fury*. While in the current chapter we examined Faulkner's work only through Brooks's lenses, in the next, we will explore what Faulkner's modernist novel reveals about attentive reading without the immediate mediation of the New Critics, to understand what aspects of Faulkner's modernist production appealed to the New Critics and how it influenced their thinking. Drawing on insights from Sound Studies, we will see that Faulkner not only sets the ground for the New Critics' practice of unselfing but pushes it to its limit. He skillfully manipulates form to morph readers into aural echo chambers, where the lingering presence of "stubborn back-looking ghosts" resounds. For Faulkner, the ultimate reader perceives what is absent, discerns the unheard.

Chapter Two

"I Wrote This Book and Learned to Read"

Sound, Fury, and William Faulkner's Negative Audition

> When we read to ourselves, our ears hear nothing. Where we read, however, we listen.
>
> —Garrett Stewart

The figure of the urn, it is well known, was central to the New Critics' thinking. However, as we have seen in the previous chapter, the meaning carried forward by this trope in the New Critical body of work is quite surprising. The urn is usually interpreted as symbolizing the New Critics' view of the literary text as a perfected, self-enclosed artifact, but a closer look at its placements and functions undermines this very assumption. Following the urn in Cleanth Brooks's *The Well-Wrought Urn* and his interpretation of William Faulkner's work, we witnessed how, against expectations, the urn bespeaks a New Critical preoccupation with loss; a theory of the reader's active participation in the creation of the literary work; and both an ethical and a disciplinary readerly protocol.

Within this context, the New Critics are revealed to have understood the literary text and its reader as urns of sorts. The literary work hovers between life and death, requiring the reader to divest herself of animation and transform into an empty urn in which the text can come to life. And though this readerly subjectivity—a ghostly, deadly one—might appear to be utterly pessimistic, I suggested it opens up an ethical possibility in the spirit of Jacques Derrida's "hauntology": Brooks identifies in Faulkner a gesture toward a radical form of encounter with the literary text as an alterity.

In this chapter, I return to Faulkner's oeuvre, once again pulling on the thread of the urn, which was a figure of great significance for him as well. Here, I temporarily bracket the New Critics' readings of Faulkner and follow the urn to examine the writer's own depiction, conceptualization, and manipulation of the reading process. I suggest that the New Critics felt a proximity toward Faulkner's work as they deftly identified in it a view of the reader that corresponded with, and perhaps even initiated, their now paradigmatic model of the unselfing, attentive close reader. In Faulkner's case too we find that the urn leads to a dialectical theory and practice of reading. More specifically, Faulkner's recurrent resort to the urn image, either explicitly or implicitly, points to literature's potential in cultivating a specifically acoustic sensibility to otherness, a form of reading-listening that may have paved the way for, and is still traceable in, close reading. The profound connection between the New Critical model of reading and Faulkner's work will be further underscored in the following chapters, as we witness how frequently Faulkner's body of work accompanies the transnational journeys of the New Criticism, the two converging around their shared archetype of the "urn" reader. An avowed admirer of Keats's "Ode on a Grecian Urn," Faulkner referred to the poem and the urn at its center in various of his works (such as *Flags in the Dust*, *Sartoris*, and *Go Down, Moses*). He also famously declared that "if a writer has to rob his mother, he will not hesitate; the 'Ode on a Grecian Urn' is worth any number of old ladies," and even crafted his own version of the "Ode" for his lover, Meta Carpenter.[1] Surprisingly, the triangulation between the Southern critics, the author they promoted, and the figure of the urn has not received much scholarly attention.

When Faulkner's interest in the urn was nevertheless explored, scholars have taken the writer's frequent gestures toward "Ode" to mean that, like the New Critics, he understood the literary text to be an autonomous, unfading, and exceedingly well-formulated aesthetic object. In that vein, André Bleikasten claims, in alluding to Brooks's *The Well Wrought Urn*, that Faulkner "strove for . . . the wholeness and perfection of the 'well-wrought urn,' sometimes even subscribing to the extreme idealistic assumption . . . that, if the world exists at all, it is destined to end up in or as a book, the Book: 'it takes only one book to do it . . . it's one perfect book, you see. It's one single urn or shape that you want.'"[2] Bleikasten understands Faulkner's superimposition of the "perfect book" onto the "single urn" as a testament to the writer's idealistic aesthetic view. In a like manner, Fredric Jameson criticizes Faulkner for overly manipulating form at the expense of plot in the spirit of the purported New Critical ideal of literature as a perfected aesthetic object. For Jameson, Faulkner "construct[s] a mystery which is the result only of the author's withholding of information, rather than latent in the plot itself" in agreement with the New Critical vision of literature as an "artifact" from which "nothing stands out, there are no excesses either way . . . no extra stylistic frills, no 'extrinsic' or extraneous content poking out of the pillowcase."[3]

Using similar vocabulary, Richard Godden, a prominent Faulkner scholar, critiques the author for producing mystery and an accompanying readerly difficulty in the service of a sadistic obsession with crafting too well-wrought a text: "Many are the close readings of Faulkner, generally conducted under some version of a celebratory modernist rubric, whereby 'difficult' is translated as 'rich,' 'dense,' or 'complex.' . . . Rather, Faulkner's 'difficulty' . . . is driven by his penurious habit of secretion—a habit which demands the reader attend closely in order to recover, from Faulkner's choked, subverted, underarticulated, and yet imperious prose, inferences of a tale that is not being told."[4] According to Godden, the demand Faulkner's work makes on the reader to "attend closely" is fruitless. It is merely the heavy price she must pay for Faulkner's excessive formalism: "Faulkner's 'difficult' writing is not pleasurable, and reading him is often an intolerable labor. Impressionistically, the experience can resemble running on the spot, only to find that you are descending, and have been button-holed in a pit."[5]

Godden's paradigmatic view can find support in Faulkner's own introduction to *The Sound and the Fury*, the novel that will be my main concern in this chapter and which Faulkner lovingly depicted as his "most gallant and the most magnificent failure."[6] In this introduction, Faulkner describes the novel as a well-crafted vase: "There is a story somewhere about an old Roman who kept at his bedside a Tyrrhenian vase which he loved and the rim of which he wore slowly away with kissing it. I had made myself a vase. . . . It's fine to think that you will leave something behind you when you die, but it's better to have made something you can die with."[7] Against the backdrop of Faulkner's fascination with Keats's ode, and his own comparison between a "perfect book" and a "single urn," it is quite clear that he has a specific "vase" in mind. *The Sound and the Fury* is not any "Roman vase"; with this work, Faulkner felt, he had reached the creative pitch he was aiming for in crafting his own urn.

Faulkner's description reinforces the notion that the urn represents for him an important aesthetic principle. If it is the novel's lasting impact that he wanted to stress, as suggested by the critics above, a vase seems like a commonsense choice of metaphor given the longevity of this artifice. But Faulkner's vocabulary around the "Tyrrhenian vase" is far more morbid and far less stable than one would expect from a writer advancing a view of literature as a beacon of "wholeness," with "no excesses either way."

If we follow that image through, Faulkner's love for his novel eventuates not in its endurance as an unchanged object, but in its material decay; the Roman's kisses wear the vase "slowly away." And this object is not made to outlast the author in its eternality, but to perish with him; it is a thing to "die with," rather than to leave "behind." These ghostly undertones, which follow Faulkner's descriptions of the urn throughout his work, and which distinguish his urn from Keats's Romantic "cold pastoral" granted with "eternity," call for a reconsideration of Faulkner's purported transcendental aesthetics, which such critics as Jameson and Godden attribute him with. Instead, I suggest that the urn echoes for Faulkner not only "wholeness and perfection," but also—I would venture to say mostly—a ghostly theory of reading, a conceptualization of the reader's mental work as providing an empty space for ostensibly absent entities to resound.[8]

As the following pages will suggest, Faulkner is even more committed to the idea of the reader as receptacle of ashes than Brooks had predicted. Brooks, we recall, models his view of the ideal reader on the fictional character of the suicidal Quentin Compson (*Absalom, Absalom!* and *The Sound and the Fury*), whom the New Critic suggests acts as an exemplary reader within Faulkner's diegetic world. Brooks turns specifically to this morbid character since he believes that Faulkner encourages his reader to utilize her attention as a way to turn herself into a vessel for the dead, namely, to unself for the sake of animating the lifeless text.

But Faulkner does not only think of his reader as a Quentin of sorts, an echoing "empty hall," metaphorically. Instead, he takes the acoustic aspect of this depiction literally.[9] For Faulkner, the reader's work of attention signifies a labor of sonic imagination; the attentive unselfing reader is she who brings the text to life by producing its soundtrack, by making the novel's voice heard within her silenced self.[10] Faulkner understands ethical listening to involve an attunement to sonic stimuli that one is socially and bodily taught to register as inaudible. And in order to render oneself open to sounds that usually remain beneath the threshold of acoustic awareness, one must, in following Faulkner's implicit instructions, provisionally transform into an empty vessel in which these silenced voices can resonate.

Consequently, to use Garrett Stewart's terminology, Faulkner structures his work to provoke in the reader a unique form of "inner audition," which entails the "evocalization" of absent-presence sounds, ones that haunt the text but do not positively appear on the page, like an unmentioned cry or an unspecified ticking of a clock.[11] In this way, Faulkner trains his audience to aurally and mentally perceive entities that are ostensibly absent but, with the right ear, reveal themselves to be palpably there. My reading, then, continues in the footsteps of exciting recent explorations into Faulkner's "auditory experimentalism," but broaches the subject through the question of readerly listening.[12] That is, to paraphrase Julie Beth Napolin's astute call for a shift in modernist studies from "Who speaks?" to "Who hears?" I ask not "who" Faulkner attunes to but "how" he invites his readers to listen.[13]

To do so, I delve in the first section below into Faulkner's soundscape and explore what I call "ghostly sounds," vocalities that can only be realized through readerly negative audition. Next, I examine two instances in *The Sound and the Fury* where Faulkner activates such readerly audition through the internal monologues delivered by the characters Benjy and Quentin. While these sections may initially appear to diverge from the central theme of attention, they lay the necessary groundwork for a deeper understanding of this readerly state, as we see in the following section. There, I elucidate Faulkner's conceptualization of attention as ventriloquizing alien voices, and turn to the volatile link between readerly listening and race in the novel, centering around the analysis of Reverend Shegog's preaching scene. Finally, I conclude by revisiting the affinity between the New Criticism, Faulkner, and close reading.

More broadly, through Faulkner, alongside other writers who will appear in following chapters, I wish to expand our understanding of the relationship between the New Criticism and modernist production by looking at the two through the lens of close reading and the close reader. I propose that the burgeoning and provocative model of the close reader brought about nothing less than a new literary archive. Modernist writers reacted to the New Critical model of close reading by formally constructing their works to challenge the local version of this praxis; other writers responded to the New Critical protocol by building their texts to fit it; and in yet different instances, the New Critics were inspired by modernist production's own theorization of the reading process, as was the case with Faulkner in the US.

Ghostly Sounds and Negative Audition

Faulkner's fictional world is saturated with echoing sounds; on her dying bed, Addie Bundren of *As I Lay Dying* famously hears Cash's saw going "Chuck. Chuck. Chuck.";[14] *Light in August* opens with Armstid's wagon reaching Lena Grove with "the sharp and brittle crack and clatter of its weathered and ungreased wood and metal";[15] and Old Ben in "The Bear" is recognized by the young Isaac through "a moiling yapping an octave too high . . . leaving then somewhere in the air that echo of thin and almost human hysteria, abject, almost humanly grieving."[16] While these sounds strike a haunting tone in the ears of Faulkner's characters—signifying Addie's approaching death, Lena's dangerous journey, and Isaac's uncanny encounter with nature—they are not delivered as an enigma to readers. The text presents itself as capable of registering and communicating to the reader the sounds of the saw, the wagon, and the bear through onomatopoeia ("Chuck. Chuck. Chuck."), through a detailed description of the sound's qualities ("thin . . . abject, almost humanly grieving"), and through alliteration ("sha<u>r</u>p and b<u>r</u>i<u>tt</u>le <u>cr</u>a<u>ck</u> and <u>cl</u>a<u>tt</u>er").

But what of those sounds in Faulkner's work that are not delivered to the reader through language? What readerly protocol emerges from these nonlinguistic vocalities? Karl F. Zender hints at this kind of textual sonority when he distinguishes two central sound representations in Faulkner's oeuvre: a reconciling representation, which expresses the "reciprocity between the self and the other," and a hostile one, which stands for "an invasion of the self *by* the other" [emphasis in original]."[17] The Gothic vocabulary Zender employs in describing Faulkner's "invasi[ve]" sounds gestures at textual presences that can be felt but not located.

Tellingly, it is *The Sound and the Fury* that marks the shift in Faulkner's soundscape for Zender, who identifies in the novel the author's painful recognition that the natural and bestial world around him is autonomous and cannot be controlled by human imagination.[18] Indeed, the sounds in this work invade the reader, force themselves on the reader's perception; and yet, what Zender does not consider is that these ghostly sounds, though perhaps experienced as inimical by the characters, are devised to have a different impact on the reader.

Even if the sounds in *The Sound and the Fury* are borne out of a lamentation for a lost world, the readerly experience formally provided by this text is one of ethical potentiality, compelling the reader to acknowledge through the senses the porous quality of one's ontology and the presence of muted beings in the world. In a similar vein, Napolin notes that, for Faulkner's narrator, "The story [functions] as a medium of aural memory: depersonalization, becoming someone else, being-inhabited by lost voices as a condition of having a voice in the present."[19] What Napolin identifies in the case of the narrator, who is "inhabited by lost voices," reveals itself in the current context to be true also of Faulkner's reader, who is encouraged by the novel to inhabit erased sounds.

The ethical charge of Faulkner's sonic-induced experience brings us back to Derrida. In his 1984 lecture on Joyce, titled "Ulysses Gramophone: Hear Say Yes in Joyce," Derrida conceptualizes the positive charge of a negative or absent sound.[20] He makes the ostensibly idiosyncratic argument that behind Joyce's repetitive yes, especially pronounced in Molly Bloom's final soliloquy, he hears a laughter: "With one ear, with a certain hearing [ouïe], I can hear a reactive, even negative yes-laughter resonate," and "through the telephonic lapsus that made me say or hear *ouï dire*, 'hear say,' it was the *oui rire*, 'yes laughter,' which was making its way, as well as the consonantal difference from the d [of *dire*] to the r [of *rire*]. These, moreover, are the only consonants of my name."[21]

Derrida discusses here the phenomenon of hearing what is materially absent, a "negative" form of "hearing," or what could be called a negative audition. If one listens carefully to *Ulysses*, Derrida claims, this laughing "vibration" becomes "the very music of *Ulysses*."[22] And this imagined soundtrack proves important to him because it highlights the playfulness embedded in the novel, which, Derrida claims, is read with excessive gravity, especially by scholars. This unheard "music" also underscores the ethical valence of Joyce's work; both laughter and the affirmative "yes," Derrida asserts, are acts of response; they are always part of a dialogue with an Other, whether external or internal. As Anca Parvulescu puts it, for Derrida "*Yes* stands in need of an other that comes before it, an ambiguous, undetermined structural necessity. It is to this other—not necessarily a somebody or a something—that one responds."[23] Hence, according to Derrida, by attending to or imagining the laughter that emanates from *Ulysses*, the reader takes part in the novel's consistent dialogical gestures, in its reaching out for the Other.

What I find important in Derrida's discussion of negative audition is the recognition that sound can emerge from a text and even hold ethical significance without being explicitly inscribed in or described by the words on the page. Faulkner also works to activate negative audition in his reader as an ethical practice, compelling the reader to cultivate an acoustic attention to what is not on the page, which is an ability to radically open oneself up to sounds and voices that are literally and metaphorically on the verge of audibility. In comparison to *Ulysses*, however, *The Sound and the Fury* provokes negative audition in a way that is far less subjective. One need not be the founder of deconstruction to experience negative audition in Faulkner, since his novel is fully organized around the conjuring of imaginative ghostly sounds in the reader's mind.

A paradigmatic example of Faulkner's negative audition invocation can be found in the first section of *The Sound and the Fury*, a novel whose title ineluctably summons up a consideration of sonority. Yet, as Laura R. Davis aptly notes, although the novel's title "overtly references the senses, most critics have focused on the fury rather than on the sound."[24] What comes into view if we do respond to the novel's titular invitation, is its soundscape's work of impressing itself on the reader's mind. As we shall see, delving into Faulkner's conjuring of negative audition will lead us to his implicit theory of attentive reading and its potential ethical implications, along with this practice's affinity to close reading.

In the opening part of the novel, Benjy, the youngest of the Compson siblings, depicts his experiences following his grandmother's death, which he was never informed about but apprehends through the senses of hearing and smell.

> I could hear mother, and feet walking fast away, and I could smell it. Then the room came, but my eyes went shut. I didn't stop. I could smell it. T. P. unpinned the bed clothes.
> "Hush." he said. "Shhhhhhhh."
> But I could smell it. T. P. pulled me up and he put on my clothes fast.
> "Hush, Benjy." he said. "We going down to our house. You want to go down to our house, where Frony is. Hush, Shhhhh."
> He laced my shoes and put my cap on and we went out. There was a light in the hall. Across the hall we could hear Mother.
> "Shhhhhh, Benjy." T. P. said. "We'll be out in a minute."
> A door opened and I could smell it more than ever, and a head came out. It wasn't Father. Father was sick there.
> "Can you take him out of the house."
> "That's where we going." T. P. said. Dilsey came up the stairs.

> "Hush." she said. "Hush. Take him down home, T. P. Frony fixing him a bed. You all look after him, now. Hush, Benjy. Go on with T. P."
> She went where we could hear Mother. . . .
> We went down stairs. The stairs went down into the dark and T. P. took my hand, and we went out the door, out of the dark. . . .
> "I can't take you down home bellering like you is." T. P. said. "You was bad enough before you got that bull-frog voice. Come on."[25]

The most salient feature in this exchange, appearing ten times in different variations, is the attempt to silence Benjy. Such comments as "Hush," "Shhhhh," and even T. P.'s "I can't take you down home, bellering like you is," overwhelm the text in this moment, as they do much of Benjy's section and the ones to follow. In fact, over 100 hushings directed at Benjy can be found in *The Sound and the Fury*.[26]

In the spirit of narratology, it seems pertinent to ask what the function of this silencing might be. Clearly, it is not there merely to inform us that Benjy is crying, as one mention of this fact would have sufficed. It also does not advance the plot much, definitely not enough to account for its compulsive repetition; we do not need to be constantly reminded that Benjy is crying to understand why he is sent out of the house in a time of mourning. The actions his crying propels, such as Dilsey walking up the stairs, do not bring about any significant change of events.

Undoubtedly, the repetition of the hushing onomatopoeia adds a profound sense of urgency and anxiety to the passage, but beyond this affective significance, the repetitive silencing gestures communicate, via negation, the nature of the scene's fueling force, namely, Benjy's sound. Put differently, it is Benjy's impact on the events around him that disappears once the silencing gestures are removed from the text—as I took the liberty to do for the purpose of demonstration.

> I could hear mother, and feet walking fast away, and I could smell it. Then the room came, but my eyes went shut. I didn't stop. I could smell it. T. P. unpinned the bed clothes.
>   []---[]
> But I could smell it. T. P. pulled me up and he put on my clothes fast.

"[]." he said. "We going down to our house. You want to go down to our house, where Frony is. []."

He laced my shoes and put my cap on and we went out. There was a light in the hall. Across the hall we could hear Mother.

"[]." T. P. said. "We'll be out in a minute."

A door opened and I could smell it more than ever, and a head came out. It wasn't Father. Father was sick there.

"Can you take him out of the house."

"That's where we going." T. P. said. Dilsey came up the stairs.

"[]" she said. "[] Take him down home, T. P. Frony fixing him a bed. You all look after him, now. []. Go on with T. P."

She went where we could hear Mother. . . . We went down stairs. The stairs went down into the dark and T. P. took my hand, and we went out the door, out of the dark. . . . "[] Come on."

In this subtracted version, Benjy "hears," "smells," sees, and follows T. P. down the stairs and into "the dark," but he does not act independently on his surroundings. He appears to be a passive, unemotional, and purely receptive subject, who cannot express himself via spoken language and therefore cannot orally express himself at all.[27]

Yet, as we know from the full version of the passage, Benjy—and specifically his cry—is the propelling force of this scene: it motivates T. P.'s haste ("T. P. . . . put on my clothes *fast*"; "We'll be out in a minute"), it pulls one of the mourners away from the grandmother's side to request that Benjy be taken "out of the house," it sends Dilsey up the stairs, and in a larger context, it draws all of the Compson brothers to the servants' house and leads them to the novel's central scene where Caddy climbs up the tree in her "muddy . . . drawers."[28]

The hushes, then, are where Benjy's emotional presence resides, and yet the cry itself is never positively represented in the passage above as in Benjy's chapter as a whole—neither through onomatopoeia nor description, nor even through a simple internal comment. The cry is only communicated via negation, either in the form of hushes or through comments such as "I can't take you down home bellering like you is," which is itself, interestingly, formulated as negation. Even though it might appear that Benjy's subjectivity unfolds in full on the page through his detailed internal dialogue, his affective nonlinguistic yet vigorous vocal expression exists not in the text but as a sonority reverberating between the novel and the reader's mind.

Without the hushes, Benjy stands the risk of appearing to be, as Philip M. Weinstein writes, in a passive state of "continuous alienation—he is clothed, fed, seated, kept in or out of the house, summoned, concealed."[29] But the passage's continuous work of silencing points to Benjy as an active rather than a reactive participant in the scene; he propels the actions around him. That is, Benjy's medium of agency, even if limited, is compressed into the signs of its negation, and with each such "hush," Faulkner calls on, one may even say automatically triggers, his readers' attention to the absent-presence cries that provoked it.

This negation strategy is thrown into relief especially when the first section of the novel is set against the backdrop of the fourth, where Benjy's cry is described in explicit detail (for example, "Suddenly he wept, a slow bellowing sound, meaningless and sustained"; "But he bellowed slowly, abjectly, without tears; the grave hopeless sound of all voiceless misery under the sun").[30] Faulkner could have similarly portrayed Benjy's bellows in the opening section, yet he chooses to conjure rather than represent, thus training his reader from the onset to listen differently; the reader is called on to take in and give voice to Benjy's cry as a counter to those around him who mostly "concern themselves . . . with suppressing his crying," as Ted Roggenbuck argues.[31]

Benjy's is not a generic cry; it invades the reader's mind in its acute specificity molded by the text's form. The number of silencing gestures informs the reader of the duration of the cry: it begins when Benjy recognizes the smell of death and continues as he is dressed and as he walks down the hall all the way to the servants' rooms. The cry's amplitude is signaled through diegetic distance: Benjy is loud enough to be heard not only in the adjacent room, but also downstairs, which prompts Dilsey to climb up and try to calm Benjy down. The novel also informs its reader of the cry's unique quality via T.P.'s vexed comment about Benjy's "bullfrog voice."

As if anticipating that the reader is liable to think of Benjy's presence in the world as placid due to the neutral tone of his internal monologue, Faulkner makes clear that Benjy's "bellering" is acoustically low-pitched and clamorous. In fact, as the final scene of the novel—when Benjy's cry, motivated by a subtle change in the route home, forces all characters back into a strict routine—implies, it might just be the case that Benjy's voice and its tonality are the determining factor of the family's very way of life. What we encounter here is Faulkner's formal strategy for making Benjy's presence, mobilized through his cry, felt without rendering it legible through language. Faulkner engraves it into the text as a haunting ghostly sound, transforming the novel into a readerly echo chamber.

Unlike the reader, however, the characters within the diegetic world of *The Sound and the Fury* need not engage in any mental imagining in order to hear Benjy. On the contrary, effort is required if one wishes to avoid hearing his voice. As we have seen, the protagonist's cry reverberates far and wide, penetrating the perception of people around him whether they like it or not; it arouses compassion, rage, and brings about dramatic changes of events. On the morning of his suicide, for example, Quentin—the Compson's eldest brother—recalls the moment when Benjy's cry invaded the sister's (Caddy's) wedding, causing her to rush away and calm Benjy down.

> Only she was running already when I heard it. In the mirror she was running before I knew what it was. . . . Then she was across the porch I couldn't hear her heels then in the moonlight like a cloud, the floating shadow of the veil running across the grass, into the bellowing. She ran out of her dress, clutching her bridal, running into the bellowing where T. P. in the dew Whooey Sassprilluh Benjy under the box bellowing. Father had a V-shaped silver cuirass on his running chest.[32]

Hearing Benjy "bellowing" is a communal act—no one can escape it, not even the bride on her wedding day. His voice reaches everyone within his soundscape before they can even decipher "what it was."

Indeed, the ear is an organ prone to penetration. As Lacan reminds us, the ear, as differentiated from the eye and mouth, is always physically open: "I must . . . point out to you the difference between *making oneself heard* and *making oneself seen*. In the field of the unconscious, the ears are the only orifice that cannot be closed. Whereas *making oneself seen* is indicated by an arrow that really comes back towards the subject, *making oneself heard* goes towards the other. The reason for this is a structural one [emphasis in original]."[33] What constitutes sound as a collective experience is the structure of the ear as a sensory organ. While the human subject can eliminate light through the shutting of the eyes, avoid food by closing the mouth, and deflect touch via movement, the ear cannot close, it is always open to the Other and we can only cover it externally. Sound is by nature intrusive; it is often unavoidable, much like Benjy's cry, invading both the characters in the story world, and the "inner audition" of the reader.[34]

Yet Faulkner's sonic world does not always follow Lacan's principle. While Benjy's voice penetrates everyone's perception, other auditory stimuli in *The Sound and the Fury* encroach on specific ears alone. This is the case with Quentin, who is imprisoned within a body that cannot help but hear the sound of clocks. All other characters in the novel can ignore that ticking and yet the reader is called on to enlist in the protagonist's perceptual experience. Intensely exposed to Quentin's emotional reactions to that clock's intolerable repetition, the reader only seldom receives a full depiction of the sound itself and is thus urged to negatively hear the ticking via its imprint on Quentin's experience.

To differentiate from Benjy's cry, however, the reader's internal echoing of the clock does not work to amplify human sound; its ethicality lies in a willingness to puncture Quentin's hellish perceptual isolation by internally echoing a sound usually silenced by sensory habitation. That is, the reader is asked to alleviate Quentin's acute loneliness by joining in acoustically. After all, the tick-tock haunts and fragments Quentin's experience to such a degree that, in the moment of his drowning, he thinks: "the road empty in darkness in silence the bridge arching into silence darkness sleep the water peaceful and swift not goodbye."[35] "Silence," "empty," and "peaceful," are escapes from an overwhelmingly loud world, which is populated by Benjy's bellowing, the mumbling of the past's ghosts, and above all, the repetitive din of moving time.

> When the shadow of the sash appeared on the curtains it was between seven and eight oclock [sic] and then I was in time again, hearing the watch. It was Grandfather's and when Father gave it to me he said . . . I give it to you not that you may remember time, but that you might forget it now and then for a moment . . .
>
> It was propped against the collar box and I lay listening to it. Hearing it, that is. I dont [sic] suppose anybody ever deliberately listens to a watch or a clock. You dont [sic] have to. You can be oblivious to the sound for a little while, then in a second of ticking it can create in the mind unbroken the long diminishing parade of time you didn't hear.
>
> Father said that. That Christ was not crucified: he was worn away by a minute clicking of little wheels.[36]

The traditional interpretation of Quentin's suicide, rooted in Sartre's famous essay on *The Sound and the Fury*, locates its cause in "chronological metaphysics": Quentin can imagine no future and is thus a captive of a haunting past and an enclosed present.[37] In the current context, however, Faulkner's metaphysical preoccupation reveals itself as rooted in phenomenology, in a lived-sonic experience.

The sound of his pocket watch is the first external stimulus to reach Quentin in the morning, forcing him out of his dream world and "into time." Immediately following is Quentin's thought about the isolated quality of his sensory experience. Others, he ponders, are capable of being "oblivious to the sound for a little while," but he cannot avoid it. Just as Christ is seen by his father, Quentin is tortured not by one definitive act of human violence ("Christ was not crucified"), but by a repetitive inhuman mechanical sound ("worn away by a minute clicking of little wheels").

This sensory experience stands in stark contrast to the paternal instructions Quentin receives on inheriting the watch: "I give it to you not that you may remember time, but that you might forget it."[38] Quentin, of course, cannot, and he conveys the involuntary nature of his sensory experience through exchanging the verb "to listen" with "to hear" when he describes his interaction with the watch's ticking: "I lay listening to it," he says, and immediately corrects himself, "Hearing it." Listening, for him, is associated with choice and agency, which are the domain of others around him. "I dont suppose *anybody* ever deliberately listens to a watch or a clock. *You* dont have to [emphasis mine]." The "you" that surrounds Quentin—including the reader who might be called on by this pronoun—can choose to unlisten to the sound of the clock. Quentin, on the other hand, does not "listen," he unwillingly "hears" the clock; the sound invades his ear.

Clearly, it is not the ear as an orifice that governs Quentin's inability to ignore the clock, but his mind. More specifically, as prominent cognitive psychologists and neuroscientists claim today, this is the work of attention. The brain, and its novelty detector neurons, differentiates between predictable ongoing noises and novel ones. And the tendency of the mind, these scholars suggest, is to tune out repeated sound patterns and make salient to consciousness only those that are distinct from their environment.[39] Quentin, against this backdrop, appears to suffer from attention disorder, perceiving "the old" rather than attuning to "the new"; he is perceptually porous to that which should be unheard. But Faulkner probes in the reader a different state of attention. As we have seen through Benjy's "ghostly" cry, which he urged the reader to hear, Faulkner encourages a perception precisely of that which is considered insubstantial, either socially or perceptually.[40] Similarly, Faulkner propels the reader of *The Sound and the Fury* to reactivate her ability to hear the ghost of the clock ticking.

Once the reader is reminded of the ticking of time, it becomes much harder for her to unremember this familiar sound. Put differently, Faulkner plays with negative audition through sonic reactivation. The text mentions the ticking of the clock but does not provide us with a robust representation of this sound in proportion to its centrality within the diegetic world. The text reads: "the watch ticked on," "I heard a clock strike the hour," "the clock struck three," "the chimes began," "the chimes ceased," but the words "ticking" and "clicking" are the closest the novel gets to an onomatopoeia of the watch's sonority.[41]

Similarly, the text presents the reader with very few descriptions of the clock's acoustic properties. Instead, Faulkner trusts that the reader cannot resist echoing this absent-presence sound as a consequence of the mere mention of the ticking, accompanied by Quentin's inevitable receptivity to it. For instance, when Quentin enters a clock shop, we are told: "The place was full of ticking, like crickets in September grass, and I could hear a big clock on the wall above his [the shop owner's] head . . . I went out, shutting the door upon the ticking . . . I could hear mine, ticking inside my pocket, even though nobody could see it, even though it could tell nothing if anyone would."[42] Quentin's watch allegedly sounds "like crickets in September grass," but the protagonist's sonic experience is, in actuality, far removed from this simile; rather than something pastoral, Quentin takes the watch's sound to be unbearably regular, unstoppable—nothing like the cyclical, seasonal chirping whose appearance in Quentin's description probably bespeaks his desire for a different, more amenable soundscape.

The clock does not function for Quentin on the level of signification ("it could tell nothing" to anyone who could see it), but rather on a somatic level, haunting him thus that even when he tries to "shut the door upon the ticking" of the shop, the sound invades him anew from "inside [his] pocket." As we shall see below, Quentin here mimics Faulkner's own self-proclaimed attempt, during the writing of the novel, to "shut the door" upon sounds, only to then be visited by other sonorities. Being penetrated by sound is undoubtedly a frustrating and even violating experience, as Zender suggests. And yet it has an ethical purchase as well. This is especially evident in the case of Faulkner's readers, who, by surrendering themselves to the ticking of the clock, learn, if only momentarily, to discern sonorities designed to be forgotten. This provides Quentin with a you who, like himself, is not "oblivious to the sound," maddening as it might be.

In his sensitive analysis of the novel, Weinstein also identifies Benjy and Quentin as the two main figures through which Faulkner pulls the reader into *The Sound and the Fury*.[43] And though Weinstein does not analyze sound in the novel, his narratological analysis of the two protagonists' "voices" gestures toward the novel's negative audition. He writes,

> If a coherent voice is a protective skin—protective because it subjectifies and makes instrumental some of the sayings of a culture while resisting others—Benjy and Quentin emerge naked. In their different ways they have no filters, can do little but suffer and die. Quentin's silent voice compels us, like Benjy's, in its radical undefensiveness. Faulkner proposes through such candor a uniquely intimate relationship with the reader. Benjy's lack of project and Quentin's desperately confused project disarm our own project, and we enter—as it were, naked ourselves—into the pathos of their lives.[44]

Indeed, Quentin and Benjy are naked, not only in their lack of cohesive internal voice, but also in their orientation to sound: Benjy is stripped of his main form of oral communication—his cries—via repetitive gestures of silencing, and Quentin is revealed to have no acoustic "skin," and to thus be sonically penetrable.

Faulkner leverages precisely this sonic "nakedness" to create a "uniquely intimate relationship with the reader"; he prompts readers to suspend their filters, to render porous their perceptive skins, and to internally echo the novel's ghostly sounds. Indeed, this might be a painful process, becoming aurally vulnerable and "naked ourselves." But it is through this move that readers can amplify Benjy's suppressed cry, counter Quentin's sensory isolation, and slowly acquire the skill of listening otherwise.

Silence, Race, and Unheard Music

What, then, is the conceptualization of the reading process that arises from Faulkner's negative audition? What relationship between mental activity, sound, and text does he consider conducive? And how does this conceptualization relate to the New Critical practice of close reading discussed in the previous chapter? The kind of audition that *The Sound and the Fury* advances is counterintuitively rooted in silence. The reader is urged to hear Benjy's cry through the attempts to suppress it, and to perceive the ticking of Quentin's clocks in a movement opposite to mental habits of sonic erasure. There is, then, a nuanced dialectic that Faulkner imagines between silence and the reader's capability to act as an echo chamber.

In his introduction to *The Sound and the Fury*, this dialectic unfolds further as Faulkner depicts the writing process of the novel. After failing attempts to find a publisher for *Sartoris* (1929), his earlier novel, he notes a change: "One day it suddenly seemed as if a door had clapped silently and forever to [sic] between me and all publishers' addresses and booklists and I said to myself, Now I can write. Now I can just write."[45] Like Quentin, Faulkner closes the door "silently" to create a physical barrier between himself and the external loud world; in this sonic environment, he can "just write."[46]

However, as Faulkner goes on to articulate, the shutting of the door on the sonic stimuli, as in Quentin's case, does not eventually close off sound. In fact, it is the vocalities that emerge from silence that sustain Faulkner's ability to write, and, as the very first sentence of the introduction reveals, his capacity to read as well: "I wrote this book and learned to read."[47] He elaborates on this enigmatic statement.

> I discovered then that I had gone through all that I had ever read, from Henry James through Henty to newspaper murders, without making any distinction or digesting any of it, as a moth or a goat might. After *The Sound and The Fury* [sic] and without heeding to open another book and in a series of delayed repercussions like summer thunder, I discovered the Flauberts and Dostoievskys and Conrads whose books I had read ten years ago. With *The Sound and The Fury* [sic] I learned to read and quit reading, since I have read nothing since.[48]

The experience Faulkner describes is not far removed from Derrida's hearing of Joyce's laughter. With *The Sound and the Fury*, Faulkner can *hear* a facet of the texts he most loves "in a series of delayed repercussions like summer thunder."[49] This sound—this re-percussion—appears to him not in the external texts, the books in their materiality, but in the "Flauberts and Dostoievskys and Conrads" as they inhabit him internally. That is, writing the novel behind closed doors, Faulkner auditorily perceives the books within him.

In a later interview, Faulkner returns to the word "thunder" to describe once again the voices that one hears during the reading process: "Music," he says, "would express better and simpler, but I prefer to use words as I prefer to read rather than listen. . . . That is, the thunder and the music of the prose take place in silence."[50] The reading process, for Faulkner, consists of sound and silence simultaneously: it is the lack of external auditory stimuli that enables the "thunder and music" of the alterities one carries within to make their presence felt. Silence allows the reader to become an echo chamber, to be perceptually present to what is ostensibly not there.

This dialectic brings us back full circle to Faulkner's referral to *The Sound and the Fury* as a vase in his introduction to the novel: "There is a story somewhere about an old Roman who kept at his bedside a Tyrrhenian vase which he loved and the rim of which he wore slowly away with kissing it." This depiction hints at Faulkner's morbid view of art, not only in terms of literature's creation ("I made myself a vase") but also in relation to its consumption. If *The Sound and the Fury* is Faulkner's vase-urn, then reading it—"kissing" the vase—is what brings about its slow destruction.

However, bleak as this affinity may seem, *The Sound and the Fury*'s negative audition throws a different, positive light on Faulkner's novel-as-urn analogy. For Faulkner, the ability to read and write ethically is bound up with the capacity to open up aurally, to perceive the past, the dead, and dead sound, to internally hear the "Flauberts and Dostoievskys and Conrads" without interacting with the material books themselves, to hear Benjy's cry through its negation, and to sense "the thunder of prose" in silence. The urn, then, stands for the ethical, acoustic position of both reader and writer-as-reader who are willing to make space for absent-presence sonorities within them even at the price of a provisional self-deadening. Turning oneself into an urn, an empty echo-chamber for silenced voices, allows one to "die with" the work in order to hear it.

Keats's "Ode" itself, we should recall, similarly knots together art, sound, silence, and death. The pleasure afforded by art in "Ode" is tethered to the object's lifeless status and to its invitation for the consumer to animate it via audition. The viewer of the urn confesses,

> Heard melodies are sweet, but those unheard
> Are sweeter; therefore, ye soft pipes, play on;
> Not to the sensual ear, but, more endear'd,
> Pipe to the spirit ditties of no tone.[51]

The urn cannot make its melodies heard because it is static. However, music "unheard" by the "sensual ear" is in no way unfelt or nonexistent; as the opening stanza states, the ode's legend "haunts." In fact, the experience—of attuning to these absent-presence sounds—is "sweeter," "more endear'd" than registering "heard melodies." This perceiver is not alone in her capacity to sense the silent "soft pipes"; the "spirit ditties of no tone" also participate in this negative audition.[52] Faulkner's ghostly ethics of reading do not map perfectly onto Keats's Romantic depiction of the phenomenology of art consumption. Yet Faulkner's gesture to "Ode" in his introduction to a novel so deeply preoccupied with unheard sounds further underscores his ongoing interest in and profound commitment to the amplification of vocalities of a different ontology.

Writing about the ethicality of *The Sound and the Fury*, however, is not without its potential pitfalls. After all, the bulk of the novel consists of internal monologues by three white men of the Southern elite. Readings with an eye to racial and gender bias have highlighted how this white male narrative voice, though different from the inanimate sound at the center of this discussion, similarly conjures the question of listening. As various scholars have noted, Caddy, the beloved sister centering this family drama, is consistently mediated via her brothers' psyche without being given the opportunity to speak in her own voice.[53] And the Gibson family, the Black American domestic workers who materially and emotionally sustain the Compsons, take center stage only in the fourth section of the novel, via Dilsey's character—the Gibson's matriarch. But even Dilsey is not given the authority of first-person narration and is instead depicted by an external, third-person voice.

For contemporary Black scholars, such as Joanna Davis-McElligatt, this is part of what Faulkner's more general "narratological thingification of Blackness" entails.[54] Faulkner presents Blackness as "a disabling contaminant, a marker of the nonhuman, and a sign of permanent degeneracy and abjection,"[55] which leads her to ask if reading Faulkner has any value for Black people in the first place: "If Faulkner had no interest in Black futures, and therefore no stake in shaping Black presents or coming to grips with Black pasts, what could a reading of his work possibly have to say about Blackness and Black futures?"[56] Recent retorts to these and similar claims include Susanna Hempstead's demonstration that Caddy's independent voice does appear in the novel through the cracks in the brothers' internal discourse, and Dorothy J. Hale's argument that the excessive lyricism that accompanies Faulkner's withdrawal from internal dialogue in Dilsey's section attests to the "social fact that some social positions resist representation by the white, male novelist."[57]

Nevertheless, the novel's ethicality remains a bone of contention, especially in the intersection of voice, sound, and listening. Thus, for example, Kristin Fujie demonstrates that Black voices and sounds in the novel are consistently instrumentalized "as conduits, or mediums, through which Faulkner and his white characters gain access to embodied sensation and psychological interiority."[58] In the context of her overall investment in Faulkner's critique and examination of human instrumentalization, Fujie demonstrates that Black characters in *The Sound and the Fury* serve as a vessel through which white male characters introspect—a glass or window to look through rather than at, with the final object of interest being the white characters themselves.

In the current case as well, Fujie's insightful interpretation raises the urgent question of *who* the object of perception is. Can we speak of Faulkner's commitment to amplifying silenced sounds in the reader when he grants no voice to Caddy or Dilsey? Or when he attunes internally, as we have seen in the scene of his silent writing, to the absent-presence sonorities of only the paragons of Western white hegemony (the "Flauberts and Dostoievskys and Conrads" within him)? A way into this conundrum begins with recognizing a subtle discrepancy in *The Sound and the Fury* between its diegetic world and narration, on the one hand, and the novel's labor of cultivating sonic sensitivities, on the other. I claim that the latter paradoxically grants the reader tools for reading or listening to the novel against itself. Put differently, by tuning his readers to such ghostly sounds as Benjy's and Quentin's, Faulkner also, perhaps unwittingly, prepares his readers to access a kind of counteracoustics in his writing that was never intended to be audible, to register sounds in the novel that have been, or are bordering on being, muted out.

In that sense, I am following in the footsteps of Aliyyah I. Abdur-Rahman, who invites us to listen to Faulkner's description of racialized sound in terms of a resistance that potentially runs counter to the work's explicit intensions.[59] And I further take my cue from Davis-McElligatt, who suggests, from an Afropessimist standpoint, that we approach Faulkner not in an attempt to "locate an authentic or real Black presence" in his fiction ("it is not there," she contends).[60] Instead, she urges us to "extricate" from Faulkner's "narrative nonexistence the trace of Black life formation."[61]

Indeed, as I now move to demonstrate, *The Sound and the Fury* presents a scene toward its end that plays out this tension, when a racialized voice is placed on the brink of erasure by the narrator and the mediating events, until the practice of negative audition forces it back in, compelling us to resurrect Black sound from "narrative nonexistence." The scene's potential stands out especially when approached with an ear to the burgeoning theoretical reflections on race and the sonic, which identify sound and aurality as potential loci of resistance, or what Fred Moten calls "a radical breakdown."[62] Faulkner's novel, I suggest, offers us not an ethical world but an ethical readerly sensibility that would allow us to evocalize what has been silenced from the page.

In one of the most racially volatile scenes of the novel, Dilsey, her two children, and Benjy visit the local church for the Easter service, anticipating the arrival of the "big preacher" from St. Louis, Reverend Shegog.[63] The narrator, who in this fourth and final section establishes a third-person distance from the characters' consciousness, carefully builds the scene as a vivid soundscape via a successive mention of pleasant sound sources: "Most of the women were gathered on one side of the room. They were talking. Then the bell struck one time and they dispersed to their seats and the congregation sat for an instant, expectant. The bell struck again one time. The choir rose and began to sing."[64] Shegog is placed in the scene against this orchestrated sonic backdrop.

> It was not until the choir ceased singing that they realised that the visiting clergyman had already entered, and when they saw the man who had preceded their minister enter the pulpit still ahead of him an indescribable sound went up, a sigh, a sound of astonishment and disappointment.
>
> The visitor was undersized, in a shabby alpaca coat. He had a wizened black face like a small, aged monkey . . . the six children rose and sang in thin, frightened, tuneless whispers.[65]

The Reverend is depicted as an "aged monkey" in a narrational ambivalence that leaves unclear whose description it is—the narrator's, the community's, or both.[66] These shifting possibilities amplify the objectification at the center of the scene; all participants—writer, narrator, and congregation included—seem to take part in questioning the preacher's humanity, which would explain not only the community's "disappointment," but also its "astonishment" and the children's "frightened" responses.

Tellingly, Shegog's devaluation is signaled by a muffling and a distortion of sound, a modification made especially noticeable by the vibrant sonic environment that he enters. When the congregation recognizes the visitor, their singing abruptly pauses. The bell's harmonious tunes are replaced with an "indescribable" sound, and the choir's singing transitions into "tuneless whispers." Auditory reduction and perceptual depreciation come together to signal a metonymy between the hushing of sound in the church and a potential collective silencing awaiting Shegog.

Indeed, when the reverend begins his sermon, the congregation, mediated by the narrator, dismisses his words, attending to them as a spectacle; "they listened at first with curiosity, as they would have to a monkey talking."[67] But then, a change occurs.

> They began to watch him as they would a man on a tight rope. They even forgot his insignificant appearance in the virtuosity with which he ran and poised and swooped upon the cold inflectionless wire of his voice, so that at last, when with a sort of swooping glide he came to rest again beside the reading desk with one arm resting upon it at shoulder height and his monkey body as reft of all motion as a mummy or an emptied vessel, the congregation sighed as if it waked from a collective dream and moved a little in its seats. . . .
> Then a voice said, "Brethren." . . .
> With his body [Shegog] seemed to feed the voice that, succubus like, had fleshed its teeth in him. And the congregation seemed to watch with its own eyes while the voice consumed him.[68]

Stephen Ross astutely notes that the congregation's deep listening, in contrast with listening for pure "curiosity," begins when Shegog shifts to a voice "separate from its source," a voice "as sound," which opens with "Brethren."[69] Per Ross, "the radical separation of voice from speaker and (sometimes) from speech itself" grants the scene its potency, as "nowhere in Faulkner's oeuvre are the presence and power of voice more beautifully conceived."[70] Indeed, as André Bleikasten adds, Shegog's sermon "induces a vision," which is "the only experience of spiritual enlightenment recorded in the whole book."[71]

But what brings about this change? What causes the congregation to awaken "from a collective dream" and the shift of Shegog's "voice" into "sound"? The unique wording chosen to describe Shegog's production of "the voice" is significant, especially in view of Faulkner's investment in the figure of the urn. At the reading desk, we are told, Shegog transforms into a "mummy," an "empty vessel"; he deadens himself to entertain a "voice" that is external to him, one that fully "consume[s]" and fleshes "his teeth in him." It is the same semantic field that Faulkner traverses to conjure the morbid image of his novel as a vessel following him to the grave.

In terms of perception, then, Shegog's scene is one of complex layering: the more trivial structure of a preacher speaking and an audience listening is substituted with an arrangement of double negative audition. Shegog listens to a higher-frequency divine voice that has no material presence, and consequently provokes the congregation to awaken from a "collective dream" and surrender to what we can think of as a lower-frequency voice that was at the immediate risk of being discarded as "insignificant," or worse, as ontologically unworthy.

The scene lends itself to the logic Moten proposes in his book *In the Break*, which centers, as Akira Mizuta Lippit succinctly puts it, the "phonic substance . . . that erupts from the depth of two 'peculiar institutions' (slavery and literature) and opens onto the history and catastrophe of slavery in America"; the acoustics that Moten follows and gives voice to—one of cries, moans, and prayers—demonstrates, for him, that "objects can and do resist."[72] As Moten writes, "While subjectivity is defined by the subject's possession of itself and its objects, it is troubled by a dispossessive force objects exert such that the subject seems to be possessed—infused, deformed—by the object it possesses."[73]

Indeed, if Shegog is made the object of both the community and the narrator, he is undoubtedly an object that acoustically resists. Shegog himself is made to feel the dispossessive force of sound when an external ghostly voice "fleshe[s] his teeth in him." And the congregation is drawn in, "infused," by the subject they objectified, when "the voice" ventriloquized by Shegog not only awakens them, but also goes on to literally enter and echo within their bodies: "[T]he voice [sounded by Shegog] died in sonorous echoes between the walls . . . sinking into their hearts and speaking there again . . . they just sat swaying a little in their seats as the voice took them into itself."[74]

Finally, narration itself, which is most clearly accountable for the Reverend's objectification, is overcome by the Reverend's voice. The sermon, which takes up more than three pages, makes for the longest monological direct speech (rather than internal monologue) in the novel, with a progressive diminution in narrational comments and mediations, as if the tables have turned and it is now "the voice" that silences the narrator, leading the novel to its key experience of spiritual epiphany. Through the lens offered by Moten's conceptualization, then, the novel's narrator can be seen as dispossessed by the sonic force of its object, by a voice that "deform[s]" the novel's own power structure.

Similarly, Faulkner's readers are called on not only to perform negative audition but also to witness an act of such listening. When Faulkner was asked by Malcolm Cowley about his writing process, he confessed, "I listen to the voices . . . and when I put down what the voices say, it's right. Sometimes I don't like what they say, but I don't change it."[75] Like "the voice" that occupies Shegog, Faulkner too is haunted by "voices," and requests his readers to lend themselves to a similar sonic experience. But, as in Shegog's scene, this act of perceptual surrender is one of political surrender as well; one cannot know what voices will take possession even when one does "not like what they say," as in the case of the novel's narration, overcome by a voice it politically strives to undo. Paradoxically, then, *The Sound and the Fury* provides its readers with a practice of listening that might enable them to hear those very voices that the novel, with its racial and gender bias, had silenced, as has nearly happened in Shegog's case.

Fujie was perhaps right then in claiming that Black sound serves in the novel as a medium. But for Faulkner there could not be a more ethical position than that of an auditory conduit, a position he himself tries and urges his readers to occupy. In this context, it seems pertinent to conclude with Erik Steinskog's suggestive conceptualization of sonic counterhistory.

> [There exists the] possibility of a hidden tradition—hidden, that is, from the hegemonic, Western literate tradition—of an underground, or perhaps of a counter-history. Perhaps *the* counter-history is a sonic one, with the sonic playing the role of the other in opposition to the written [emphasis in original]. Sound rather than sense, some would say, in that the sonic is often understood as non-signification, found within studies of poetry but reduced in importance when dealing with meaning of texts. The figure of "the lower frequencies"—a figure from a literary text but also heard, for example, in dub—plays into this "hidden" history, almost as a kind of ghost story.[76]

Through its invocation of negative audition, then, *The Sound and the Fury* instructs its readers in how to attune themselves to these counterhistories, counter perhaps even to the novel itself.

Close Reading History

At this point, it has become evident, I hope, how Faulkner's implicit guidelines for reading correspond with, or set the ground for, Brooks's hauntological New Critical protocol: for both novelist and literary critic, the reader's ethical attunement to the literary text as alterity is imagined as predicated on an unselfing process of a specific sort, a bestowing of one's life force on the literary work as a living-dead entity. More so, for both, this readerly practice emanates from the specific histories, and counterhistories, of the Southern United States, from its violent past of exploitation and abuse and its postbellum ghostly existence of decay and disintegration.

After all, Brooks and Faulkner's exemplary close reader, Quentin Compson, is able to function as an urn, to dispossess himself so that the dead can dwell inside him, since, to quote from *Absalom, Absalom!*, "[H]e was born and bred in the deep South . . . the deep South dead since 1865 and peopled with . . . ghosts."[77] As Hortense J. Spillers beautifully puts it in terms of Quentin's auditory sensibilities, "Along the course of the narrative, Quentin keeps thinking that he will never hear anything else his whole life, will never have to hear anything else, cannot but hear and have heard through his sinews, his muscle-build, on the pulse of the nerve, what his elders obsessively repeat about the South."[78] Quentin has become an astute close reader in New Critical terms because he grew up in a living-dead culture, one that is haunted by the "sin of slavery," in Faulkner's terms. As Brooks and Faulkner suggest, then, if readers are to follow in Quentin's footsteps when they engage with a text—as Faulkner's manipulation of negative audition and Brooks's cognitive readerly protocol direct them to do—they may learn to attune themselves to entities that are not clearly present, to practice the difficult task of listening to the ghosts of the past.

Indeed, the perceptual attunement to a lost past is what opens *The Sound and the Fury*. The novel might form the impression of recording its characters' psyches in the pure present, giving us direct access to their minds as they unfold right there on the page, but the text, as we have seen, is also inhabited by sonic presences, such as Benjy's cry and Quentin's ticking watch, that resist fitting into that mimetic present. These are the voices of the past that echo through the work even when they are not directly inscribed in it, thus encouraging readers to attend to a hauntological stimulus.

That these sonorities are linked to a lost past, to a history, is evident already in the opening scene of the novel, which has the problem of sound at its heart. In the first page of *The Sound and the Fury*, the readers encounter Benjy as he accompanies Luster, his fourteen-year-old Black caretaker, while the two are searching for a lost quarter along a fence that borders a golf course. Suddenly, Benjy overhears the golfers call for their caddies.

> Through the fence, between the curling flower spaces, I could see them hitting. . . . Luster came away from the flower tree and we went along the fence and they stopped and we stopped and I looked through the fence while Luster was hunting in the grass.
> "Here, Caddie." He hit. They went away across the pasture. I held to the fence and watched them going away.
> "Listen at you, now." Luster said. "Aint [sic] you something, thirty three years old, going on that way. After I done went all the way to town to buy you that cake. Hush up that moaning. Aint [sic] you going to help me find that quarter so I can go to the show tonight."[79]

Benjy hears what is not there. He hears the name of his older sister, Caddy, in the golfers' call for their caddie. This ghostly echo reminds Benjy of his beloved sister's disappearance eighteen years earlier, when she left home to get married and was abandoned by her husband when he realized that her baby was not his own. Benjy's capacity, or perhaps compulsion, to hear Caddy's absence is immediately made to replicate in the reader's mind. Benjy's cry, which bursts out in response to the echo of Caddy's name, appears only through its negation in Luster's imperative to "hush up that moaning," a tendency, as we know, that will continue throughout the first section.

Like Benjy, like Quentin, like Shegog, Faulkner's readers, who form the infrastructure for Brooks's model, are asked to conjure absence through negation, to pay attention to what once was, and is now ostensibly gone. The historicity of close reading, then—a practice so frequently chided for being ahistorical—takes on a specific shape through Faulkner's depiction of and instructions to his reader, and from the New Critical creed. This historicity is not rooted in context (a demand that the reader explore the historical backdrop against which a work is written), in content (an emphasis on the marks left on the plot, characters, or narration by historical events), or in form (a view of literary style or structure as expressing historical pressures), but in close reading's imagined ability to sharpen the reader's sensibility to absent-presences, to the echoes of what is ostensibly lifeless but in fact has a story to tell, a voice to sound.

In the upcoming two chapters, we will delve into the practice of close reading in Brazil, where echoes of another history intertwine with the New Critical creed. There, the violence is not only rooted in the legacy of slavery but also emerges from the complexities of postcoloniality. And yet, in Brazil too we will encounter the paradoxical desire and imperative to unself, to suspend one's subjectivity while engaging with the literary text. And while in this section, we engaged with a literary oeuvre that set the stage for the New Critical readerly protocol, in the following section we will look at literary attempts to challenge, parody, and offer alternatives to this mode of reading.

Part II

Brazil: The Unsavaged Reader

Chapter Three

Unsavaging

Afrânio Coutinho's *Nova Crítica* and the Problem of the Brazilian Exact Reader

> Whoever observes the intellectual situation in Brazil these days, senses more and more the need for a *redressement*, [the need] to rectify tendencies and vices that have been long with us . . . a certain inclination to praise improvisation and the innate qualities of the spirit, to laud and lead to a mental agility dangerously opposed to the qualities of meditation, patience, and study, all resulting in a true catastrophe to intelligence.
>
> —Afrânio Coutinho

The image of the reader developed by the anglophone New Critical creed is one of an achieved spatial void. As we have seen so far, the North American New Critics liken the reader to an urn, a vacant vessel, an echo chamber, an empty hall. They propose, quite counterintuitively, that this self-imposed state of absence is to be generated not by absent-mindedness, as idiomatic language might suggest, but through the labor of attention: the reader's intense focus is imagined literally to pull the reader out of herself and toward the text. This process, which I have referred to as "unselfing," requires intense self-control, and encapsulates a complex tension between pain and reward, whose nature changes in accordance with the sociopolitical and cultural-historical contexts in which close reading as a technique of the self was implemented.

Cleanth Brooks's fantasy of the emptied reader, which drives his interpretation of William Faulkner's work, is fueled by and immersed in the US North-South divide and violent history of enslavement, making the figure of the ghost—the haunting past and haunting dead—an inseparable part of his narrative about the relationship between the literary text and its consumer. Consequently, the dialectics of unselfing obtains within the US a specific form: the reader's achieved unselfing takes on the meaning of a temporary death, and her gain is theorized as an unmediated encounter with alterity and a cultivated attunement to muted voices and absent presences.

Traveling south to Brazil in the 1950s, close reading carries with it this powerful potential for unselfing and reselfing readerly identity. However, Brazilian intellectuals and writers ascribe different and profoundly local qualities both to the self that needs to be voided, and to the self that is constituted through close reading as the preferred approach to literary interpretation. In Brazil, too, the practice advanced by the New Criticism absorbs the weight of a violent past, but now it is the conflict of the colonized that creeps into the figuration of the reading process. The Brazilian New Critics venture to extract from within the reader—to unself through training in disciplined attention—a "savaged" tendency for "distraction." Their project is explicitly emancipatory: through their own version of close reading, the local New Critics aim to prove the West wrong in claiming that the Brazilian people are incapable of attentive analytic thought. Yet their endeavor is plagued with postcolonial ambivalence; rather than challenging the perception of the Brazilian mind as defective, the South American New Critics operate from the colonial assumption that an internal savage prone to distraction inhabits the Brazilian mind, and attempt to "cure" this condition.

Through close reading, the Brazilian New Critics work to refashion the Brazilian reader as fully civilized by describing and fostering the inherent powers of attention these readers can and do bestow on literary texts. Thus, whereas the North American reader was encouraged to make space for the haunting dead, the Brazilian reader is imagined to undergo a kind of self-extraction: a variation of unselfing that I think of as "unsavaging." As I will show, it is precisely the credit that the Brazilian New Critics give to "the savage within" that registers their own deep internalization of colonial ideology, a bias that compromises their emancipatory political program. While they use cognitive language to describe close reading and its positive effects, their theory of mind remains underdeveloped since their real investment is not in exploring the reader's interaction with the literary text, but in disciplining and "mending" the Brazilian subject. Yet, what I find intriguing and perceptive in the Brazilian (as well as the Israeli) New Critics is that they immediately identify the anglophone New Criticism to be not a purely aesthetic project, but one with self-formation at its heart, very much in contrast with the long history of the theory's reception in the anglophone world. While in the US it is rare to find interlocutors who recognize the plastic political potential of close reading, these international intellectuals identify it from the get-go.

The Brazilian case strongly demonstrates the New Critics' unique conceptualization of the affinity between history, reading, and the mind, a conceptualization that remains consistent transnationally. Close reading is traditionally understood as, and criticized for, being apolitical, since the New Critics vocally favored a focus on the text over an engagement with the work's production and reception circumstances. But for the Brazilian New Critics, as well as for the North American and Israeli New Critics, history and politics lie in the reader herself rather than in the text or context. They take history to impress itself on the very structure of the mind, such that its reshaping through habituated processes of reading constitutes a political act, shaping the reader's engagement not only with the text but with its surrounding reality as well. And since this praxis is imagined as remolding the subject through a process of self-suspension, the past and its political present make themselves mostly felt through deliberate acts of negation: those parts of the reader's self that the New Critics imagine to require extraction symbolize for them remnants of the past embedded in the reader, which come into view during the reading process.

In that spirit, the Brazilian New Critics imagine the prolonged Brazilian history of domination and exploitation to have left its mark on the colonized mind, making it susceptible to distraction. And they choose to define the affliction forced on them as cognitive—a problem of attention—rather than ethical or evolutionary, since this understanding renders the purported savagery amendable. If the problem of savagery, a postcolonial carryover, is only a tendency toward dispersive "butterfly-like" thought processes (as we will see it called), then unsavaging, and consequently self-emancipating, is simply a matter of replacing those habits with an orderly, attentive form of thought.

The chapter will follow the Brazilian New Criticism, the *nova crítica*, from its formation in the early 1950s to the establishment of its model of the unsavaged, "exact reader," pivoting around the movement's key thinker, Afrânio Coutinho, quoted in the epigraph. However, the discussion will begin a century earlier with José de Alencar's eminent *Iracema*.

This nineteenth-century novel demonstrates that Brazilian culture has not always revered "attention" as the paradigmatic readerly state and clarifies what kind of readerly model the New Critics were trying to negate in their forceful entry into the cultural scene in the mid-twentieth century.

I will conclude with an analysis of the modernist counterreaction to the *nova crítica*'s readerly model in the form of João Guimarães Rosa's 1964 short story, "O espelho" ("The Mirror"). Rosa's modernist story presents an allegory, or better yet a stinging satire, of the unsavaged reader and brings to the fore this figure's internal paradox. But even more importantly, "The Mirror" demonstrates that the New Criticism in Brazil, as we have seen in the US and will see in Israel, functioned as a generator of literary production, a process the following chapter will continue to explore through the work of Clarice Lispector. The *nova crítica* was not only influential in the public debates it spurred, the institutional changes it brought about, and the model of subjectivity it put into circulation; it also functioned as a galvanizing force for literary experimentation, inciting writers to respond to the model of the exact reader through a body of work centering the (un)savaged reader.

A Reader Cradled in the Hammock

Illiteracy and colonial rule are firmly linked in the Brazilian context. Unlike Spanish America—and various other colonies for that matter—Portugal forbade any press activity in Brazil and ensured that no printing press existed in the colony from its "discovery" in 1500 by Pedro Álvares Cabral all the way to 1808, when the Portuguese court, fleeing from Napoleon, relocated to its South American colony.[1] For three centuries, texts concerning Brazil were printed in Portugal only, and even later, had to be authorized by the censors, representatives of the king and of the Church. The consequential low circulation of written works in Portuguese, together with an intentional prevention of a proper education system and a systematic neglect of Brazil's large rural areas, far removed from urban processes of written form standardization, led to historically low rates of literacy, which the country is still battling.[2] In Brazil, then, imagining a capable reader is a profoundly political enterprise, interweaved with national independence and postcolonial sentiment.[3]

José de Alencar's foundational novel, *Iracema: lenda do Ceará* (*Iracema: A Legend of Ceará*), exemplifies the intentional combination of readerly acumen and national autonomy that characterized nineteenth-century Brazilian literature's idealized reader.[4] There is hardly a work more emblematic of nascent postcolonial Brazilian literature than this 1865 romantic masterpiece.[5] The novel's very title is an anagram of "America," the home continent of Brazil, recently independent (1822). The novel follows the love affair of Martim, a Portuguese colonizer, and Iracema, a young Tabajara indigenous woman. This national allegory—not untainted by colonial tropes—portrays Brazilian autonomy as deriving its force from the admixture of the indigenous native and the European colonizer. This implicit claim reaches a crescendo toward the end of the novel when the two protagonists who represent these geocultural identities give birth to Moacir, "the first child born in Ceará."[6] And since factually the territory that is now the Brazilian state of Ceará has been long-inhabited by natives, Moacir's status as a "first child" lends itself to be read symbolically as marking "the beginning of the Brazilian people" and setting "national history in motion," as Naomi Lindstrom concisely puts it.[7]

Marisa Lajolo adds to our understanding of Alencar's canonical work that *Iracema* depicts not only the archetypical national Brazilian subject, but also the exemplary Brazilian reader: "José de Alencar set in circulation an array of readerly characteristics that have since become a commonplace in tradition, if not in the occidental one then at least in that of Brazil and in José de Alencar's work itself."[8] As Lajolo points out, Alencar conducts his most intense work of "reading pedagogy" in his prologue to the novel's first edition, which opens with the intimate appeal to the reader as "my friend."[9] In this letter-like introduction, Alencar poetically describes the kind of reader he expects his novel to encounter and the kind of experience he hopes this novel will incite.

Lajolo explicates the gendered and class-related characteristics of *Iracema*'s imagined reader, who, unlike the novel's protagonist, is an upper-middle-class white man, who is able to depend on the service of his wife and servants to allow him time for leisurely reading. But Alencar also leverages this figure to make an important statement about the mental state required of his interlocutor in engaging with the book, a mental state, as we will see, very different from the one the New Critics will theorize a century later as necessary for a productive reading process to take place. In his prologue, under the valance of a romantic imagining of his novel's future scene of consumption, Alencar provides an implicit set of instructions as to how one should engage with his text.[10]

> Este livro o vai naturalmente encontrar em seu pitoresco sítio da várzea, no doce lar . . . Imagino que é a hora mais ardente da sesta. . . . A natureza sofre a influência da poderosa irradiação tropical, que produz o diamante e o gênio, as duas mais brilhantes expanções do poder criador. . . . A dona da casa, terna e incansável, manda abrir o coco verde, ou prepara o saboroso creme do buriti para refrigerar o esposo, que pouco há recolheu de sua excursão pelo sítio, e agora repousa embalandose na macia e cômoda rede. Abra então este livrinho, que lhe chega da corte imprevisto. Percorra suas páginas para desenfastiar o espírito das cousas graves que o trazem ocupado. . . . O livro é cearense. Foi imaginado aí, na limpidez desse céu de cristalino azul. . . . Escrevi-o para ser lido lá, na varanda da casa rústica ou na fresca sombra do pomar, ao doce embalo da rede, entre os múrmuros do vento que crepita na areia, ou farfalha nas palmas dos coqueiros.

> This book will naturally find you in the picturesque meadows, in your sweet abode. . . . It is probably the most blazing time of Friday. . . . Nature is under the dominion of the potent tropical irradiation, that which produces both the diamond and the genius, the two most brilliant instantiations of creative powers. . . . Your wife, loving and tireless, commands that a fresh green coconut be opened for you, or prepares a delicious mousse of *buriti* to freshen her husband, who had just returned from his excursion and now reposes, cradled in his hammock, soft and snug. You then open up the book which reached you unexpectedly from Corte. You scroll through its pages to distract your spirit from the serious matters that keep it preoccupied. This book is Cearánian. It was envisioned there, under these lucid crystal blue skies. . . . I wrote it to be read there, on the porch of a rustic cabin or in the garden's fresh shade, in the sweet rocking movement of the hammock, among the murmurs of the wind crisping through the sand, or rustling the branches of the coconut tree.[11]

I have included the original text and its translation for this quote, as I will do selectively for various quotes in this and the upcoming chapters when the analysis will delve into the nuances of specific word choices or stylistic elements. This holds true for Alencar's description of his ideal reader, who is imagined as primarily tranquil. The reader is located on a porch within northeastern Ceará, rocked by the hammock and embraced by the murmuring wind, the chirping birds, and the coconut trees' rustling branches. These do not function as a mere context to be erased by an attention-absorbing narrative. Instead, Alencar imagines this medley of sounds, images, and sensations to be present for his reader, whose interaction with the literary text is interwoven with the body's soft snuggle, with the harmonic temperature of a commingled shade, wind and sun, and with nature's sonic pleasures.

The absorption of these conditions is assumed by Alencar to then produce a mental state of "distraction" (*desenfastiar*; literally, to unbore or relieve), which the author metonymically ties with a movement of thought. Mimicking the back-and-forth rocking of the hammock and the "crisping" motion of the wind and sand, the reader's mind is imagined to wander, straying "from the serious matters that keep it preoccupied." Intensity in this context is depicted as external, emanating from the Brazilian "potent tropical" climate, which, if surrendered to, can produce creativity, intellectual force, and beauty (*o diamante*). The link between tranquility of mind and imaginative thought is already communicated by the object at the center of Alencar's reading scene. The Brazilian hammock (*rêde*), as Luís de Câmara Cascudo demonstrates in his ethnographic work, is not only long associated with meditation, dreams, and a deep observation of nature, but also functions in the popular imaginary as a metaphor for the plasticity of the Brazilian mind and body.[12] Put another way, a wandering, distracted mind and readerly aptitude go hand in hand for the author of *Iracema* and are both characteristics associated with social and intellectual standing.

Little less than a century later, a group of Brazilian literary critics will wage war against Alencar's image of the ideal Brazilian reader, and by extension, the Brazilian citizen. More specifically, the Brazilian New Critics will labor to undo the association between valuable reading and distraction, condemning the latter as epitomizing supposed racial and intellectual weakness, and ardently promoting a readerly effort of attention predicated on mental, rather than environmental, intensity. In order to achieve this goal and replace Alencar's "commonplace" readerly model, these critics will leverage and adapt the anglophone theory of New Criticism and its key practice of close reading. I will return to Alencar's opening scene toward the end of this chapter, to demonstrate how it was rewritten by the key leader of the Brazilian New Critics. But for now, suffice it to say that Alencar's romanticized mind-wandering will become for the Brazilian New Critics an urgent problem to be solved.

As with any other cultural goods, the travels of the New Criticism into Brazil depended on material border-crossing. The central agent to carry New Critical close reading into the continent's largest country in the late 1940s is the prominent and contentious literary critic Afrânio Coutinho (1911–2000), who studied medicine, but made the bold decision to pursue a career in literary studies that later earned him the prestigious title, "the father of modern Brazilian literary criticism."[13] Coutinho grew up in the city of Salvador, the capital of Bahia, which is located, like Alencar's Ceará, in the Brazilian northeast (*nordeste*). This area has not only been historically populated by indigenous communities, as Alencar stresses, but was also the first region in Brazil to be colonized and functioned as a central port in the Atlantic slave trade. This history of oppression afflicted the region with continuous poverty and violence, evident to this day.[14] Coutinho's *bahiano* background will haunt him throughout his career, as noted by Cunha e Silva Filho, making it difficult for him to enter the Brazilian intellectual milieu of Rio de Janeiro.[15] Coutinho, then, as Alencar, ventures on his mission of rethinking the New Criticism and the Brazilian close reader burdened by questions of national and regional identity and by a history of oppression.

Coutinho returns to Brazil in 1947, after spending five years in the US as the editor of *Reader's Digest*'s Brazilian edition. During his time abroad, he also attends courses at Columbia University as a visiting scholar, and arrives back in Brazil deeply impressed by the New Criticism.[16] This is so much the case that in 1948, a year after his return, Coutinho initiates an extensive literary campaign explicitly aimed at introducing into Brazilian cultural circulation his local version of the theory, which he titles the "nova crítica." In two decades, he publishes eight books dedicated to the nature of Brazilian literary criticism (*Por uma crítica estética* [1954], *Da crítica e da nova crítica* [1957], *A crítica* [1958], *Conceito de literatura brasileira* [1960], *No hospital das letras* [1963], *A tradição afortunada* [1968], *Crítica e poética* [1968], and *Crítica e críticos* [1969]); edits the prestigious literary journal, *Coletânea* (1951–1960); edits a six-volume renewed historiography of Brazilian literature, *A literatura no Brasil*, which radically changes the face of the field (to be discussed in the next chapter);[17] and brings about an institutional transformation, which culminates in 1967 with his establishment of the first autonomous literature department in Brazil, at the Universidade Federal do Rio de Janeiro (UFRJ). All through this time period, from 1948 to 1966 to be exact, Coutinho also persistently publishes his Sunday column, "Correntes cruzadas" ("Cross Currents"), in the literary supplement of the daily newspaper, *Diário de notícias*, which becomes his most popular presentation of the *nova crítica*'s principles.[18]

Coutinho was not alone in his interest in the New Criticism; the Brazilian scholars Sérgio Buarque de Holanda (SBH) and Antônio Cândido were likewise central players in the local reception of the theory. During the 1940s, Holanda spent a year in Washington, and came back with "a whole little library about Anglo-American New Criticism," making him, in Antonio Arnoni Prado's words, "one of the most fecund interpreters of New Criticism to ever develop in Brazil."[19] And the legendary Antônio Cândido was invested in the New Criticism in an attempt to link together formalism and sociology, a combination that allowed him "to maintain [his] distance and yet learn from the Anglo-American theory," as his student, Robert Schwartz, has claimed.[20] However, to differentiate from Coutinho, SBH and Candido were significantly ambivalent about the merits of New Criticism and, most importantly in the current context, devoted very little of their discussions about aesthetics and literary criticism to the figure of the reader and the practice of close reading. Coutinho, on the other hand, was intensively preoccupied with defining the attributes of the efficacious Brazilian reader in line with the New Critical pedagogy.

Coutinho's intense work was fruitful; his extensive critical oeuvre left an indelible mark on Brazilian intellectual life and positioned him as a key cultural figure of his time to later be consecrated as a symbol of modern Brazilian literary criticism. As João Cezar de Castro Rocha puts it, "The recent history of literary criticism in Brazil knows many versions, but almost all overlap in pointing to the same moment as the origin of its modernization: the polemics initiated in 1948 by Afrânio Coutinho."[21]

Impact notwithstanding, the basic precepts Coutinho presents in his critical body of work may seem quite unoriginal. He advocates for an "intrinsic" reading of literature rather than a focus on context; an institutionalization, democratization, and professionalization of the field; and a methodological shift that would make the reading of literature more systematic and less dependent on subjective impressions, all presented as interdependent pursuits. Various scholars, including Coutinho himself, have pointed out that these principles could be labeled structuralist or formalist, as much as New Critical, even though Coutinho continually quotes and mentions in his writing, and with special force in "Cross Currents," various

New Critics from Cleanth Brooks, Robert Penn Warren, and Allen Tate to Robert Bechtold Heilman, R. P. Blackmur, and John Crowe Ransom. In this spirit, Denis Heyck claims that "the unique feature of the *nova crítica* is its combination of Anglo-American new critical principles with a remarkably wide variety of other intellectual influences and concerns," among them Russian Formalism, the Spanish Stylistics School, and Benedetto Croce's aesthetics.[22] And Coutinho himself does not perform in his oeuvre many detailed analyses of literary works, which could demonstrate the specificity of the method or aesthetic view he advanced. In fact, it is mostly Coutinho's adversaries who claimed his work was uniquely New Critical. They did so by deprecating his ostensible parochial imitation; Álvaro Lins sardonically writes, "The true thinkers of New Criticism are certainly not like their post-boys from the provincial backland of South America, who pick up such cultural movements . . . as others buy certain North American machines long-ago constructed, eroded and done for."[23]

Hence, when Coutinho's *nova crítica* project is examined in retrospect, it is usually discussed in the context of disciplinary institutionalization in Brazil, or the emergence of new scholarly trends. That is, Coutinho's cultural contributions are thoroughly documented and historicized but without attention to his theory's specific affinity with the American New Criticism and its view of readerly subjectivity.[24] But this is selling short Coutinho's shrewd perception and interpretation of the signature New Critical model of unselfing. By following closely Coutinho's descriptions of his version of close reading—its aims and modes of operation—I wish to reveal Coutinho's astute adaptation of the New Critical readerly practice to the local Brazilian cultural, historical, and political context.

Coutinho's sophistication lies in his vocal identification of the Anglo-American New Criticism as a social rather than merely aesthetic project, and of close reading as a method of subject-formation contingent on the faculty of attention, over and above the North American critics' explicit statements regarding the apolitical nature of their theory and practice, discussed in the earlier chapters. This is a highly keen and original understanding of the New Critical project, one that only decades later will emerge in the anglophone world.[25] In that vein, Coutinho reinforces the view that this present book advances, which identifies a pedagogical core to the New Critical enterprise.

Yet, as I briefly mentioned above, Coutinho's work is double-edged. On the one hand, he cannily conceptualizes the mind as a historically construed and plastic apparatus that carries the marks of the past but can also be reformulated via a reading praxis; on the other, he leverages close reading as a technique of the self for a dubious Brazilian civilizing mission, very much in a colonialist spirit, presenting the New Critical method as a cure for Brazilian intellectual inferiority. Coutinho's terms also speak to this ideological paradox. He inconsistently describes this assumed Brazilian inferiority as "national," brought about by a history of colonial rule, and as inherent to the Brazilian "race," as in the example quoted in the epigraph ("the *innate* qualities of the spirit"). Via these internal contradictions, Coutinho exhibits what Du Bois famously called a "double consciousness"; he structures his critical project around a continuous "measuring [of] one's soul by the tape of a world that looks on in amused contempt and pity."[26]

It is, I argue, precisely this complexity that established Coutinho as such a pivotal cultural figure. By harnessing the unselfing technique, which underlies the New Critical reading method, to the construction of a Brazilian self, he was able to inject the politically charged and then-timely issues of subject-formation, postcolonial identification, and national identity into the ostensibly esoteric question of literary methodology.

Butterfly Dispersion

To understand Coutinho's reworking of the New Critical technique of the self, we must consider not only what the *nova crítica* was promoting, but also—perhaps mostly—what it was working against. We recall that Rocha above identifies Coutinho as the initiator of "polemics," and he is undeniably right in referring to Coutinho's writings with this term. All through his work, and with particular urgency in "Correntes cruzadas," the Brazilian critic was out to pick a fight, with his proclaimed opponents being the *críticos de rodapé*, or "footnote critics" (the abovementioned Álvaro Lins was a lead nemesis). The "footnote critics"—thus termed because of their reviews' location on the newspaper's margins—were established Brazilian cultural figures who traditionally published their literary commentary in newspapers and addressed the public and the academic professionals as one. They functioned, in Rocha's terms, as "cultural mediators" between high culture and the public, offering guidance to readers, educated or not, in their interactions with the literary text.[27]

However, for Coutinho and his later adherents, *rodapé* literary commentary served as the most typical example of all that is faulty in Brazilian letters: it was written by amateurs, they claimed, who never studied literature systematically and was hence subjective and impressionistic. *Rodapé* criticism, Coutinho writes, is a "criticism without objective criteria, either a simplistic, superficial commentary beside the point of the book, or a relativist one whose sole criteria is personal taste or pure sensory impression. That is, both journalistic and impressionistic criticism do not make sense."[28] Over and above its quality of interpretation ("beside the point," "relativist," "impressionistic"), what the *nova crítica* thinkers found most troubling in *rodapé* criticism was its flagrant exhibition of what they took to be a general, widespread Brazilian mental inadequacy for analytic reading, or, as Coutinho provocatively puts it, an "inaptitude of our race for speculative meditation."[29] Coutinho does not hesitate to diagnose the mental work exhibited by the *críticos de rodapé* as a disability or chronic sickness, paradigmatic of Brazilian readers writ large. The Brazilian readership, he argues, suffers from a severe "degeneracy" in comprehension capabilities, an internal "degradation," "mental immaturity," and a "disorder of spirits" as quoted in the epigraph, all made starkly evident by the *rodapé*'s reviews.[30]

Coutinho's view undoubtedly has an essentialist component to it. But the Brazilian critic also, somewhat counterintuitively, holds that the "innate" defects he identifies in the Brazilian reader have been historically and socially constructed. More specifically, he takes the Brazilian state of "degeneration" to have been inscribed into the local mind by centuries of colonial oppression, thus putting forward an insightful conception of consciousness as the surface on which history and political power struggles are marked.[31] Coutinho maintains that being under prolonged oppression has impeded Brazilian mental capabilities such that, for example, the systematic depriving of a sense of control has entrenched in the Brazilian subject—Coutinho does not distinguish between indigenous people and descendants of colonizers—a tendency toward mental dependency. In his words, "As far as culture is concerned, our condition as a colonialized people is made evident, among other symptoms, by our preoccupation with serving a master. We have yet to truly achieve intellectual maturity, which would grant us independence from the eminent culture-producing peoples of the West."[32] He further clarifies that "improvisation and impressionism, the natural substitutes of method, are spontaneous recourses in incipient civilizations, but they become mental vice when stratified and normalized into the realm of education."[33]

Per Coutinho, then, one of the devastating results of colonialism is a transgenerational mental pathology, a "symptom" of "intellectual

[im]maturity" that has been ossified into a "racial inaptitude": "Since the country's colonization was based on extractive economy, the colonizer has utterly neglected mental education, even that which is elementary, undetectable, done in passing. They did not create strong intellectual traditions, and even less so construed organizations that constitute the material armor of the people's intellectual and educational work: universities, libraries, museums, presses, and various instruments compatible thereof, without which culture is a hollow word."[34] Coutinho's goal, then, in battling *rodapé* criticism is of considerable scope; he is aiming to cure his people from what he perceived as the mental malady of colonialism. Heyck writes on this issue, "Coutinho could not accept the notion that Brazilians were inherently inferior; he had to find an external cause that, once found, could be uprooted."[35]

Indeed, Coutinho merges the aesthetic New Critical principle of literature's autonomy with his project's drive toward establishing an independent national literature, or, more specifically, an autonomous mind for the local reader. If the Brazilian reader could prove capable of reading literature as an autonomous object—a process he believes requires systematic and analytic thought in contrast with "personal taste" or "pure sensory impression"—she will thus prove her independence from the history of colonization inscribed on her mind.[36]

Charging his objection to *rodapé* criticism with such political valence, Coutinho propelled the issue of Brazilian literary interpretation into the center of public concern. During the 1950s and 1960s, a heated debate took place, on and off the pages of daily newspapers, in which leading cultural figures from both sides of the barrier participated, including Eduardo Portella, Euríalo Canabrava, Lêdo Ivo, Wilson Martins, Fábio Lucas, Fausto Cunha, Nelson Werneck Sodré, and Álvaro Lins.[37] The debate had such a strong cultural presence that, Heyck argues, "it helped to determine the state of the national critical mind that came to prevail during the sixties."[38] One might be surprised that a conversation about the nature of literary criticism reached such proportions. But the fact is that centering this deliberation was not only the question of literary interpretation or method; instead, this was predominantly a debate about the literal contours and capabilities of the "Brazilian mind."

Indeed, it is in the mind, rather than the text, that the problem begins. According to the *nova crítica*, at the center of the Brazilian "degeneracy" is a specific cognitive tendency: a Brazilian proclivity for distraction, or what Coutinho calls, a "dispersive and butterfly-like form of thought,"

> Tudo conspira entre nós contra o trabalho do espírito, mesmo em relação aos mais bem-dotados. Em primeiro lugar, a deficiente formação, fruto de autodidatismo, responsável pela ausência de disciplina mental, pelo espírito de diletantismo, pela falta de persistência em perseguir os objetivos colimados, pela inexistência de metodologia, pela atitude dispersiva e borboleteante da inteligência, pelo virtuosismo personalista, pela tendência ao enciclopedismo, ao poligrafismo, às generalidades.
>
> Everything conspires amongst us against the work of the spirit, even with regards to our most talented. First, our deficient formation, the result of autodidacticism, which is responsible for our lack of mental discipline, our dilettante spirit, our lack of persistence in pursuing aspired goals, our insubstantial methodologies, our dispersive and butterfly-like form of thought, our idealization of the personal, our tendency towards encyclopedism, graphomania, generalizations.[39]

As we have already seen, here too Coutinho blurs the lines between the inherent and the historical. He counts among the "everything" that operates against the Brazilian's "work of the spirit" social reasons such as the flawed education system ("deficient formation"), but mingles it with "spirit[ual]" tendencies such as "lack of mental discipline" and "idealization of the personal."

The resulting portrait exhibits the Brazilian mind in constant erratic movement, at times producing excessively ("graphomania") and at others coming to unexpected halts ("lack of persistence"). When the Brazilian mind does progress, its movements are unsystematic, advancing in a "dilettante" and unmethodological manner. Fueling this irregular mental motion is a particular motor, a "dispersive and butterfly-like form of thought."[40] Coutinho admits himself to have suffered from this same ruinous inclination, to which he found a cure in the North American university. As Castro Rocha narrates,

> In his 1952 inaugural speech in Colégio Pedro II, Coutinho acknowledged that, before his encounter with the North American university, his perspective was one of a dilettante, precisely because he was wanting in methods and concentration: "My scatter and lack of direction were substituted with

strong conviction and linearity. The vice of butterflying around without rest, so common amongst us, and which was mine as well, was opposed by a tendency to restrict one's vision under the assumption that no one serves well many lords."[41]

Rocha vividly depicts this scene but does not linger on the question of attention it raises. What Coutinho is most wanting in, as a paradigmatic representative of the Brazilian "us," is methods and concentration, the former presented as the generator of the latter. While the intellectual problem Coutinho attests to is the "vice" of "scatter," here again associated with a mental "butterfly" movement, its resolution per Coutinho is a method that enhances a "restrict[ion] of one's vision."

Tellingly, and in line with the political valence this pedagogical project carries for Coutinho, he puts even the question of mental aptitude in terms of servitude.[42] For Coutinho, the question is not only which, but how many "lords"—how many stimuli—can the Brazilian mind answer to. And he claims that what derives the Brazilian mental degeneracy is a tendency toward serving too many lords, a tendency toward distraction—etymologically pointing to erratic movement (from the Latin *distrahere*, to "draw in different directions"). The solution, he insists, is to be found in the North American university. In that spirit, throughout his writings, Coutinho endorses university education as a means not of acquiring knowledge but of method acquisition. For him, methods of reading are trained forms of engagement with literature that, with repetition, become part of the reader's more general habituated praxes. Hence, a method that enhances concentration can be internalized to reshape the mind and "oppose" the vice of distraction.

In his book, tellingly titled *Na hospital das letras* (*In the Hospital of Letters*), Coutinho reiterates his view of the Brazilian condition as an illness.[43] He writes, "[This book is] a hospital for the vices and deformations of our professional activity. Here we diagnose and reproach various aspects of our moral and social diseases, in the hope that, in the future, the healing process of the university will not allow for the transmission of this devastating virus."[44] The readerly "devastating virus" Coutinho detects results, as we have seen above, from external ("social") and internal/ized ("moral") causes intertwined. Hence, a proper reading method might function as a suitable antidote since it works both intrinsically and extrinsically: it is externally incorporated into and adopted by the reader, but then becomes an integral part of her form of being in the world.

Indeed, Coutinho refers to the reading method he promotes as a "cure" (*esforço de "redressement,"* as in the epigraph) or "remedy" (*remedio*) for the Brazilian problem of distraction, "scatter and lack of direction."[45] He writes, "Our issue at hand is one of methods. It is only through a radical change of methods that we will be able to remedy our detrimental mental habits, which are responsible for the faults in our intellectual production."[46]

Coutinho's cognitive language ("our detrimental mental habits," the vice of "scatter") and his solution in the form of a "method" may convey the sense that his writings offer a comprehensive readerly theory of mind. However, as we will soon see, Coutinho's theory is notably underdeveloped, unlike what we have seen with Brooks in the previous chapters. The reason is that Coutinho is implicitly driven by the ideological assumption that there is a savage within the Brazilian self that is in need of extraction before any reading can take place. Consequently, the Brazilian New Critic is first and foremost interested in self-discipline and self-civilization, rather than in an exploration of the full interchange between the literary text and the reader's mind. This ambivalence slowly emerges as we follow Coutinho in the description of his "remedial" reading method, which, as we would expect from a New Critic, is close reading.

Exact Reading

Coutinho often referred to close reading by its English title, making evident his dialogue with the anglophone New Critics. However, as we shall see, he also assigned to this praxis a local Portuguese title, "*leitura exata*" ("exact reading"). In the years since, close reading has been popularized in Brazil as "*leitura de perto*" (literally, "reading from close by"), a term that, though departing from Coutinho's translation choice, attests to the *nova crítica*'s impact on Brazilian culture. While in the Hispanic world bordering Brazil no local term for the New Critical method has gained cultural traction, Coutinho and his followers were able to insert close reading into the local critical tradition and discourse.[47]

Following the semantic field Coutinho structures around close reading in the Brazilian context is significant for understanding the meaning it has accrued. Coutinho writes,

> Various recent works acknowledge that the movement called nova crítica (New Criticism [English in the original]) ... acquired public importance beyond the circle of pioneers who gave rise to

it. Emphasizing an intense, exact and accurate analysis of literature (close reading [English in the original]), or, more explicitly, "the examination of the literary work in order to understand each of its parts and in order to establish the relationship between them and the whole and amongst themselves" (George Arms), it positions the critic in front of the poem as a poem, in front of the work of art as a work of art.[48]

Via the little-known North American literary critic, George Warren Arms, Coutinho reiterates the traditional New Critical emphasis on the unity of the literary text (the fourth and fifth chapters will display the unique amplification of this precept in the context of the Israeli New Criticism). What is particular in Coutinho's presentation of close reading is its rendering in terms of visual perception. We recall that Coutinho depicts the problem of distraction and its methodological solution in terms of light; the vice of "scatter" or "dispersion" is to be opposed by a tendency to "restrict one's vision." This same metaphorical field envelopes the *nova crítica*'s reading method as well. For Coutinho, close reading is a form of engagement with literature that manipulates the subject's point of view in space ("positions the reader *in front* of the poem") and is contingent on intensity ("*intense*, exact and accurate analysis"). The close reader's mental ray of light coalesces toward a single point—the literary work—rather than spreading outward in various directions.

In the quote, Coutinho links "intensity" with the adjective "exact," and though the former is undoubtedly important to his conceptualization of the New Critical method, it is the latter that he returns to when translating close reading into Portuguese. In another column dedicated to his vision of literary criticism, he precedes the term "close reading" with a translation in parentheses, referring to it as "leitura exata." The method he advances, which, he maintains, centers "a movement in progress whose development awaits all those who believe in criticism," is "oriented toward an 'exact reading' (close reading [English in original]) of the literary work of art and toward the discovery and interpretation of its intrinsic aesthetic content."[49] This is a revealing word choice on Coutinho's part, which betrays his expectations for this mode of reading. As in the English, the adjective *exact* refers to an action done with great care and rigor, from the Latin *exactus*, "precise, accurate, highly finished."

The proximity of this term to positivist vocabulary is not accidental. In contrast with (or perhaps simply more explicitly than) their Anglo-American precursors, the *nova crítica* thinkers openly aligned themselves with scientific discourse and thought.[50] Their imagined reader is one who approaches the text with "the expertise that accompanies scientific investigation," in the words of Eduardo Portela, one of Coutinho's followers, or who applies to literature "a scientific method" and introduces "discipline and order" into the text, according to Euríalo Canabrava, the analytic philosopher who zealously supported the *nova crítica*.[51] The result is indeed an "intensity" of reading. As Coutinho puts it, once again thinking of the reading "eye" as an intense beam of light, close reading is a "method that penetrates to the intrinsic core or esthetic essence of the work of art,"[52] or, as in the quote above, one that "discover[s]" the work's "intrinsic aesthetic content." Exact reading intensifies, focalizes, and narrows down the reader's mental field of vision.

Coutinho views the readerly concentrated thinking "ray" as synonymous with "attention."[53] In discussion of F. R. Leavis, one of the British founding fathers of the New Critical approach, Coutinho writes that "Leavis focuses his powerful critical instrument on the supreme works of George Eliot, Henry James and Joseph Conrad, using for the investigation of their intimate nature all recourses available . . . but subordinates them all to a focal attention to the text itself."[54] Leavis' "powerful" reading is thought of in terms of perceptual "focus," in which one stimulus alone ("the text itself") attracts the whole of one's "critical instrument." In the same spirit, Coutinho writes in a different column that he has learned "the technique of focalizing on the poetic structure from John Crowe Ransom, Allen Tate, Cleanth Brooks and R. P. Warren."[55] This might explain why, as Heyck points out, though it was never fully clarified what Coutinho or his followers meant by "a literary scientific method," when Coutinho did address this topic, he defined scientificity as "an objective and ordered state of mind before the work of art."[56] The reader's "ordered state of mind" and her position in space ("before the work of art") come together once again to generate an "exact" reader.

Still, as in the English, *exact* should not be glossed only with the adjective *exactus*. It also has its etymological roots in the Latin verb *exigere*, which literally means "to drive or force out," for example, to exact revenge or exact a promise from someone. In Portuguese, the verb *exigir* similarly signifies the act of imposing a demand or command on someone. Indeed, the process of turning the Brazilian reader "exact" involves for the thinkers of the *nova crítica* a complex, and politically charged, process of extraction. Indeed, *leitura exata* is most characterized by what it forestalls the reader from doing; it is imagined to guide the reader toward suspending—annihilating if possible—her internal distracting force, which is imagined by Coutinho to be almost animate: "This reaction is a product of a new mentality created by the diffusion of higher academic education. These studies necessitate professional rigorous thought and a changed spiritual attitude, which are the adversaries of dilettantism, improvisation, amateurism, infantility. Undoubtedly, the university will put an end to the old mentality. But we must not lose heart in vigilance, for the devil has a thousand breaths."[57]

Coutinho focuses here, as elsewhere, on the role of higher education in solving the Brazilian problem of distraction. The question arises, then, if he indeed entrusts the responsibility for unselfing (for *exacting* distraction) to the reader, as I have so far suggested, or if he takes it to be the institution's task. As his quote suggests, Coutinho believes the university should advance "rigorous thought and a changed spiritual attitude," but these institutional exercises should be oriented toward an ultimate end of modifying the reader's mind, creating a "new mentality," so that the reader, outside and independently of the academic context, could continue in her process of self-discipline.

In this vein Coutinho writes elsewhere, "the decade of the 1950s in Brazilian literature should be considered [the decade] of Brazilian criticism. It is the moment in which we acquired the exact consciousness/understanding (*a consciência exata*) of criticism's relevant role in the realm of literary production and creative writing, a function of the discipline of the literary spirit."[58] Namely, Coutinho's end goal is the production of an "exact consciousness" as a result of the disciplining of the "spirit." And the self-discipline he imagines hinges on self-suspicion; Coutinho advised the exact reader to be in a constant mental state of "self-vigilance" (*autovigilância*) in order to fight off the "old" mentality as soon as it makes its presence felt.[59] This effort must be exerted perpetually since Coutinho is uncertain if this internal impulse can ever be altogether extracted; it is nothing less than a "devil [with] a thousand breaths," which awaits a moment of inattention to rise again, but whose eviction is the very condition of possibility for a Brazilian "new" mind. The *nova crítica*'s paradox begins to emerge: self-surveillance and self-censorship are construed as self-improving.

If these descriptions of exact reading still strike you as vague, you are not alone. As Heyck mentions, Coutinho was (and is) criticized for leaving obscure what interpretative procedures his version of close reading entails. But the reason is not as simple as mere carelessness. Coutinho does not specify exact reading's interpretive protocol since, as we have seen, he follows a unique and original understanding of his North American mentors' technique. While the standard dictum is that "the Poem itself—this is what the New Criticism purported to be about,"[60] Coutinho understands the New Critical project to be pedagogical to the core, revolving around the reading-subject rather than the aesthetic object, "the poem itself." The process to be detailed, then, is not what one needs to do with the text while reading, but what the reader must do to herself while engaging with the literary text.

Simply put, the main goal of the New Critical enterprise, in Coutinho's eyes, is to create via exact reading better readers, who will become better Brazilians. And he makes clear this view as early as his May 30, 1948 column, with which he will later choose to open his volume of collected columns. There, he focuses in particular on the work of I. A. Richards, writing the following:

> More than ever, and more than any other, the movement of New Criticism confirms the conviction that literary criticism is the art of reading and teaching how to read literature, both prose-fiction and poetry. The work of I. A. Richards, a point of departure for New Criticism (1923), with his *Meaning of Meaning, Principles of Literary Criticism, Practical Criticism, Interpretation in Teaching* . . . and *How to Read a Page* . . . leads us to conclude that it is guided by one dominant line of investigation, made explicit in the title of the final work in this list—*How to Read a Page*, and its subtitle—*A Course in Effective Reading*. This idea dominates the movement as a whole.[61]

How to Read a Page is usually considered a relatively minor work by Richards that functions as a "manual of sorts. . . . Richards presents his readers with a set of exercises to enable them to read better . . . rather than adhering to the critic's role of subsequent comment," as Helen Thavanthiran puts it.[62] For Coutinho, however, enabling readers to read better is the fundamental role of the critic.

Coutinho takes the New Critical pedagogy a step further, maintaining that learning how to "read better" is intertwined with learning how to *be* better, on an intellectual, an ethical, and a political level. He declares that "[t]he process of turning oneself into a better literary artist is inextricably linked with turning oneself into a better man."[63] Coutinho does not differentiate the "literary artist" from the scholar or reader. All agents in the sphere of Brazilian letters can and should leverage his proposed reading method to mend their minds (battle their "detrimental mental habits") toward a "creation of a critical conscious for our literature . . . in Departments of Philosophy and Letters. . . . From there will flourish better poets, better novelists, better critics, better researchers and hard-working intellectuals."[64] Coutinho highlights the New Critical roots of his pedagogical project by echoing Richards's words almost verbatim: "Generally put, the new attitude questions any criticism of assertions, and instead aims to teach how to *read* literature [emphasis in original],"[65] adding that "[t]he University is first and foremost a spiritual attitude. A technique. Of work, of thought, of action. And our revolution will be one of methodology or it won't be at all."[66]

Coutinho's terminology surprisingly foreshadows Foucault's later work on technologies of the self, which I discuss in the Introduction as a possible vocabulary for understanding the mechanism of New Critical close reading. Foucault follows the archeology of methods "which permit individuals to effect by their own means, or with the help of others, a certain number of operations on their own bodies and souls, thoughts, conduct and way of being, so as to transform themselves in order to attain a certain state of happiness, purity, wisdom, perfection or immortality."[67] Contrary to interpretations that insist on detecting in Foucault's theory a clear dichotomy between power and subversion, Foucault does not impose a value judgment on these praxes, focusing instead on exposing their historical and ever-changing nature, along with their regulatory and pleasure-producing mechanisms. Coutinho does not offer a historical analysis of reading as a technique of the self, but he undoubtedly presents exact reading as such a practice, "A technique. Of work, of thought, of action." Coutinho discusses the "new attitude" he proposes as a "technique" to be deployed by the reader not only in order to perform better analytical literary work, but also, and most importantly, to self-improve the Brazilian's mode of being in the world. That is, unselfing one's distracting "devil" during the reading process creates attentive Brazilian subjects, whose improved intellectual production will potentially grant them independence from the "eminent culture-producing peoples of the West."

What Coutinho does not attend to, exact as he may be, is that the Brazilian as a distracted dilettante is itself a colonial fantasy. That is, Coutinho's pedagogical plan, as I implied all along, is fueled by a complex political, postcolonial dynamic that must be reckoned with. The *nova crítica*—objection notwithstanding—reverberated strongly with Brazilian readers, mostly from the intellectual bourgeoisie, since it saw and presented itself as a patriotic endeavor. It is not accidental that Coutinho identifies the Brazilian reader as faulty in her capabilities of analytical thoughts, and that "distraction" specifically, as related to "amateurism, infantility," and an animalistic mind ("butterfly thought"), is at the core of this "degeneracy." Clearly, the *nova crítica*'s attempt to mobilize readerly subject-formation for the purpose of Brazilian "modernization" is a byproduct of an identification with the colonial viewpoint, and hence mired in the forms of racism and colonialism from which it is trying to escape. To put it in James Baldwin's poignant words, "People are trapped in history and history is trapped in them."[68]

Coutinho orchestrates exact reading as an unselfing "cure" aimed to allow the Brazilian reader to rid herself of the history of colonization trapped in her mind. But in thus striving to release Brazilian people from the colonial gaze, Coutinho demonstrates the degree of his own internalization of that contemptuous viewpoint; he is trapped in history. In this gap, the figure of the savage storms in.

Savage Sloth

Coutinho's work arrives in a Brazil primed for a deliberation about subject formation—the country was experiencing a drastic political change that rendered malleable the contours of national identity, with which the *nova crítica* attempted to engage. "Correntes cruzadas" is first published more than a century after Brazil's independence (1822), and three years after the simultaneous end of World War II and of Getúlio Vargas's eight-year dictatorship (1945). These later occasions mark the beginning of what will later be called *República Populista* ("Populist Republic"), an eighteen-year period characterized by a tentative democratic governance in Brazil, which will come to an abrupt closure with the 1964 coup d'état and consequent twenty years of military regime. Despite political instability, this era exhibited cultural openness and provided new conditions for thinking through the urgent postcolonial question: how should Brazilian identity be imagined?

Within this context, Coutinho harkens back, wittingly or not, to *Iracema*'s opening scene. This revisitation makes evident what Coutinho hopes to alter in Alencar's popularized image of the reader, while also exposing the colonial views that haunt exact reading. The *nova crítica*'s architect maintains many of the elements in Alencar's scene—the blazing Brazilian sun, the reading in nature, and the question of attention versus distraction—but he changes the definition of readerly capability and explains why the process of unselfing is necessary for a "proper" Brazilian reader to come into being. He does so by ventriloquizing the nineteenth-century Brazilian critic, Tristão de Alencar Araripe Júnior. Coutinho writes,

> Imbuído das ideias do determinnismo [sic] geográfico, tão caras à sua geração e à época do materialismo naturalista, Araripe Júnior tentou explicar, certa feita, o precoce envelhecimento ou esgotamento do intelectual brasileiro como sendo uma consequência da influência do meio físico . . . "Neste imenso Brasil, aos raios candentes dêste sol tropical, ou imitamos o selvagem que vai buscar no ócio e na oscilação da rêde uma trégua contra os elementos devorantes do clima, ou exaltamo-nos, como único meio de adquirir alguma atividade, e consumimo-nos em pouco tempo . . . na extração dos elementos, no preparo do embasamento, consome ele toda a seiva indispensável à ideação do livro" . . . Não há dúvida que é sensível a influência do meio, [mas] . . . [a]s coisas sociais devem ser mais ponderáveis, não havendo como não há profissão intelectual organizada.

> Imbued with the ideas of geographic determinism, so dear to his generation and to the era of naturalist materialism, Araripe Júnior tried to explain, once, the premature aging and debilitation of the Brazilian intellectual as a consequence of his physical environment. . . . "In this immense Brazil, under the blazing rays of the tropical sun, one can either imitate the savage that takes refuge from this devouring climate in sloth and in the oscillation of the hammock, or intensify one's actions as the only way to achieve one's goals, thus quickly exhausting oneself . . . in the extraction, in the preparation of the foundation, [the Brazilian intellectual] has already exhausted all the mental-juice necessary for making sense of a book." . . . Undoubtedly, the environmental influence is significant, [but] . . . social reasons must also be taken into consideration, as we are lacking an organized intellectual profession.[69]

Both Araripe Júnior and the abovementioned Alencar link the Brazilian climate with the intellectual and creative forces of the reader located therein. While Alencar finds the "potent tropical irradiation" productive, Júnior takes this physical environment to be the cause for the here-undisputed problem of the "debilitation of the Brazilian intellectual."

Coutinho diverges from both in vesting social reasons with responsibility for the Brazilian difficulty in "making sense of a book." Elsewhere he makes clear that while "Araripe Júnior was early to identify . . . the Brazilian bad habit of leaving the mental faculties of imagination in disarray before tropical nature . . . the phenomenon of tropical disorder is long standing . . . and it is the sole tradition that generates our dispersive spirit."[70] For Coutinho, then, the Brazilian "spirit" is just as generative of the national problem of mental "disarray" as the lack of "an organized intellectual profession," if the two can at all be severed.[71]

Over and above these differences, Coutinho's choice of Júnior's vocabulary makes sense. The former too is highly preoccupied with what he finds to be the "debilitation of the Brazilian intellectual," and he similarly links this local predicament to the question of "intensity." Rather than an external intensity to be succumbed to, as in *Iracema*, both Coutinho and Júnior imagine intensity to be a quality of the action to be taken by the reader—Júnior asks that the intellectual "intensify one's actions" and Coutinho promotes "an intense, exact and accurate analysis of literature." For both critics, intensity functions as a counterforce to Brazilian "nature," a literal one for Júnior and a metaphorical one in Coutinho's case.

Through Júnior's words, then, Coutinho introduces a violent split into Alencar's reading scene. In *Iracema*'s prologue, the enjoying subject ("the sweet rocking movement of the hammock") and the thinking subject ("I wrote it to be read there, on the porch") are one and the same, both benefiting from the "intensity" of the Brazilian climate. For Coutinho, on the other hand, these two subject positions cannot coexist. Instead, they are antithetical forms of self-comportment: one characterized by "sloth" and "savage[ry]," and the other by "intensi[t]y," "exhaust[ion]," "extraction," and "making sense of a book."

The latter model jibes well with the depiction of the close or "exact" reader we have encountered above: this subject pushes against the temptation to indulge distraction on the hammock in order "to achieve one's goals." But what this paragraph adds to our understanding of exact reading is the identification of the abstract and ostensibly cognitive tendency for "butterfly thought" with the specific image of the "savage." The national "degeneracy," "lack of mental discipline" and "dilettante spirit," which so unsettle Coutinho, and which exact reading is designed to extract, are exposed as associated with the colonial ur-signifier of the Brazilian native. It is the savage that Coutinho, via Araripe Júnior, derides for taking "refuge from this devouring climate in sloth and in the oscillation of the hammock," and for renouncing in advance any attempt to "make sense of a book." To put it differently, Coutinho bisects Alencar's reader using a Cartesian dualism invested with a local political charge: the embodied pleasure-seeking "savage" is constructed as the binary opposite of the hard-working thinking reader.[72]

That would explain why in his writings Coutinho describes the Brazilian's faulty cognitive tendencies as related to "instinctive forces," "unconscious, savage-like, virginal, primitive forces," and "innate qualities of spirit."[73] The long-standing colonial pejorative conception of the Brazilian native as a savage—primitive, infantile, lazy, unconcentrated, intellectually inferior, animalistic—is found to be at the heart of Coutinho's project of reader-formation. When the *nova crítica* encourages the Brazilian reader to suspend or, even better, utterly "exact" her distractive and destructive forces, a process done in the name of postcolonial mental liberation, it is in fact a demand that she unsavage, that is, empty herself of supposed "innate," "savage" tendencies.

The identification of the indigenous with the body, and as the other of intellect, is a well-known colonialist trope. In fact, Antônio Cândido suggests that the tension between the "barbarian" and the "acculturated" undergirds the whole of Latin American culture, as can be viewed in Domingo Faustino Sarmiento's seminal *Facundo: civilización y barbarie* (*Facundo: Civilization and Barbarism*, 1845), and Euclides da Cunha's *Os sertões: campanha de Canudos* (*Backlands: The Canudos Campaign*, 1902).[74] In the same vein, the abovementioned Buarque de Holanda (though disagreeing with Coutinho on many other grounds) similarly internalizes the colonial viewpoint and complains that "leisure [in Brazil] is worth more than business, and that productive activity is in itself less valuable than contemplation and love."[75] What Coutinho nevertheless adds to this notorious hierarchical dichotomy is the matter of mental focus. Against the backdrop of his ongoing association of mental effort with light, Coutinho dichotomizes "savage" dispersion and "exact" attention. In coping with the overcentralized Brazilian sunrays, one can either "imitate the savage" and perform a metaphorically opposite mental movement of decentralized thought (here translated as "sloth") or choose the path of the intellect and intensify (etymologically "tighten") one's mental "rays" to an even higher degree than the sun.[76]

In this context, the paradox centering the *nova crítica* enterprise is brought into full relief. The local New Critics strive to dispel the colonial myth of the Brazilian as unable to engage in rigorous, analytical thought, not by exposing the basic falsity of this argument, but by educating Brazilians in how to detect and remove their own pathology of distraction from within in order to create in its stead a spiritual attitude of "rigorous thought" via "higher academic education" and its exact method of intense focus and unselfing. It follows that in order to transform into a sovereign Brazilian reader, unconstrained by the colonial grip, the Brazilian subject must detach herself from what the *nova crítica* defines as most essentially Brazilian: improved readers are ones who extract their innate Brazilian tendencies from within, and thus become independent, universal (or simply "neutral" Western) readers.

In the spirit of the dialectics depicted at the opening of the chapter, the Brazilian New Critical method of unselfing guarantees the reader an intense encounter with the literary text, and an enhancement of overall concentration and attention capabilities; the price, however, is equally high. What has been internalized as most profoundly Brazilian, must be violently and continually extracted. It is precisely into this caesura that the renowned Brazilian writer João Guimarães Rosa injects his intricate critique of exact reading. Rosa brings us back full circle to the image of the reader as a spatial void with which we began this chapter, demonstrating that the process of unsavaging is, too, fueled by a fantasy of self-depletion, which, if taken seriously, may amount to an utter self-annihilation of the reader.

The Jaguar Reader: Guimarães Rosa

João Guimarães Rosa—the celebrated, polyglot, Brazilian modernist—is often compared to James Joyce in the context of world literature, with his 1956 masterpiece, *Grande Sertão: Veredas*, classed as "the Brazilian *Ulysses*."[77] Yet, within the North-South comparatist framework, as several critics have maintained, Rosa's work bears much more of an affinity with Faulkner's oeuvre. Both writers locate most of their writing in a detailed fictional universe, which, in Rosa's case, is modeled on the Brazilian Sertão, the most inland, poorest part of the Northeast region (*nordeste*), reminiscent of Faulkner's South. The *nordeste*, we recall, also encompasses the abovementioned city of Salvador, Coutinho's birthplace.[78]

And yet, the point of contact between Faulkner, Coutinho, and Rosa that I wish to linger on in the next few pages is only tangentially linked to the geocultural backlands at the (implicit or explicit) center of these bodies of work. Instead, I wish to focus on a short story by Rosa, "O espelho" ("The Mirror"), which is atypically located in an urban setting. The story follows a scientist who tries to erase his bestial attributes from his mirror-image, a protagonist, I propose, who stands for the exact reader.[79] While Faulkner's work, as I have discussed in the first two chapters, was perceived by the New Critics and indeed lends itself to be read as facilitating unselfing, Rosa's short story closely follows a spectacularly failed attempt at suspending one's internal savage during the reading process. With Faulkner and Rosa, we see how the project of New Criticism has been, in fact, inseverable from processes of literary production and circulation, both in terms of how the critics responded to novelists, and how novelists responded to the critics. For example, while the New Critics rewarded Faulkner with canonization for his work's suitability to their reading practice, the Brazilian *nova crítica* provoked in Rosa a literary response—whether intentional or not—as we shall also see in the following chapter with the case of Clarice Lispector.

"O espelho" was first published in 1962 at the precise middle, the heart, of Rosa's short story collection, *Primeiras estórias* (*First Non-Stories*).[80] In that same year Coutinho was finally elected to the prestigious Brazilian Academy of Letters (*Academia Brasileira de Letras*) following two previous rejections—a historical moment that marks, according to both Heyck and Rocha, the general victory of the *nova crítica* and its method of reading over more traditional Brazilian forms of literary analysis.[81] These are also the heydays of the third wave of Brazilian modernism, to which Rosa is usually taken to pertain (along with Lispector). The first wave of Brazilian modernism preceded Rosa by about four decades, and indeed his oeuvre differs in various ways from that of the pioneers of the 1920s. However, Rosa markedly shares with them a "posthuman affiliation," to quote Gabriel Giorgi.[82]

It is well-known that the metaphor of anthropophagy has been central to Brazilian modernism from its inception in the 1920s—making its debut in Oswald de Andrade's 1928 iconoclastic *Manifesto antropófago*—to its later 1960s manifestations.[83] In de Andrade's *Manifesto*, the avant-garde poet calls for the devouring, absorption, and transformation of European culture into and through the Brazilian experience, in an attempt to "challenge the binary opposition of civilization versus barbarism, highlighting the dual history, indigenous and European, of contemporary Brazil," in Susan Basnett's words.[84] Following his footsteps, the early Brazilian modernists—in a radical move of resistance and in reaction to a postcolonial anxiety of influence—reappropriated the European stereotype of the Brazilian as a savage, and urged Brazilians to brazenly "cannibalize" Western culture into their own; to devour hegemonic culture not via imitation emerging from a sense of inferiority, but from a position of power that allows for creativity and play. In contrast, then, with the viewpoint that Coutinho exemplifies, according to which Brazilian "savagery" should be amended through acculturation, the Brazilian modernists strove to expose the cultural and political potency embedded within the "the cannibal instinct," in de Andrade's words.[85]

Rosa continues in this anthropophagic modernist tradition by insisting on the cannibal, the bestial, and the insane as the locus of truth and knowledge. Coutinho, for his part, can be said to have had stylistic preferences very close to those of Rosa and the 1920s modernists (for example, he too was invested in reinserting the baroque style of the colonial period into the Brazilian canon), but the leader of the *nova crítica* insisted on drawing a clear line of demarcation between his work and that of the modernists, both early and late. He believed that the avant-garde aesthetics that emerged from the anthropophagic movement exacerbated the "degeneracy" of the Brazilian reader. Brazilian modernist works, he claimed, incite a readerly state of mind utterly opposed to the one that accompanies exact reading: "Since these assertions might seem barbaric, the above signed [Coutinho] would like to make clear that no personal mark is imprinted on his position with regards to modernism. . . . With its [Brazilian modernism's] aesthetics of liberty, its rebelliousness, its negativism . . . it endorses tendencies very typical of the Brazilian nature and habits . . . our tendencies towards indiscipline, towards disorder, and towards disobedience to methods and norms."[86]

Coutinho pairs together the Brazilian aesthetics that openly structures itself on indigenous culture with what he understands to be a "savage" reading practice. It is his conviction that modernist works "endorse" the unacculturated "tendencies" that plague the Brazilian reader from within: "disorder," "disobedience," and "indiscipline." So, the "savage," for the *nova crítica*, is taken to disturb Brazilian culture from both sides of the literary equation: that of the text and that of the reader. It engenders "rebellious" texts and "disordered" readers, and should thus be kept in check in both realms (which is why Coutinho makes clear in the paragraph above that *his* assertions are anything but "barbaric").

Rosa's "The Mirror" forces its reader to rethink the *nova crítica*'s association of worthy engagement with literature and the suspension of the "savage," or, if possible, its overall extraction. This is not to claim that Rosa intentionally wrote this story as a direct response to the *nova crítica*'s theory and practice. More likely, "The Mirror" records on the page the culturally circulating demand to unsavage, and, wittingly or not, reacts to it. As we shall see, Rosa's engagement with the figure of the savage is not only modernist-cannibalist in nature; it engages with the specific contours of the *nova crítica*'s unselfed exact reader.

"The Mirror" is recounted by a first-person narrator who commits early on in the story to the task of revealing his "true countenance," which is hidden, he is certain, in the mirror.[87] As Anna Pacheco argues, this narrator places his confidence in *scientificismo*, the belief that the scientific technique can and should be extended to examine the whole scope of human behavior.[88] It is hardly surprising, then, that Rosa's protagonist chooses to accomplish his formidable task by using empirical methods alone. This positivist inclination resonates with the *nova crítica*'s project, but the question of literature could seem quite removed from the concrete object at the heart of this story. Yet the mirror is to be understood in the context of this work not only literally but also allegorically. Yudith Rosenbaum suggests we read the mirror as standing for the literary text, and, I would add, for the reader's responsibility, according to the Brazilian New Critics, to "penetrate" the aesthetic essence of the image.[89]

The tension between the denotative and symbolic meanings of "the mirror" appears already in the first line of the story. There, the narrator advises his listener (both an anonymous interlocutor and the reader) that he is not about to provide her with a story in the conventional literary sense (*uma aventura*) but to present a scientific *experiência* based on rational and systematic research.[90] To differentiate from English, the Portuguese *experiência* stands for both "experiment" and "experience." So, while the narrator is trying to establish a binary distinction between the scientific (his exploration of the mirror) and the subjective (a depiction of a personal experience or adventure), Rosa's reader is already instructed to suspect that the two are inseparable.

The adventure of Rosa's narrator begins when he encounters, in a public bathroom, a "repulsive, utterly hideous" image in the mirror, which he shockingly discovers to be his own reflection.[91] This self-proclaimed "impartial investigator, absolutely neutral," does not back away from the challenge of comprehending his baffling experience of self-estrangement, and plans a scientific experiment to expose the "real self" that lies behind what he concludes must have been a "false mask."[92] This coping mechanism, the story reveals, holds social capital. By dealing with the situation through logic, the narrator understands himself to establish a superiority over children, animals, and, most importantly, the "primitive" inhabitants of the Brazilian Northeastern *interior* (backlands). "They" are all afraid of mirrors and superstitiously believe that "when you are alone you should never look into a mirror during the small hours of the night, for sometimes, instead of your own reflection, some other, frightful visage may appear there."[93] The narrator, of course, is beyond these fears. Though he admits to be himself from the *interior* (as is his interlocutor, the reader's avatar in the diegetic world), the narrator insists that, in contrast with his former neighbors who satisfy themselves "with fantastic nonexplanations," he is "a materialist, a rational person who keeps his feet and paws on the ground."[94] In his scientific experiment, he is positive he will act as "a hunter of my true form, driven by disinterested, even impersonal curiosity; not to say a scientific urge."[95]

The terms Rosa's narrator uses for his self-description match perfectly with the traits attributed to the exact reader: he is rational, impersonal, scientific, and objective. As Coutinho writes, "the man of letters must subordinate himself to his observations as does the physicist and the biologist . . . [to] the careful and objective observation of facts, the verification of their consequences and the progressive accumulation of their results . . . whenever we thus operate in literature, we conduct science."[96] Moreover, we will soon see, the narrator of "The Mirror" works ardently to detach himself from all beings he considers "primitive."

And yet, quite a few elements in the narrator's monologue destabilize this exact self-portrait. Why, for example, would such a "rational person," a scientist, allow himself to grow an animal's foot, even if only metaphorically ("his feet and *paws* on the ground")? And why would he, a perfectly neutral observer, imagine himself to be a "hunter" of all things ("a *hunter* of my true form")? After all, searching for prey or being prey can hardly be viewed as disinterested positions; they both threaten to invite the body along with its desires and anxieties back into the realm of presumed scientific impartiality. It seems that Rosa is stealthily calling on his readers to take with a grain of salt the narrator-protagonist's authoritative speech and categorical statements by allowing the denigrated animal-child-native to speak through his allegedly "disinterested, even impersonal" language.

While this linguistic play takes place behind his back, the narrator continues in his endeavor, unaware and undisturbed. As one would expect of an exact reader, instructed to focus his attention outward while performing internal self-censorship, the procedure Rosa's narrator chooses for discovering his "true form" is the slow "annulment" of irrelevant and distracting layers from his reflected image.

> Sendo assim, necessitava eu de transverberar o embuço, a transverberar daquela máscara, a fito de devassar o núcleo dessa nebulosa—a minha vera forma. Tinha de haver um jeito. Meditei-o. Assistiram-me seguras inspirações. Concluí que, interpenetrando-se no disfarce do rosto externo diversas componentes, meu problema seria o de submetê-las a um bloqueio "visual" ou anulamento perceptivo, a suspensão de uma por uma, desde as mais rudimentares, grosseiras, ou de inferior significado. Tomei o elemento animal, para começo. . . . Meu sósia inferior na escala era, porém—a onça.

> As it was, I had to penetrate the veil, see through that *mask*, in order to expose the heart of the nebula—my true countenance. There must be a way. I pondered. I was rewarded by a positive inspiration. I concluded that since the disguise of the external face was composed of diverse mingled elements, my problem was to submit those to a "visual" blockage or perceptive annulment, blotting out each element one at a time, beginning with the most rudimentary, the grossest, the least meaningful. I took the animal element as a start. . . . My inferior double in the scale of evolution was—the Jaguar.[97]

By selecting self-reflection as the aesthetic object under examination in this story, Rosa is brilliantly able to put on display the self-imposed procedures that exact reading entails. And he produces a narrator who, like Coutinho, imagines analytic thought in terms of an intense light: in order to "penetrate" the aesthetic object the protagonist must "see through" the mask and behind "the veil." The same is true for the process of unselfing, presented as an integral part of the *experiência*. The task of internal self-policing requires "visual" blockage, which will lead to the necessary suppression of the internal Other, a "perceptive annulment, blotting out each element one at a time."

As in the case of the "ailing" Brazilian reader, Rosa's narrator must reengineer his "perception" to be able to correctly engage with his object of examination. And tellingly, he refers to the deceptive illusion created in the mirror due to his faulty perception by the reputable New Critical term, "affective fallacy" (*preconceito afetivo*).[98] To mend this default, Rosa's protagonist sets to "blot out" the four elements he believes most severely distort his accurate vision: the bestial, the familial, the emotional, and the psychological. He begins with the "animal element," very much in the spirit of Coutinho, emphasizing its malignant effect on his analytic thought by repeatedly depicting its worthlessness, "beginning with the most rudimentary, the grossest, the least meaningful. I took the animal element as a start."[99] But this excessive depiction of unimportance in fact only indirectly points to the animalistic as eminent, functioning as a means for Rosa to signal that he shares neither his narrator's nor Coutinho's view that the bestial must be eliminated for a valuable thought process to take place. Rosa further underscores this position by identifying specifically "the Jaguar" as his narrator's "inferior double." Through this figure, he stealthily inserts into "The Mirror" an intertextual reference to his earlier novella *Meu tio o iauaretê* (*My Uncle the Jaguar*), published only a year prior.[100] There, he negotiates the very differentiation between the jaguar and the human, forcefully questioning the anthropocentric notion that the animal is the inferior of the two, and creatively countering the colonial viewpoint of the Other as bestial.[101]

In contrast with the implied author, at this point of the story Rosa's narrator is still blind to the disintegration of the premises underlying his own experiment. In fact, the story reveals, our protagonist has finally become, after a long and ardent process, a master at unselfing, "excluding, abstracting, and extracting," as he had hoped.[102] He has been successful in "excluding" the internal Brazilian "primitive" (bestial, immature, emotional) while simultaneously accentuating his "intellectual" faculties (impersonal, grounded, rational). The "savage" is now subordinate to rational thought, a process that entails constant mental effort and self-control: "It was principally in a *mode* of focus, in a partially peripheral vision, that I had to acquire agility: to look without seeing. Without seeing, in 'my face,' the *relic* of the beast [emphasis in original]."[103]

It is the narrator's "peripheral vision"—what occurs on the outskirts of his gaze—that poses the biggest danger to accuracy (revealing his "true" countenance), and consequently requires stricter discipline; he must attempt to avoid those parts of the visual field as much as possible, "to look without seeing." That this visual training is conducted via the manipulation of attention specifically is made clear by the narrator's comment to his interlocutor: "You don't see that your face is merely a perceptual, deceptive motion. You don't see because you are inattentive, dulled by habit."[104] In contrast, Rosa's narrator is doubly attentive. He is able to focus his mental efforts so intensely on the object under scrutiny, that is, his own reflection in the mirror, and to suppress any relic of subjective particularity to such an extent that he has become a "transparent contemplator."[105] Even Coutinho, I would guess, could not have described in more accurate a term his ideal Brazilian reader.

The narrator's perceptual victory, however, is quick to pass. As it does throughout the story, language sets up a trap for its speaker. Rosa's protagonist reveals, startled, that his metaphor of "transparency" has concretized. Instead of exposing his *vera forma* in the mirror ("discovery and interpretation of [the] intrinsic aesthetic content," in Coutinho's words), Rosa's narrator finds that his reflection had disappeared altogether. Nothing at all appears as his reflection; or, put differently, a forceful "nothing" is the only thing now staring back at him from the looking glass: "I will simply say that I looked into a mirror and there was nothing there. I saw nothing. . . . Had I no features, no face at all? I touched myself repeatedly. But there was only the unseen. The fictive. Without visible evidence. What was I—the transparent contemplator? . . . I turned away abruptly. So agitated, I could scarcely stand and almost fell into an armchair."[106] Coutinho's process of self-vigilance ends for Rosa in self-annihilation. Without the familial, emotional, and psychological—but most importantly, the bestial—the reading subject is erased and with it the object under scrutiny. To take Rosa's implications seriously would mean concluding that the Brazilian exact reader is in danger of becoming no reader at all, unsavaging herself out of existence. And indeed, for Rosa, in this text specifically and in his body of work more generally, critical thought is embedded within the bestial, the corporal, and the subjective, incorporated by the leper, the child, the outcast, and the savage.[107] These figures are not, for him, the others of thought, but form the very locus of apprehension.

The juxtaposition of the *nova crítica*'s understanding of "attention" with "The Mirror"—a comparative reading this short story seems to call for—sheds light on Rosa's implicit conceptualization of readerly attention. In one of his rare interviews, five years after the publication of *First Non-Stories*, Rosa maintains, "Many people say it's difficult to read my work. It's not difficult. And it's not necessary to read aloud, like many people I know, to apprehend. It's enough to read, read attentively. You think you don't understand, but mentally you do. Understand?"[108] This typically Rosa-esque enigmatic answer suggests that, for him, "read[ing] attentively" entails allowing some internal alterity to read for, or with, a more conscious "you." While one *you* thinks, "I don't understand," another mental *you* does. This statement might seem to jibe with Cleanth Brooks and Faulkner's New Critical conceptualization of ghostly readerly attention as suggested in the first two chapters; they too understand this mental state to facilitate receptiveness to alterity. However, for the North Americans, the close reader must deaden herself—suspend her subjectivity during the engagement with the literary work—for the alterity of the text to speak through her. For Rosa, on the other hand, alterity always already resides in and is intermingled with the reader's subjectivity such that one must be alive rather than dead to oneself, internally attentive, in order to fully "understand" the literary work.

Rosa's conceptualization of the internal, animalistic alterity appears most clearly in the last and surprising segment of "The Mirror." After years of fearfully avoiding mirrors so as to not confront his "nothingness" once again, Rosa's narrator accidently encounters one. To the amazement of the narrator, from that encounter emerges not self-transparency, but a fuzzy image, a mysterious and barely emerging "not-quite-face."

> Pois foi que, mais tarde, anos, ao fim de uma ocasião de sofrimentos grandes, de novo me defrontei—não rosto a rosto. O espelho mostrou-me. Ouça . . . sim, vi, a mim mesmo, de novo, um rosto; não este, que o senhor razoavelmente me atribui. Mas o ainda-nem-rosto—quase delineado, apenas—mal emergindo, qual uma flor pelágica, de nascimento abissal. . . . E era não mais que: rostinho de menino, de menos-que-menino, só. Só. Será que o senhor nunca compreenderá?"

> It was only later, years later, after I had gone through a period of great suffering, that I confronted myself again—but not quite face to face. The mirror showed myself to me. Listen . . . yes, I

saw myself again, my face, a face; not this one which your reason attributes to me. But a not-quite-face—scarcely outlined—barely emerging, like a pelagic flower born of the abyss. . . . And it was no more than: a child's small face, even less-than-a-child's. And nothing more. Will you ever understand?[109]

In a sophisticated play on words that is quite difficult to render in English, Rosa brings back the image of the jaguar into this uncanny final scene. When calling on his fictional interlocutor and his reader to pay attention, this time via sound rather than vision, he implores them to "Listen"—in Portuguese, "*Ouça.*" Through this word, Rosa subtly engraves into the text the word *onça* (jaguar), identical except for the inversion of the *n* into a *u*. The proximity in both sound and orthography between "*ouça*" and "*onça*" brings closer together the less-than-a-child and the jaguar's face staring at the narrator from the mirror. Both are not the "true self" that the narrator hoped to find in the mirror via his experiment, but a self that cannot be detected by "reason" alone since it does not obey the basic logical law of identity, according to which each thing is the same as itself; what the narrator encounters in the mirror is simultaneously "my face" and "a face." "The mirror showed myself to me," he declares, a "myself" that is not identical with "me."

The miraculous reappearance of the narrator's mirror image implies that, for Rosa, the dimension of "extraction" in exact reading is nothing less than impossible; and "The Mirror" makes manifest that the extraction in question is specifically Brazilian. Though Rosa's protagonist labors to present his story as universal—leaving himself, his interlocutor, and their place of encounter unnamed and unspecified—behind his back the story is presented as deeply entrenched in the Brazilian context; in fact, the text guides the reader to identify the protagonist's attempt to hide his background as motivated by a particularly Brazilian history. The protagonist's "*interior*" roots along with his choice to marginalize them and distinguish himself from the "primitive" and superstitious inhabitants of the Northeast attest to the link between his desire to exclude, abstract, and extract his internal "bestial" part, for supposedly disinterested scientific reasons, and his wish to sociologically and intellectually distance himself from Brazilian "backwardness," thus conceived due to an internalization of the colonial gaze. That is, what Rosa's protagonist tries so ardently to unself is his own self-debasing view as savage, an internal transgenerational remnant of colonial oppression.

Against this backdrop, the differences between Coutinho and Rosa heighten. Both astutely perceive colonial history to impress itself on the colonized's sense of self well after political independence. But while Coutinho adapts the anglophone New Criticism to the Brazilian setting by conceptualizing exact reading as a tool to suspend what he takes to be the colonially generated tendency to be distracted, Rosa, in a distinctly Brazilian modernist spirit, reclaims the internalized stereotype, positioning bestiality at the center of Brazilian readerly capability. Put differently, Rosa pushes against the perception of the Brazilian savage as an inherently unintellectual sloth by depicting this purported savagery as what enables the Brazilian to read, and read well. After all, it is the people of the *interior*, which the narrator most identifies with the "veil" to be "annulle[d]," who have recognized in the mirror/text, way in advance, what the narrator will come to perceive only years after his experiment: "[W]hen you are alone you should never look into a mirror during the small hours of the night, for sometimes, instead of your own reflection, some other, frightful visage may appear there."[110] Under these conditions, "to read attentively" comes to depend not on an extraction of Brazilian "savagery," but on a receptiveness to it.

It is important to note that Rosa does not do away with close reading, that is, the *nova crítica*'s recommended processes of "discover[ing the literary work's] intrinsic aesthetic content." "The Mirror" invites the reader to engage with the New Critical reading practice through its play on words, complex metaphoric structures, and delicate work with paradoxical forms. Moreover, without his scientific efforts (*experiências*) to solve the enigma, Rosa's narrator would never have experienced (*experienciar*) his significant encounter with the "not-quite-face." What Rosa does seem to imply through his latent dialogue with the *nova crítica* in "The Mirror" is that exact reading's imperative to unsavage stands the risk of undoing the Brazilian reader and the text altogether. Instead, if indeed distracted "butterflies" or hammock-rocking "savages" exist or have been placed within the Brazilian mind, they may allow for the reader to perceive in the text "a pelagic flower born of the abyss." On this note, Rosa's narrator ends his story.

> Será este nosso desengonço e mundo o plano—interseção de planos—onde se completam de fazer as almas?
> Se sim, a "vida" consiste em experiência extrema e séria; sua técnica—ou pelo menos parte—exigindo—o consciente alijamento, o despojamento, de tudo o que obstrui o crescer da alma,

> o que atulha e soterra? . . . E o julgamento-problema, podendo sobrevir com a simples pergunta:—"Voce chegou a existir?"
>
> Sim? . . . Disse. . . . Solicito os reparos que se digne dar-me, a mim, servo do senhor, recente amigo, mas companheiro no amor da ciência, de seus transviados acertos e de seus esbarros titubeados.
>
> Sim?
>
> Can this disjointed world of ours be the plane—the intersection of planes—where the finishing touches are put to our souls?
>
> If so, then "life" is an extreme and serious experience; its technique—or at least part of it—demands a conscious jettisoning, a clearing away, of whatever obstructs the growth of the soul or buries it under rubble? . . . And the problem-judgment survives in the simple question:—"do you exist yet?"
>
> Yes? . . . Tell me. . . . I welcome any objections you may design to express to me, your obedient servant, a newly made friend and your companion as a lover of science with all its misguided successes and its halting quantum jumps forwards.
>
> Yes?[111]

Rosa's repetition of and conclusion with a "Yes" is reminiscent of Joyce's famous "yes I said yes I will Yes."[112] However, Rosa injects this Joycean gesture with hesitation and interrelationality, posing the "yes" as a question to the reader. Indeed, the final lines of the story seem to approach Rosa's Brazilian exact readers directly. Themselves working to suspend their internal savage during the reading process, the exact readers are now forced by Rosa to come face to face with the limitations of their technique of "conscious jettisoning" and "clearing away."

The narrator, an easily relatable "companion as a lover of science," demands their personal response on the question of self-censorship. What is the best "technique" for their "extreme and serious experience/experiment" of reading? Coutinho, in his sophisticated adaptation of close reading into exact reading, mobilized the process of unselfing, which he finds buried under the anglophone theory, to free or empty the local reader of her detrimental, inherited and, he claims, "savage" tendencies of distraction. He exhibits a complex fusion of postcolonial rebelliousness with blind internalization, keen readings with broad generalizations, a national commitment to independence with a desire to discipline and control. In response, Rosa sets out on a fantastic thought experiment, forcing his (exact) readers to ask: what would happen if we were indeed able to fully extract the internal "savage" while reading? Would it gaze back at us from the mirror-text? Would one at all *exist yet* without engaging with its presence?

These questions will persist into the following chapter, where we will encounter Clarice Lispector's own modernist response to the imperative to attentively unsavage. Rather than parodying the exact reader, Lispector will take this reader's attention to task, and press on it so hard as to transform it into inattention. If we want to touch the savage—the "wild heart" of the text—we must, she will claim, "read distractedly."

Chapter Four

Exact and Exhausted Reading

Clarice Lispector and Catching the Apple in the Dark

> Do not read what I write as a reader would do.
> —Clarice Lispector

> We have to be careful when we read Clarice Lispector.
> —Hélène Cixous

When Otávio thinks back to the moment he first met his wife, Joana—the protagonist of Clarice Lispector's 1944 debut novel, *Perto do coração selvagem* (*Near to the Wild Heart*)—he relates an encounter quite at odds with the traditional romantic-type scene.[1] They are strangers who happen to both be visiting a bookstore at the same time, when an elderly man comes through the door, "his fat body shaking, his skull weepy."[2] His gestures are all geared toward soliciting Joana's sympathy: "I got a boo-boo. . . . It hurts. . . . I took my medicine like a good boy, it's a little better . . . aren't you going to say you feel sorry for me? . . . aren't you even going to say 'poor little thing'?" Joana seems to succumb and utters "poor thing," which leads the old man to consider "the game over" and turn laughing to the door. But the game is not over. As soon as he moves away from the table, Joana picks up "a thick little book" and throws it "with all her strength" at the back of his head. Shocked, the man turns around in "vague terror" only to hear Joana's biting response: "Forgive me. A little lizard there, above the door . . . I missed."³ Yes, Lispector's novels are designed to hit you over the head—to violently jolt your mind—precisely at the moment when they have gained your trust. And in spite of this violence (or perhaps as a result of it), Lispector's reader, just like Otávio, often finds herself falling in love.

As the title of her first novel predicts, Lispector's oeuvre will consistently orient itself toward the "wild heart." On different occasions, Lispector explicitly states that her main endeavor in writing is to approximate that elusive core of existence, which she refers to as the "thing" or "truth" and considers untamed and unruly. This "wild" core has been read by scholars as metaphysical, existential, and theological, but it is most commonly understood as psychological; in line with her work's close affinity with High Modernism, Lispector is said to plumb the depths of the unconscious psychological self.

This trait has also gained Lispector criticism for detaching herself from local Brazilian histories and realities by imitating the colonizer's modernist tradition of apolitically focusing on the internal world. Lending itself to such critique, Lispector's first novel declares its "wild" title borrowed from the ur-European modernist, James Joyce, whom we've encountered in the previous chapter, and whom she quotes in the novel's epigraph, "He was alone. He was unheeded, happy, and near to the wild heart of life."⁴ However, the simple act of translating Joyce's "wild" into the Portuguese *selvagem*, and giving it prominence as the title that would launch her literary career, bespeaks Lispector's deep investment in the charged Brazilian cultural-political history.

The word *selvagem* carries within it and stems from the word *selva*, meaning "woods," "forest," or "jungle." In the Brazilian context, the "selva" immediately connotes not only the local geography of the Amazon rainforest, but indigeneity more generally, whose deprecating view by the colonizer ingrained itself into language. Thus, *selvagem* functions not only as an adjective (*wild*) but as a noun as well, which denotes "savage," and features in most iterations of the colonial binary between the "civilized" white and "uncivilized" native.

As we have seen in the previous chapter, the idea of the Brazilian as "savage" carried forcefully over into the postcolonial twentieth-century, and was generalized from the figure of the indigenous into the Brazilian citizen per se. When Lispector, then, explicitly proclaims via the title of her first book the aspiration to come near the "wild," "savage" heart, she is making a decidedly political statement, cleverly demonstrating how

Joyce's words in translation expose the Western canon's own instability: the "savage" that the West is positioning itself against is found at the very core of its literary canon. This chapter will trace Lispector's engagement with the Brazilian "wild," not through its representation in her fictional world as either psychological or not, but through her response to the Brazilian New Critical view of the local reader as besieged by internal *selvagem* forces.⁵

In the previous chapter, we encountered the *nova crítica*'s midcentury self-contradictory project, which strives to ardently battle the colonial stereotype of the Brazilian as the other of intellect, but simultaneously adopts the colonial assumption that the Brazilian is prone to a "savage-like," distracted form of reading and thinking. To dominate that internal proclivity, Afrânio Coutinho, the *nova crítica*'s founder and principal thinker, encourages the local close reader to be in a constant state of self-vigilance against the appearance of those "unconscious, savage-like, virginal, primitive forces," which threaten to bring about an unfocused, "butterfly-like form of thought."⁶ This self-mastery process, which I have termed *unsavaging*, is aimed at creating a new and improved Brazilian close reader, who will perform what Coutinho terms *exact reading* by being intensely attentive to, rather than distracted by, the words on the page.

Lispector, on her end, is quite skeptical about this readerly protocol. In fact, as in the case of her protagonist Joana, the Brazilian writer carefully plans a pedagogical blow to her exact reader's head by means of "a thick little book." Carefully maneuvering genre expectations, Lispector forces the reader to abandon her earlier reading habits and enter into a "wild," new "reading pact" with her text, one that calls back the distractive "selvagem" into play. That is, while the *nova crítica* presents the labor of attention as enabling mastery over internal wildness, Lispector tempts her readers into distraction, the only mental state she believes that can bring them close to the "wild heart" of the literary work.⁷

Lispector's "thick little book," which this chapter centers on, is *A maçã no escuro* (*The Apple in the Dark*, 1961), a novel published two decades after *Near to the Wild Heart*, at the height of the *nova crítica* in Brazil.⁸ There, Lispector taps into and exaggerates her exact reader's habits of engagement with the text, only to then frustrate them. This clever process of unceasing impediment works to tire out the reader and to set the stage for Lispector's radical alternative to exact reading that I term *exhausted reading*.⁹ This is a mode of engagement with the work that hinges on the reader *exhausting*, that is, completely using up her mental resources oriented at attentively focusing on the text as the *nova crítica* demands, a process that leaves her *exhausted* to such an extent that she is forced to let go of the self-discipline required for exact reading.

The resulting state of mental lassitude echoes an earlier, nineteenth-century Brazilian readerly model—Alencar's distracted reader on the hammock, discussed in the previous chapter—and gestures toward a reading in a dreamlike state; an ad hoc reading that centers on the now and at least partially abandons the attempt to master the meaning of the text. Lispector, then, does not do away with exact reading in her work. On the contrary, she dialectically depends on this practice's hyperbolic form in order to develop from within it a new mode of interaction between reader and text—a move reminiscent of Lispector's use of Joyce's words, which she employs only to then unsettle the tradition they represent.

My argument takes its cue from Emília Amaral, Benedito Nunes, and Ângela Fronckowiak, who astutely identify Lispector's investment in molding her own "ideal reader." While these critics do not linger on the cultural context in which this political-poetic move is conducted, I suggest that Lispector intervenes in her readers' mode of interaction with the text as a response to the very specific readerly model that was circulating in Brazilian culture during her literary career.[10] This reaction reaches a peak of sophistication with *The Apple*, a novel that forcefully demonstrates that Lispector does not simply resist the general "discourse of precipitated deciphering . . . a protocol of reading, used as early as Antiquity," in Amaral's words.[11] Instead, Lispector is engaging with her immediate cultural surroundings that were saturated at the time with the *nova crítica*'s readerly imperatives.

The previous chapter's discussion of the modernist João Guimarães Rosa revealed how the *nova crítica* did not only incite a heated cultural debate in Brazil, but also generated a body of literature that was responding to the ideas and readerly guidelines advanced by the local New Critics. Rosa, we observed, challenges the *nova crítica* by parodying the process of unsavaging. He demonstrates that when the bestial elements of the self are excluded, with them goes subjectivity itself; for Rosa, through unsavaging, the Brazilian exact reader censures herself out of existence. Facing the imperative to extract the distracting savage, Lispector is less preoccupied with the value of the animalistic (though this too is present in her work), and more concerned with the hunt itself.

"Extracting" the savage from within, as we have seen, signifies for the *nova crítica* the bringing under control of this unruly internal force, a process that should allow for the close reader to pay full "attention" to the words on the page. However, as the *nova crítica* thinkers never made completely clear what this "attention" entails, Lispector's fictional manipulations imply that she imagines the exact reader to perform a similar hunting gesture in relation to the text as well: just as the reader is directed to catch and hold tight to the internal *selvagem*, so too, she predicts, will the reader try to bring under control the words on the page by fully hunting down their meaning. As mentioned above, while the *nova crítica* identifies "savagery" as an impediment to reading located within the reading subject, Lispector sees the *coração selvagem* as the beating heart or "truth" of the literary work. And so, as a mirror image to self-unsavaging, Lispector suspects attentive reading to insinuate an attempt at grasping and bringing under control the wild "thing" at the center of the work.

Lispector's *crônica*, published two years prior to *The Apple*, expresses her skepticism about the ability or value of hunting down the "wild heart" of the literary text. In *A pesca milagrosa* ("The Miraculous Catch of Fish"), she compares the art of writing to that of reading.[12]

> Então escrever é o modo de quem tem a palavra como isca: a palavra pescando o que não é palavra. Quando essa não-palavra morde a isca, alguma coisa se escreveu. Uma vez que se pescou a entrelinha, podia-se com alívio jogar a palavra fora. Mas aí cessa a analogia: a nãopalavra, ao morder a isca, incorporou-a. O que se salva então é ler "distraidamente."
>
> Writing, therefore, is the use of a word as bait: the word fishes for what is not a word. Once this non-word takes the bait, something has been written. And when the between-the-lines has been caught, the word can be thrown away with relief. But this is where the analogy breaks off: the non-word, when taking the bait, incorporates it. What remains, then, is to read "distractedly."[13]

The *nova crítica* presents meaningful reading as a process of overcoming nature, taking captive one's innate internal savage. Lispector too comes near this sematic field when she compares reading and writing to hunting, in this case fish. However, the practice of "catching" that she imagines is inherently impossible. As a bait, the word is there to attract meanings, connotations, and affects that are beyond the utterable, but once the "fish" eats the "bait," the two entities, the word and the nonword, are forever combined. Consequently, the reader cannot avoid the word, which should have been in fact "thrown away with relief." If one tries to engage the nonword directly, without deviations—these attributes that the *nova crítica* attaches to attention—the nonword would disappear within the word. The reader can hence only tangentially touch the "nonword" if she engages the text askew, in what the *nova crítica* took to be a savage-like state: in a mode of distraction. Namely, while the *nova crítica* insists that attention will allow the reader to penetrate "to the intrinsic core or aesthetic essence of the work of art," Lispector maintains that only "reading distractedly" can make palpable, never penetrable, what she takes to be the work's essence.[14]

As I hinted above through Joana's bookstore scene, Lispector explores the question of reading from early on in her career. Though much of this chapter will focus on *The Apple* as a work that throws into stark relief Lispector's strategy of questioning the privileged status of exact reading in Brazilian culture, it will end by expanding its view toward other texts from Lispector's body of work. I will first look at the *nova crítica*'s critique of *The Apple* in Coutinho's famous edited historiography, *A literatura no Brasil*. I will then shift to the novel's own formal devices used to conjure what I call "exhausted reading," as an alternative to exact reading that dialectically emerges from the *nova crítica*'s technique. And I will conclude by taking into consideration Lispector's abovementioned *Near to the Wild Heart*, in addition to *A paixão segundo G.H.* (*The Passion According to G.H.*, 1964), to suggest that her ongoing investment in readerly response emerges from an understanding of reading as a praxis of self-formation, similarly to the Brazilian New Critics.[15]

Reading, for Lispector, is a place where gendered, ethnic, racial, and national identities are negotiated, not only through what is written or understood, but also through the interplay of the reader's mental state and the work's surrender or resistance to the reader's strategies. Maneuvering responses to her texts, then, grants Lispector the rare opportunity to offer readers new possibilities of being in the world.

Lispector's Deceptive Opacity

One of the *nova crítica*'s most significant contributions to Brazilian letters is *A literatura no Brasil*, an impressive six-volume historiography of Brazilian literature, edited by Afrânio Coutinho. First published between 1955 and 1959, and republished multiple times, *A literatura* offered a provocative new genealogy of Brazilian literature. In the spirit of formalism and the New Criticism, quoting René Wellek and T. S. Eliot in his introduction, Coutinho presented a stylistic periodization of Brazilian literature centered on genres and forms, rather than on historical and political events. In addition, he advanced the radical notion that local Brazilian literature had its own unique features well before national independence.[16] In terms of structure, *A literatura* provided a general introduction to each period's aesthetics and themes, and a detailed account of its key writers. The project brought together the best of Brazil's critics, who wrote entries about their period or writers of specialization, and though they were not all proclaimed followers of the *nova crítica*, the movement's spirit and editor's hand were very much felt, as the entry dedicated to Lispector's work evinces.

Within *A literatura*, Lispector is located as expected under the prose-fiction of the *era modernista* (modernist era). Preceding her section is the one dedicated to modernist poetry, the spearhead of the *nova crítica*'s project. As we saw in the previous chapter, Coutinho was no fan of the Brazilian modernist tradition that affiliated itself with the "anthropophagic" impulse. However, he and his followers venerated another group of modernist poets, *Geração de '45* ("the 1945 Generation"). This group included celebrated poets such as Domingo Carvalho da Silva, Lêdo Ivo, and Geir Campos, who produced stern and well-wrought, concise and impersonal poetry, with a strong focus on form, in open dialogue with anglophone high-modernist poetry. That the *nova crítica* favored this group is immediately made evident in *A literatura*, where the task of producing the 200-page summary of Brazilian modernist poetry, from the vanguardists of the 1920s to the 1960s concrete poets, is given to a major figure of the 1945 Generation itself, Péricles Eugênio da Silva Ramos. But these poets' singular style was not only publicly championed by the *nova crítica*, it also, as suggested by José Guilherme Merquior, functioned as the very prototype around which they developed their method of reading. Merquior writes, "Since this generation surged more or less simultaneously with the introduction of the *nova crítica* into our culture, the two immediately tried to unite. The aesthetics of '45 formed a counterpart to aesthetic criticism, which then proved itself equipped to uncover the structure of the poem."[17] In this too, then, the *nova crítica* follows the American critics who modeled their aesthetic theory on modernist poetry. And it is precisely for that reason, as we saw in the first two chapters, that following the New Critics as they read prose can be so enlightening. When these critics venture out of their comfort zone, their moves more readily reveal their project's aesthetic, but also ethical and political values.

The qualities the Brazilian New Critics found in the poems of the *Geração de '45* correspond to the mental state they hoped to cultivate in their reader. In *A literatura*, these poems are praised (by a member of the group, we recall) for being "disciplined," "balanced," "well governed," "universal," "formally rigorous," and "intellectual."[18] The Brazilian critics believed that the formal discipline of these poems would enhance the kind of self-discipline they were expecting their exact readers to perform. This is further supported by Coutinho's vocabulary of praise for the poets of '45 in his *Correntes cruzadas*. In his view, their texts demonstrate an admirable "preoccupation with language, with the careful search for the accurate word and image."[19] He employs similar adjectives to describe his ideal reader, who is expected to conduct an "exact and accurate analysis of literature (close reading)," and a "careful and objective observation of facts," as discussed in the previous chapter.[20] The form of these poems, then, is understood to encourage the reader to similarly engage with language in a "disciplined" and "well governed" form, "accurate[ly]" organizing the words on the page into a stable whole, and "careful[ly]" suppressing any possible (and perilous) "savage" interferences from within.

As *A literatura* veers from poetry to prose-fiction, Lispector's aesthetics is depicted as the "wild," ungoverned mirror-image of the *Geração de '45*. Her work is compartmentalized, together with that of the abovementioned Guimarães Rosa, and the novelist Adonias Filho, under the subsection *Instrumentalismo* ("Instrumentalism"). These writers are said to have focused their work, published from 1945 onward, on the "exploration of form and language" and to have been metafictionally invested in examining the very "instruments of their work." While these attributes are celebrated in the section dedicated to Guimarães Rosa and in a more modest fashion in that of Filho, Lispector's twenty-three-page entry consists of a detailed, work by work, examination of the writer's "incapacities," "weaknesses," and "failures."[21]

In charge of Lispector's entry, which was added to *A literatura* in its second edition, was Luiz Costa Lima, one of the pivotal figures in the importation and adaptation of Structuralism into the Brazilian scene in the 1960s and '70s.[22] As we will see in the Israeli context as well, the later arrival of the New Criticism into Brazil made it almost contemporaneous with Structuralism, a simultaneity that highlighted and amplified the similarities between the two movements and brought about an affinity between the intellectuals who subscribed to these theories and methodologies. Deepening this rapport in the Brazilian case was the Structuralists' and New Critics' joint position on the opposite side of the traditional *crítica de rodapé* in the famous cultural debate mentioned in the previous chapter.[23] In this spirit, Costa Lima's disparagement of Lispector's work bespeaks many of the *nova crítica*'s values and readerly expectations.

At the time of the entry's publication, Lispector's oeuvre had yet to acquire the international fame it enjoys today. And though Costa Lima acknowledges Lispector's position as a renowned "introspective novelist" within Brazilian culture, he refuses to be impressed. Her work's manifold flaws, he asserts, all emerge from a fundamental problem of *opacidade* ("opacity"), which presents itself via her characters, language, and plot, but mostly through the perceptual and epistemological response Lispector compels in her reader. Per Costa Lima, Lispector's work systematically deprives the reader of a "clear" view of the fictional world, which renders her oeuvre nothing less than "deceptive." More specifically, he argues that Lispector's narrator confines the reader to the internal world of the characters, who are self-involved and hence socially isolated ("Lispector's characters . . . cannot go beyond themselves"), detached from the tangible fabric of everyday life ("Lispector is . . . unable to embed her word in the concrete"), and overly intellectual, and thus excessively abstract in their thought-processes ("tend to intellectualize and thus turn false since they are incapable of showing more than thoughts, reflections and small cruelties").[24]

Costa Lima consequently argues that Lispector's readers, who are affixed to the characters' point of view, hardly get information about the surrounding diegetic reality since the characters are simply uninterested in the details of the everyday world. This tendency makes Lispector's characters "false"—merely representations of psychological states of mind—and hinders the novel from "going beyond the singular" to represent a world in its totality. Even worse, Costa Lima continues, is that Lispector's characters are not only trapped in their own minds, they also lack the agency to break out of this entrapment for more than a few moments of grace, giving readers a sense that human autonomy is questionable: "[G]iven the characters' delusional intellectualization, the consequent falsehood of their conduct, the lack of respect for the characters' autonomy, and the reduction of reality to its subjective-intellectual dimension, [Lispector's] setting is unreliable."[25] In other words, per Costa Lima, Lispector propagates in her work nothing less than a false view of human subjectivity as idiosyncratic, thought-oriented rather than action-oriented, and agentless.

Costa Lima goes on to maintain that Lispector's deception on the level of characterization and world-building finds its match in her language, which functions as a "trap."

> A linguagem de Lispector contém como que uma armadilha: a sua simplicidade enganosa, podendo dar ao leitor a impressão de uma planura sem fim, de uma superfície horizontal. . . . Poderíamos mesmo dizer que essa linguagem comum, revestindo aparentemente um desenrolar de ocorrências, é um correlato, ao nível da linguagem, da opacidade do mundo. Assim como esta é clara e familiar, parecendo ter conseguido sufocar por inteiro qualquer expressão perigosa de vida, assim a palavra usual parece não dizer nunca mais do que diária e mecânicamente repete. Engano, tôda a clareza tem seu reverso e mesmo na coisa comum podem-se condensar perguntas que não se desejam.
>
> Lispector's language contains a kind of trap: its simplicity is deceptive, giving the reader the impression of an endless plateau, of a horizontal surface. . . . One might even say that this simple language, apparently covering the unfolding of events, corresponds, on the level of language, to the opacity of [Lispector's] world. Just as [this world] is clear and familiar, apparently successful in fully stifling any dangerous expression of life, so too the simple word appears not to say anything more than what it daily and mechanically repeats. Well, wrong [literally, deceit], this clarity has its very reversal, and even within the most common of objects undesired questions could be concealed.[26]

My aim is neither to argue with nor against Costa Lima's view of Lispector's oeuvre. Instead, I want to linger on his vocabulary's strong resonance with the *nova crítica*'s protocol of exact reading. As we saw in chapter 3, Coutinho establishes a binary between distraction and attention throughout his writings: the first being the pivotal characteristic of a Brazilian savage tendency, and the latter characteristic of the unselfed, acculturated close reader. The basic metaphor Coutinho utilizes to describe this dichotomy is that of light, comparing the readerly thought process to rays hitting the page. While the distracted savage is said to suffer from the vice of "scatter" or "dispersion," the close reader is able to "restrict [her] vision."[27] That is, Coutinho imagines exact reading to "remedy" the Brazilian reader by repositioning her in space "in front of the poem," so that her mental ray of light, rather than dispersing sideways, will focus with intensity on the work of art.[28]

It is telling, then, that Costa Lima centers his critique of Lispector on the tension between "opacity" and "clarity." In fact, the various attributes that make up Lispector's "opacity," per Costa Lima, link back to the "savage" tendencies the *nova crítica* was trying to restrict through exact reading. As we recall, the *nova crítica* postulates that the Brazilian subject engaging with texts is prone to abstractness ("our tendency towards . . . generalizations"), and to subjectivity ("our idealization of the personal," or "*subjetivismo*"), inclinations that can be deemed "curable" only under the assumption of considerable agency on the part of the subject (the individual's ability to deliberately suppress one's internal alterity).[29] It is to be expected, then, that Costa Lima would fault Lispector for interfering "in the autonomy of the characters"; without the capacity to choose and neatly navigate one's own fate, any attempt at unsavaging is futile.

But what most bothers Costa Lima is Lispector's play of appearances. Her texts give the "illusion" of clarity, provide an impression of an open visual field just right for exact reading, "an endless plateau . . . a horizontal surface," which would encourage the Brazilian reader to rest assured that his distracted tendencies will not be activated, and perhaps, consequently, let down her guard against the internal wild. Costa Lima thoroughly inspects every one of Lispector's published works to date, and among them identifies *The Apple in the Dark* as "the most characteristic of her novels," which brings to "maximum force" Lispector's faults of deceptive opacity.

Putting aside Costa Lima's value judgment, he has a point. The novel is indeed dialectical: it first appears to lend itself perfectly to the *nova crítica*'s imperative of vigilant attention, but then turns out to systematically bring this mode of reading to an abrupt halt. This orchestrated rhythm of frustration, though viewed in *A literatura* as a lack, can also be seen as a means for mobilizing the mind-set associated with exact reading to produce a different reading experience. That is, though Costa Lima uses his terms to accentuate the "incapacities" of *The Apple*, he discerns what I believe are in fact prominent qualities of the text. Costa Lima writes,

"In her best novel . . . Lispector shows, to the point of exhaustion, her unresolved potentialities and limits."[30] Indeed, examining the novel without the *nova crítica*'s value judgment unexpectedly leads the way to the novel's own strategy of readerly exhaustion.

In *The Apple*, Lispector sets a "trap" in order to motivate her reader to employ exact reading, with its tendency to "catch," to its maximum degree. She does so only to then expose the limitations of this method and direct the reader toward an alternative pattern of engagement with her novel. All in all, Costa Lima knew what he was saying.

What's the Catch: A Genre in the Dark

How does one begin to describe *The Apple*? It is not only Costa Lima who shrewdly identifies *The Apple* as concealing a "trap" at its heart. Hélène Cixous, one of Lispector's most passionate and persistent readers, contends that "*The Apple in the Dark* is a most deceptive book. It is represented as a novel, but it is the opposite. It is a mystical path of such density that it becomes perhaps even more unreadable than *The Passion*. The book is double."[31] Cixous's analysis focuses on the novel's network of libidinal economies, but the question of genre, which she does not delve into, leaps out of her quote as well; *The Apple* presents itself as "a novel" when it is in fact a "mystical path."

Similarly, Vilma Arêas and Berta Waldman argue that "one can quite easily identify [in *The Apple*] elements of the epic mixed with those of the farce, the western, the mystery movie or book, with those of the *folhetim* novel and the romance novel—a variance established within what seem to be the contours of a crime fiction, an expectation that ends up being thwarted."[32] And Benjamin Moser observes in his introduction to *The Apple* that "the detective-story setup is a flimsy pretext for the real drama, which is linguistic and mystical."[33] These critics all recognize the novel as setting up a genre expectation to be unfulfilled, but do not ask what this repetitive disappointment does to and in this novel.

Lispector saw *The Apple* as her best-crafted novel, whose 400 pages saw eleven drafts during the long years of its production and failed publication attempts.[34] The book's deception, then, is not accidental; as we will soon see, Lispector aims to masquerade her book, especially through its first chapter, as a distinct combination between the crime novel (presenting a mystery to be solved) and an allegory (displaying elements whose meaning must be supplemented from the outside). Since both the crime novel and the allegory stimulate in the reader a vigilant anticipation for details that will bring the riddle of the text to a closure, Lispector relies on these genetic forms to fully activate her exact reader's heightened attention.

The readers meet *The Apple*'s protagonist, Martin, when he becomes a fugitive from the law after attempting to kill his wife. He tells himself that he has committed this crime to avenge his partner's adulterous affair, but later on in the plot he comes to the realization that his reason was in fact much more abstract and existential; the murder was his way of forcing himself out of normative society, the world of "dead language" and "the speech of others."[35] Martin flees the big city to hide from the police and finds himself aimlessly wandering the backlands of what seems to be northeastern Brazil (the *sertão*, mentioned in the previous chapter). During these days of rumination, he makes up his mind to embark on an attempt to abandon his language, along with his very humanity, for the sake of inventing a speech of his own ("his reconstruction had to begin with his own words").[36]

With this decision in mind, Martin reaches a farm called *Vila Baixa*, owned and sternly managed by a woman, Vitória, who lives with her cousin, Ermelinda. Without disclosing the reason for his presence on the property, Martin requests and is given a job as a farmworker, although he admits to being an accomplished engineer (readers will later know this to be a lie; in his previous life, Martin was in fact a statistician). On the farm, Martin develops a sexual relationship with both Ermelinda and the *mulatto* woman who works there, and he becomes the object of Vitória's sexual fantasies. This does not prevent him from carrying out his plan of self-dehumanization, and he shifts from identifying with rocks to becoming-cow in a Deleuzian sense. Vitória is, from the outset, suspicious of the fact that an engineer from the city had decided to take a job on the farm. One day, a regular guest at the house, a character referred to as "the professor," confronts Martin with these suspicions and, with Vitória's support, informs the police of the fugitive's whereabouts. Martin is arrested and learns that his wife, whom he thought he had killed, has survived his murder attempt. The novel ends with the protagonist's decision to continue his journey of self-creation in jail and to write there "a book of words" where he will have "the courage to leave unexplained what cannot be explained."[37]

Lispector's genre deception begins as early as the novel's mysterious title, *The Apple in the Dark*, which intimates a story of great passion and a lurking danger. The title also gives the impression that knowledge is concealed, awaiting the reader to bring it into light (only later will the reader learn the title to be an epistemological assertion; knowledge in the novel is by essence in the dark). The novel's first line similarly promises a deliciously captivating narrative: "This tale begins in March on a night as dark as a night can get when a person is asleep."[38] Martin is depicted standing on the porch, looking anxiously outside so as "to not miss anything that was going on."[39] His alert gaze focuses specifically on a Ford parked at the driveway of a deserted "put up for sale" hotel to which he arrived, the readers are told, "two weeks before."[40] The Ford, they learn, belongs to "a German" who, along with "a servant" ("if he *was* a servant"), is the only other guest in the building.[41] Though Martin reminds himself that he is ready to set off on a "new flight" if the "two men should seem too curious about the identity of the guest," he falls asleep.[42]

Then, suddenly—the air "in suspension"—Martin realizes that he had just heard the roar of the engine, "the car had disappeared."[43] The startled protagonist quickly calculates that "it would take some time for [the German] to get there and return with the police," and fearing that "the servant . . . would at this very moment be outside the door of that very room with his ear alert to the slightest movement," Martin decides to "slip away."[44]

> Without looking back, guided by a slippery adroitness of movement, he began to climb down the balcony by placing his unexpectedly flexible feet on the outcroppings of the bricks. . . . Now only his spirit was alert. . . . with a soft jump that made the garden gasp as it held its breath, he found himself in the middle of a flower bed, which ruffled up and then dosed up. With his body alert the man waited for the message of his jump to be transmitted from secret echo to secret echo, until it would be transformed into distant silence. . . . The night was delicately vast and dark.[45]

With this suggestive final sentence, *The Apple*'s first chapter ends. It animates a diegetic world of "alert" ears, spirits and bodies, "secret echoes," mysterious villains, a man on the run, and a plausible police chase. The chapter raises various questions and with them the expectation that their answers lie dormant in the following chapters: who is the mysterious German, why is he searching for Martin, and why are the details about his national identity and his car's manufacturer important enough to be mentioned? What and who is Martin running away from, and what is his goal? This world and its mysterious question-clues solicit tension and suspense ("made the garden gasp as it held its breath") not only in its characters but also, importantly, in its readers.

The exact reader, we know, is already subsumed in a sense of constant danger that necessitates vigilance and surveillance, making her especially susceptible to the kind of suspense triggered by *The Apple*'s opening. Both the reader and Martin are on the run, the latter from the police, the former from herself. The need, then, to attend to the details of the text for search of clues about Martin's crime and the German's identity, and to survey the protagonist as he attempts to escape, bring into harmony the *nova crítica*'s call for the reader to attend to the text and keep watch over the possible reappearance of her internal savage. Lispector presents the reader with a literary form that pushes the mental states exact reading requires to their utmost extent; she has prompted her reader to immerse herself in an intense mode of "catching," both the internal savage and the clues of the text.

However, following the first chapter, all of the reader's expectations and consequent efforts at attending to the hints hidden in the text, turn out to be in vain. In the hundreds of pages to follow, the German is never mentioned again, nor is his servant or the notorious Ford. Martin's crime is revealed right off the bat, without any need for scrutinizing attention, and turns out to be a failed crime at that. And the rest of the novel, rather than continuing the opening heightened tone of suspense, dwindles in emotional register into a philosophical treatise about the nature of subjectivity and language.

Following the escape from his forlorn hotel, Martin finds himself treading across the "heart of Brazil," a desert-like landscape that, though never located geographically, brings to mind the Brazilian northeastern backlands. This space, which in the Brazilian imaginary carries a mythic quality of being outside the reach of the Law, in the general sense of the word, enables Martin to plunge into an intense attempt to overcome the limits of the self: "With this enormous courage the man had finally stopped being intelligent."[46] As a consequence, the text itself teeters on the brink of intelligibility as it tries to depict through language a man wishing to abandon the symbolic altogether: "The man had rejected the speech of others and did not even have a speech of his own."[47] The narrative overflows with bizarre descriptions ("[T]ime was fortunately passing by with dogs sniffing at the street corners"), with quasi-nonsense metaphors and similes ("His muscles contracted savagely against the dirty conscience that had formed itself about the fingernail"),[48] with seeming contradictions ("[A]s if not understanding were a kind of creation"; "the man was his own Prohibition"),[49] and with amorphous statements ("[H]e knew it was the sun that was inflating his words").[50] To this list, one can add ossified clichés, repetitions, and aphorisms, which stand at the center of Arêas and Waldman's exploration of the novel, mentioned above.[51]

Though the beginning of the novel has undoubtedly left a strong mark on the reader (that phenomena called "primacy effect"), one would assume that, with time, the reader would accept the novel's change of character and slowly let go of her expectation that the novel functions as a crime mystery.[52] But *The Apple* makes sure to consistently reactivate the reader's heightened attention via rhetorical gestures that anticipates the forthcoming of a dramatic statement or moment, in line with the first chapter's mode. These anchors usually open with an emphatic marker: "Suddenly," "Unexpectedly," "For the first time," "That's it, yes!," "Yes! . . . Stunning victory," "Oh God!," or "He finally confessed."[53] These lexical cues, comprised of temporal expressions, exclamation points, and factlike assertions, give the reader the impression that she had just encountered a segment of great significance within the text—a moment of revelation, or a resolution to a fundamental problem. It can only be expected, then, that the Brazilian exact reader would pause at these segments of the text, scrutinize them, and then flag them as conquered. If not the criminal, then at least the "essence" of the text, as Coutinho puts it, may be caught or "penetrated," a "clear" ray of light can finally be shed on the text: what is the goal of Martin's journey? What has he gained or understood?

Unfortunately, these cues quickly and consistently turn out to lead nowhere. *The Apple* retreats from its promise of certainty and nullifies its previous self-assured statements in a variety of crafted ways. The promises, for example, that "it was a silence as if something were going to happen beyond a man's perception" leads to a "few trees were swaying, and the bugs had already disappeared"; and the suspenseful assertion that "for the first time since he [Martin] had started walking, he stopped," ends with "then he started walking again."[54] A similar disappointment follows many of the characters' epiphanies, which are almost always camouflaged by the omniscient narrator in an intentionally ambiguous free indirect discourse. This is the case when the novel appears to finally reveal what has led the protagonist to murder his wife (not yet knowing that his attempt had failed): "Then—by means of a great leap of a crime two weeks before he had taken the risk of having no security, and he had reached a point of not understanding."[55] The factlike tone of this phrase along with its poetically concise vocabulary ("a great leap of a crime"), gives the impression of a final resolution. Yet a page later, this assertion is invalidated when we witness Martin thinking: " 'Crime?' No. 'The great leap?' These did not sound like his words, obscure, like the entanglement of a dream."[56] This revelation is followed by another one, brought about by Martin's confrontation with the backland's stones, which he treats as his audience. The protagonist requests: "Try to imagine a person . . . who did not have the courage to reject himself. Therefore, he needed an act which would make other people reject him, and he himself would not be able to live with himself after that."[57] By this logic, Martin committed his crime in order to be expelled from the world of the known. But a moment later, the narrator of *The Apple* adds, "It is quite possible that he [Martin] had been lying to the stones."[58] The novel never ceases to exhaust.

Lispector adds to *The Apple* another fragrance of mystery via the indefinite quality of its constitutive elements, what Costa Lima calls the "generality" of the novel. The characters, objects, and geographical places that populate the novel—"the German," "the Ford," "the heart of Brazil," "the professor," "the farm"—are left unspecified enough to imply that they stand for something bigger than themselves. This form, which might be called allegorical, enhances, like the novel's thrilling opening, a vigilant quest for clues. One must be on guard in order to solve the mystery of these generalities, which may help in either understanding the initial crime story or the "meaning" of the novel, what it aims to say. And indeed, as evidenced by the scholarship on this work, this poetic principle triggers a critical tendency to view *The Apple* as an allegory and to fill in its gaps. Yet, as in the case of the alleged crime story, Lispector's diegetic world is built to disappoint: each such abstract element hints toward at least two contradictory meanings, making it impossible to fully decipher the allegorical riddle.

Martin, for example, is given no last name throughout the novel, and the readers know almost nothing about his appearance, age, or his former life apart from the fact that he has a son from the wife he tried to murder, and that he used to be a statistician (why does he lie that he is an engineer, a job as suspicious as a statistician for someone looking for a job on a farm? This too is a question raised to be unanswered). In response, Kristin Pitt suggests that Lispector's Martin is an iteration of

José de Alencar's protagonist in his Brazilian national allegory *Iracema*, mentioned above and discussed in the previous chapter.[59] Since the former Martin represents the Portuguese colonialist, Pitt reads Lispector's text as an allegorical rewriting of hegemonic "narratives of conquest and discovery."[60]

From a different point of view, critics such as Beatriz de Castro Amorim and Mara Negrón-Marrero focus on the apple symbolism and on Martin's rebirth, and consequently view the protagonist as standing for the biblical Adam, and Lispector's novel on the whole as a subversive retelling of the Garden of Eden narrative.[61] By contrast, Maria José Somerlate Barbosa claims that Martin is only a parody of the biblical Adam, and that he in fact exemplifies aggressive modern patriarchy.[62] Specifying this claim, Rebecca E. Biron argues that Martin represents social violence rooted in Brazilian patriarchal traditionsy.[63] However, Hélène Cixous takes Martin's crime to represent the exact opposite. For her, the protagonist's attempted murder stands for the cables and ropes that one has to aggressively cut in order to break loose of the hegemonic order: "Given the nature of his crime, one could think that Martin is a real man. In fact, everything is reversed. A close reading shows that he is the most feminine of all characters."[64]

Benjamin Moser too finds Martin to be the oppressed, rather than oppressor, through the figure of "the German." He writes, "The word 'German' in a work by a Jewish writer of the 1950s, was not a neutral description, especially when applied to a figure of harassment and oppression. And 'Ford,' the only brand named in the book, suggests Henry Ford, the notorious anti-Semite whose racist writings were widely distributed in Brazil. Both names suggest that the German's victim must be Jewish."[65] Martin, then, is a man and a woman, an oppressor and an oppressed, an Adam and an anti-Adam.

This small sample testifies to the novel's internal mechanism of soliciting an expectation for catching the villain on the level of plot or catching the meaning on the level of theme. But the contradictory nature of these various "solutions" speaks to the insolvability of this riddle. This is not to say that these readings are in any sense wrong, but to suggest that the carnivalesque dance that appears when these different readings are put together acts out a tension inherent to the novel: *The Apple* at once encourages and frustrates its attentive readers. This might explain why the criticism around *The Apple* is replete with its depiction as "difficult" to read. Júlio César Vieira and Osmar Oliva, for example, open their article on the novel with a description of its reader,

> Reading *The Apple in the Dark* . . . is experienced first and foremost as a challenge. The uninformed reader, accustomed to the plot linearity of the traditional narrative, tends to find it difficult to follow the progress of this book, which the author claims to be her most structured. . . . The model-reader of this novel, to use Umberto Eco's term (2004), must be prepared to accompany a slow movement, rife with reflection, to which the reader must be attentive if s/he is to perceive the richness of the text in question.[66]

The thinkers of the *nova crítica* have been right, then. Lispector sets a trap for her readings through a "deceit of language." *The Apple* is structured thus that it keeps its readers "uninformed"—or, more accurately, misinformed—which causes them "to find it difficult" to follow the plot. To adjust, Vieira and Oliva suggest, these readers "must be attentive"; but it is a unique kind of attention that this novel invites, to which I will now turn.

Exhausted Reading

Lispector's repetitive false alarms make palpable for the readers their own cognitive process involved in exact reading, their exercise of disciplined attention toward comprehension ("catching" the text), accompanied by a constant sense of vigilance and lurking danger. Precisely by making this effort felt, *The Apple* also raises the question about the afterlife of such "intense" attention; that is, what happens when such a cognitive effort is excessively prolonged and systematically hindered?

Following another false cue ("That was it—he had felt victory"), the novel reads, "That was what it was, then. And Martin asked himself with intensity and pain, 'could that be all it was?' because his truths did not seem to be able to bear attention for a long time before they became deformed . . . it was at the cost of a certain control, then, that Martin stuck to one truth only and with difficulty erased all others. (Without him realizing it, his reconstruction had already begun to gasp)."[67] According to *The Apple*, controlled attention involves an erasure and a sort of cognitive stiffness ("Martin *stuck* to one truth"). But his effort to hold on through attention to an ostensibly stable "truth" eventually leads to a "deformation" of these momentary understandings. In fact, as we have seen above, the novel consistently presents a temporal waning of any "truth" or answer found by its narrator or characters. *The Apple* is an ouroboros; a moment after establishing something solid, it undoes its very foundation, burns the bridges it builds.

Lispector herself suggests a metaphor for this temporal manipulation when reverting to Martin's sense of time via another outlandish simile: "Time was fortunately passing by. So much that it was like the meal one eats in the daytime, and then goes to bed and wakes up vomiting in the middle of the night . . . everything going so well! . . . But in the middle of the night you would suddenly wake up vomiting."[68] The novel's movement forward is marked by a repeated vomiting of its own history. It deceives the reader to think that "everything [is] going so well," only to find time and again that all expectations of order have been demolished.

Lispector is interested precisely in that liminal space of transformation from "intensity" and "attention" to where mental focus begins "to gasp," just like the garden. This awkward temporality is in keeping with Lispector's general doubt about the possibility of predicting any sort of future (fictional or concrete) based on the past or present. Just before her death in 1977, she translated *Le Bluff du Futur* (*The Bluff of the Future*, or in Portuguese *O Blefe do Futuro*) by French economist Georges Elgozy, in which he attacks "futurology" as "the modern disease of naively assuming that the future is strictly determined by the past, when history, whether modern or ancient, in fact teaches us that it is the unexpected that always occurs."[69] *The Apple* resists "futurology." The hyperbolic state of attention it elicits, and this mind-set's eventual inadequacy, exhaust the reader into loosening her tight grip on both the internal savage and the text's meaning.

The languished reading of *The Apple*, which follows the "intense" initial one, involves a lingering in the moment. Having learned that conclusive answers, declarations, and decisions are consistently revoked in the novel, the reader is encouraged to engage with Martin's revelations without being tempted to declare them understood; to read in a state of fatigue. This unique practice can also be thought of as an ad hoc reading: an engagement with the current segment of the literary text without the intervention of any "anticipatory urge," to borrow Bruno Carvalho's term.[70]

Instead of "catching" and shedding "intense" light on the text, Lispector suggests a quick distracted caress of the "non-word" or "truth," which is itself, like the internal savage, always unruly and in the dark.

In another *crônica*, *Escrever, humildade, técnica* ("Writing, Humility, Technique"), Lispector explains that any finite "catch" of the literary text is impossible, and that any contact with the true "non-word" requires a different kind of touch altogether.

> Essa incapacidade de atingir, de entender, é que faz com que eu, por instinto de . . . de quê? procure um modo de falar que me leve mais depressa ao entendimento. Esse modo, esse "estilo" (!), já foi chamado de várias coisas, mas não do que realmente e apenas é: uma procura humilde . . . Quando falo em "humildade" refiro-me à humildade . . . que vem da plena consciência de se ser realmente incapaz. E refiro-me à humildade como técnica . . . só se aproximando com humildade da coisa é que ela não escapa totalmente.
>
> This incapacity to attain, to understand, makes me instinctively . . . what? It makes me search for a mode of communication that would lead me more immediately to understanding. This mode, this "style" (!), has been called many things, but never what it truly and solely is: a humble quest . . . when I speak of "humility," I refer to the humility . . . that arises from a full awareness of one's true incapability. And I refer to humility as a technique. . . . only if we approach the thing with humility, will it not utterly escape us.[71]

Instead of a "catch"—since to "attain" is beyond possibility—Lispector offers a "quest." And this reading "technique," a distinctly *nova crítica* term, involves precisely those characteristics associated with the detrimental *selvagem*, a sense of incapacity (*incapacidade*) and, as we saw above, distraction (*distração*). However, Lispector's choice of words also points to her deeply dialectical approach to the practice of attentive reading. Both "*in*capacidade" and "*dis*tração" are structured around and dependent on the lexical root which they then negate. One must diverge from a certain track to be distracted (*dis-tractus*), and must not grasp to be incapable (*in* + *capax*, "able to hold much"). In other words, the mind-set that she calls for is inherently linked to (rather than cancels out) its opposite; distracted or exhausted reading is a result of an engagement with an attentive one.

Indeed, at the end of *The Apple*, Martin adopts an "incapable" and "distracted" attitude toward the truth (the apple), very much akin to the one Lispector, through a long process of exhaustion, provokes her reader to accept: a humble search that leads to a momentary "catch," vague and ephemeral, that involves not the *nova crítica*'s exalted light and clarity, but dim uncertainty.

> Because understanding is a mode of looking. Because understanding is an attitude. Just as he now stretched his hand in the dark to catch the apple, and felt his fingers so ungainly [*desajeitados*] for the love of the apple. Martin did not search for the name of things anymore. It was enough to have known them in the dark. And to rejoice in it, ungainly. And later? Later, when he reenters clarity, he will see the things in his hands, and will identify their false names. Yes, but by then he would have already known them in the dark, like a man sleeping with a woman.[72]

Echoing how the *nova crítica* and Costa Lima describe meaningful reading in terms of light and "clarity," Lispector too presents "understanding" as a mode of "looking," as an attitude toward the "thing" under inspection. But, as she illustrates through Martin, this mode of looking, of "catching" the apple, is intrinsically linked for her with the *un*gainly, or in Portuguese, the *un*ordered (*des-a-jeito*). That is, the comprehension toward which *The Apple* is steering its readers requires a certain abandonment of control, and can thus only occur in the state of blindness, in the dark, or while "sleeping," the latter bringing to mind bodily pleasures and desires ("like a man sleeping with a woman").

Bringing the catch into "clarity" provides one with a sense of control and possession; knowledge is "in his hands" and is "identif[ied]," but like the fish and the nonword, truth slips away under light, and its appearances (its "names") are "false." At the same time, it is important to note, throughout her conceptualization of an alternative to exact reading, Lispector never stops engaging, manipulating, distorting, and playing with the concepts and ideas of the *nova crítica*. If the *nova crítica* suggests that the wild needs to be caught and restrained through attention, Lispector suggests that in order to come near the wild heart of the text, one must enhance that specific effort of attention all the way to the point of distraction, and keep humbly searching for the *selvagem* while knowing its unattainability.

Reading Subjectivity

That Lispector enters into conversation with exact reading in *The Apple* might be doubted when we consider that during the years of the novel's writing, Lispector was far from Brazil. Following her husband in his world tours as a diplomat, Lispector begins writing *The Apple* in 1951, while in Turkey, continues it in England, and brings it to a close in Washington, DC, just before returning to Brazil in 1956. In truth, however, during her years abroad, Lispector stays closely attuned to the occurrences in Brazil. One might even say she never fully left home: "I lived mentally in Brazil, I lived on borrowed time," she confessed about her experience abroad.[73]

During her years in "exile," as she refers to it, Lispector visits Brazil frequently, remains highly involved in the world of Brazilian print media to the extent that she is offered a personal column in the prestigious magazine *Manchete*, and is in constant touch with the intellectual milieu that admired her since *Near to the Wild Heart*—she regularly corresponds with Fernando Sabino, Erico Verissimo, and Rubem Braga, for example, and hosts in Washington such prominent Brazilian figures as San Tiago Dantas, João Cabral de Melo Neto, and Augusto Frederico Schmidt, to name just a few.[74] Moreover, during these same years, Lispector writes her acclaimed short story collection, *Laços de família* (*Family Ties*), which describes with great accuracy the Brazilian upper-middle-class Rio of the time, demonstrating once again how au courant she was with the Brazilian scene.[75]

Finally, and perhaps most importantly, it makes sense that Lispector would find the *nova crítica*'s project compelling, since she was always invested in the central question these critics raised about the link between forms of reading and subject formation. In *Near to the Wild Heart*, with which this chapter opens, Lispector characterizes the protagonist and her partner, Joana and Otávio, through their unique approach to literature. Their ways of being in the world are expressed through their reading mode, which in turn perpetuates their subjectivity. This is so much the case that Joana's reading mode can be said to bring their marriage to its end.

Lispector dedicates the chapter *A pequena família* ("The Little Family") to a description of a reading scene, which marks a key moment of change in the couple's relationship. The chapter's title sets the wrong readerly expectation, a tendency we saw exacerbated in *The Apple*. Hinting at a possible tightening of the emotional link between husband and wife, the title in fact reveals itself to denote the upcoming birth of Otávio's child from his mistress, leading to the couple's divorce. The vast majority of the chapter follows Otávio at his work desk, laboring over his article on Civil Law; indeed, he views this process as "labor." Otávio understands himself to be an "intellectual worker" (*um trabalhador intelectual*) who must abide by certain rules of work (*a regra de trabalho*), and goes back and forth between reading and writing as the two main and inseparable tasks that comprise his endeavor;[76] he writes down his thoughts, reads them, rereads the notes he had written the day before, and ends up picking out of the library the primary source he is working with, Spinoza's *Ethics*.

Surprisingly, however, instead of encountering there the writings of the Jewish Dutch philosopher, he finds another text awaiting his reading within the book: "A page from a notebook was tucked between its pages. He looked at it and discovered Joana's uncertain handwriting. He leaned over it avidly. 'The beauty of the words: God's abstract nature. It is like listening to Bach.' . . . Joana always caught him off guard."[77] This encounter with Joana's readerly comments jolts Otávio, and he finds himself utterly unable to further his "work." His wife's words conjure her presence "in her moments of *distraction* [emphasis mine], her face white, vague and light. And suddenly great melancholy descended over him. What exactly am I doing? He wondered and didn't even know why he had attacked himself so suddenly. No, don't write today." Joana's "distracted" reading, which Otávio associated with her very "presence," brings about an irremediable interruption in his process of intellectual labor ("he had attacked himself so suddenly"). However, alongside its aggression, this caesura is also experienced by Otávio as a relief: "Otávio felt almost happy. Today someone was giving him time off [literally, "rest," *descanso*]." This sense of freedom leads Otávio to write his wife a counternote ("telling her he wouldn't be home for lunch. Poor Joana"), and he heads off to meet his lover, Lídia.[78]

Joana's entire selfhood—her physical presence, her ambience, her characteristic mien of engaging things—is compacted into her readerly comment, which stands in stark opposition to Otávio's ways of thinking and being. Setting the ground for Lispector's future disagreement with the *nova crítica*'s advancement of attention as the preferred readerly mental state is her depiction of Joana's distracted mode of reading as productive, creative, and politically subversive. Joana's sensate reading, being able to see and hear the text ("The beauty of the words," "It is like listening to Bach"), appears to Lispector to be a vein of approaching texts not sufficiently explored, one outside "the comfort of order."[79] Indeed, when embarking on his intellectual endeavor at the beginning of the chapter, Otávio thinks to himself, "What fascinated and terrified him about Joana was precisely the freedom in which she lived," to which he later adds: "Joana thought without fear and without punishment. Would she end up mad or what?"[80] Joana's distracted reading method speaks to her "wild" agency, especially against the backdrop of Otávio's deeply internalized social order.

In fact, if any of the two protagonists is closer to the exact reader, then in its historical moment of constitution, it is Otávio. The husband is depicted as being constantly on guard against diversions from what he considers to be his central line of thought ("he'd allowed his pen to run a little freely in order to rid himself of the persistent image or idea that may have decided to dog him and stanch his main stream of thought").[81] He also feels himself to be under tight internal supervision, which he relies on to orient his thoughts ("Now he was going to work. As if everyone was watching approvingly, closing their eyes in their assent: yes, that's right, very good").[82] Otávio's engagement with the text is anything but "distracted" or "restful"; it requires militant self-discipline ("Well, now order. Pencil down, he told himself, free yourself of obsessions. One, two, three!"), and is experienced as constraining and hostile ("Like that, like that, don't avoid it . . . yes, yes, that was it, don't avoid myself, don't avoid my handwriting, how light and horrible it is, a spider's web").[83] In fact, Otávio himself recognizes the dichotomy between his and Joana's reading modes, and pits his own vigilance against her alleged lethargy ("I'm an intellectual worker, Joana is asleep in the bedroom. . . . She has been defeated by sleep, defeated, defeated").[84] This is not to say that Lispector simplistically views Otávio's interaction with the text as unworthy. She puts in his mind and notes Spinozian ideas that are pivotal to her oeuvre.[85] But it is already in this early work that we see Lispector beginning to form an image of a reader who shies away from mental self-control even at the price of being called "mad," considered "defeated," or, with the *nova crítica*, labeled "savage."

Lispector will once again signal her view of reading and self-formation as intertwined in *The Passion According to G.H.*, published in 1964, only three years after *The Apple* and simultaneously with the *crônicas* mentioned above. She begins *The Passion* with a note "to possible readers," where she openly discusses the readerly subjectivity she believes her text demands and can form.

> Este livro é como um livro qualquer. Mas eu ficaria contente
> se fosse lido apenas por pessoas de alma já formada. Aquelas
> que sabem que a aproximação, do que quer que seja, se faz

> gradualmente e penosamente—atravessando inclusive o oposto daquilo que se vai aproximar. Aquelas pessoas que, só elas, entenderão bem devagar que este livro nada tira de ninguém. A mim, por exemplo, o personagem G. H. foi dando pouco a pouco uma alegria difícil; mas chama-se alegria.
>
> This book is like any other book. But I would be happy if it were only read by people whose souls are already formed. Those who know that the approach, of whatever it may be, happens gradually and painstakingly—even passing through the opposite of what it approaches. They who, only they, will slowly come to understand that this book takes [literally "pull out"] nothing from no one. To me, for example, the character G.H. gave bit by bit a difficult joy; but it is called joy.[86]

Reading "forms" subjectivity. Not through its content, but through the interaction between the "approach" the book solicits and its responsive or irresponsive reader. As we have already seen in *The Apple*, Lispector's approach evolves over time. Hers is a challenging and exhausting reading mode precisely because of its dialectical nature, traversing through its very opposition.

Lispector engenders a readerly exhaustion that stems from intense effort and a readerly distraction born out of vigilant attention. But most importantly, and in implicit yet strong response to the *nova crítica*'s demand to unsavage, Lispector insists that the readerly "technique" she aims for will require no self-undoing: it will pull out "nothing from no one." While the *nova crítica* urges the reader to exact the savage from within, Lispector exhausts her reader into engaging with distraction in order to experience an invaluable "difficult joy."

∽

Quite a while after I had first put on paper my long-brewing thoughts about *The Apple*, I was surprised to find these ideas reflecting back at me from a different book altogether. This uncanny encounter occurred when I read a critical work on the master of suspense, D. A. Miller's *Hidden Hitchcock*—how apt indeed. In this enticing book, Miller argues that a unique game of attention takes place between Hitchcock and his viewers, and I could not help but feel that Lispector is winking at me from her famous "between-the-lines." Miller writes,

> In his supremely lucid narrative communication, nothing deserves our attention that his camera doesn't go out of its way to point out . . . but as anyone who has seen a Hitchcock film knows, the director primes us to be considerably more alert than his spoon-feeding requires. In addition to our instrumental attention, we find ourselves possessed by a watchfulness that seems to have no object or use. . . . A strangely futile vigilance, it irritated our vision only by virtue of being palpably in excess of what we are being *asked* to see; ready to be as observant as Sherlock Holmes, we are challenged with the most elementary cases. . . . I postulate a game he [Hitchcock] would be playing with that absurdly, pointless watchful spectator . . . and whom I call the Too-Close Viewer. . . . It is as though, at the heart of the manifest style, there pulsed an irregular extra beat, the surreptitious "murmur" of its undoing that only the Too-Close Viewer could apprehend.[87]

In *The Apple*, a very different "extra beat" awaits the "Too-Close" reader. While Miller identifies in a dazzling variety of films "a perverse counter-narrative" that only the excessively alert viewer can apprehend ("a small continuity error made on purpose, or a Hitchcock cameo fashioned so as not to be seen, or a narrative image secretly doubling for a figure of speech in the manner of a charade"), Lispector confronts her readers—"possessed by a watchfulness that seems to have no object or use"--with a static, at times nonsensical, narrative that depicts via language a protagonist's attempt to undo traditional communication.

And yet, Lispector's ghost speaks through Miller's book. After all, she chooses to masquerade *The Apple* as an allegorical detective novel precisely in order to prime her readers to "be considerably more alert" than required. This is her way of bringing about "a strangely futile vigilance" that "irritates," or exhausts, her reader "by virtue of being palpably in excess" of what that reader is "being *asked* to see." With the bait of Martin's unknown crime, the German's threatening identity, the mysterious servant, and the protagonist's courageous escape, Lispector enjoins her Brazilian readers to "be as observant as Sherlock Holmes," in Miller's words, or as observant as Coutinho's exact reader. But, as in the case of Hitchcock, these readers are doomed to find their arduous attempts futile; they encounter nothing but "the most elementary cases," or, in Lispector's novel, no case at all. *The Apple* never reveals who the German or his servant were, and Martin's crime, as we now know, turns out to have been a "failed" one. It is no coincidence that Lispector's technique of "deceit" reverberates through a study of Hitchcock; this momentary coalescence intimates once again that she is manipulating the effect of suspense specifically for the sake of turning "pointless" the efforts of her culturally construed "watchful" reader. And so, while a "Too-Close Viewer" is born in front of Hitchcock's screen, a specifically Brazilian exhausted reader emerges as she leafs through *The Apple*, in the dark.

In the upcoming final two chapters of this book, I will sketch the contours of the Israeli reader who emerges both from the works of local intellectuals affiliated with the New Criticism and from those of modernists who anticipate and respond to the New Critical model. With Coutinho and Lispector, we have seen how the Brazilian interpretation of close reading circles around the open wound of colonialism and its accompanying image of the distracted savage. In the Israeli context, it is the specter of social disintegration that casts a shadow over the figure of the reader. There as well, we encounter a "Too-Close" viewer, but one whose preoccupation is different. Instead of extracting the savage from within, the Israeli reader is urged to synthesize the myriad elements of the literary text into an excessively coherent whole, as a response to an anxiety from an impending social breakdown.

Part III

Israel: The Unlocalized Reader

Chapter Five

Unlocalizing

The Tel Aviv School and the Israeli Crisis of Social Disintegration

> A text is a body of language full of gaps, ellipses, unlinked units, to be read and understood, i.e., to be filled out and reorganized in the mind of the "proper" reader.
>
> —Ziva Ben-Porat and Benjamin Harshav

> There is a need to return to something stable but today expectations are diminished. The center has broken down and it makes it impossible to present a comprehensibly ordered picture of Israeli society.
>
> —A. B. Yehoshua

There are few Hebrew writers as closely associated with a specific political stance, a militant right-wing one at that, as Uri Zvi Greenberg (UZG) (1896–1981). Known as the "poet of the Revisionist [Zionist] movement" and himself a member of parliament, UZG (or *Atzag* as he is referred to by his Hebrew acronym)—with his fervent modernist-expressionist work—was a central figure in the pre- and early-independence Israeli cultural arena. His political commitment, however, was not without its price; as the critic Orit Meital has demonstrated, since UZG's activism and journalistic publications left no doubt as to his political agenda, his complex poetry too was almost always read (and still is) in the narrow terms of the national Zionist project. More precisely, Meital shows that around the 1930s, a persistent critical tradition of reading UZG's poems as national allegories was established, assuming that they recount the Zionist struggle—the poems' singular form or content notwithstanding.[1] In that sense, UZG's reception bespeaks the more general tendency in pre-1970s Israeli literary criticism to examine Hebrew literature solely through the lens of a teleological Zionist ideology: a critical perspective that takes Hebrew literature to always portray what is believed to be the ineluctable historical movement toward a "national revival" in a Jewish, Hebrew-speaking, Israeli state.

It was a well-orchestrated and irreverent move, then, on the part of Benjamin Harshav (formerly, Hrushovski) to publish in 1968, in the very first volume of his journal, *Ha-Sifrut* (*Literature*), a lengthy article on UZG's poetry, analyzing its rhythm in explicitly apolitical formalist terms.[2] Harshav was the founder of the Tel Aviv School of Poetics and Semiotics, which will be the focus on this chapter, as it played a key role in the introduction of the New Critical method of close reading into Israeli scholarship and culture. In that context, Harshav presents his alternative to the Israeli nationalist tradition of interpretation in terms of a new mode of reading, "an accurate and detailed analysis . . . from close by."

שירתו של אורי צבי גרינברג היא אחת התופעות הגדולות ויוצאות הדופן בתולדות השירה של עם ישראל. . . . הזיקה הנועזת של שירתו לאידיאולוגיד ולפוליטיקה גרמה לכך שרבים ראו אותו מצדדים אלו בלבד. . . . על כל פנים, על אופיה השירי של שירת גרינברג יודעים אנו מעט. דומה שהגיעה השעה למחקר המדוייק והמדוקדק, שיגש לשירה הזאת מקרוב, ויראה אותה כפי שהיא. לשם כך עלינו לוותר על הקריטריונים האידיאולוגיים (הספרותיים או הפוליטיים) ועל האסנציאליזם, המדבר על "גרינברג" כאילו היה משורר מונוליטי אחד.

The poetry of Uri Zvi Greenberg is one of the most monumental and exceptional phenomena in the poetic history of the people of Israel. . . . His poetry's brazen affinity with ideology and politics made it so that many have viewed him solely through these perspectives. . . . In any case, we know very little about the *poetic* nature of Greenberg's poetry. The time has come for an accurate and detailed analysis of this poetry, one that would approach it from close by, to see it as it is. For that to occur, we must give up ideological criteria (both literary and political) and the essentialism that presents "Greenberg" as if he were one monolithic poet.³

As I will go on to discuss, Harshav's thinking and the overall work of the Tel Aviv School (the TA School from here on), were deeply indebted to Czech Structuralism and Russian Formalism, among other theoretical orientations, all advocating for a break with "ideological criteria" when approaching literature. But Harshav's vocabulary echoes specifically the New Critical method of reading, urging the reader, in the spirit of their critique of the intentional and affective fallacies, to "give up" both readerly "ideological" agendas and an "essentialist" view of the writer for the sake of practicing close reading: an "accurate and detailed analysis" from "close by."

In this chapter, I argue that the New Critical method of close reading in its Israeli iteration—one which reaches its peak not with Harshav but with his students at the TA School, Menakhem Perry and Meir Sternberg—involves self-suspension via attention, as we have seen in the American and Brazilian cases as well. But while it was subjectivity as a life force that the reader was instructed to hold off through attention in the American case, and the internal "savage" that the Brazilian thinkers strove to remove from the reading process, the Israeli critics—in an endeavor to battle the historically established habit of reading any Hebrew work as a national allegory—urged the reader to perform what I call "unlocalization." Meaning, the Israeli reader was required to detach during the reading process from her stance regarding the reigning local Jewish narrative, that of Zionism. Instead, in this iteration of unselfing, the reader was to cognitively engage with literature, and with Hebrew literature specifically, for its formal "poetic" nuances and, most importantly, to attentively expose the work's "integrational" structure, a pivotal term in the Israeli adaptation of close reading.

The centrality of "integration" in the conceptualization of close reading is highly telling, since it gives voice to the paradox I find at the heart of the Israeli version of this method: though close reading was designed to mold an apolitical reader, it was adopted in order to help resolve a national political crisis. More specifically, the Israeli version of close reading was informed by the acute internal conflicts that surfaced within the ostensibly unified young nation of the late 1960s–1970s. During that time, the concept of social disintegration in its various Hebrew articulations (*pizur* [dispersal]; *hitparkut* [falling apart]; *shever* [breach]; or the Hebraized version of disintegration, *disintegratzya*) saturated the political discourse.

Concomitantly, the Israeli version of close reading was conceptualized in diametrically opposite terms as necessitating a mental effort of "integration," the word itself hinting at this method's covert political undertones. The Israeli critics who adopted the New Critical method instructed their readers to invest attention—a mental state, as we have seen, which was associated with close reading from the outset—in the task of linking together to the maximum degree the various elements of the text. Paradoxically, this unlocalized, analytic reader, proficient in integration, was imagined to provide a possible solution to the exceedingly local Israeli internal struggles by uniting, if only in thought, the distinct sectors of the increasingly balkanized Israeli society.[4]

To be clear, my claim is not that the Israeli thinkers associated with the New Criticism intentionally deceived their readers, presenting their project as cognitive when it was in fact deliberately designed as political. Instead, I believe that political and social anxieties lodged themselves into the Israeli unselfing project independently of any one New Critic's individual decision. The TA School openly proclaimed its intention to construe an unideological, attentive reader, but pervasive sociopolitical pressures left their mark on the enterprise, shaping its internal contradiction: the unlocalized, apolitical reader was imagined in terms of an acutely local and political problem that haunted these critics.

We witnessed similar internal contradictions in the North American and Brazilian cases as well. In the first, simultaneously with an explicit declaration of disinterest in the reader, we identified a deep investment in shaping a reader who could undo her own presence. And in the Brazilian context, the cognitive work of attention, imagined to free the Brazilian reader from the colonial grip, was found replete with derogatory colonial tropes. Interestingly, an intellectual movement deeply engaged with the literary device of paradox—the textual fusion of the like and the unlike—seems to have developed a reading method structured precisely around such paradoxical tensions.

The chapter focuses on what I call the long 1970s (1967–1984), during which the TA School's version of close reading, with its aesthetic and political values, occupied the national cultural center. And yet, the gradual process by which the New Criticism was accepted in the Israeli sphere began two decades earlier. Already in the 1950s, there gathered in Jerusalem a new coterie of vanguardists, to be later known as the "Statehood Generation" poets, who functioned as one of the gateways through which the New Criticism entered the Israeli sphere.[5] One of the founders of this literary circle and its flagship journal, *Likrat* [*Towards*], was Harshav, who served as the key intellectual of the group. His cofounder was Natan Zach, the dominant Israeli poet of the 1950s–1960s, and the leader of the Statehood Generation, who was also responsible for articulating the group's poetics (a third founding member, Yehuda Amichai, who did not fully abide by Zach's imperatives, will be discussed in the following chapter).

After years in which Jewish culture in the *Yishuv* steered away from anything anglophone following the British mandate (1917–1948),[6] Zach—later to become a scholar of modernist English and American poetry—openly modeled *Likrat*'s poetics on that of Ezra Pound and T. S. Eliot, suggesting from the get-go that his project was not at all apolitical; after all, via Pound and Eliot, Zach strives to position himself as part of the white hegemonic Anglo-American West specifically. A central venue through which Zach familiarizes himself with American High Modernism is the seminars given at the Hebrew University by Shimon Halkin, the legendary chair of the Hebrew Literature Department. Halkin, who was the teacher of Zach, Harshav, Amichai, and later on Menakhem Perry, was an Eastern-European immigrant who spent most of his life in New York; he was an ardent reader of contemporary American literature, fluent in the work of Eliot, a translator of Walt Whitman, an admirer of both American romanticism and modernism, and highly versed in the New Criticism.[7] And though his sociocultural interpretations of Hebrew literature were very much infused with the abovementioned Zionist teleological ideology, his students testify that in the classroom, he was a New Critic par excellence. The literary critic Ariel Hirschfeld plainly puts it: "The Halkin era was characterized by its affiliation with the dominant trend of Anglo-American mid-century literary studies, the school of New Criticism."[8]

Halkin's students—the *Likrat* Statehood Generation poets—emphatically relied on the lyrical "I," a move that for a long time was taken to reflect Zach's call for a poetry representative not of the Israeli national collective, but of the universalized individual ("I'm a citizen of the world," Zach declares in one of his celebrated poems).[9] However, as Michael Gluzman demonstrated, the Statehood Generation's focus on the poetic "I" was not in fact an apolitical universalizing move, but an expression of a particular political melancholia, which he terms "the melancholia of sovereignty."[10] He finds in Statehood Generation poetics traces of the "sense of loss and lack" that permeated Israeli society after the War of Independence and the establishment of the state in 1948. Expanding on Gluzman's argument, I believe that the universal antinationalist thrust that manifested itself in the poetry of the 1950s and '60s spread in the 1970s, via Harshav and Zach among other cultural figures, into the realm of literary criticism, to carry there as well an implicit political valence. In the 1970s, the "melancholia" Gluzman keenly points to is converted into anxiety: the fear that the fragile unity that had provided Israeli society with the illusion of national coherence is in a rapid process of erosion. In response, the Israeli critics adopted close reading, adding to it a particular political dimension: it was to transform Israeli readers into cognitively astute "citizens of the world" who would hence be able to participate in the specifically national mission of unifying the internally conflicted Israeli society of their time.

I will return to the 1950s and early 1960s, with *Likrat* and Zach as central players, in the following chapter, but in the current context I focus on Harshav and his legacy, since it is with the TA School that the Israeli iteration of New Critical close reading gains substantial cultural currency. This is due to the fact, among other reasons, that Harshav was the only one of Halkin's students who went on to study with a New Critic in North America. After his BA at the Hebrew University, Harshav did graduate work at Yale under the guidance of the celebrated New Critic and Czech Structuralist René Wellek, and returned to Israel in the mid-1960s with an in-depth knowledge of the New Criticism and Structuralism, in addition to a profound acquaintance with phenomenology and formalism (the poet Moshe Dor recalls that already in the 1950s, the *Likrat* members "were inspired and terrified by [Harshav's] erudition").[11] Against this backdrop, Harshav founds in 1967 the Department of Poetics and Comparative Literature at Tel Aviv University (simply referred to in Hebrew as *Ha-Chug Le'torat Ha-Sifrut*, The Department of General Literary Theory), which became a leading voice in Israeli and international literary scholarship ("there are many centers of literary scholarship in the world," writes Alan Mintz in 1984, "but there are few as energetic and concentrated as the Department of Poetics and Comparative Literature at Tel Aviv University").[12]

Within his newly formed Department of General Literary Theory, Harshav establishes the Tel Aviv School of Poetics and Semiotics, from which would emerge some of the most important Israeli literary scholarship and scholars. As the department's title and school's name evinces, Harshav structures them as theoretically rigorous, in an attempt to move away from Halkin's Hebrew Literature Department and the nationalist, impressionistic, and biographical interpretation style it represented for him.[13] Yet Halkin's (and Wellek's) New Criticism had a strong, even if more covert, presence in the scholarship produced at Harshav's young TAU department. Undoubtedly, on the macrolevel of the theoretical and historical study of literature, the department was deeply invested in Structuralist thought in its different variations, which governed its widely read English journal *Poetics Today* and its preceding version *Poetics and Theory of Literature* (*PTL*).[14] However, on the microlevel of studying the single text—what Harshav called the subfield of "interpretation"—the School drew heavily on the New Critical practice and theory of close reading (Harshav's "reading from *close by*"); we may recall in this context the affinity between the New Criticism and Structuralism that we saw in Brazil as well.[15] Nevertheless, the TA School's association with the New Critical creed has often escaped notice within the current literature on the subject. Aside from Brian McHale and Eyal Segal's essay on this matter, this lack of recognition has hindered a comprehensive understanding of the TA School's role within the broader transnational discourse I map out in this book.[16]

I begin my discussion with the establishment of the Department of General Literary Theory in 1967 in the immediate aftermath of the Six Days War, and end in the mid-1980s, when Harshav leaves permanently for the US and Israeli literature breaks with New Critical thought and aesthetic criteria.[17] I devote the first section of the chapter to the exploration of the New Critically informed Israeli protocol of close reading, termed "maximalist reading." I follow Harshav's students—Menakhem Perry and Meir Sternberg (who later became central cultural figures)—and their imperative to "maximize" the text as related to the concept of attention-as-integration. The second and third sections discuss the 1970s' translated and local prose-fiction, produced against the backdrop of the Israeli 1960s shift away from poetry with the emergence of a new generation of prose-fiction writers, famously dubbed by Gershon Shaked "The New Wave in Hebrew Literature."[18] More specifically, the second section demonstrates how Perry and Sternberg also followed the American New Critics in their admiration for William Faulkner, but adapted their readings of his oeuvre to fit the Israeli model centered on unlocalizing, integration, and the labor of attention. In the third section, I focus on the work of A. B. Yehoshua, a writer who famously models his work on Faulkner's. I show how the critical discourse around Yehoshua's work—a discourse deeply informed by Israeli New Critical readings of Faulkner—reveals the latent link between the imperative of cognitive and formal integration, and the angst over social disintegration.

Before diving in, let me add an important note on the concept of unlocalizing. In contrast with the "haunted" and "unsavaged" self, terms that suggest very locally specific processes of self-formation, the "unlocalized" self calls more strongly into question the difference between the process of "unselfing," which I suggest underlies the method of close reading writ large, and the well-known categories of "impersonality" and "universalization," long associated with the theoretical and creative literary movements centering this book, that is, the New Criticism and Modernism. In other words, the question arises, in what ways is the "unlocalized" reader different from the universal or impersonal subject thoroughly discussed in the context of modernism? I engaged this question briefly in the Introduction but would like to add here a few more words of clarification.

The model of modernist impersonality is inseverable from the figure of T. S. Eliot, the spiritual forefather of the New Criticism, and, as mentioned, of the *Likrat* group as well. Eliot famously claimed in "Tradition and the Individual Talent" that "poetry is not . . . the expression of personality, but an escape from personality."[19] The meaning of this statement has been often flattened, as Jewel Spears Brooker shows when unpacking Eliot's dialectics. However, over and above the intricacies of Eliot's philosophy, his claim underlies the widely accepted view that impersonality served as a model for both modernist aesthetics and the New Critical thought.[20] In that sense, it may seem that "unselfing," that is, suspending one's subjectivity, and "unlocalizing," that is, detaching from local affiliations, are nothing but other iterations of Eliot's "escape from personality." However, the term *impersonality* and its often accompanying *universalizing* are consistently used as if applicable to any modernist or New Critical text, time and place notwithstanding. In contrast, the North American, Brazilian, and Israeli iterations of unselfing demonstrate that the process of suspending subjectivity, which governs the method of close reading, is exceedingly historical and local. Following the global circulation of the New Criticism, one realizes that processes of "universalization" are not universal, that processes of "depoliticizing" are molded by specific political circumstances, and that any undoing of the self is burdened and formed by the long local history of self-conception.

The umbrella term of *unselfing* and the specific *unlocalizing*, then, distinguish themselves from *impersonality* by emphasizing their geohistorical contingency, their underlying assumption that history haunts any attempt on the side of the subject to strip herself of context. In that vein, though *unlocalizing* might sound like a general term, the ideological agenda that the Israeli New Critics requested their reader suspend during the reading process is ideologically and temporally specific—the teleological Zionist narrative that prevailed in the allegorical literary interpretations of the 1960s—and the reasons for molding the local iteration of close reading around this form of ideological unselfing is fueled by particular political, historical, and social conditions. Somewhat counterintuitively, then, it was only a distinctly local Israeli reader who could fully grasp and participate in the self-formation praxis of unlocalizing.

Attention-as-Integration

The Israeli 1970s are famous for their radical political and social instability, witnessing dramatic military events and significant revolts against the established power structures, predominantly controlled by Jewish Israelis, particularly those of Ashkenazi (Central or Eastern European) descent. A pivotal moment was the Six Days War in 1967, which not only dissolved clear national borders but also precipitated a series of profound societal shifts. Shortly thereafter, the Mizrahi uprising emerged, involving Jews of North African or Middle Eastern descent, who, despite their integral role within the broader Jewish identity, have historically confronted social and economic disparities in comparison to their Ashkenazi counterparts; this contention found a vocal outlet in the early 1970s through the local Black Panthers movement. Additionally, this era witnessed the significant rise of a public voice among Israeli Arabs,[21] the devastating toll and impact of the Yom Kippur War in 1973, and the consequent game-changing elections of 1977, where the Labor Party lost to the right-wing "Likud" party for the first time since the establishment of the state. Under these conditions, the fractured nature of the young and immigrant-based nation was exposed, and the widespread ethnic, cultural, linguistic, and religious tensions, along with their accompanying prejudices and discrimination, rose to the surface.

These changes were experienced as a threatening process of "disintegration," especially by the white liberal left that was losing its political standing, a group that included the majority of the Israeli intellectual milieu, and specifically the scholars and writers this chapter follows. This is, for example, how Ariel Hirschfeld describes the 1970s: "[T]he political turnover [the Likud's ascendency to power] shook up [Israeli] society's profile. That moment made it possible to view Israeli society as an assemblage and not as one thing; an assortment of ethnic groups (*edot*) and communities, settlements and regions, a rabble of human beings who could be very different from each other."[22] In the same spirit, the critic Nissim Calderon states that "since 1977 . . . a new and lasting chapter in the social life of Israelis has opened . . . the melting-pot dream was torn apart and exposed violence, resentment, and deafness. It is a deafness of one cultural code to another."[23] Gershon Shaked remarks that "[s]econd generation Zionists no longer saw themselves as a unified group of adolescents, but as a fragmented group, craving unification."[24] And when the celebrated "New Wave" writer, Amos Oz, engages this issue, he locates the roots of this disintegration in the years following the 1967 Six Days War: "When you build a home, one made to endure for generations, and you build it for tenants of different tastes and lifestyles, you must take it all into consideration . . . even if the existential threat hovering above us would have ended with the war of 1967, we should have come up with an 'architectural decision,' but we avoided that decision. Now the building is about to collapse."[25]

Similarly, Hanna Soker-Schwager, in her analysis of Yaakov Shabtai's canonical novel, *Zikhron devarim* (*Past Continuous*, literally, "memorandum"), which "captured the portrait of Israeli society [of the 1970s] and predicted the turnover of 1977," claims that the author centers his work on a "torn subject" who is haunted by the "three foci of conflict in the Israeli political reality of the 1970s . . . the forefathers' generation versus that of the 'lost' sons . . . , the ethnic struggle between Ashkenazi and Mizrahi Jews, and the Israeli-Palestinian conflict."[26] And Hannan Hever characterizes the entire 1970s as haunted by a fear of a sociopolitical "apocalypse," expressed through a split between "the need to warn against the dangers awaiting the Israeli collective, and the premonition that the right political move will not be made in the 1970s."[27]

In this "apocalyptic" atmosphere of fragmentation, the Israeli government of 1968 also implemented a new policy in the education system called, unsurprisingly given the immediate political context, *integratzya chinukhit* (School Integration); this program, whose title had since been conventionalized into an Israeli idiom, included placing students from privileged and underprivileged ethnic and socioeconomic (solely Jewish) groups together in Israeli middle schools in order to increase educational equality and decrease social divides.[28] Both the concept of and the anxiety over social (dis)integration were thus omnipresent.

It is precisely this conflicted and fractured political climate that Harshav returned to from Yale in the mid-1960s, to find a receptivity to his work's deep investment in "integration" and "disintegration" in their various semantic forms. However, his was an explicitly apolitical engagement with these concepts. As highlighted earlier, Harshav established the TA School within his newly formed Department of General Literary Theory, fostering a scholarly environment that produced notable figures like Ziva Ben-Porat, Itamar Even-Zohar, Perry, and Sternberg (the latter two of whom will receive further discussion shortly). In the context of the TA School, Harshav developed his overarching theory, which he tellingly called "Integrational Semantics" (a term he began utilizing in the 1970s and adopted as the official title in the 1980s).[29] In McHale and Segal's words, Integrational Semantics functioned as the "'big tent' under which nearly the whole range of Tel Aviv poetics research gather[ed]."[30]

Importantly, both this theory and the research it yielded were conceived of by the TA scholars as "scientific" in the sense of the German *Literaturwissenschaf*, whose aim is "a systematic and integrated study of Literature."[31] This scientific aspiration was expressed via the very title of the School's flagship Hebrew journal, *Ha-Sifrut: riv'on le-mada ha-sifrut* (*Literature: A Quarterly Journal for the Science of Literature*). The opening words of the journal's manifesto state: "This journal, first of its sort in Hebrew, brings both good tidings and a challenge. Good tidings since it launches a new phase in the study of literature in Israel. A challenge, since it would demand of us the development of a systematic discipline at the highest scientific level possible today."[32] The scientific urge of the TA School did not preclude it from having a declared national goal. As the manifesto makes clear, the school strove to introduce the national literature into the realm of World Literature, and to radically expand the category of Israeli literature so that it includes voices previously considered as Other, like those of Yiddish and Arabic literature, restoring the multilingual formation of Jewish literature in general and of Israeli literature in particular: "The question closest to our hearts: does Hebrew literature in its multiple forms, and the texts produced by the people of Israel in Yiddish and other languages, receive a literary examination as careful and comprehensive as that accorded in relation to other literatures?"[33] In that sense, the school engendered a much-warranted revolution in the sphere of Hebrew literary criticism. It strove to dislodge literary interpretation from its Zionist teleological confines and opened the door to a more capacious and multilingual conception of Jewish and Israeli, rather than solely Hebrew, literature.

Yet the TA School aimed to achieve its national goal precisely by avoiding any national imprint on its methodology. In order to make sure that Hebrew, Israeli, and Jewish literatures were not read as Zionist "tools of indoctrination" or "vehicles of ideology," to quote Ben-Porat and Harshav, the school organized itself around the image of an "'epistemic' reader, who does not impose his own idiosyncrasies but who constructs only such meanings which can be justified from within a given text."[34] This unlocalized reader does not impose her Zionist, Jewish, or Israeli identity on the text, but is able to look at it through a disinterested, analytic, and systematic lens. One of the implicit goals of the TA School, then, was to produce such a "scientific," nonidiosyncratic reader of Israeli literature via their reading method. To do so they made their appeal to the New Criticism since, like their Brazilian contemporaries, the school's members astutely recognized the pedagogical impulse embedded in the North American creed and method.

Yet the TA School's interaction with the New Critical theory was in no way one of passive reception. The Israeli scholars modeled much of their approach on Wellek, whose *Theory of Literature* served in many ways as the School's "Bible."[35] Like Wellek, the School's members were invested in the intersection between East European literary theory and Anglo-American ideas, and in that spirit, they brought foreign sensibilities to bear on close reading as well. They titled their practice "maximalist reading" and "attached reading" interchangeably (terms whose etymology I will return to), and reconfigured the method in accordance with Roman Ingarden's phenomenology, a theory that stresses the active realization (*Konkretisierung*) of the text by the reader.

More specifically, the TA scholars believed the American New Critics depicted the reading process in too static a light, imagining the reader to perceive the literary text in one stroke as a fixed and unchanged entity. As Menakhem Perry writes: "The Anglo-American 'New Criticism' is based, essentially, on a static vision of the poem," neglecting the "temporality of the reading process."[36] As a response, the TA School relied on Ingarden and zoomed in on the reader's cognition in order to render the dynamic nature of reading. It was this exploration of the New Criticism through a phenomenological lens that allowed the TA School to be ahead of its time and develop a reader-response theory before and in tandem with such reception theories as Wolfgang Iser's (who later become among the School's central interlocutors).[37]

I would like, however, to go beyond the TA School's explicit presentation of its method as an enhancement of the New Critical one. Instead, I would suggest that the Israeli emphasis on the active role of the reader in "realizing" the text was not only a revision of close reading, but also a recognition of the impulse already implicit in the New Critical theory. As I have shown in earlier chapters, the American New Critics themselves were implicitly invested in the reader's active process: they instructed the reader in producing the text as an ostensibly "static" independent entity via her arduous cognitive process of attention as self-depletion. Similarly, the Israeli critics strove to mold an "unlocalized" reader by educating her in utilizing "attention-as-integration," that is, suspending national and parochial identification and investing cognitive efforts in the integration of the text. Even more so, while the TA School overtly celebrated the reader's role in text creation, the Israeli critics, like their North American counterparts, veiled their vision of close reading as a transformative process of shaping the reader's subjectivity. The affinity between the Israeli and North American critics is further underscored by the TA School scholars' propensity to publish extensively in English, as the quotes in the forthcoming pages will evince.

For the TA Scholars, integration is both the basic characteristic of literature and the main end of close reading. In that spirit, Harshav and Ben-Porat assert: "a work of literature is a certain set of language elements, called the text. A text implies a whole network of linkings between elements, to be made by the reader."[38] Here as elsewhere, it remains ambiguous in the TA School's writings whether the "linkings between elements" are an inherent trait of the literary work to be uncovered by the reader or a result of the reader's active mental construction: is integration to be "made" or to be "found" by the reader? The former option would imply, in the spirit of Russian Formalism, that "literariness" is an intrinsic feature of specific texts. Under this assumption, the reader should be instructed in identifying rather than engendering links. The latter option is more radical. It implies that the close reader should be endowed with the ability to produce "linkings" where they might never have been before. It is this possibility that arises from Ben-Porat and Harshav's later definition of literature, which I quote in the epigraph: "[A] text is a body of language full of gaps, ellipses, unlinked units, to be read and understood, i.e., to be filled out and reorganized in the mind of the 'proper' reader."[39] Meaning that works of literature consist of "unlinked units," and it is the reader—whose mind has been made "proper"—who is responsible for reorganizing the text into a "network of linkings." As we shall see, a middle ground between the two options can be found in TA theory, as it was in the American and Brazilian cases as well: the reader is indeed trained in forming rather than recognizing connectivity, but she is also directed toward texts that are assumed to encourage this mental endeavor. That is, the TA School endorsed the creation of, and educated its readers to favor, literary works that fit with what they conceived of as an aesthetics of attention. However, before exploring what formal features the TA critics identified as inducing integration, it is pertinent to first follow their perception of the mind of the "proper" reader.

Maximalist Reading

It is here that we arrive at the intersection of attention, integration, and maximalization. For the TA Scholars, close reading signified a maximal realization of possible intratextual links, a task contingent on the reader's capacity to attend. In "An Outline of Integrational Semantics," Harshav writes: "Though some of the specific techniques as observed here may be conventions of literature, and the close and exhaustive attention to the details may be borrowed from literary interpretation, there is nothing literary about semantic integration itself. We merely attend to a 'maximal reading' of the text. The technique of this very elementary example of semantic integration is valid for any text containing scattered elements for the presentation of one reference or one *fr* [frame of reference]."[40] To differentiate from the examples above, Harshav is explicit here about the generative role of the reader in constructing textual links. Literature appears more integrated than other texts not due to its unique nature (its "literariness"), but as a result of reading "conventions." When engaging with literature, readers are taught to "maximize" the links between "scattered elements," a "technique" that could potentially be applied to any text whatsoever. The basic readerly activity responsible for producing integration, we are told, is "close and exhaustive attention to the details." And this mental task is so familiar and engrained that we should "*merely* attend" in order to perform a "maximal reading."

Still, Harshav sets the bar very high as to what the reader's attention should achieve: "[W]e may speak of an ideal 'maximal' meaning of a text, based on the assumption that all possible interconnected constructions of meaning are necessary and that there is a maximal functionality to all elements and orders of elements in a text."[41] Ideally, then, the "proper" close reader will realize via attention "all possible interconnected constructions of meaning" and prove functional "all elements and orders of elements in a text." Clearly, Harshav and his colleagues are well aware that no "ideal" readers truly exist, but in presenting this horizon of expectation, they pedagogically outlined a model to strive for, if not to achieve.

The understanding of attention as the labor of maximal integration explicates the TA School's choice to translate the English "close reading" into both *kri'a tzmuda* ("attached reading") and *kri'a maximalit* ("maximalist reading"), interchangeably. "Maximum" connotes of course both quantitative and qualitative abundance. And indeed, the School conceptualized close reading at its *best* as the assembling of *the greatest number* of textual elements under one interpretation, or, in the School's terms, the creation of *rav-kishuriyut* (maximal linkage) among elements, described as *tivnut* (patterning). I will mostly employ the term *maximalist reading*, since it translates more easily into English, while *kri'a tzmuda* holds a range of connotations in Hebrew that are difficult to consolidate into one English term.

The term *tzmuda* resonates in Hebrew with two central meanings, an adjectival and a verbal one. The adjective *tzamud* resembles the English *close* but denotes a tighter physical proximity, significantly "closer" than the Hebrew term for *close*, that is, *karov*. *Tzamud* hints at being attached, having an intimacy with the text (perhaps even an overbearing one). Accordingly, the TA School's scholars demanded of their readers a forensic examination of the text, a scrutiny of details considerably more intense than that exhibited in the American or Brazilian cases. The second meaning of *tzamud*, as a participle derived from the three-letter verbal root *tz-m-d*, evokes the verb *le-hatzmid*, which signifies coupling, pairing, bringing elements together, namely, an act of consolidation or unification, and this is where "integration" comes into play. The school's members imagined the process of reading first and foremost as an act of centralization, of "exhausting" or "maximizing" the possible connections between the apparently "peripheral" details of the text and its core, or between the work's larger units, such as subplots, and its overarching structure (as I mention in the introduction, the "exhausted reading" we encountered in the Brazilian context appears here too, albeit in different form).

While Harshav sets the theoretical foundations for the ideal of maximalist unlocalized reading, the majority of his work was not conducted in the field of "interpretation" (as we have seen in Coutinho's case as well) but in those fields he referred to as "poetics" and the study of "literature generally, in its historical existence." In fact, in his work on the meaning of sound patterns in poetry he implicitly casts doubt on his own assumption that in a literary work "all possible interconnected constructions of meaning are necessary and that there is a maximal functionality to all elements and orders of elements in a text."[42] Nonetheless, his conceptualization (rather than practice) of literary interpretation as dependent on attention-as-integration became deeply ingrained in the TA School scholarship, embraced and amplified by his students and colleagues.

This is already evident in the 1971 volume of *Ha-Sifrut*, where the section "Important Figures in Literary Theory" is dedicated to I. A. Richards. The opening article is written by Naomi Tamir, then completing her dissertation on the British thinker under the guidance of Harshav.[43] However, as the article openly declares, its agenda was not to focus on the British scholar in isolation, but to demonstrate his theory's inextricable link to both the North American strand of New Criticism, and to Czech Structuralism. Tamir aspires to bring Richards's theory in line with Wellek's view of the literary object in *Theory of Literature* (1948), and Monroe C. Beardsley's in *Aesthetics: Problems in the Philosophy of Criticism* (1958), as well as to free Richards from the American New Critics' allegations that he defined the work of art "through its creator and consumer while ignoring the work itself."[44] In response, she labors to demonstrate that Richards too saw the literary work as autonomous. Tamir writes,

> From my selective readings in Richards' oeuvre, there arises a theory of literature that views the poem as an autonomous and complex object in which every element must fit in with the rest and serve a purpose, be functional. The various elements maintain reciprocal relations and are interdependent. . . . The power of poetry is in its minute, delicate details and their interconnections, which is why poetry necessitates an intensive, recurring reading practice that involves attention to the smallest of details. . . . Even though his critics did him no justice and distorted several of his ideas, Richards' theory was able to influence the field enormously: it was able to direct attention to the work of literature itself, to its complex language, to what distinguishes it from other phenomena.[45]

Tamir's vocabulary attests to her TA School interest in "integration," which leads her to depict Richards's work in terms quite distinct from the conventional view. Instead of focusing on his pedagogical project, ahistoricity, or psychological orientation—the traditional lens through which his "practical criticism" is described—Tamir understands the import of Richards's vision to lie in his assumption that in the poem, "every element must fit in with the rest and serve a purpose, be functional. The various elements maintain reciprocal relations and are interdependent." This is, of course, almost a verbatim repetition of Harshav's dictum, and it implies that the poem is essentially integrated: in the poem "every element *must* fit," and "the various elements *maintain* reciprocal relations" (emphasis mine). Immediately following, however, when the term "attention" enters her vocabulary, Tamir presents a different view. The poem's elements are not essentially interrelated, since they "necessitate" a reader who will conduct the "intensive" labor of integrating these details.

By and large, Tamir leaves veiled the prescriptive thrust of the TA School's theory, as it is communicated through Richards's theory. She never fully admits to the mental education required for "attention to the smallest of details" to take place. This pedagogical facet comes most forcefully and explicitly to the fore in the influential work of Menakhem Perry, who is considered to be "more than any other member of the Tel Aviv School . . . directly involved in the creation of cultural opinion and fashion in Israel," according to Alan Mintz.[46] Perry writes,

> [T]he drama of reading will push to the focus of attention "unconsidered and unnoticed details, from the rubbish heap, as it were, of our observations" (to borrow Freud's wording in "The Moses of Michelangelo"), and these accumulated details will suddenly "click" into a convergence that will offer us a new key to the main aspects of the story. And the other way around: only in light of a decision to raise the threshold of exhaustion will my reading proposal be considered effective and preferable. Anyone not seeking a maximal reading will have no need for my reading hypothesis.[47]

For Perry, the reader must "decide," and is guided by him to do so, to "raise the threshold of exhaustion" for the various "rubbish heap" details to appear linked together. Perry openly sketches the reciprocity between the reader's active and education-based capacity to "focus attention" and the view of the story as integrated. It might be surprising to encounter Freud of all thinkers in Perry's lexicon, but it is a TA School Freud, one who is focused on fully exhausting the functionality of details occurring in the patient's oral or written text, a debatable view in the context of Freud's psychoanalytic theory more generally.[48]

What Perry, however, leaves vague in his description of "the drama of reading" are the attributes that qualify a text as suitable (or unsuitable) for the labor of attention and the process of integration. He thus guides his reader to assume that "details will suddenly 'click' into a convergence" in any text sufficiently attended to. He repeats this claim more clearly in a much later text, published in 2017, where he argues that all texts are amenable to maximalist reading, independently of their form, content, or even "literariness."

> בשלושים השנים האחרונות . . . הפעלתי, מתוך מגמה חתרנית, קריאה הנחשבת בדרך כלל ל"קריאה כספרות"—בשדות אחרים. . . . כאשר "קריאה מקסימלית" ביומנו האישי של שרת מדהימה אותנו . . . הולך ומתבהר שמה שנחשב כמייחד את הספרות הוא במידה רבה תוצר של אסטרטגיית קריאה, וכי את ייחודן של השירה ושל הסיפורת—דבר שאנו חשים בו אינטואיטיבית, ואינו תוצר של מרכיבים מהותניים—יהיה עלינו לתאר באופן אחר.

> Over the past thirty years . . . I've subversively implemented a reading practice considered "literary" to texts from other fields. . . . When [the result of] a "maximal reading" in Sharett's personal diary shocks us . . . it clarifies that what is considered unique to literature is in many ways a result of a reading strategy, and that we should describe the singularity of poetry and prose-fiction—something we intuitively sense, and is not a result of intrinsic elements—in different terms.[49]

Beyond the specificity of Moshe Sharett's diary to which Perry refers here—another example of an aesthetic analysis of a political text, but outside the scope of my current exploration—in this version of maximalist reading, it is the reader alone who confers unity on the various details of the text via her capacity to attend. In the context of this formulation, maximalist reading is a "strategy" that fits all texts, notwithstanding their genre or formal attributes.

This is the version that McHale and Segal rely on when they claim, "Tel Aviv poetics is *constructivist* in spirit. . . . [C]onstruction implies the process by which readers *make* meaning, in a strong sense of that phrase, by interacting with texts. They do so by linking up textual elements . . . and producing *patterns* of meaning, then integrating these patterns into even more comprehensive patterns of meaning—hence the term *integrational semantics* [emphasis in original]."[50] Though McHale and Segal do not discuss what "attention" means for the TA critics, their vocabulary points to the roles conferred on the reader's mind by the TA School: the reader is taught to construct meaning by "linking up textual elements" and "integrating" them into patterns of increasingly larger scope. However, McHale and Segal seem to accept Perry's declaration that the school did not single out specific texts or formal features as more generative of this mental process (and indeed, throughout his career, Perry interprets "non-literary" texts such as diaries and court rulings to corroborate his claim).[51] But Perry's claim is qualified when examined alongside the literary archive of work taught and researched in the context of the TA School, especially during the 1970s and 1980s.[52]

In contrast with Perry's universalist take, the TA School showed a clear preference for performing maximalist readings on highly stylized modernist texts, like those by William Faulkner or A. B. Yehoshua, while other literary works were deemed unsuitable for maximalist reading, as I will demonstrate in the next chapter dedicated to the fiction of Yehuda Amichai. Unpacking the characteristics that qualified a literary work for the effort of maximalist reading not only offers a better understanding of the TA School's definition of attention, but also provides important insights into the political impulse that drove the School's investment in the process of unlocalizing and mental integration.

Faulkner: A Riddle of Unity

In 1962, following William Faulkner's death, the Israeli literary critic Shimon Grodzensky, himself an American highly versed in the New Critical idiom, mourns on the pages of the Israeli Hebrew-language daily *Davar* the striking absence of Faulkner translations into Hebrew. In the process, he introduces Faulkner's work to the Israeli audience as bound to the history of the New Criticism.

> It appears that not even one of William Faulkner's works has yet been translated into Hebrew, and it's no wonder. It would take a true artist to translate his unique style into Hebrew. . . . Faulkner is the son of his land [the South], which

was shaped by a captivating dramatic and tragic history. The defeat of the South in the Civil War was not only military and political. . . . Yet, for years, this pain did not find its expression either in literature or in historical or political thought. It was a given that the defeat of the South signified the victory of justice, progress, and national unity over stagnation, conservatism, and the cruel abuse of the black slaves. It is only in the twenties and thirties that other voices came rising from the South. In Nashville, Tennessee, there came together the "Fugitives," a group of poets and thinkers, among which were two of the most brilliant minds of American literature: Allan Tate, and John Crowe Ransom. . . . The position occupied by this group can too easily be judged as reactionary and even "fascist" . . . but one thing is beyond doubt: the positive and fruitful influence this "Southern renaissance" had on American literature, which became richer in content, perspectives and dimensions. . . . Faulkner is the most momentous and productive figure to grow out of the South.[53]

In Grodzensky's view, Southern culture, along with the New Critics and Faulkner, stand on the side opposite to "national unity." That is, for him, Faulkner—as the predominant literary voice in the "Southern renaissance" generated by the New Critics—speaks to the acute pain experienced by the disintegrating South in the aftermath of its horrendous history of violence. I believe that it is precisely the link Grodzensky identifies between Faulkner and social disintegration that granted Faulkner his canonical position in Israel of the 1960s–1980s; and indeed, Grodzensky's review marks the beginning of his oeuvre's entry into the cultural center.[54]

During the 1960s and 1970s, one after the other, *The Town*, *The Mansion*, *The Reivers*, *The Unvanquished*, and *Light in August* were translated into Hebrew, followed by "A Rose for Emily," "Barn Burning" (by the School's own Yael Renan), "The Bear," "Was," *Sanctuary*, and *As I Lay Dying*.[55] These translations received immediate positive attention and were embraced not only by the Israeli readership but by many Israeli writers as well; New Wave novelists such as Amos Oz, Binyamin Tammuz, and later on David Grossman acknowledged their reliance on Faulkner as an aesthetic model, a move that was most pronounced in the work of A. B. Yehoshua, as I will discuss below.[56]

The TA School critics played a crucial role in this rapid and impressive process of Faulkner's canonization, attesting once more to their close affinity with the American New Critics. Like their American colleagues, the Israeli scholars were invested in writing scholarship about Faulkner, in translating and publishing his books, in inserting his oeuvre into the academic curricula, and in advancing his reputation via popular newspaper reviews. This investment in Faulkner cannot be detached from what Chana Kronfeld describes as the overall "shift in the dominant extrinsic modernist model from a Russian and French one . . . to the Anglo-American prototypes" in Israel of the 1950s and 1960s.[57] However, the School's focus on Faulkner was specific even within the Anglo-American canon; in fact, their advancement of Faulkner was successful to such an extent that he became the most widely translated and studied High Modernist in Israel for most of the 1970s and 1980s, superseding such canonical writers as James Joyce and Virginia Woolf.

In that vein, Faulkner figured heavily in *Ha-Sifrut*, more than any other Anglo-American writer: *Light in August* was analyzed in three consecutive early issues (1968, 1970, 1971),[58] and "A Rose for Emily," which was briefly discussed by Perry and Sternberg in their seminal article "The King through Ironic Eyes" (1968), later became the primary example in their theory of "Literary Dynamics" (1979).[59] Moreover, the celebrated journal *Siman Kri'a* (*Exclamation Mark*), founded and edited by Perry from 1972 to 1991, opened its first issue with Perry's own translation of "A Rose for Emily" (under the pseudonym Rachamim Nof), and with Yael Renan's translation of "Barn Burning." Renan, who was a central faculty member of the department, also included *The Sound and the Fury* as a key example in her famous article on the Formalists' defamiliarization, published in *Siman Kri'a*'s second issue (1973), which was later followed by Perry's publication of Faulkner's translated *The Wild Palms* with Siman Kri'a Publishing House. In addition, the TA School's members regularly taught Faulkner's novels and short stories in required undergraduate courses in the department, a pedagogical tradition that trickled down to the Israeli high school system of the 1980s and is still traceable today.[60]

Yet, unlike Grodzensky's reading of Faulkner, the TA School depicted the writer in explicitly apolitical terms, detaching him from the Civil War's "dramatic, fascinating, and tragic history." Instead, they highlighted the ostensibly neutral (that is, apolitical) formal features of Faulkner's work and the cognitive work they believed it enhanced. In that spirit, for example,

Perry's (brilliant, I must add) interpretation of "A Rose for Emily," to be discussed below, endeavors to prove that Faulkner's depiction of Emily as associated with the "old traditional South" does not function as a historical and political commentary but rather as a rhetorical device used to induce readerly surprise in the story's end.[61] These apolitical readings of Faulkner were informed by the School's aspiration to mold a form-oriented reader disengaged from her national affiliations.

For Perry and Sternberg in particular, Faulkner's strength lay in improving the reader's capacity to integrate via his work's attention-provoking form; Faulkner's texts, they claimed, present themselves as disjointed, while implicitly informing the reader as to how they could and should be made cohesive. Along these lines, Sternberg reads *Light in August* as a novel that gives the impression of depicting two unrelated plotlines when in fact, he claims, it leads the sufficiently attentive reader to notice their allegorical integration; and Perry interprets "A Rose for Emily" as intentionally providing the reader with two contradictory characterizations of Emily, only to then manipulate the close reader into unifying them into a complex picture of her as a single figure. According to Perry and Sternberg, for this unique Faulknerian structure to be "realized," it must be met with a "proper" reader, whose mind is trained enough in attention-as-integration to accurately follow the text's implicit instructions.[62] As a consequence, they viewed Faulkner's work as a fertile practice ground for the reader's cognitive labor of attention-as-integration, ameliorating her general capacity to skillfully engage with literature more generally. This makes Faulkner's work, of course, especially conducive to maximalist reading, in contrast with Perry's comment above that this "strategy" is contingent solely on the reader, rather than on the literature she reads.

Faulkner's ability to disguise integration as fragmentation, which the TA scholars so deeply appreciated, was never given a name in the school's context. In a later stage, the literary critic Nili Levi suggested that it be called "a dismantled center" structure, when harkening back to the TA School's work on Faulkner in order to characterize the writing of Yehoshua Kenaz (A. B. Yehoshua's contemporary).[63] Though thought-provoking, Levi's term may be partly deceptive since "the center" in Faulkner, as seen by Perry and Sternberg, only *appears* to be "dismantled" in the eyes of untrained readers. Instead, I suggest referring to this formal structure as one of "difficult integration": a structure which, on the level of plot, characters, or theme, is designed to present the reader with a challenge of integration.

Interestingly, Frederick Jameson recently characterized (or, more accurately, admonished) Faulkner's work in terms similar to those of the TA School: "This is the deeper structure of Faulknerian cataphora, to construct a secret and a mystery which is the result only of the author's withholding information, rather than latent in the plot itself. . . . In Faulkner, only the reader is inflicted with this mystery."[64] For Jameson, the Faulknerian model is emblematic of a modern catastrophe, the loss of historical storytelling, or *récit*, but for Perry and Sternberg, there is nothing more productive than inflicting the reader with mystery.[65] It is precisely the challenge to solve the mystery, constructed through form, which forces the reader to come face to face with the problem of integration, and to practice her mental capacity for attention. Interestingly, we have seen that literary mystery and readerly suspension were also central to the discourse provoked by the New Critical conceptualization of attention in the US and Brazilian cases, via Faulkner's *Absalom, Absalom!*, Rosa's "The Mirror," and Lispector's *The Apple*. Mystery and readerly attention, we learn here as well, go hand in hand.

Difficult Integration

To digress for a moment from Faulkner, we can already note that Perry and Sternberg implicitly view good literature as literature that poses integration as a difficult yet conquerable readerly assignment. This is articulated in their famous "The King through Ironic Eyes," the key text of their coauthored theory of "Gap Filling." In this study, Perry and Sternberg turn to the biblical story of David, Uriah, and Bathsheba (2 Samuel 11), which, they claim, encourages the reader to shift uneasily between two "mutually exclusive systems of gap filling," that is, two paradigms that can explain many of the story's details but cancel each other out. The text encourages the reader to develop two hypotheses about David: that the king thinks Uriah knows about his affair with Bathsheba, or that he believes Uriah does not know. Obviously, David cannot hold both beliefs simultaneously, but the text, Perry and Sternberg insist, provides the reader with equally compelling evidence to support each of these contradictory options. The result, the critics claim, is that the reader strains her attention in an effort to assemble and unify the story's details until she finally realizes that even though only one option can be true in terms of the diegetic world, both hypotheses lead to a similar negative judgment of David's personality. If

David decided to kill Uriah even though the latter does not know about the affair, then the king would be a "cruel tyrant"; and if he murdered Uriah because he was terrified of the latter's reaction to the affair, then the king would be a "weak, colorless figure."[66]

This semblance of disintegration enables the Bible to attract the reader's attention and manipulate her into lingering with the subtlety of the text, thus allowing her to sense the moral judgment passed on a God-elected king, which can only be communicated with extreme innuendo. What seemed then like a text that lacks unity, that resists the unification of its various details, is revealed when due attention undergirds the process of integration, to be a tightly organized text, one that shrewdly uses its internal tension to propel the reader to integrate on a higher level: David is seen "through ironic eyes" no matter what he thought about Uriah. In this sense, as McHale and Segal point out, Sternberg and Perry's "The King through Ironic Eyes" emphatically resonates with the New Critical notion of "irony," identifying literature's strength in its ability to balance contradictory elements.[67]

Sternberg's 1970 analysis of *Light in August* locates Faulkner's "difficult integration" not in the work's depiction of character motivation as in the biblical story, but in plot structure. And while the role attention plays in "difficult integration" remains implicit in "The King through Ironic Eyes," it is openly discussed in Sternberg's piece. *Light in August*, Sternberg claims, invites the reader to understand the novel in two seemingly unrelated ways: as the story of Joe Christmas, and as that of Lena Grove. This is not a case of "mutually exclusive systems of gap filling" since these two hypotheses are not contradictory; nevertheless, *Light in August*, like David's story, makes it intentionally difficult for the reader to reconcile the interpretive possibilities she is presented with into a cohesive whole.

Traditionally, Sternberg explains, novelistic integration is viewed as driven by causal relations, by the consistency of the protagonist or narrator's identity, or by a stable "focus of interest."[68] But in *Light in August* the two protagonists, Grove and Christmas, never so much as meet one another, giving the sense that the novel is split into two distinct narratives and thus lacks coherence. In Sternberg words, *Light in August*'s "different centers of gravity, progressing in chiefly distinct narrative paths do not focus [the reader's] attention or interest, but work to scatter it, pulling it in different and even opposite directions."[69] Indeed, Sternberg claims, many have fallen prey to this distracting thrust, leading to the widespread critical assumption, spearheaded by Malcolm Cowley, that the "Faulknerian novel is frequently loose, even fractured, and characterized by a pronounced disunity."[70]

However, a sufficiently skilled reader (such as Sternberg himself) will notice that the novel itself signals the reader as to how to counter this mental "scatter": if one attentively follows the novel's instruction, Sternberg demonstrates, it is revealed that *Light in August*'s two plotlines are closely knit via "allegorical cohesion."[71] That is, these plotlines are metonymically and metaphorically similar, even if utterly detached in the diegetic world. For example, both narratives portray a preoccupation with the "movement of escape" and "the experience of foreignness," a similarity the novel flags to the reader through what Sternberg calls "repetition clusters."[72]

> העיקרון המרכזי בקומפוזיציה של הרומאנים של פוקנר הוא ניפוצם המכ
> של חלק או של מרבית הקישורים דמויי-המציאות בין התבניות דמויי
> המציאות . . . כדי לעודד את הקורא, או אף לאלצו, לחפש דווקא
> הקישורים הספרותיים גרידא (אשכולות הפיגורות והחזרות, האנאלוגי
> ברמותיה השונות של היצירה, התמטיקה), להפנות את תשומת לבו אלי
> ולהעמידו על משמעותם או משמעויותם.

> The central principle of composition in Faulkner's novels is the intentional shattering of part or most of the reality-like linkages between reality-based narrative frames . . . in order to encourage the reader, or even coerce him, to look for purely literary linkages (clusters of figurative language, repetitions, analogy in the different layers of the text, thematic elements), [to] direct the reader's attention to them [the literary links], so as to expose him to their meaning or significance.[73]

It seems that Sternberg views the reader's mind as primarily reactive rather than active; the novel "encourage[s]" and "even coerce[s]" the reader to pay attention to allegorical literary links. But the more Sternberg depicts this process, the clearer it becomes that only a maximalist reader can accurately realize the novel's instructions, such that the agency in reaching unity shifts between the text's guiding powers and the reader's capacity to attend. *Light in August*, he writes, "directs the reader's attention" to seeing its allegorical coherence, and "only a reader who fully realizes the text's potentials [of unity] can grasp the meaning of these [analogical] links and the light they shed on the work."[74]

The second section of Sternberg's article is a spectacular performance of the critic as a maximalist attentive reader, while also demonstrating how these readerly reactions are provoked by Faulkner's artful design of difficult integration. According to Sternberg, in *Light in August*, and even more so in *The Sound and the Fury*, while Faulkner intentionally makes the unification of the narrative difficult, he never abandons his struggling reader.[75] The reader, he claims, approaches the text with "the basic assumption or hypothesis . . . that the work is unified,"[76] and Faulkner, for his part, "organizes the sequence of the plot units in order to direct the reader more precisely to the units he must juxtapose . . . so as to strengthen the reader's assumption [about textual unity] and prevent his discouragement."[77]

Sternberg further underscores his argument through a dialogue with the American critic Frank Baldanza, who similarly identifies clusters of repetitions in *Light in August*, but claims that "their influence on the reader may be largely without his conscious attention."[78] In response, Sternberg argues the a lack of "conscious attention" to analogical unity is likely to occur in traditional novels, like those of Jane Austen for example, which are "tightly integrated through reality-like linkages," and therefore not impressing the analogical unity on the reader's mind (though, he adds, a reader qualified in "a full, rich reading" would notice these as well).[79] But it is much harder to not consciously attend to analogical unity in *Light in August*, since no other integrational paradigms are to be found: "The writer *forces* the reader . . . to make purely literary linkages" (emphasis mine).[80] In that sense, *Light in August* serves as a pedagogical tool: it "develops in the reader a specific awareness of analogical linkages between elements," making her more aware of the process of unification and more skilled in its execution. To wit, *Light in August* forces the reader to practice her skills of attention as unification, and it takes a skilled reader to "follow the text's instruction."[81] After all, as the beginning of his article makes clear, Sternberg is able to identify in *Light in August* the analogical unity that escaped so many proficient critics, Cowley included, thanks to his own skills of maximalist reading.

In a similar vein, Perry's 1974 reading of "A Rose for Emily," published in *Siman Kri'a*, focuses on the apparent incoherence of Faulkner's work, a feature expressed in this short story, he contends, via Emily's personality. And Perry too positions himself early on in the article in opposition to the tradition of "inattentive" readings common in response to Faulkner's "best short story."[82]

> During these years [the 1930s], "A Rose for Emily" served as an example of Faulkner's weakness as a writer. . . . Critics saw it as no more than a horror story that does not point to any abstract meaning "beyond it." . . . Lionel Trilling wrote that "'A Rose for Emily' is . . . a trivial story in its horror, since it signifies nothing." . . . The psychopathological view of Emily . . . [also] does not exhaust what the story constructs, and does not stand alone at the center of the reader's attention. . . . The story orchestrates a clever system of techniques structured to provoke readers to build around Emily a set of "high" meanings, understanding her actions as principled, ideological, and value-laden, and see her as a monumental figure (even if controversial). . . . While construing her psychopathological facet, the story also makes sure to shift it away from the reader's center of *attention* [emphasis in original]. . . . When I speak of the rhetoric of "A Rose for Emily," and of literature more generally, I mean the ways in which the story controls the reader's response, making him realize specific potentialities rather than others.[83]

The same tension we have seen in Harshav and Sternberg appears in Perry's depiction of the reader's attention as well. On the one hand, "A Rose for Emily" is treated as an agent capable of controlling the reader's attention, implying that the reader's response relies not on how experienced a reader she is, but on the story's deliberate formal manipulations ("the story orchestrates a clever system of techniques structured to provoke readers"). In that spirit, Perry cites scholars of cognitive psychology in order to justify the story's ordering of elements: due to the cognitive "Primacy Effect," for example, Faulkner's readers will be more impacted by Emily's dramatic funeral than by her unkempt home. On the other hand, as evinced by the opening of Perry's article, most critics' attention did not accurately respond to the story's "clever system of techniques." As a result, these critics were unable to grasp the story's crafted cohesion, and consequently, its overall meaning.

Only a specific reader, then, practiced in integration, can attune her attention correctly, and Perry will guide her in doing so. This idea falls in line with Perry's later claim, quoted above, that "what is considered unique to literature is in many ways a result of a reading strategy," shifting the agency from the text to the reader. One of Perry's footnotes reconciles these two thrusts: "[W]hen I refer to the *reader's* response, I do not mean the subjective response of one reader or another, but the responses that can be deduced from the *work itself* [emphases in original]."[84] It is the encounter, then, between a "clever" work that both challenges and guides the reader's attention and a reader practiced in the "reading strategy" of integration that allows the work's cohesion to appear. And, as we have seen, for the TA School critics there is no work that better promotes such a reader-text exchange than Faulkner's.

Early Marriage and *Late Divorce*: Faulkner and Yehoshua

Sternberg and Perry's readings of Faulkner systematically steer away from the "tragic history" at the heart of Faulkner's work, as mentioned above. Their reading of his oeuvre as offering a fertile ground for practicing attention-as-integration—a reading conducted under the umbrella of Harshav's "Integrational Semantics"—can therefore seem purely formalist, that is, apolitical and ahistorical. After all, their interpretations imply that if one reads Faulkner properly, maximizing the integration of the work's scattered elements, one will become a more attentive reader of literature more generally, no political strings attached.

However, this understanding of Harshav, Perry, and Sternberg is partial at best. In truth, the School's choice to follow the American New Critics in centering on Faulkner—whose work the Israeli critics depicted as enhancing readerly integration—had everything to do with the American author's depiction of a culture in a state of disintegration. This social condition resonated strongly with the racial, ethnic, and religious rifts and anxieties that were exposed during the 1970s in the very fabric of Israeli society, anxieties that found an implicit expression in the TA School's "scientific" theory. This political facet of maximalist reading reveals itself when the school's analyses of *Light in August* and "A Rose for Emily" are translated into the Israeli rewritings of Faulkner and their local critical reception.

At the center of Faulkner's literary adaptation into Hebrew stands the work of A. B. Yehoshua, who began publishing short stories in 1962 and transitioned to novelistic form in the late 1970s with *Ha-me'ahev* (*The Lover*, 1977) and *Gerushim me'ucharim* (*Late Divorce*, 1982).[85] This genre transition, explained by critics as a shift from Kafkaesque allegories to a stream of consciousness technique, was precipitated, as Yehoshua himself repeatedly declared, by his reading of Faulkner, both in the original and in translation. And Yehoshua's fascination with the American author cannot be understood without the mediation of the TA School. Not only did Yehoshua feed off their public endorsement of Faulkner, but he was also personally engaged with the TA School's projects: he regularly published reviews and essays in *Siman Kri'a*, and his own work has been edited from the early seventies onward by Perry's publishing house.[86]

When this close affiliation is taken into consideration, it turns out that Yehoshua not only espoused the TA School's understanding of Faulkner as cultivating a maximalist attentive reader, but also shrewdly identified this pedagogical capacity as holding national significance. As a consequence, Yehoshua makes it clear that he mobilizes Faulkner's training of the reader in integrating the ostensibly fragmented text, not only in order to enhance her capacities as a reader of literature, but also for the sake of instructing her in cognitively uniting the fractured Israeli body politic.

This political conception of "difficult integration" plays itself out most emphatically in Yehoshua's Faulknerian novels, where the tension between unity and disunity is presented to the reader both through an ostensibly fragmented narrative structure organized around internal monologues, and via the diegetic world that depicts a society on the verge of, yet never fully in, disintegration. In this manner, Yehoshua's work vacillates and functions as a point of conjunction between the two meanings of "integration" that circulate in Israeli culture during the 1970s: on the one hand, the desire to cultivate a cognitively integrating reader and a body of Israeli literature that would aesthetically provoke this mental labor; and on the other hand, the anxiety of social disintegration that permeates the public discourse. The easy intermingling of the two in Yehoshua's work attests to the political shadow that haunts the seemingly purely "scientific" research of the TA School.

This is not to say that Yehoshua's work did not itself engage in political repression at this point in time. As Dror Mishani recently demonstrated, Yehoshua of the 1970s and early '80s steered away from the question of *Mizrahi* exclusion, which bore upon him personally, and presented his Israeli-Arab characters in highly ambivalent light, in line with the values of the Israeli liberal left of his time.[87] Yehoshua, after all (very much like the abovementioned Zach), aligned himself via Faulkner with masculine, white, and Western modernism, thus breaking away from anything Levantine. However, unlike the TA School critics who promoted his work, Yehoshua explicitly engaged with the political gaps opening up around him.

There is nothing new in claiming that Yehoshua's *The Lover* and *A Late Divorce* depict the fragmentation of Israeli society in the 1970s. In fact, these novels are regularly read as national allegories, very much in the vein of the interpretive tradition the TA School was fervently trying to battle. *A Late Divorce* follows the story of Yehuda Kaminka's return to Israel from the US. Yehuda returns to seek a divorce from his wife, Naomi, who is hospitalized in a mental ward, only to ultimately be murdered by his wife's friend. This narrative, which slowly unfolds through a series of the family members' internal monologues, is conventionally taken to allegorically portray the disintegrating Israeli social fabric.

Shmuel Huppert's review, "The Centre Cannot Hold," is paradigmatic in this regard, claiming that the novel's "disintegration reaches beyond the personal to the collective. Naomi, who, losing her sanity, tries to murder her husband, embodies the violence of her family, and of Israeli society, whose tribal-traditional-fatherly center no longer holds it together. . . . The Kaminka family, and schizophrenic Naomi, are a symbol of the conflicts, violence and self-destruction that characterize Israeli existence."[88] Similarly, Yosef Oren argues, "What the plot and story [of *A Late Divorce*] are missing can be fully complemented if we recall that the novel's events parallel those of the state," and Haim Chertok states, "In both *A Late Divorce* and *The Lover* [Yehoshua] seems to use [the family] as a figure, almost a trope for the conflict and disintegration of Israel as a whole."[89] What these critics, however, do not take into account is the affinity between Yehoshua's obsession with social disintegration and the TA School's ideal of maximalist reading. They also rarely discuss the link Yehoshua might have found between Faulkner's own investment in the American social dismantling and his own, and the ways in which Yehoshua formally thematized the fluctuation between unity and disunity in both novels.[90]

The truth is that Yehoshua is attracted to Faulkner's novels precisely because they deal with (dis)integration both formally and thematically. He makes that clear when explaining in retrospect—tellingly, to his American interviewer, Joseph Cohen—that his interest in Faulkner's narratological "method of multiple voices" was fueled by a political preoccupation.

> [Faulkner's] monologue provided a form to mirror . . . the gradual crumbling of the center of national values and cultural experience, a process that only intensified in the eighties. . . . Because the ideological center of Israel was dismantling

itself, we [the writers of the 1970s] felt we didn't have the possibility of really representing the Israeli society through an authoritative, controlling, single voice. . . . We felt that if you really want to represent Israeli reality in the 1970s—and this was our starting point—you have to bring it to the reader through different voices. There was no authority anymore as there had been in the 1950s and 1960s. . . . In the 1970s, when I started to write my novels, I felt incapable of taking the controlling position and responsibility of an omniscient narrator who can really control the novel and speak on behalf of one hero.[91]

Like Sternberg and Perry, Yehoshua identifies Faulkner's work as structured around difficult integration: it presents the reader with a fictional reality refracted "through different voices." But while the TA Scholars depict *Light in August*'s unrelated plotlines or the contradictory character depiction in "A Rose for Emily" in a manner that highlights the cognitive challenge these puzzles impose on the reader, Yehoshua depicts the Faulknerian apparent fragmentation in narratological terms that right off the bat hold political implications.

Yehoshua focuses on Faulkner's technique of internal dialogue and views the mental labor this perspectivism demands of the reader as mirroring a social and political crisis. The reader is forced by Yehoshua to slowly and patiently put together the various details and motivations that arise from each internal monologue in order to get a picture of the novels' overall occurrences, following Perry's command to "push to the focus of attention unconsidered and unnoticed details." As Joseph Cohen puts it, "the puzzling over required of the reader by *A Late Divorce* is similar to the suspense that develops in a detective novel" (recall how in chapter 4 we have seen a similar genre, the crime novel, playing a role in Lispector's own manipulation of attention).[92] Yet this process, per Yehoshua, is political, providing the reader with a sense of "the gradual crumbling of the center of national values and cultural experience." That is, Yehoshua's withdrawal from an "omniscient narrator" is designed to reflect and impart to the reader the "dismantling" characteristic of the "Israeli reality in the 1970s."

Where Yehoshua remains loyal to the TA School is in his assumption that, while Faulkner's ostensible fragmentations provide an "experience" of disintegration, they in fact reveal an essential structural integration. He conveys this belief when he states the following:

> [The] center has now collapsed and we cannot act as if it still exists. In the coming years we will have to find our way in an Israel that no longer has a center. . . . There is a need to return to something stable but today expectations are diminished. The center has broken down and it makes it impossible to present a comprehensibly ordered picture of Israeli society. . . . He [Faulkner] exemplifies the best of world writers. It is unfortunate that in the modern world, there are more "theme-writers" than "world-writers." But it is no longer possible to close off a universe the way Faulkner did. . . . I am a "theme" writer. I would be happy if I had a world, but I don't. The problem today is to find a "theme" capable of filling the void of a "world" that is no longer there. . . . Again, I return to Faulkner. The actions in his novels can occur within a three-mile radius, there are all those family connections, and other kinds of connections, such as those between *Absalom, Absalom!* and *The Sound and the Fury*.[93]

Yehoshua's "world" diverges from the meaning denoted by "world literature" in current scholarly discourse. For Yehoshua, "world writers" are those capable of unifying in their literary work a sphere of life, a social group, notwithstanding its internal incoherence. In contrast, he places his own oeuvre under the category of "theme" literature, which leans on a central topic to fill "the void of a 'world' that is no longer there."

However, this binary does not hold. On the one hand, Yehoshua gives the impression that his and Faulkner's diegetic universes are altogether different. In Yehoshua's fictional world, the "center has now collapsed" and "a 'world' . . . is no longer there," while Faulkner is able to "close off a universe" brimming with "connections" of various kinds. Yet, despite these avowed differences, Yehoshua ultimately chooses Faulkner's "world" literature as his model, subsequently hinting at his underlying desire, or even hope, to be able to "present a comprehensibly ordered picture of Israeli society" against all odds. That is, by emulating Faulkner's "world" literature on the level of point of view and plot structure, Yehoshua is trying to "close off" via aesthetic means an Israeli universe that is socially breaking apart, and thus to forge a reader who will be able to (re)integrate her dismantling sociopolitical world. All told, and as I quote in the epigraph as well, Yehoshua writes that "there is a need to return to something stable," and that he "would be happy if [he] had a world."

The word *world*, then, functions for Yehoshua on both an aesthetic and political level: it is the political Israeli reality that pushed him to adopt a new aesthetic form, and via this form he aspires to shape a reader who will be able to cognitively integrate "an Israel that no longer has a center." This is also what Yehoshua understands Faulkner to have achieved: the American writer succeeded, through his internal monologues, to depict an integral picture of the American South, without neglecting to convey its disintegration. This view is very much in line with Eric Sundquist's famous argument, presented in his book aptly titled *A House Divided*, about Faulkner's "sequester[ed] modes of consciousness," which grant his novels a "disintegrated yet tenuously coherent form," representing an acute political schism within American society—"the sectional conflict over slavery that grew into the Civil War."[94] According to Sundquist, as explained by John F. Desmond, Faulkner's formal structure "is largely determined by Faulkner's struggle with the race question, so that narrative unity/disunity stems directly from his strategies of confronting this theme."[95] Yehoshua, who similarly identifies and carefully (though only partially, to recall Mishani) depicts deep racial, national, religious, and class gulfs in Israeli society, turns to Faulkner's "sequester[ed] modes of consciousness" because they produce a "disintegrated yet tenuously coherent form," as the TA School claimed about Faulkner's work more generally, which responds to a nationally "divided" house.

Yehoshua locates Faulkner's ability to balance unity and disunity not only in the technique of internal dialogue, but also in Faulkner's choice to focus on the social structure of the family specifically. To emphasize the schisms in Israeli society, Yehoshua recounts that "in Israel all you have to do is take a walk Friday afternoon in Jerusalem and pick seven or ten people in the street and ask each of them, what is your political program, what is your cultural program: you would find huge gaps, unbelievable distances between people who had been walking on the same pavement just an hour before."[96] This social formation could have easily functioned as the model for Yehoshua's long-1970s novels, following Israelis who randomly share the same geonational space. But Yehoshua follows in Faulkner's footsteps and centers each of his novels on one family alone since he believes it is this character system that allowed the American writer to form a "closed off universe," even if destabilized.

According to Yehoshua, "all those family connections" portrayed in *The Sound and the Fury* and *Absalom, Absalom!* permitted Faulkner to depict a universe "within a three-mile radius" and to forge a continuity between the different Yoknapatawpha novels. And indeed, as in Faulkner's novels, the families at the core of *The Lover* and *Late Divorce* symbolize in their particularity the decay of the larger social structure, and openly speak to questions of race and social class. But while Faulkner's families usually represent one social class within the overall structure of the South, Yehoshua's families are more diverse, consisting of different social types, to represent Israeli society more generally.[97]

In *The Lover*, for instance, Dafi, the daughter of Adam, the protagonist, is the representative of the young Israeli generation; she has an affair with Na'im, one of the first Israeli Arabs to appear in mainstream Israeli literature with his own distinct voice (even if a threatening one, potentially shattering the family/national structure),[98] and is the granddaughter of Veducha, who having been born in the year that stands for the birth of the "Zionist dream" (1881), lends herself to be read as the embodiment of Zionism more generally.[99] Similarly, in *A Late Divorce*, Dina, Yehuda's daughter-in-law, is marked by her religiosity against the backdrop of the overt secularism of the Kaminka family, and Refa'el Calderon, Yehuda's son's lover, stands out as a Mizrahi Jew against the family's self-proclaimed Ashkenazi-European superiority.[100]

These different social types constantly enter into violent conflict with each other, but Yehoshua's families never disintegrate altogether, testifying once again to the writer's vacillation between the wish to communicate disintegration and the desire to resist it. In fact, as Nehama Aschkenasy argues, the fate of Yehoshua's families as presented at the end of his novels is far more optimistic than Faulkner's. In *A Late Divorce*, for example, "[T]he family does survive the trauma of the divorce, the sudden death of the father, and the hysterical times that the narrative has recorded. . . . It seems that if in Faulkner's fictional South the lost time is unredeemable and irretrievable, Yehoshua's novel does offer a modicum of hope for the future, albeit imbued with anxiety, sadness, and regret."[101]

Yehoshua further communicates his entrapment between and investment in the imperative to integrate, informed by the TA School, and the anxiety of utter fragmentation, via the two epigraphs opening the second and ninth chapter of *A Late Divorce*. The first, by Yeats, gives voice to the dismantling force that permeates the novel's narration and plot: "Things fall apart; the center cannot hold; / Mere anarchy is loosed upon the world."[102] By contrast, the final quote by Eugenio Montale expresses the uncanny sense that under apparent fragmentation there lies cohesion: "I still am haunted by the knowledge that, / whether separate or apart, we are one thing."[103] The readerly work Yehoshua finds necessary for navigating these two thrusts is hinted at in the first epigraph in the novel, taken from Quentin's monologue in *The Sound and the Fury*: "Benjy knew it when Damuddy died. He cried. *He smell hit. He smell hit* [emphasis in original]." As discussed in chapter 2, Benjy is known for his capacity to compensate via his senses for the difficulty in unifying the various pieces of information he receives from his environment: he "smells" Damuddy's death, and "hears" Caddy's absence. Yehoshua's novel similarly demands of the reader an extraneous integrating effort, yet she is encouraged to face that challenge not through her senses but through her cognition, in line with the ideal of the attentive maximalist reader.

As in the case of Faulkner's *Absalom, Absalom!*, Yehoshua places his ideal reader within the diegetic world of *A Late Divorce*, providing us with a glimpse into his conceptualization of the reading process. His model, it turns out, fits neatly with the TA School's idea of the close reader as straining her attention in order to consolidate apparently marginal details into a coherent narrative. In Yehoshua's eighth chapter titled "*Yom shabbat?*" ("Saturday?"), the only one framed as a question or riddle, the readers encounter the world as filtered through the consciousness of Yael, Yehuda's daughter. She presents herself as the one responsible for "zealously assembling" the "tiniest facts" of the event leading to Yehuda's death, what she calls "the story."[104] However, Yael is horrified to discover that she is unable to recall the occurrences of Saturday, the day preceding the murder. The chapter diligently follows her obsessive attempts to "retrieve" that day in order to "centralize," bring "clarity," and "join" together the narrative's parts, notwithstanding her husband's attempts to convince her that this process is of no importance: "Now you're really going off the deep end. Don't tell me you're still looking for that day."[105] The chapter reads,

> Saturday? Saturday? Suddenly, halfway through the story, I'm stuck and can't go on . . . somehow I lost it—I, who tended each one of those days like a priest at the altar; who stubbornly salvaged them, forever frozen in clarity, from the passage of time; who zealously assembled [literally, centralized] and preserved their story person by person and day by day down to its last detail, color, smell, fragment of conversation, article of clothing, shift of mood and of weather . . . collecting snatches of memory like the last feathers from a torn quilt . . . yet as soon as I reached Saturday I drew a blank, I blacked out completely,

> the music stopped . . . my mind wouldn't work . . . I'm trying to think logically about it. . . . I suppose I cooked for the Seder . . . if only I remembered what I made, I could reconstruct the whole day.[106]

When Kedmi, Yael's husband, humorously declares during the chapter that he intends to write a book, she quickly responds: "I will be your first reader."[107] Indeed, Yael is an ideal and maximalist reader in the TA School's sense. She labors to "collect" and "assemble" into a coherent narrative the smallest of the details in the "story"—"color, smell, fragment of conversation, article of clothing"—salvaging them "from the [story's] rubbish heap" in Perry's words.

Yael is invested in a labor of unification, of "reconstructing" the texture of a "torn quilt," or of harmonizing the "music" that momentarily "stopped." To do so, Yael does not turn to her senses as Benjy does but relies on the "work" of her "mind"—"think logically about it," she commends herself; in other words, she must attend. This mental endeavor is finally accomplished when Yael's cognition works doubly, straining to decipher two riddles simultaneously: both Saturday's occurrences, and the mysterious reason that propels Kedmi to hide the details of his phone call conversation with her father's young lover, Connie.

> He's hiding something. That smile of his. What's come over him? There's something between them. There has to be. He'd never been so calm otherwise. What is he up to? Can it be . . . is she really capable of turning off and leaving us the . . . but *what face superimposes itself* [emphasis in original]? I can hear the ring of the telephone in the distance . . . how strongly the memory of it flickers on . . . of course! How did I ever forget it? Was it that morning? A call from the prison. That man—that prisoner—that murderer of his—had escaped. . . . Now I remember. Saturday. I have it![108]

While Yael tries to estimate the probability that Connie has left them with her toddler, that is, with Yael's half-brother ("is she really capable of turning off and leaving us the . . ."), she also keeps in mind the chapter's imposing question ("Saturday?"). These two puzzles burden Yael's cognition, and we can sense her mental effort through the sudden change in punctuation and the frequent turn to ellipses and italics ("Can it be . . . is she really capable of turning off and leaving us the . . . but *what face superimposes itself?*). The protagonist's intense concentration finally generates a third image—a sudden cognitive insight—that "superimposes itself" on the two queries: On Saturday, Yehuda, Yael, and Kedmi were busy tracing Kedmi's client, "that prisoner—that murderer of his," who had escaped from prison to the dismay of his lawyer.

Yael thinks of this information in terms of possession, "I have it!" which attests to the sense of victory and relief Yehoshua imagines one to experience with the process of difficult integration. Later on, Yael will conclude: "[A]t least it [Saturday] joined all the others, stubbornly salvaged from the passage of time, forever frozen in clarity, beamed with them on that one bright screen down to the last detail."[109] Like Sternberg and Perry in their reading of Faulkner, the protagonist is able to reconstruct the cohesiveness of an apparently fragmented story with her mind, to force a deviant part to "join all the others."

The figure of the maximalist reader appears once again, and much more bluntly, in *A Late Divorce*'s tenth chapter. This chapter, titled *Ha-layla ha-acharon* ("The Final Night"), was written with the rest of the novel but excluded from publication until 2010, due to what Yehoshua and Perry describe as a mutual writer-editor conclusion that the chapter was not "in unity" with the rest of the novel. "The Final Night" delineates the internal monologue of the family's dog, Horace, who is a "theoretician of literature" named after none other than the great Roman poet; this chapter is much more humorous, sarcastic, and fantastic than the previous—it even rhymes—which led to Yehoshua's hesitations about its publication: "I did not include this final chapter in the novel since I was afraid that its surreal nature would ruin the credibility of the novel as a whole."[110] Perry, on his end, confessed "to have participated, along with other friends, in the writer's equivocations," and, along with Yehoshua, to have believed that the "Final Night" did not "advance the plot of *A Late Divorce*."

Later, the two change their minds, but the terms in which Perry explains his 2010 counterdecision are still in sync with the School's ideal of integration.[111] For Perry, "The Final Night" should now be printed since, he revealed, it in fact "provides a new 'code' for understanding the novel . . . as a final chapter [it] acts like a magnet that reshuffles the novel as a system by attracting various details from the novel as a whole."[112] This statement echoes Perry's more general notion of maximalist reading as a process of pushing one's "focus of attention" until a sudden "click" or "convergence" offers the reader "a new key to the main aspects of the story."[113] The debate around the chapter's publications, then, takes place in terms of its integration into the novel's larger system, and in that manner, acts out the chapter's plot, which has Horace meta-analyze the reader's work of interpretation generally and integration specifically.

As Perry astutely notes, "'The Final Night' is a parody of several writers and scholars (including me)." The chapter rethinks, through sarcasm, the efficiency of the theory advanced and developed by Perry and the TA School. The chapter also, as Perry asserts, functions as a "self-parody": "A. B. Yehoshua is smacking A. B. Yehoshua through the dog," making fun of the writer's obsession with the "Faulknerian monologue."[114] Indeed, all along the chapter, Horace engages in dialogue with what seems like the reader or the writer, both holding to a TA School standard of "click"-inducing literature: "What would you like me to be? A dog or a symbol of a dog? . . . First person? Second person? Maybe third? . . . I would leave with one wolf-like howl . . . but who would provide you with the code?"[115] That this "code" refers to the TA School's idea of solving the riddle of the text as a unity is made self-evident later on, when Horace mockingly says: "Should I turn the reader into a dog? With great pleasure. Gap filling? Be my guest. The reader as the constructer of meaning, I've heard of that as well."[116] This process, so clearly reminiscent of Perry and Sternberg's Theory of GapFilling, is ridiculed by Horace, who insists that no stable order can ever be found, neither in the world nor in texts: "Imitation of what? Of stream of consciousness? Don't make me laugh. Installing a microphone in the brain or soul, you will get nothing but a whirlpool. Not gaps but abysses. Splashes of thought smeared all over quivering objects, voices opened up into sounds, shards of information hiding in memories, emotions snuggling unordered, no organization."[117]

Yehoshua's conclusion on the level of the literary text—"no organization" can be found by a "reader as the constructer of meaning"—has bleak implications if we take into consideration Yehoshua's hope to use Faulkner's novelistic form in order to provide the reader with tools to mentally overcome or solve Israeli social disintegration. While Yael's cognitive efforts are a success story ("I have it!"), Horace suggests a much grimmer point of view: "not gaps, but abysses" are to be found in the specifically Israeli "anarchy . . . loosed upon the world." When Perry and Yehoshua, then, decide that the final chapter should be excluded since it might "ruin the credibility of the novel as a whole," they might have had a point; "The Final Night" is indeed incompatible to a certain degree with the novel's overall project of demonstrating the feasibility of difficult integration and maximalist reading on both an aesthetic and political level.[118]

∼

I would like to conclude with a personal anecdote that I believe illustrates well the complex yet intimate relationship the TA School maintained with the American New Criticism. During my freshman year at the department of Poetics and Comparative Literature founded by Harshav, we were given a memorably challenging task in the obligatory survey course, "Literary Theory." At the time, Menakhem Perry was the department's chair, and in this specific assignment, we were handed an article with the writer's name removed (very much in the spirit of I. A. Richards), and were asked to decipher, via the article's methodology and theme, the school of thought it was borrowing from.

The article was titled "The Inverted Poem: On a Principle of Semantic Composition in Bialik's Poems," and though it was printed in Hebrew, we were uninformed as to whether this was a translation or the article's original language. The essay's author, we later revealed, was Perry himself. But this was the early 2000s and we were not yet accustomed to the internet as a source of knowledge. Instead, we faced what proved to be a difficult riddle through endless conversations, struggling together to pin the article down: was it in dialogue with Structuralism? Reader-Response theory? Formalism? Finally, after much debate, my study group settled on the New Criticism, and we were quite sure we had it right. In the following section, however, our instructor's expression suggested otherwise: "I'm deeply disappointed to say that the class unanimously failed," she said. "With no exceptions, you all chose the New Criticism, but the article clearly corresponds to the Tel Aviv School of Poetics and Semiotics." She was right, of course; but she was simultaneously wrong. The class's mistake gave voice to a genuine resemblance and an international-theoretical dialogue whose importance has been, for the most part, discounted, as exemplified by my instructor's response.

The TA School critics have consistently refrained from admitting to their close affinity with the New Criticism, in contrast with their open embrace of structuralism, formalism, and phenomenology. This might account for the scarce scholarship on, or even mention of, the relationship between these two key theoretical schools. Undoubtedly, as discussed earlier, differences exist between these schools' premises and praxes. However, I would suggest that it is rather the similarities between them that have motivated this disavowal of kinship. At the heart of the TA School's project, as well the New Critical one, there lies an unspoken pedagogical thrust, a will motivated by sociopolitical and historically grounded anxieties to form a new subject through close reading. But in contrast with the TA School's self-proclaimed apolitical, "scientific" motivation, the ideological one found its way into maximalist reading over and above these critics' explicit intentions through, I would suggest, their highly astute understanding of the North American praxis as a technique of the self.

The New Critical pedagogical legacy is evident in the TA School's lexicon, its image of the reader, its aesthetic criteria, and its interpretations of Faulkner's work that informed Yehoshua's oeuvre. These convey together a will to design an Israeli subject who would be able to cognitively construct a unified whole out of the conflict-ridden Israeli reality of the long 1970s. That is, the urge to integrate, which governs Harshav's capacious Integrational Semantics and is then amplified in Sternberg's and Perry's investigations of Faulkner, expresses a social anxiety that whispers through the school's reading method. "The center has now collapsed and we cannot act as if it still exists. In the coming years we will have to find our way in an Israel that no longer has a center," said Yehoshua.[119]

And so, if social disintegration was understood as a given reality, unchangeable through political action, then the only way to "find our way in an Israel that no longer has a center" had to be cognitive, mobilized by the capacity to construct unity where it seemed to be, or indeed was, missing. In the following chapter we will see how the TA School's imperative of attention-as-integration influenced the reception of another canonical Israeli writer of the time, Yehuda Amichai. In his prose-fiction, and in contrast with Yehoshua, Amichai constructed a style that clearly privileged distraction and *un*integration. But his too, we shall see, was not only a stylistic choice. His push against integration was highly political, invested no less in finding a way to navigate "an Israel that no longer has a center."

Chapter Six

Maximalist Reading Gone Wild

Yehuda Amichai and Creative Unintegration

> Politically speaking, Amichai was much more radical than his delightful decorations, witty jokes, and sarcastic puns might lead us to believe. Unconstrained cynicism and nihilism, even under the semblance of docility, are never far from the surface.
>
> —Benjamin Harshav

> One must be a real literary critic in order to not derive any pleasure from Yehuda Amichai's short story collection, *In This Terrible Wind*.
>
> —Natan Zach

In 1978, Yehuda Amichai, by then a prominent figure within Israeli culture, was asked in an interview with Dan Omer to discuss the relationship between his poetry and prose fiction.[1] Seemingly neutral, this question was in fact highly charged, touching on the mixed reception of his short story collection (*Ba-ru'ach ha-nora'a ha-zot* [*In This Terrible Wind*], 1961) and two novels (*Lo me-akhshav, lo mi-kan* [*Not of This Time, Not of This Place*], 1963; and *Mi yitneni malon* [*Would I had a Lodging Place*], 1971), which stood in stark contrast to the admiration his early poetry elicited. "I would say that prose fiction is the soil on which my poetry grows," Amichai answered, suggesting a close and intrinsic affinity between the two.[2] Indeed, when one reads Amichai's *Shirim 1948–1962* (*Poems 1948–1962*) alongside the contemporaneous *In This Terrible Wind*, similarities abound.

This is especially true for Amichai's signature stylistic trait, metaphorical language.³ The figures, symbols, and unexpected analogies that appear in his poems in a condensed, compact fashion stretch out and spread sideways in his short-story collection; more specifically, the figurative language in his narratives—which I will term "concatenated" metaphors—sprawl horizontally from tenor to vehicle, or from one tenor/vehicle to another in a dreamlike manner that involves a constant shift in the grounds of figurative mapping.

The unique dialogue between Amichai's verse and narrative is evident, for example, when we read side by side the poem "Avi" ("My Father") from *Poems 1948–1962* and the short story "Mitot avi" ("The Times My Father Died") from *In This Terrible Wind*. The first, a six-line poem, opens with a startling image: the speaker's father (or his memory) is wrapped in white paper like two "slices of bread" in a sandwich.

זֵכֶר אָבִי עָטוּף בִּנְיַר לָבָן
כִּפְרוּסוֹת לְיוֹם עֲבוֹדָה.

כְּקוֹסֵם, הַמּוֹצִיא מִכּוֹבָעוֹ אַרְנָבוֹת וּמִגְדָּלִים,
הוֹצִיא מִתּוֹךְ גּוּפוֹ הַקָּטָן—אַהֲבָה.

נַהֲרוֹת יָדָיו
נִשְׁפְּכוּ לְתוֹךְ מַעֲשָׂיו הַטּוֹבִים.

> The memory of my father is wrapped in white paper
> like slices of bread for the workday.
>
> Like a magician pulling out rabbits and towers from his hat,
> he pulled out from his little body—love.
>
> The rivers of his hands
> poured into his good deeds.⁴

Without delving into a full analysis of this dense poem, I would like to linger on its opening figure. Within the context of Jewish culture—and in that of Amichai's poetry which consistently (and iconoclastically) engages with traditional Jewish sources—the white "wrappings" of the father carry two impactful connotations. The father would have been covered in white in the synagogue, wearing the traditional white prayer shawl, *tallit*, during the morning prayers (*Shacharit*) or on Yom Kippur. And the evocation of "good deeds" in the final stanza (*ma'asim tovim*), brings to mind Yom Kippur specifically, a time of atonement for one's "meritorious deeds" (in the words of the central prayer: "Our Father, our King, be gracious to us and answer us, for we have no meritorious deeds").

Hence, the first shade of meaning granted to the father's white "wrappings" resonates with life; one asks for forgiveness during Yom Kippur in order to be inscribed in "The Book of Life" (*sefer ha-chayim*), which is also why Jews traditionally wear white on that day, to purify themselves and prove themselves pure when facing divine judgment. But the father, as we know from the speaker's work of remembrance ("The *memory* of my father"), is no longer among the living, so that his "wrappings" now stand for the white shroud (*tachrichim*) in which deceased Jews are buried. Finally, with Amichai's typical antipathos, these two weighty meanings (life and death; atonement and memory) are put together within a simple, quotidian image: the speaker's father and his memory are wrapped in white paper, like a sandwich he takes to work. The father, along with his "good deeds" and "love," is present to the speaker not as a consecrated memory that arises solely on special occasions, but as a nourishing memory that continually follows him in his everyday life.

The short story, "The Times My Father Died," opens with the very same paradoxical image of the living/dying father wrapped in white.

ביום-כיפור אחד עמד אבי לפני בית-הכנסת. טיפסתי על כיסא כדי לראותו היטב מאחור. קל יותר לזכור את עורפו מאשר את פניו. עורפו נשאר קבוע ולא משתנה. פניו תמיד מוזזים בתנועת דיבור, כשפיו כשער בית אפל, או כדגל מתנופף. פרפרי-עיניים, או עיניים כמו בולי-דואר על מכתב פניו שתמיד נשלח למרחקים. או אוזניו שהן כמיפרשים בים אלוהיו. או כי היו פניו אדומים כולם, או לבנים כשערו. וגלים שעל מצחו, שהיה חוף קטן ופרטי ליד ים התבל. . . באותו יום-כיפור עמד לפני עסוק כל-כך באלוהיו המבוגרים. כולו לבן בתכריכיו. כל העולם נשאר לידו שחור, כמקום שהיתה בו מדורה ונשארו אבנים שחורות. הרוקדים הלכו, המזמרים הלכו, אבל האבנים השחורות נשארו. וכן נשאר אבי, לבוש בתכריכיו הלבנים. זו היתה המיתה הראשונה שאני זוכר.

One Yom Kippur my father stood in front of me in synagogue. I climbed up onto the seat to get a better view of him from the back. His neck is much easier to remember than his face. His neck is always fixed and unchanging; but his face is constantly in motion as he speaks, his mouth gaping like the doorway of a dark house or like a fluttering bug. Butterfly eyes, or eyes like

> postage stamps affixed to the letter of his face, which is always mailed to faraway places. Or his ears, which are like sails on the sea of his God. Or his face, which was either all red, or white like his hair. And the waves on his forehead, which was a little, private beach beside the sea of the world . . . That Yom Kippur he [the father] stood in front of me, so very busy with his grown-up God. He was all white in his shrouds. The entire world around him was black, like the charred stones left after a bonfire. The dancers were gone and the singers were gone, and only the blackened stones remained. That's how my father, dressed in his white shroud, was left behind. It was the first time I remember my father dying.[5]

"The Times My Father Died," as its title implies, follows the various moments in which the protagonist experiences his father as dying (e.g., "He died when they [Nazi soldiers] came to arrest him," "He died when we left Germany to emigrate to Palestine," "My father died many times more, and he still dies from time to time").[6] The first among these instances occurs in the synagogue during Yom Kippur, and it is here that what was insinuated in "My Father" is spelled out: the father's white *tallit* are explicitly depicted as *tachrichim* (shrouds), forcing to the fore the double meaning of the white "wrappings."

However, what stands out in the transition from poetry to prose is the expansion of Amichai's metaphorical structure. In the short story, Amichai allows the affinity between the color white and his father to stretch out almost endlessly, a movement the text metafictionally engages with through its gestures toward a geographical drifting (or "sail[ing]") away: the white of the *tallit* and *tachrichim* expands now to the father's face ("white like his hair") that is like a letter (in a white envelope, per the convention), mailed to faraway places; and the ears are like "sails"—again, prototypically white—that cross the boundless "sea of his God." White also stretches into its opposite, the mouth that is like a "dark house," and the entire "black" world around the father that is like "charred stones left after a bonfire." These similes are multiple (*x* is continually described as being like *y* and like *z*), and they also blend into other images: the mouth is like a "fluttering bug," a metaphorical vehicle that is then transformed with slight change into the adjective modifying the tenor, the father's "butterfly eyes." Similarly, "the world" is described through the vehicle of an extinguished "bonfire," but that vehicle in turn becomes the subject of the following autonomous sentence: "The dancers were gone and the singers were gone, and only the blackened stones remained." We find that Amichai's account of the difference between his poetry and prose is painfully accurate in its metaphors: his prose fiction is indeed a wide horizontal plane from which a vertical, condensed poetic plant emerges.

And yet, this extraordinary affinity of images notwithstanding, the continuum between Amichai's poetry and prose fiction is severed in the scholarship around his work. As Michael Gluzman recently noted, "The love for Amichai's poetry was and still is reflected in the research around it; [his poetry] receives extensive critical attention," while his prose fiction "has been forgotten almost entirely."[7] Gluzman explains this scholarly split in terms of the trauma Amichai's prose fiction gives voice to: the "ongoing, boundless" trauma of the War of Independence, an expression that was incongruent with the Statehood Generation's imperative of repression. I would like to turn the spotlight on another facet of the Israeli disavowal of Amichai's prose fiction, with a focus on *In This Terrible Wind*.

Amichai produced his short stories precisely when the New Critical ideal of maximalist integrating reading, which we followed in the previous chapter, and the minimalist aesthetics it was associated with, began to take root in Israeli culture via the Hebrew University and the *Likrat* literary group (to recall, the avant-garde Statehood Generation poetic circle of the 1950s). In this context, Amichai's metaphorically abundant stories were deemed "loquacious," "wild," and "uncontrolled," and later on—in the context of the Tel Aviv School of Poetics and Semiotics (TA School), where "maximalist reading" was conceived—were systematically ignored. These stories did not jibe, nor were they meant to, with the maximalist readerly expectation of integrating all the elements in the text and their interconnections through the mental labor of attention. In fact, Amichai's figurative language was devised precisely to bring about a unique state of distraction, which I would like to think of as "creative unintegration," borrowing from the psychoanalyst Donald Winnicot.[8] As we have witnessed in "The Times My Father Died," and as we shall continue to see in this chapter, the metaphors of *In This Terrible Wind* work to instigate "distraction" in its most basic sense of pushing the reader's thought thread sideways (from the Latin *dis* [away, aside], *trahere* [to draw], as noted in earlier chapters), rather than guide her from and toward a solid integrating center.

This is not to say that *In This Terrible Wind* was written in explicit response to the full-fledged creed of maximalist reading, as we have seen, for example, in the case of Guimarães Rosa and the Brazilian "exact reading" (*leitura exata*). After all, the clear formulation of this praxis within the Tel Aviv School would occur only a decade later. Instead, Amichai publishes his short stories when the foundation on which maximalist reading would develop is first set in place: that is, when "integration" is first imagined as a characteristic of both the mental effort a sensitive reader should practice and the quality of a good work of literature. In this context, Amichai theorizes and provokes in his prose fiction a mode of reading that works against the binary of integration/disintegration, which in the Israeli context would become a cultural "road not taken."

But Amichai's "creative unintegrating" reading not only cultivated and conceptualized a different aesthetic experience; it also carried a particular political valence. As discussed in the previous chapter, anxiety about social disintegration was central to the development of maximalist reading. And Amichai's stories, as well, are fraught with the political, social, and economic conflicts that surfaced in the Israel of the early 1960s and further intensified in the following decade. Yet Amichai's proposed political solution, communicated via form, is not integration. Instead, his poetics urges the reader to linger with scatter, and to explore its potentiality. More specifically, by linking together extremely distant realms via common grounds that continually and systematically shift, Amichai encourages the reader to reevaluate the fundamental premise that a stable denominator is a prerequisite for relationality to be established, whether between members of a community or between elements in a metaphorical concatenation. This politically implies an acceptance of difference as an essential and nondetrimental attribute of Israeli society and advances a search for more tentative and particular points of affinity.

It is important to note that the investigation of Amichai's politically charged invitation to practice "unintegrating" reading, and the ways in which this offer was declined in Israel of the 1960s and 1970s, does not aim to criticize the *Likrat* milieu, Amichai's early critics, or the TA School scholars for neglecting Amichai's prose fiction. Aesthetic criteria change in accordance with a multitude of cultural, historical, political, and social parameters, and it would be absurd to insist that Amichai's prose fiction holds some universal and atemporal value that should have been identified. Instead, I believe that the critical division between Amichai's poetry and prose fiction is important to follow since it exposes the reading norms in Israel during the 1960s and 1970s, and the aesthetic and political reasoning that deemed a work of literature culturally valuable during that time.[9]

In the first section of this chapter, I follow the reception of Amichai's poetry and prose fiction—and specifically the poem "Geshem bi-sde krav" ("Rain on a Battlefield")—first in the context of the *Likrat* group and later within the TA School, in order to trace the attributes assigned to his short stories' metaphors when read through the Israeli New Critical lens. The second section attempts a reading of Amichai's *In This Terrible Wind* that sets aside maximalist expectations. This reading focuses on the story "Pgishat ha-kita" ("Class Reunion") in order to follow its "concatenated" rhythm, to unpack its distracting mechanism, and to ask what the political implication of its form might be. The two sections together suggest that the apparent dichotomy between Amichai's poetry and prose fiction should be reconfigured as a continuum, such that the breadth allowed by narrative form can be seen as bringing to full fruition the horizontal thrust that inhabits Amichai's poetry as well. Against this backdrop, Amichai's body of work as a whole ultimately articulates an alternative to the New Critically informed Israeli practice of maximalist reading, one that is grounded in distraction rather than attention (as we have seen in Lispector's case as well) and calls into question the very notion of full integration.

Minimalist Aesthetics and Maximalist Reading

One of the most committed and persistent advocates of Amichai's poetry was Benjamin Harshav, whom we met in the previous chapter: the intellectual visionary behind both the *Likrat* group and the TA School. The two met as students at the Hebrew University (both frequenting the New Critical seminars of Shimon Halkin), and Harshav was among the first to read and appreciate Amichai's poems, as the poet himself recalls.[10] Harshav was also the one to introduce Amichai, formerly Ludwig Pfeufer (his name before his family's escape to Israel from Germany in 1936), to the *Likrat* group. "The old literary establishment did not accept him," Harshav writes, so much so that the then prominent literary editor Ephraim Broida shamelessly declared, "One cannot publish him [Amichai], because he simply does not know Hebrew." In that spirit, Shlomo Tzemach sardonically hypothesized, "If I were to be asked (as critics must be asked): what is the asset of Amichai's poetry? I would honestly reply, I haven't a clue,"[11] and B. Y. Michali insisted that Amichai "cuts off the thread of experience, and deadens it in its prime."[12]

In contrast, Harshav and the other members of the *Likrat* avant-garde circle found Amichai's poetics exciting and surprisingly aligned with theirs, even though he was almost a decade older than most of them. He was regularly asked to contribute poems to *Likrat* from 1952 onward, and the journal's modest publication house was responsible for the poet's 1955 debut collection, *Akhshav u-va-yamim ha-acherim* (*Now and in Other Days*), which won him rave reviews, and proved to be his springboard into public acceptance. Finally, Harshav, along with his partner Barbara Harshav, an acclaimed and prize-winning translator proficient in Hebrew, Yiddish, and French, undertook together the task of translating an extensive collection of Amichai's poetry into English, an invaluable contribution to Amichai's global reputation.[13]

Harshav was especially enthusiastic about Amichai's metaphorical language, which he read as revealing a surprising common ground between ostensibly unrelated domains: "Amichai's strength lies not in the singular metaphor, but in the ongoing collision between two expansive fields of meaning."[14] This account resonates with the New Critics' famous definition of paradox as the "hanging together of the like with the unlike," which, as mentioned in earlier chapters, the American critics identified in abundance not only in the Metaphysical Poets but in the work of T. S. Eliot and Ezra Pound as well.[15] And indeed, Amichai not only read and admired the American modernists, but his alliance with their paradoxical thrust via his metaphors made his work attractive to Harshav and Natan Zach (whom we met in the previous chapter as the leading poet of the "Statehood Generation" and the cofounder of *Likrat*) and, later on, to the TA School critics, all affiliated with the New Critics. For that reason, while critics such as Tzemach claimed this premeditated "collision" to be "nothing but a prank, a trick of the tongue," the *Likrat* group and the TA School members, who modeled their theories on both Anglo-American and Israeli (Statehood Generation) modernisms, were fascinated by Amichai's unexpected "metaphorical bridges."[16]

Harshav was highly invested throughout his career in exploring the structure and function of metaphor, an interest that was interwoven with his concern for the mental process of attention-as-integration. Metaphor for him was a formal device that intensified attention, especially when it confronted the reader with the challenge of "difficult integration"—one structured to appear just *nearly* impossible, as discussed in the previous chapter—by forcing together highly distinct frames of reference. For that reason, he discusses Amichai's poetry in the same article in which he claims that T. S. Eliot's startling juxtaposition of "the city" and "the hospital" in "The Love Song of J. Alfred Prufrock" successfully "activates the reader's sensibilities and the interpreter's dialectical negotiating."[17] In the same vein, Harshav argues that Amichai's poem, "Va-hagirat horai" ("And My Parents Migration"), encourages difficult integration: "His [Amichai's] mode is direct statement, which often may be taken as a literal sentence . . . but has to be integrated metaphorically in the basic *fr* [frame of reference]."[18]

Harshav's view was shared by Zach, who similarly identified Amichai's metaphorical sensitivity to be the key property of his poetics, and the one that best engages the reader's mind. In discussing Amichai's poem "Le-orekh ha-sdera she-eyn ba ish" ("Along the Deserted Boulevard"), Zach claims that Amichai chose a child as the poem's speaker since "the child's network of associations is much more expansive than that of an adult, who knows the 'right' place of things in the world and is thus limited in the number of reasonable connections that could be made between them. On the other hand, not knowing the [right] place makes possible the most surprising couplings."[19] For Zach, these "surprising couplings" are Amichai's way of producing "gesture via poetry," a concept he explicates by quoting the American New Critic, R. P. Blackmur: "Gesture, in language, is . . . that play of meaningfulness among words . . . which is defined in their use together. . . . He [the poet] must do this by making his written words sound in the inward ear of his reader, and so play upon each other by concert and opposition and pattern that they not only drag after them the gestures of life but produce a new gesture of their own."[20]

In other words, according to both Harshav and Zach, Amichai's poetry activates the reader's mind or "inward ear" in a productive fashion (which may bring to mind the exploration of audition and attention in chapter 2). But this was not the case for them with regard to his prose fiction. Immediately following the publication of *In This Terrible Wind*, Zach confesses that the collection is extremely enjoyable. As he remarks sarcastically in the epigraph to this chapter: "One must be a real literary critic in order not to derive any pleasure from Yehuda Amichai's short story collection, *In This Terrible Wind*." Still, it is not pleasure that Zach seeks most in a literary work of art, but rather precision, lucidity, and condensation.[21] As he writes in his influential modernist manifesto, which was to describe the poetics of the Statehood Generation and was modeled on Pound's aesthetic creed—the poet should "resist excessive figuration . . . resist the use of the poetic figure if it serves only as an embellishment or an explanatory example, if it lacks a basic expressive impulse, or if it is not 'toned down' . . . by humor, irony, or self-directed humor. Favor 'wit' [English in the original Hebrew], lack of solemnity, the restraint of figurative creativity, and emphasize the human voice, the voice of the subject who is given life in the poem."[22] In that spirit Zach concludes that

> Amichai's image [in *In This Terrible Wind*] is wonderful when it develops his story or "moment" . . . and it is not good—or far less good—when it serves as a linguistic ornament alone, dimming [the story's] lucidity, or giving the reader the sense that life cannot be touched through words. . . . [At times], Amichai does not know how to concentrate on the crux of the matter, wrap himself around the storyline, and get rid of the fluttering excess for the benefit of more solid and rocklike "materials."[23]

Zach perceptively identifies the formal structure of Amichai's prose fiction metaphor or "image" as working through "excess." But he considers this quality to be a flaw, and deems Amichai's metaphoric expansion a "linguistic ornament." Since Zach values "solid and rocklike" materials along with an aesthetic and mental "concentration," he finds Amichai's "fluttering excess" problematic, dimming the story's (and the reader's) "lucidity."

That Zach was invested in editing out Amichai's "fluttering excess" is made evident through the production and reception history—or myth—surrounding the poem, "Geshem bi-sde krav" ("Rain on a Battlefield"). I qualify the term "history" since a heated debate is still ongoing about the poem's creation process. Today, "Rain on a Battlefield" is one of Amichai's most frequently quoted poems (at times ad nauseam), read aloud in almost every Israeli Memorial Day ceremony and memorized by the majority of Israeli schoolchildren. Yet in contrast with its current warm (and stifling) embrace by the state, the poem held a revolutionary and iconoclastic status at the time of its publication. As articulated by Menakhem Perry (who we know from the previous chapter as one of the prime movers of maximalist reading among TA School members): "The poem was seen as a blunt antithesis to the multitude of earlier poems about the casualties of the Independence War. . . . The dead [in Amichai's poem] did not lecture in the ears of the nation, their blood did not call out from the land, they did not return as red roses, or wake up and walk. . . . The poem emphasized what they did *not* do" (emphasis in original).[24]

Amichai's poem, in other words, forcefully resisted the national Israeli myth of the heroic death, the notion that "it is good to die for our country," in Joseph Trumpeldor's notoriously fictionalized words.[25] However, Zach and Harshav, and later on Perry as well, found the poem captivating not only because of its subversive politics, but also, and perhaps mainly, because it fit with their ideal of a "rocklike" poem that enhances readerly "concentration." The poem reads,

גֶּשֶׁם יוֹרֵד עַל פְּנֵי רֵעַי;
עַל פְּנֵי רֵעַי הַחַיִּים, אֲשֶׁר
מְכַסִּים רָאשֵׁיהֶם בַּשְּׂמִיכָה—
וְעַל פְּנֵי רֵעַי הַמֵּתִים, אֲשֶׁר
אֵינָם מְכַסִּים עוֹד.

> Rain falls on the faces of my friends;
> on the faces of my living friends,
> who cover their heads with a blanket—
> and on the faces of my dead friends,
> who cover no more.[26]

"Rain on a Battlefield" evades figurative language altogether; presenting instead a strong literal image.[27] According to Harshav and Perry, and the literary critic Dan Miron as well, "Rain on a Battlefield" arrived at its acute succinctness through an editing process conducted by Zach in the 1950s.[28] As Perry puts it, "[Zach] erased" additional lines in the poem that "diverged from the imagistic thingness" in order to create "a unique Amichaian poem in the spirit of Ezra Pound."[29] Hana Amichai, the poet's partner, avidly insists that the poem, along with the others included in *Now and in Other Days*, was "refined, polished, and ready for print" before Amichai even joined *Likrat*, adding that Amichai was never edited, neither then, nor later on.[30]

What is significant for me in this debate is not whether Zach in fact edited the poem (and book) or not. What is crucial instead is that the debate gives voice to the degree of cultural privilege that the concise minimalism of this poem received, such that it became worthwhile arguing over who is responsible for its ultimate form. One can clearly notice this preference, for example, in Harshav's reflections on *Now and in Other Days*: "Natan Zach helped with the selection of the poems, and edited the book. As I learned at the time, Natan shortened some of the long, loquacious [*dabrani'yim*] poems, and tried instead to emphasize the succinct few-lines-long image (as in the case of 'Rain on a Battlefield'). Amichai accepted the editing, and this is how his familiar style was established, one that combines the dramatic monologue and the succinct witty images."[31]

The reliability of Harshav's assertion about the editing process notwithstanding, his word choice expresses the concern that Amichai's poems run the risk of being "loquacious." They hold the potential to encompass textual excess. This property, as we know, can stand in the way of maximalist reading which, as Harshav will later explain, "assumes that all elements of the text, as well as the order of all elements, are *functional* to its meaning" (emphasis in original).[32] By the same token, Harshav's repetition of the word "succinct" as a quality to be "emphasized" hints at his view that "Rain on a Battlefield" counters Amichai's potential "loquacious" thrust, bringing to mind Zach's complaint about Amichai's stories' "fluttering excess." By the end of the paragraph, the ambivalence around the poem's status comes strongly to the fore: Harshav describes "Rain on a Battlefield" as establishing Amichai's "familiar style" immediately after he had presented the text as a product of a one-time editing process. Though Harshav is well aware of and admires Amichai's tendency toward the "ongoing collision between two expansive fields of meaning," he does not include this property in his account of the poet's "familiar style." There is something in Amichai's "loquacious" metaphor that is simultaneously appealing and appalling.

The same ambivalence about "Rain on a Battlefield" as both exemplary and exceptional is present in Perry's much later maximalist analysis of the poem in 2016. From a distance in time, Perry makes explicit the reasoning behind his, Zach's, and Harshav's preference for this poem specifically from Amichai's overall oeuvre. At first, Perry depicts "Rain on a Battlefield" as an exception to the rule in Amichai's early work, where usually even a four-line poem, Perry notes, "includes a plethora of images, similes, and metaphors."[33] And yet, Perry chooses to open his article, which sets forth to analyze Amichai's overall poetics, with a reading of none other than a "Rain on a Battlefield."[34] In explaining his curious choice, Perry indicates that the poem embodies a "key attribute of Amichai's poetics": the depiction of the living as dead as a protest and reaction against the Israeli tradition of portraying the dead as still alive. But this explanation comes across as insufficient. After all, Perry goes on to name many other examples of poems that corroborate his claim (e.g., "Ahava Ide'alit" ["Ideal Love"], "Elohim merachem al yaldey ha-gan" ["God Has Pity on Kindergarten Children"], "Lo ka-brosh" ["Not Like a Cypress"]).

Instead, I would suggest, Perry focuses on the atypical "Rain on a Battlefield"—in the spirit of Zach and Harshav—because it fits more easily with the minimalist aesthetics and maximalist reading he advanced in the sixties and seventies. Perry writes: "The traditional understanding of the poem as emphasizing the difference between the living and the dead soldiers . . . is a product of 'flat reading' [*kri'a raza*, literally, "thin" reading], which leaves many elements in the poem neglected and unaccounted for. A maximalist reading, on the other hand, that wishes to raise the bar of the text's exhaustion, will search for a theme that will turn these elements functional and informative."[35] As Perry's meticulous interpretation shows, "Rain on a Battlefield" is especially amenable to a reading that strives "to raise the bar of the text's exhaustion" precisely because of its atypical "succinctness." Its minimalism, not only in size but in eliciting potential connotations and associations, allows for the functionality of each and every element to be "accounted for," thus integrating all of the elements of the poem under one unified interpretation. In addition, the poem's succinctness leaves much to be discovered by the reader, and thus provokes her to activate the mental capacity of attention as integration. As Perry states, "in this fashion, attention is shifted from the contradiction between 'life' and 'death,' and a mysterious equivalence is revealed."[36] Interestingly, as in the case of Lispector's *The Apple in the Dark*, discussed in chapter 4, when close reading encounters an ostensible literary "excess," the question of "exhaustion" comes to the fore: Will this literary abundance exhaust the reader? Will it get in the way of the reader's exhaustion of the text's potential?

Perry powerfully demonstrates his skillful attention as he zeroes in on the smallest of the poem's sparse details to demonstrate that "Rain on a Battlefield" draws a similarity, rather than discrepancy, between the living and the dead. He focuses on the order of the poem's elements (that is, it opens with what is shared by the dead and the living—the rain on their faces—rather than on their dissimilitude), the location of line breaks (the adjectives "dead" and "alive" are deemphasized by the position of the relative pronoun "who"), the specific cultural connotations of the "blanket" as an "ostensibly insignificant detail" (alluding to the military-blanket used to cover the dead in the battlefield), and the ambiguity of the Hebrew term *al-p'nei* ("on the faces of"), which could idiomatically mean "*over* my friends" or literally signify their faces.

The maximalist reader, then, such as Perry, whose attention is finely tuned to follow the text's cues, is guided by "Rain on a Battlefield" to synthesize its seemingly disparate elements—those left "unaccounted for" by "flat-reading"—into a unified whole. So, this Amichian poem proves to be an ideal textual ground for a maximalist reader to demonstrate and practice her abilities. If Amichai's "atypical" poem is structured to fit perfectly with an attentive integrating reading, then it is clear why his short stories—abundant in heterogeneous metaphorical figures, changing common-denominators, and shifting associations—were considered too hefty to be integrated into one solid "rocklike" center. Against this backdrop, it might be easier to understand why the scholars of the TA School—in stark distinction from their ongoing investment in publishing, studying, and translating Amichai's poetry—never discussed his prose fiction, neither in *Ha-Sifrut* nor in *Siman Kri'a*.[37]

The affinity between figural minimalism and maximalist interpretation is made explicit in Boaz Arpali's 1971 *Siman Kri'a* article devoted to Amichai's poetry, which would later develop into his book, *Ha-prachim ve-ha'agartal* (*The Flowers and the Urn*; this translated title, which figures on the book's jacket, leaves no doubt as to Arpali's dialogue with the New Criticism).[38] The article, based on the dissertation Arpali was writing under the guidance of two prominent members of the TA School (Itamar Even-Zohar and Yosef ha-Ephrati), relies heavily on Harshav's Integrational Semantics and the TA School's practice of maximalist reading. Arpali's main claim is that the "basic composition" behind the various formal phenomena in Amichai's poetry is that of the " 'catalog,' 'list' or 'series.' "[39] As a consequence, the "central method for grasping [Amichai's] poem as a whole is a search for a common denominator. . . . The various elements in the catalog . . . first appear disconnected or unrelated to the poem's explicit theme . . . but the key meaning of the poem is created via the link between these various elements through a common theme."[40] According to Arpali, it is the tension between the various elements in Amichai's poems that "encourages the reader to understand the link between them as metaphorical."[41] That is to say, Amichai's catalog is conducive to integration.

Later on in his book, Arpali would argue that in Amichai's oeuvre, even poems whose "surface" appears "chaotic" are in fact catalog-like in their "deep" structure.[42] Yet, for Arpali, Amichai's compositional method is also risky; the catalog is always on the verge of "running wild," and Amichai labors to "solve" this "problem" via formal means: "[Amichai] curbs the 'wildness' of the poem by using restricting forms such as quatrains or sonnets. . . . Another way is constructing the poem around familiar structures . . . that are imposed on the composition and organize it. This is why, for example, an overarching metaphor is frequently created. . . . The difficulty in articulating a common denominator . . . is what guides the reader's attention to the various concrete elements of the catalog themselves."[43]

Though Arpali attributes to Amichai the view of his figural "catalog" as potentially "wild" (Amichai "curbs the 'wildness' of the poem"), this is obviously Arpali's notion, as his vocabulary evinces. The catalog, he argues, must be "restricted" by minimalist forms such as the quatrains or sonnets in order for the metaphorical link it instigates to remain under control. And once this "wildness" is "constrained," Amichai's aesthetics fits with the process of "difficult integration": by forcing the reader to face the "difficultly of articulating a common denominator," Amichai's poems "guide the reader's attention" to the minutia of the text, and in that manner aid her in maximizing their meaning and arriving at integration, that is, "a common denominator."

Arpali reiterates his claim, borrowing from Amichai's own metaphor in the poem "Mifkedet ha-um be-veit ha-natziv bi-Yrushalayim" ("The U.N. Headquarters in the High Commissioner's House in Jerusalem"), which reads, "And the thoughts pass overhead, restless, like reconnaissance planes."[44] Arpali writes, "[Amichai's] reader's thoughts are like an airplane hovering above a surface marked by various points, ruins of buildings perhaps; this viewer's eye can perceive lines that connect these disparate points, imagining walls, buildings, fences, or even an ancient city or military encampment. . . . The poem utilizes a series of devices to encourage the reader to connect the various elements."[45] In its constricted lyric form, Amichai's catalog "encourage[s]" integration. It creates a perfect perspective, here described in physical terms, for the perception of links and connections between apparently discrete elements, which in fact belong to one structure (they are like ruins of one building or city). But it follows that Amichai's "wildness" might prevent precisely this process.[46]

The question, then, remains *how* Amichai's "wild" metaphors work to hinder the reader's work of "connect[ing] the various elements." If he uses "a series of devices" to restrict his own wild potential, what is Amichai's opposite mechanism for dis-concentrating the reader from "the crux of the matter," to quote Zach?

"Distract the minds of people": Creative Unintegration

The effort to integrate appears at first to stand at the very center of Amichai's short story, "Pgishat ha-kita" ("Class Reunion"), which opens the collection *In This Terrible Wind*.[47] The story follows the narrator, an

Israeli man in his thirties, as he attempts to gather his old high school friends for a reunion, fifteen years after their graduation around 1938.[48] Simultaneously, a link proposes itself between this personal project of unification and the national endeavor to establish Israeli cohesion. The narrator wanders the politically volatile city of Jerusalem in order to assemble his friends who are "scattered" like "different stations all over the world," bringing to mind both the Jewish exile and the Zionist project of *kibbutz galuyot* ("the ingathering of the exiles").[49]

During the time of narration, mid-1950s, Jerusalem was of course divided (1948–1967) between West (under Israeli rule) and East (under Jordanian rule), with a *"shetach hefker"* ("no-man's land") in between. Thus, the question of "integration" had a palpable geopolitical presence, which the narrator consistently points to: the plot frequently takes the narrator close to the border, and the story is populated by "soldiers," the symbolic "eucalyptus trees," and people who "caress the walls of Jerusalem," while also mentioning historical landmarks like the "Generali Building" and "Salameh Square" (today named Wingate Square), both tightly linked to the 1948 War of Independence in the aftermath of which the city was divided.[50] Finally, the narrative itself recalls a journey of territorial conquest, depicting in short vignettes the narrator's fleeting meetings with his old acquaintances all over Jerusalem, moving between the bank, the Hebrew University, the auto repair shop, the post office, and a children's playground, to name just a few locations.

And still, these spatial markers notwithstanding, the reader is quickly made to realize that "Class Reunion" records at best a tepid desire to conquer or integrate, if at all, both on a personal and on a national level. Not only are the schoolmates uninterested in their reunion ("Why would you need all this?"), the narrator himself confesses to be using this proposed event as nothing but a pastime: "[T]his plan of mine, to gather all my school friends from fifteen years ago, is just a branch I climb and swing on to occupy myself. Soon, God will throw my way another stone, and I will run to fetch it, forgetting all about the old one."[51] In that spirit, the story ends not surprisingly with the cancelation of the reunion by the indifferent narrator: "I'll admit to the truth, I have completely forgotten about the reunion already. The meeting did not occur. I wrote and tried but could not ingather the scattered [*le-khanes et ha-pzurim*] And they did not even sense that they were scattered."[52]

The very state of disintegration—the classmates as "scattered" like "different stations all over the world"—which premised and motivated the narrator's attempt to bring the class together as a collective is ultimately put into question: "they did not even sense that they were scattered." Moreover, the heated political debate over the exact demarcation of the city's division-line, and the national desire to unify (or integrate) Jerusalem, is presented as utterly futile: "Barbed wire fences separated one deserted zone from another. Tractors moved soil from one place to another. . . . They always cover up the marks of the past, not only those of the blood, with soil and sand."[53] Moving soil from one side of the no-man's land ("deserted zone") to the other is meaningless; the battle over territory is presented as nothing but a "cover up" for pointless bloodshed. And so, if it is not disintegration that defines the "scatter" and the plans for "reunion" that are at the heart of the story, what then is it?

Amichai's story leaves the reader with this question in mind. In fact, "Class Reunion" lends itself to be read as a sophisticated investigation into the essence of the dichotomy between integration and disintegration. Initially, the story presents itself as a narrative of integration only to then undermine this portrayal and thus challenge its own framing of "scatter" as a problem to be solved. Through this plot conceit, the story announces its deep preoccupation with, and doubts about, the meaning and merit of unification—be it mental, geopolitical, national, or social. The ambiguity around, and interest in, integration/disintegration is presented in "Class Reunion," not only through the plotline, but also—and most emphatically—through form: the story's metaphoric structure thematizes a middle-ground between these two binary poles.[54]

Amichai's metaphor, as Harshav aptly described it, continually brings about an "ongoing collision between two expansive fields of meaning," which, Chana Kronfeld convincingly demonstrates, works politically to resist the erasure of difference: "[I]n both building and drawing attention to the bridges they construct over semantic, perceptual, and historical distances, Amichai's metaphors set up arrays of tentative, novel exchange between previously alien domains, all the while maintaining, and communicating to the reader, a keen awareness of their distinctness."[55] In "Class Reunion" specifically, and in his prose fiction more generally (as we have seen in "The Times My Father Died"), Amichai takes his poetics of difference to the extreme, inflating his poems' several "bridges" into a plethora of links between "previously alien domains." And the shift between these common grounds is rooted in difference as well, such that the tenor in the first metaphor systemically changes into the vehicle in the following one, creating a horizontal associative movement, a metaphorical concatenation.

In this way, Amichai crafts a form that destabilizes the clear distinction between unification and scatter. His story speaks through metaphors, which are in essence a form that unites, but these metaphors are simultaneously made to engender a sense of scatter, to deter the reader's attempts to integrate all elements into one thematic center. Amichai creates what can be thought of as a "linked scatter," already visible in the story's first paragraph.

> יום אחד היו רגלי עסוקות בהליכה תחת השמש השורפת קוצים ומחשבות. תיקי היה מלא דברים, שרק בחלקם עמדתי להשתמש בהם. את אותם הדברים והניירות והספרים שלא עמדתי להשתמש בהם הובלתי כמו שמובילים תינוק בעגלה. כל גופי היה עסוק בהליכה ובשמיעת צעדי. רק למחשבתי היה זמן איטי ופרטי כמו לזוג אוהבים ההולכים בתוך העיסוק הרועש של העולם. אוהבים משמשים זה לזה מגן, קיר בידוד ועוגן וחומר מאיט. בכימיה משתמשים בחומר מזרז שקוראים לו קאטאליזטור. אוהבים מאיטים את תהליך העולם ודוחים את בוא-הקץ.

> One day my feet were busy walking under the sun that burned thorns and thoughts. My bag was heavy with things and words, only some of which was I about to use. I carried all those things and notes and books that I was not about to use as one carries a baby in a stroller. My whole body was busy walking and listening to my own steps. My thoughts alone moved in a time of their own, slow and private, like that of lovers walking in the noisy bustle of the world. Lovers act as a shield one for the other, an insulating wall and an anchor and a decelerating substance. In chemistry, they use an accelerating substance named catalyst. Lovers slow down the process of the world and postpone the end.[56]

The first three sentences and their figurative language set the tone and pace for the story: it is the pace of a man wandering the streets under a sun so hot that it consumes the process of thinking ("burned thoughts"). These thoughts' proximity to the "things and words, only some of which was I about to use," which he carries with him, suggests that the narrator's musings are also partly futile. And they are enjoyable as well, perhaps even nurturing, carried around like "a baby in a stroller."

Amichai's reader is invited to join this lethargically pleasant progress via a concatenated structure that constantly pushes her mind away from the matter at hand—the narrator walking around on a hot Israeli day with his bag on his back—into distant and unexpected terrains, like those of "burned" thoughts, and "listening" bodies. This sideways movement gains further force in the following four sentences. First, "thoughts" are compared to "lovers," both moving in a "slow and private" time. The conjunction of "slow" and "private" is itself baffling since the two are qualitatively different: the first refers to a physical dimension of time while the latter to its subjective experience. The vehicle ("lovers") is then elaborated on, pushing it to the center of the reader's attention through concretization: the specific movement of the lovers (which in the realm of the tenor is the movement of the narrator's thoughts) is depicted as traveling through the "noisy bustle of the world."

A significant transition occurs in the following sentence where "the lovers," the former vehicle, turn fully into the tenor of another metaphor, leaving the original tenor ("thoughts") to evaporate from the scene altogether: "Lovers act as a shield one for the other, an insulating wall and an anchor and a decelerating substance." The lovers thus receive a quadripartite vehicle, or, in more impressionistic terms, excessive elaboration: "lovers" are "a shield," "an insulating wall," "an anchor," and "a decelerating substance." Not only is the reader required to shift from imagining the temporal movement of thoughts ("slow and private") to the essence of love relations (how lovers function for each other); she is also asked to move through four vehicles depicting the latter, each carrying a wholly different set of contradictory meanings and associations, all this for a tenor that just a sentence earlier was itself the vehicle of a simile. The "shield," for example, can point to both protection and war; the "insulating wall" might echo either isolation or home; and the "anchor" simultaneously denotes stability and stagnation. By the end of this sentence, when the last "decelerating substance" appears, some of the reader's thoughts will indeed be "burned." The text has worked to cognitively "decelerat[e]" her mind and push it away from the "lovers" around whom the metaphor was built, now moving in multiple directions and activating a medley of associations.

The same rhizomatic mental movement is precipitated by the sentence that follows, with a leap via antinomies (deceleration-acceleration) from the "lovers" to an "accelerating substance": "In chemistry," we are told, "they [chemists] use an accelerating substance named catalyst." Neither "thought" nor "lovers" are mentioned here, and the entire context shifts from the depiction of a thinking man walking the streets and the intersubjective relations of lovers, to the realm of science and the space of the lab. The lovers return only in the final sentence, this time as the tenor of a simile whose vehicle is implicit: in contrast to the "catalyst" that "accelerates" processes, lovers (like an anticatalyst) "slow down the process of the world." In this way, at the end of a paragraph that formally thematized and worked to activate in the reader a slow, associative thought process, the readers are brought back to the question of rhythm; the lovers, and the wandering narrator—the people of the everyday whom Amichai persistently presents as the locus of social and political change—affect the overall "process of the world" through their ostensibly "personal" pace. This first paragraph concludes, then, with Amichai's reader guided to imagine the world as a chemical substance to which the lovers are added to slow it down, an image far removed from the narrator's thoughts that served as the "crux of the matter" only four sentences earlier.

No wonder critics such as Zach, Harshav, Perry, and Arpali were worried about Amichai's "loquacious" and "wild" figurative tendency; if we accept this first paragraph as paradigmatic, then "Class Reunion" both describes and provokes an intentionally unproductive thought process, declaring its disinterest in putting into use all the elements in the text ("I carried all those things . . . that I was *not about to use*" [emphasis mine]), in blunt contradiction with Amichai's own *Likrat* group and the TA School's maximalist imperative. In other words, the story asks its reader to imitate the narrator's purposeless and lethargic thought process.

As a rejoinder, one could claim that Amichai's metaphors are designed to decelerate the reading process, that is, to mimic the lovers who "slow down the process of the world," thereby facilitating the concentration maximalist reading entails. But the rhythm set by Amichai's metaphors is better described as idle, rather than attentive. His orchestrated shift between vehicle and tenor, with thoughts constantly maintaining a relationality between the various elements in the text, is disorienting in nature; it encourages the reader not to investigate the logic behind the connection she is presented with, but to let herself go within this associative flow. In that sense, the reading I just performed goes somewhat against the thrust of the text, in an attempt to make visible its internal mechanism rather than participate in it; but I sense that Amichai's metaphorical concatenation oozes pleasant lethargy even in this analyzed form.

That Amichai pushes away from attention toward a sideways movement of thought, namely, "distraction" in its most basic sense, is evinced one last time in this opening paragraph via his intertextual engagement with the Jewish sources, an intertextuality that doubly communicates its message so as to make it easier for the reader to grasp it during her wanderings, if at all. By slowing down "the process of the world," we are told, the lovers are "*dochim et ha-ketz*," that is, are able to "postpone the end." As Kronfeld demonstrates, Amichai's dialogue with the Jewish sources is not based in religious belief but works through "iconoclasm"; salvation for him is not divine but based on human relations, which are thematized through his dedication to metaphor as a formal device.[57] This is the case here as well. *Ha-ketz* (literally, the end, and phonetically close to the Hebrew "summer" through a shared root, *k-y-tz*, thus emphasizing the diegetic lethargic atmosphere), refers in Jewish tradition to the arrival of the messiah, that is, to the moment of final redemption. To "postpone the end," then, is a negative movement away from potentiality.

However, the attempt to accelerate the arrival of the messiah is strictly forbidden in rabbinic sources. In fact, Amichai's sophisticated game sends the Israeli reader's associations to tractate *Sanhedrin*, where it is stated that one must "divert the mind" from thinking about "the end," since by explicitly thinking of the messiah, the believer is postponing his coming.[58] Injecting this rabbinic intertext into his story through the sexually charged image of the lovers of all things, Amichai crafts a political and interrelational argument, rather than a metaphysical one. Within a given interaction (between the believer and the messiah, between the lovers, between the reader and the text), a possible redemption is embedded not in a directed effort ("calculating the end") or in focused thought (like the broiling focus of the sunrays that might "burn" thoughts), but in the capacity to think *around* the "crux of the matter." That Amichai identifies a positive potentiality in the slow, distracted, sideways thought process that he manipulates his metaphors to engender is evinced by the second meaning of "postponing the end," which arises from modern rather than biblical and rabbinic Hebrew. There, "the end" does not connote the arrival of the messiah, but the arrival of death, the termination of life. That is, "distracting" oneself from the Messiah precipitates redemption, just as thinking sideways precipitates life.

It seems that Amichai's paragraph has led me to a point of saturation in my analysis, to a fluttering excess, where I suggest that we think of the relationship the story engenders between reader and text through the relationship between believer and savior, between lovers, between the story's narrator and his classmates, and between that narrator and the world. But this is not to say that these various analogies fit perfectly with each other, or that they are utterly unrelated. In fact, my point is precisely that this proliferation performs what *In This Terrible Wind* strives to instigate in its reader: the ability to linger with loosely connected scatter. By fomenting an excess of figurations that are radically different, yet connected via a chain of association, Amichai provokes in the reader neither the effort of integration nor the anxiety of disintegration, but a third intermediate state, that of unintegration.

As mentioned above, I borrow the term "unintegration" from the psychoanalytic terminology of Donald Winnicott. The British analyst's work might seem out of place here, given that "integration" in its circulation within the TA School and its discussion of Amichai takes on a mental, formalist, and political valence, but not a psychodynamic one (though Perry occasionally refers to Freud the reader, as we saw in the previous chapter). Yet, in alliance with Amichai, Winnicott's investigation of "unintegration" opens a space for rethinking the binary integration/disintegration in contexts other than that of the human psyche.

For Winnicott, as he writes in an article published just a year after *In This Terrible Wind*, "integration" is a constructive process: "The achievement of integration is the unit."[59] In the psychoanalytic context, this "unit" is the self, but Winnicott's take on this process speaks more generally to the intense work of collecting and building that "integration" entails. By contrast, Winnicott views "disintegration" as a destructive process, "an active production of chaos." This definition sheds light on the anxiety that the prospect of such a state could elicit, as in the case of the TA School and the Israeli society of the long 1970s, portrayed in chapter 5.[60] But to differentiate from these two extremes, Winnicott characterizes "unintegration" as relaxation rather than effort: "The opposite of integration would seem to be disintegration. This is only partly true. The opposite, initially, requires a word like unintegration. Relaxation for the infant means not feeling a need to integrate, the mother's ego-supportive function being taken for granted."[61]

Unintegration, then, is a state in which the subject feels externally safeguarded from complete "chaos" and can therefore allow herself to let go of the constant struggle to hold together what seems like a fragmented self, and instead engage in a "desultory play" with the "formless": "Creativity [is] . . . a coming together after relaxation, which is the opposite of integration. . . . It is only here, in the unintegrated state of the personality, that that which we describe as creative can appear. . . . We experience life . . . in the area that is intermediate between the inner reality of the individual and the shared reality of the world that is external to individuals."[62]

Amichai's "Class Reunion" specifically, and his prose fiction more generally, calls for precisely such a "creative" encounter between text ("shared reality") and reader ("inner reality"). Amichai chooses metaphor as the basic building block of his stories—a formal device that functions through relationality—in order to provide the reader with a sense of interconnectivity; *a* and *b* are always in dialogue. However, simultaneously, he maneuvers his metaphors to transition so frequently between comparisons (*a* and *b* are compared to numerous other corresponding objects) that the work of integration, of achieving a rocklike "unit," presents itself as futile. The production of a sense of external order, which the reader cannot fully follow or grasp, opens before her the possibility of unintegration, offering the reader a safe space to play with difference and scatter rather than trying to control it. When Tzemach, then, reproaches Amichai for playing with metaphors ("[Amichai's] collisions . . . [are] nothing but a prank, a trick of the tongue"), he is absolutely right. Amichai not only handles his metaphors playfully, he also urges the reader to creatively engage with the linked scatter-play she is presented with, as I personally have felt compelled to do.

In fact, Amichai metafictionally admits in "Class Reunion" to designing a distracting scatter. The story's narrator confesses the following:

לפעמים אני נוהג כאותו תייר שבא לשכונת עניים בעיר ענייה ועטו עליו קבצנים מכל פתח ומכל סימטה. לקח מלוא-כפיו מטבעות קטנות והשליך אותן ביניהם, כדי שיתנפלו על המטבעות ויוכל להמשיך בדרכו בלי הטרדה. כך כל דברי ומעשי. אני נותן רק מטבעות קטנות של דברים ומעשים וכל מה שאני עושה הוא להסיח את דעתם של האנשים ממני.

At times I act as that tourist who arrives at a poor neighborhood in a poor town, and peddlers pounce on him from every door and every alley. He takes a handful of small change and throws it among them, so they may leap at the coins and free him to continue his way unbothered. Thus are all my deeds and words. I give away only small change deeds and words and all I do is distract the minds of people away from me.[63]

The realms of "coins" and "words" are linked in Hebrew via an idiomatic expression. Lexical-coinage is *"matbe'a lashon,"* literally "a coin of the tongue," which stands for a word-assembly that has become ossified (a cliché), rather than the act of coining a new phrase, as in English. Yet Amichai concretizes the "coin" to the extent of defamiliarizing the link between the two realms of the lexicalized metaphor: in his version, the currency coins are spread on the floor of the town just like the story's "words and deeds."

In contrast with Arpali's depiction of Amichai's "restricted" metaphors as encouraging the reader's "eye" to "perceive lines that connect these disparate points," the spreading of the linguistic coins in "Class Reunion" is explicitly oriented toward "distract[ing] the minds of people away" from the narrator, who is the alleged center of the plot.[64] And yet, in Winnicott's terms, Amichai's scattered coins are *not* disintegrating, namely, actively producing chaos. Rather than floating around like autonomous particles, his figures are always put in dialogue via metaphor (such as the "coins" and the "deeds and words" in this example). This is a loose interconnectedness, one that is constantly shifting. And in order for the reader to grasp it, she must let go of the attempt to integrate in Winnicott's sense of an unceasing labor to construct a whole.

In that regard, the function of Amichai's concatenated metaphors is twofold, activating a unique reciprocity between textual form and readerly perception. First, his vehicle-tenor chains instigate in the reader a state of unintegration, which replaces the constant effort to hold everything together with creative play. Then, this state of mind allows the reader to perceive the alternative form of relationality proposed by these metaphors: an interconnectivity contingent on the constant flux of common grounds. Imagined graphically, Amichai invites his reader to think of relationality not in circular terms, in which all the elements in a given group are connected via one shared center (the "crux of the matter") or common attribute. Instead, each of his elements shares a common denominator only with the next one, creating a horizontally interlinked series. For example, when Amichai writes that thoughts are like lovers, and that lovers are like a shield, and an insulating wall, and an anchor, and a decelerating substance, and that chemical deceleration is like postponing death, he does not expect his reader to find one common feature—a stable center—that links these various elements together. They are connected through their participation in the same chain: if a is similar to b, and b has an affinity with c, then a and c are linked, even though they might have nothing in common.

In the previous chapter, I presented the process of unlocalizing—the Israeli reader's process of detachment from the Zionist teleological narrative—as the Israeli answer to the more general imperative of unselfing embedded in the New Critical protocol of close reading. Amichai's poetics of concatenated metaphors, whose early development preceded the TA School, does not interrupt the process of unlocalizing specifically. It does, however, come in the way of the cognitive process that the school asserted should accompany this version of unselfing, namely, attention as integration. And this cognitive incongruity holds important political meaning. Amichai's unintegrational thrust unsettles the ideological assumption undergirding the school's praxis of maximalist reading.

The translation of this readerly position into political terms is not straightforward. If we were to think of Amichai's metaphorical logic in terms of the national preoccupation with cohesion, seeping from the 1960s into the 1970s, then the possibility arises that Israeli society is viewed by Amichai as rooted in acute difference and yet deeply, and horizontally, interlinked. Put differently, Amichai's form suggests that a collective can be formed without as much as a single denominator common to all its participants, and without their differences being erased. Provisional connections between particular members suffice to put in touch the various members of the group. But in order to identify such tentative linkages, the perceiver must engage in a creative, unintegrational, and horizontal thought process. She must face what seems like social scatter not from a position of anxiety or directed effort, but from a stance of relaxation and play that enables both an associative, concatenated movement from one element to the next, and a right to refuse, to say "no" to the class reunion.

To return to Harshav's quote in the epigraph above, indeed, "politically speaking, Amichai was much more radical than his delightful decorations, witty jokes, and sarcastic puns might lead us to believe. Unconstrained cynicism and nihilism, even under the semblance of docility, are never far from the surface."[65] Amichai's "nihilism," however, is not oriented toward destructive negation; it is one that, somewhat melancholically, suggests that we let go of the illusion of both a full-blown "class reunion" and an absolute disintegration (after all, the classmates did not even know they were scattered). Instead, Amichai proposes that readers attune their minds via unintegration to small-scale dialogues where the potentiality to form a chain resides.

Tumor-Like Metaphors

To conclude, I would like to revisit the Israeli reception of *In This Terrible Wind*, in the hope that it makes more sense in light of my current discussion of Amichai's short stories' poetics, its political implications, and the readerly reaction it works to invoke. One of the most important and influential responses to Amichai's 1960s prose fiction, one of very few, is Gershon Shaked's chapter on Amichai in his seminal *Gal chadash ba-siporet ha-ivrit* (*A New Wave in Hebrew Literature*, 1971). An exception to the rule, Shaked treats Amichai as an important prose fiction writer, analyzing his *In This Terrible Wind* and *Not of This Time, Not of This Place* alongside the work of A. B. Yehoshua, Amos Oz, Aharon Appelfeld, and Amalia Kahana-Carmon.[66]

However, in the spirit of the TA School (which, on the personal level, he was extremely critical of), Shaked differentiates between Amichai's poetry and prose fiction in the measure of control these genres enforce on Amichai's potentially "wild" metaphors. And he points to Amichai's abovementioned "coin" paragraph as proof of this disorderly "tendency," repeating in his critique (most probably unawares) Zach's depiction of Amichai as "not concentrating on the crux of the matter." Shaked writes,

> His [Amichai's] stories, like his poetry, are replete with metaphorical pairings, which are drawn from highly distinct realms and then, at times mechanically, linked together. Yet, if structure and length limit the possibilities of play in his poetry, the story leaves open all structural avenues, and he [Amichai] gleefully fools around with composing metaphors with no sense of measure or restraint—a liberty that is not always to the benefit of the work. In his poetry as well Amichai is inclined towards the epigrammatic metaphor . . . and thanks to the brevity imposed by the [lyric] structure (quartets, sonnets), he frequently crafts solid and brilliant epigrammatic metaphors. But this restriction is absent from his prose fiction; the epigrammatic metaphor . . . simply grows as a wild tumor that is unlinked to the overall structure and hence breaks it apart. . . . This [the coin] statement . . . is true for Amichai's form and content: a tendency to scatter phrase-coins that fragment the structure and distract the reader from the crux of the matter; even though each such coin carries its own beauty.[67]

Shaked's comments encapsulate the various responses to Amichai's prose fiction that we have seen so far, from those of the *Likrat* group poets, Harshav included, to those developed in the context of the TA School, such as that of Arpali. Amichai's success, it is assumed, is predicated on proportion: his "brilliancy" lies in the ability to link together "highly distinct realms" of meaning, but when these pairings are not "limited" by form, they grow out of proportion and become a "wild tumor" that threatens to "break [the work] apart." Though unspecified, it seems that metaphorical "wildness" signifies either an excessive number of metaphors, or an excessive distance between the "distinct realms" it binds together. And since Amichai is inclined to "play" and "gleefully fool around," he is always on the verge of losing a "sense of measure or restraint." For that reason, Shaked describes Amichai's prose fiction "form of writing" as a "constant threat": "[I]f the writer does not govern it [this writing style], it takes charge of the writer."[68]

What remains unspecified in Shaked's phrasing, and in the overall discourse around Amichai's prose fiction, is the scale used to decide where "brilliant epigrammatic metaphors" end, and "wild tumor[s]" begin. That is, at what point do Amichai's metaphors become too many or too digressive to be integrated into the "overall structure"? Against the backdrop of the current discussion, it appears that the implied agent or measure scale at stake here is the reader and her perception. As Shaked goes on to write: "At times, the narrator binds two situations in an artificial manner. . . . His eagerness to assimilate two distinct realms and formulate new and unexpected 'grounds for comparison' creates a tension so intense between these fields of meaning to the point of *imperceptibility* and improbability" (emphasis mine).[69] The two elements combined by Amichai's pairings are therefore not objectively overly "distinct"; after all, the text proves that they are in fact related. These metaphors are challenging for a reader whose "perception" is oriented toward a full integration and "use" of the various textual elements.

It is under this assumption that Shaked differentiates between "distracting" metaphors in Amichai's prose fiction and those that encourage readerly integration. In Amichai's "integrating" metaphors, "the poetic image does not grow into a wild tumor that breaks down the structure, but becomes an integral part of it, coheres it."[70] On the other hand, Amichai's "distracting" constructions, for Shaked, "can with a certain effort be perceived as probable; but they do not form an integral part of the whole. . . . Instead, they break down this structure by charging a single bead in the chain with an autonomous value, such that it is detached from the chain as a whole. These are 'small-change coins' aimed at distracting the mind from the matter at hand."[71]

Shaked is right on the mark; indeed, Amichai structures his linguistic "coins" to "distract" the reader's mind, to instigate "play" instead of a focused "thought-burning" concentration, and to confer partial autonomy on every "bead" while keeping it as part of a "chain." But, for Amichai, this mode of reading is generative and beneficial. It both questions that efficacy of integration of the kind Shaked hints at and suggests an alternative: to allow the mind to move, and perceive the potentiality embedded in asymmetrical and tumor-like structures.

For Amichai, of course, this dispersion is conjured not in the language of pathology but through the image of scattered coins on the floor. And whereas Shaked claims that when Amichai's metaphorical constructions lose proportion it is a sign that their creator did not "govern" them (they "took charge of the writer"), Amichai implies that he intentionally "fools around with composing metaphors"; he concatenates his metaphors into a long and intricate chain precisely in order to leave unlimited the readerly "possibilities of play" that open up by the creative drift of poetic, social, and political unintegration.

With Amichai's embracing notion of dialogism, unhinged by the constraints of a strict common denominator, we conclude our journey through this book. It's a journey across three distinct landscapes that, much like Amichai's tenors and vehicles, may appear entirely different, yet are intricately interconnected through numerous specific points. These lines of connection weave a network, akin to a spider's web, which becomes readily apparent when we step back and gain a broader perspective, as I have tried to offer in this book. This pattern not only outlines the various ways in which close reading has shaped us, its practitioners, but we might also be surprised to find that it forms our very own portrait.

Epilogue

New Critical Studies

Eight months pregnant, I am in labor with this book. And it is quite ironic, or perhaps simply fitting, that while I discuss the imagined praxis of emptying oneself out in order to allow space for an Other, my body is concretizing this process. My organs are literally pushed away to make room for a yet unknown entity in an ongoing process of becoming. Very Derridean indeed that my body has a clear preference for the Other over what we might call the "self" or "I." When there is a momentary blood shortage it is "I," the containing vessel, who faints, and in the battle over magnesium, my nightly leg cramps announce the victor quite plainly. Mine is not a purely ethical decision of the form discussed in the previous pages, but one only verging on the ethical, insofar as I have consented to temporarily surrender my body to—or at least share it with—another. In Maggie Nelson's perceptive words, "the soul (or souls) in utero is pumping out static, static that disrupts our usual conception of an other as a single other. The static of facing not one, but also not two."[1] Unselfing in the flesh.

Indeed, as my dual self navigates the balance between creation and vulnerability, I have endeavored to make one aspect unequivocally clear in this book about the so-called dead school of New Criticism—its lasting vitality. The relevance of this school of thought, including its theory and praxes, extends not only to the realm of literary studies and the humanities but also to writers, translators, and readers well beyond academic boundaries and beyond the confines of the anglophone world. In pursuing this aim, I have aligned myself with the emerging subfield of "New Critical Studies." This category, thoughtfully suggested to me by Laura Heffernan in a personal exchange, encompasses not only her work but also that of many scholars with whom I have dialogued in the book, such as Andy Hines, Joshua Gang, Paul Nadal, Joseph North, Rachel Sagner Buurma, Helen Thaventhiran, and others.

Within this conversation, a central goal for me was the resurrection of the New Critical reader, often considered absent by scholars studying this school of thought, as I discussed in the Introduction. Yes, the New Criticism focused on the poem as a unified object, containing an immanent and stable meaning, but what kind of reader did this model of the poem depend on? What kind of work on the self must the reader undertake in order to receive the poem in this way? Reader response theory has often been seen as a reaction to the New Criticism's focus on the objectivity of the text, but *How Close Reading Made Us* argues that the New Criticism—and this becomes especially clear in the wider, global context this book provides—has always involved work on the self, what I have called "unselfing attention."

I was only able to arrive at this insight by adopting a decentralizing, transnational perspective. As I have tried to demonstrate, joining similar attempts in the Asian context, the New Critical creed, and its practice of close reading has had an extensive and fascinating international circulation. Though I have focused on the dissemination of New Critical ideas and praxes in Brazil and Israel, I hope for this study to serve as an open invitation to further explore these intellectual travels, and especially the vibrant dialogues and cultural interactions it sparked between regions often relegated to the literary "periphery."

In the preceding pages, I introduced key figures in the global New Criticism, such as Afrânio Coutinho and Benjamin Harshav; their literary groups and institutions, including the *Nova Crítica* and the Tel Aviv School of Poetics and Semiotics; the local adaptations of close reading (*leitura exata* or *leitura de perto*, and *kri'a maximalit* or *kri'a tzmuda*); and the national-political contexts that shaped these local conceptions of readerly attention (postcoloniality in Brazil; the political and social instability of Israel in the 1970s). In these contexts, we have seen how different varieties of readerly unselfing were shaped by local political pressures, historical circumstances, and traditions of reading and exegesis. Moreover, these transnational reception histories have shed an unfamiliar light on the traditional narrative of the New Criticism in the US, compelling us to acknowledge that the link between the act of reading, politics, and self-transformation was deeply ingrained within the New Critical creed from the get-go. That is, through this exploration, it becomes evident that the North American New Critics and their counterparts in Brazil and Israel firmly believed that reshaping the reader's psyche could precipitate broader societal transformation.

Finally, we have followed together the impact that the local conceptions of the close reader's subjectivity had upon literary production and processes of translation. As I have mentioned in the book, studies of the New Criticism have often highlighted how this school's methods tend to favor specific authors and genres. My perspective, however, has honed in on a different aspect of the relationship between close reading and modernism. Engaging specific prose fiction works, I strove to show how William Faulkner, João Guimarães Rosa, Clarice Lispector, A. B. Yehoshua, and Yehuda Amichai creatively responded to or offered prototypes for the New Critical model of the attentive reader.

Notably, we have observed that these authors, well before the advent of "surface reading" or "distant reading," offered sophisticated alternatives to close, attentive reading. For instance, Lispector crafted a formal technique to fatigue her readers into a state of "exhausted reading," while Amichai ingeniously designed his metaphors to stimulate a sense of "creative unintegration" in the reader. Regardless of variations in style, culture, and language, these writers all took seriously the New Critical proposed affinity between the act of reading, subject formation, and attention, whether endorsing or challenging that association. Through this exploration, I had the opportunity to linger with lesser-known works by these authors, some of which remained untranslated or had previously received limited attention. The relative obscurity of these works is linked, as we have seen, to how they were viewed by local New Critics and their reception in a culture deeply influenced by New Critical ideas. However, it is precisely the New Critics' rejection of these works that has allowed us to discern, through their exclusion, the specific criteria by which the New Critics identified texts capable of engaging and sustaining readerly attention.

Attention, Method Wars

In this study, I navigated "close," "maximalist" "exhausted," and "unintegrated" readings, both thinking about and practicing them. I experienced firsthand the mental and physical effort required to adapt to and shift between these different reading protocols. For the New Critics, we recall, an arduous labor is necessary to unself and allow the text to speak its voice, without "appropriat[ing], or consum[ing] it," in Wellek and Warren's words.[2] But the New Critical perspective offers only one way to understand what reading attentively (or distractedly) might mean. In fact, I would suggest that the question of what reading attentively entails keeps haunting the discipline of literature precisely because it is not sufficiently attended to. Shoshana Felman memorably taught us that literary criticism acts out the very tensions of the literary work; similarly, one can also witness how what are called "the method wars" play out unspoken concerns about the meaning of attentive reading.[3] In this, I find David Kurnick's sharp article, "A Few Lies: Queer Theory and Our Method Melodramas," especially telling.[4]

Kurnick tackles the rhetoric of the method conversation, which he rightly presents as feeding on "melodramatically, binarized" and "cartoonish" sketches of the academic critic.[5] He also provocatively suggests that this rhetoric expresses an internalization of the hostile public discourse against the humanities. What is most striking for me about Kurnick's article, though, is that he clearly identifies the key role attention plays in the current method conversations, but still manages to stop just inches away from asking, seriously, what paying attention to texts entails of the reader. Kurnick's article ultimately shows signs of a different, unarticulated, disciplinary preoccupation with attention—a preoccupation with subjectivity. That is, any time we are talking about reading with, in, or against attention we are really asking a conceptual, political, and ethical question about the kind of reader our discipline imagines for itself.

Kurnick takes issue with Stephen Best and Sharon Marcus's famous manifesto on Surface Reading, which, he claims, presents itself as nonpolemical, but in fact establishes a clear binary between two lit-crit character types, "In one corner: violence, aggression, mastery, delusions of grandeur; in the other, modesty, openness, attention, curiosity, receptiveness."[6] Kurnick does not mention it, but in contrast with other alternatives proposed in the context of the method wars, Best and Marcus locate their proposal on the side of the New Critics. Franco Moretti, for example, introduces distant reading as a stark antithesis to close reading, which he admonishes as "a theological exercise—very solemn treatment of very few texts taken very seriously," while Best and Marcus align surface reading with the New Critical project: "This valorization of surface reading as willed, sustained proximity to the text recalls the aims of New Criticism, which insisted that the key to understanding a text's meaning lay within the text itself, particularly in its formal properties."[7] I mention this since, in Kurnick's terms, Best and Marcus locate the New Critics on the unexpected side of "modesty, openness, attention, curiosity, receptiveness," which, as we have seen in the previous chapters, is true but only partly, and only if we level out a good deal of complexity.

According to Best and Marcus, as Kurnick puts it, what surface readers "most insistently" do is " 'attend' to the text: they pay 'attention' to it," a claim, Kurnick emphasizes, that is made "twenty-one times in sixteen pages."[8] In response, Kurnick asks, "What kind of critic have I become? To stick with Best and Marcus's terminology . . . I have evidently put myself on the side of the symptomatic readers. And yet: I believe what I have done is, precisely, *attended* to the surface of their text, paid attention to its imagistic patterning [emphasis in original]."[9]

Kurnick raises a pertinent question: can we read against the grain and yet be considered attentive? Yet in order to provide a decent answer to this as well as many other similar queries, we must explore what attention signifies for a given "us," ask how any specific form of attention works, what it excludes, what potentialities it opens, and what subjectivity it aids in constructing. In Kurnick's own concluding words, "we should be wary of introjecting a rhetoric that offers an impoverished account of what it means to pay attention to texts," a crucial invitation, I think, but one he does not fully answer to. I have tried my best to provide an "account of what it means to pay attention to texts," at least in the modest scope of the New Criticism, and I hope this book alongside articles like Kurnick's will generate a much larger conversation about the meaning of attentive reading and its link to our very own subject formation as students, readers, and critics of literature.

The Sun

If it is so easy to be preoccupied with the question of attention without attending to the concept itself (how can one resist these puns?), what propelled the New Critics to theorize this mental state? I hereby offer a quite outlandish proposal to close this book: the sun. These days, when the world is in flames, when inconceivable heat and all-consuming fires are all around us due to ecological catastrophe and climate change, it might not be too difficult to imagine, regardless of one's location. The intellectuals and writers occupying this book were all working under a blazing sun, which forced them, I suspect, to think consciously about attention and its accompanying labor.

The sun radiates through this book. We have seen it for example in chapter 3, where the nineteenth-century Brazilian novelist, José de Alencar, could not but envision his reader facing "the dominion of the potent tropical irradiation," when engaging with his novel. His solution was to imagine the mental state required for reading as a respite from the sun, as part of a lax and inattentive practice that lowers intensity: "I wrote it to be read there, on the porch of a rustic cabin or in the garden's fresh shade, in the sweet rocking movement of the hammock."[10] Almost a century later, Coutinho, the Brazilian New Critic, also approaches the question of attention through a consideration of the Brazilian subtropical climate, but the sun directs his thoughts elsewhere. He turns, in his popular newspaper column, to another nineteenth-century Brazilian intellectual, Tristão de Alencar Araripe Júnior, who he quotes saying, "In this immense Brazil, under the blazing rays of the tropical sun, one can either imitate the savage that takes refuge from this devouring climate in sloth and in the oscillation of the hammock, or intensify one's actions as the only way to achieve one's goals, thus quickly exhausting oneself . . . exhaust[ing] all the mental-juice necessary for making sense of a book."[11] As we have seen in chapter 3, Coutinho goes on to combine Araripe Júnior's thought with colonialist ideology in his theorization of close reading or, as we have seen he calls it, "exact reading." When he conceptualizes distraction as a "savage" Brazilian tendency, then, he is thinking through the sun. This might also explain why he continually imagines attention in terms of a concentration and intensity of rays. While the distracted savage, for Coutinho, suffers from the vice of "scatter" and "dispersion," the close reader is able to "restrict one's vision."[12]

In the Israeli context, the sun appears no less brutal. We have seen in chapter 6 how when Yehuda Amichai thinks about thinking, he begins with the sun: "One day my feet were busy walking under the sun that burned thorns and thoughts. My bag was heavy with things and words, only some of which was I about to use. . . . My whole body was busy walking and listening to my own steps. My thoughts alone moved in a time of their own, slow and private, like that of lovers walking in the noisy bustle of the world." One can almost feel the heat and its effect on the mind through these lines, the sun "burned thorns and thoughts." In fact, we might think of Amichai's famous metaphorical concatenations, which we so closely followed in the chapter, as a formal concretization of the thought process that lingers and spreads sideways under the heat. Attention as a concentration of rays, as Coutinho would put it, seems impossible in an environment where light and heat are already excessively concentrated. Like Alencar, then, Amichai finds a way to conjure a reading mode and a mind-set that will counter the intensity of the sun, one that is "slow and private," that is, "unintegrational" reading.

And what does Faulkner do with the Southern sun, "cold and bright," "slanting on the broad grass," "red on it"?[13] In his introduction to *The Sound and the Fury*, which led my reading in chapter 2, Faulkner positions Benjy, of all the Compson family members, in the agonizing heat.

> Then the story was complete, finished. There was Dilsey to be the future, to stand above the fallen ruins of the family like a ruined chimney, gaunt, patient and indomitable; and Benjy to be the past . . . a pallid and helpless mass of all mindless agony under sun [*sic*], in time yet not of it save that he could nightly carry with him that fierce, courageous being who was to him but a touch and a sound that may be heard on any golf links and a smell like trees, into the slow bright shapes of sleep.[14]

For Faulkner, by the end of the novel, when all is said and done, only Dilsey and Benjy are left. And while Dilsey stands in the midst of ruins, Benjy is "under [the] sun." Faulkner's is a sun both metaphorical and concrete; Benjy is a receptacle of all the "mindless agony" to have ever existed, but he is also impermeable to such metaphors. Instead, he is acutely attuned to sensation, literally feeling, on his body, the agony of the sun, the touch of his sister, and mostly, as we have seen in the chapter, her voice: "a sound that may be heard on any golf links and a smell like trees." Through Benjy, under the sun, Faulkner conceptualizes a "mindless" attention that focuses on a sensibility to soundless sound, a negative audition.

I, too, am under the sun. Its blaze cuts through the blinds of my workspace, distracting me from the text. Pregnant with this other, I sweat and pant. But now it is finally settling down. The room is cooler.

My story is complete, finished.

Notes

Introduction

1. Edward Said, "Traveling Theory," in *World Literature in Theory*, ed. David Damrosch (Hoboken, NJ: John Wiley, 2014), 126.

2. David Kurnick, "A Few Lies: Queer Theory and Our Method Melodramas," *ELH* 87, no. 2 (2020): 349–74.

3. As early as 1983, Robert Heilman expresses his concern "with the noises of 'Brooks is dead' (or ought to be)" ("Cleanth Brooks and 'The Well Wrought Urn,'" *Sewanee Review* 91, no. 2 [1983]: 323). Decades later, Nicholas Gaskill still writes about the New Criticism: "My overall goal is not to dismiss these critics (no need to kick a school when it's down)" ("The Close and the Concrete: Aesthetic Formalism in Context," *New Literary History* 47, no. 4 [2016]: 506), and James Heffernan locates the "ashes of New Criticism . . . within the well-wrought spatiality" ("Ekphrasis and Representation," *New Literary History* 22, no. 2 [1991]: 299). About the persistence of close reading, Evan Watkins observed in the late 1970s that, "[I]n the last three decades, in practice, when we talk about individual poems, we still sound like New Critics," *The Critical Act: Criticism and Community* (New Haven, CT: Yale University Press, 1978), 5. Similarly, Jane Gallop remarks, "The fact is that for more than three decades and most recently in the theory era, literary studies in this country was dominated by the scholarly and especially the pedagogical practice of close reading," "The Historicization of Literary Studies and the Fate of Close Reading," *Profession* (2007): 182. Heather Love expresses a similar opinion in "Close but Not Deep: Literary Ethics and the Descriptive Turn," *New Literary History* 41, no. 2 (2010): 373.

4. On surface reading, see Stephen Best and Sharon Marcus, "Surface Reading: An Introduction," *Representations* 108, no. 1 (2009): 1–21. For distant reading, see Franco Moretti, "Conjectures on World Literature," *New Left Review*

1 (2000): 54–69; *Distant Reading* (London: Verso Books), 2013; "Franco Moretti: A Response," *PMLA* 132, no. 3 (2017): 686–89. On reparative reading, see Eve Kosofsky Sedgwick, "Paranoid Reading and Reparative Reading, or, You're So Paranoid, You Probably Think This Introduction Is about You," in *Novel Gazing: Queer Readings in Fiction*, ed. Eve Kosofsky Sedgwick (Durham, NC: Duke University Press, 1997), 1–41. On descriptive reading, see Love, "Close but Not Deep," 371–91. Other interesting venues include the adaptation of Clifford Geertz's "Thick Description" into literary studies, as in the work of Stephen Greenblatt, "The Touch of the Real," *Representations*, no. 59 (1997): 14–29.

5. For an extensive discussion of the tension between New-Formalism, the New Criticism, and the Digital Humanities, see Andrew Kopec, "The Digital Humanities, Inc.: Literary Criticism and the Fate of a Profession," *PMLA* 131, no. 2 (2016): 324–39.

6. Joshua Gang, "Behaviorism and the Beginnings of Close Reading," *ELH* 78, no. 1 (2011): 1–25, and *Behaviorism, Consciousness, and the Literary Mind* (Baltimore, MD: Johns Hopkins University Press, 2021); Joseph North, "What's 'New Critical' about 'Close Reading': I. A. Richards and His New Critical Reception," *New Literary History* 44, no. 1 (2013): 141–57, and *Literary Criticism: A Concise Political History* (Cambridge, MA: Harvard University Press, 2017); Helen Thaventhiran, *Radical Empiricists: Five Modernist Close Readers* (Oxford, UK: Oxford University Press, 2015); Rachel Sagner Buurma and Laura Heffernan, *The Teaching Archive: A New History for Literary Study* (Chicago, IL: University of Chicago Press, 2020); Andy Hines, *Outside Literary Studies: Black Criticism and the University* (Chicago, IL: University of Chicago Press, 2022).

7. Peter Button, "The Aesthetic Critique of Modernity in Chinese Marxism, New Criticism, and Adorno," in *Configurations of the Real in Chinese Literary and Aesthetic Modernity* (Leiden, the Netherlands; Boston, MA: Brill, 2009), 120–59; David M. Stewart, "New Criticism and Value in Taiwanese College English," *American Literature* 89, no. 2 (2017): 397–423; Paul Nadal, "Cold War Remittance Economy: US Creative Writing and the Importation of New Criticism into the Philippines," *American Quarterly* 73, no. 3 (2021): 557–95.

8. Marta Puxan-Oliva and Annalisa Mirizio, "Rethinking World Literature Studies in Latin American and Spanish Contexts," *Journal of World Literature* 2, no. 1 (2017): 7.

9. Ziva Ben-Porat and Benjamin Hrushovski, *Poética e estruturalismo em Israel*, Jacó Guinsburg (trans.) (São Paulo, Brazil: Editora Perspectiva, 1978); Ziva Ben-Porat and Benjamin Hrushovski, *Structuralist Poetics in Israel* (Tel Aviv, Israel: Department of Poetics and Comparative Literature at Tel Aviv University, 1974). The translation into Portuguese opens with an introduction by the prominent Brazilian intellectual, Haroldo de Campos, where the Israeli Tel Aviv School is presented and praised. For more, see the Epilogue.

10. David Damrosch, *What Is World Literature?* (Princeton, NJ: Princeton University Press, 2018), 22; Vilashini Cooppan, "World Literature and Global Theory: Comparative Literature for the New Millennium," *symplokē* 9, no. 1/2 (2001): 15–43.

11. Chana Kronfeld, *The Full Severity of Compassion: The Poetry of Yehuda Amichai* (Redwood City, CA: Stanford University Press, 2016), 145; Barbara Christian, "The Race for Theory," *Cultural Critique* 6 (1987): 51–64.

12. As a political choice, I will refer to the reader in the feminine throughout the chapter (as I do in the book as a whole), even when discussing thinkers who likely imagined the reader to be a white man.

13. Terry Eagleton, *Literary Theory: An Introduction*, 2nd ed. (Minneapolis: Minnesota University Press, 1996), 41.

14. John Crowe Ransom, "Criticism, Inc." *VQR* 13, no. 4 (1937), https://www.vqronline.org/essay/criticism-inc-0.

15. In my mind, the American reader-response theories as well developed out of rather than against the New Critical creed. In that sense, it is not coincidental that Stanley Fish was a student of Cleanth Brooks; see Charlotte H. Beck and John P. Rhoades, "'Stanley Fish Was My Reader': Cleanth Brooks, the New Criticism, and Reader-Response Theory," in *The New Criticism and Contemporary Literary Theory: Connections and Continuities*, eds. William J. Spurlin and Michael Fischer (New York: Garland, 1995), 211–27.

16. Grant Webster, *Republic of Letters*, 63; qtd. in John Paul Russo, *The Future without a Past: The Humanities in a Technological Society* (Columbia: University of Missouri Press, 2005), 281.

17. Karen O'Kane, "Before the New Criticism: Modernism and the Nashville Group," *Mississippi Quarterly* 51, no. 4 (1998): 683; "Literature Itself: The New Criticism and Aesthetic Experience," *Philosophy and Literature* 27, no. 1 (2003): 64.

18. I owe much of this insight to Jonathan Crary's foundational work on attention and art, which prompted me to think in depth about the link between twentieth century conceptions of reading and the cognitive work of concentration, *Suspensions of Perception: Attention, Spectacle, and Modern Culture* (Cambridge, MA: MIT Press, 2001).

19. Peter Howarth recently pointed to a similar paradox in examining the New Criticism through the concept of performativity rather than through attention: "The paradox running all through their book [*Survey of Modernist Poetry*] is that the autonomy of the poem, on which they insist, is always framed by its readers, good and bad, on whom they also insist," "Close Reading as Performance," in David James (ed.), *Modernism and Close Reading* (Oxford, UK: Oxford University Press, 2020), 48.

20. W. K. Wimsatt and M. C. Beardsley, "The Intentional Fallacy," *Sewanee Review* 54, no. 3 (1946): 477.

21. Afrânio Coutinho, *Correntes cruzadas: questões de literatura* (Rio de Janeiro, Brazil: Editora A Noite, 1953), 10. I.A. Richards, *How to Read a Page: A Course in Effective Reading*, 2nd ed. (London: Routledge & K. Paul, 1961).

22. T. S. Eliot, "Tradition and the Individual Talent," *Perspecta* 19 (1982): 42.

23. Eliot writes, "Impressions and experiences which are important for the man may take no place in the poetry, and those which become important in the poetry may play quite a negligible part in the man, the personality," "Tradition and the Individual Talent," 41.

24. Christina Walter, *Optical Impersonality: Science, Images, and Literary Modernism* (Baltimore, MD: Johns Hopkins University Press, 2014): 2.

25. Kazuki Inoue, "Ghost Psychology in T. S. Eliot and W. B. Yeats" (PhD diss., University of York, 2020), https://etheses.whiterose.ac.uk/29519/.

26. Hines, *Outside Literary Studies*, 2022.

27. Edward D. Pickering, "The Roots of New Criticism," *Southern Literary Journal* 41, no. 1 (2008): 93.

28. In that sense, I fully agree with Mark Jancovich when he contends that "the New Critics did not define the text as a fixed object. . . . Their position was that if students were to be taught to understand the workings of these broader [historical and political] processes, it was necessary to focus their attention on the texts which mediated between the contexts of production and consumption," *The Cultural Politics of the New Criticism* (Cambridge, UK: Cambridge University Press, 1993), 5.

29. For an in-depth examination of the affinity between the New Critics and Southern Agrarianism, see Pickering, "The Roots of New Criticism"; Angie Maxwell, *The Indicted South: Public Criticism, Southern Inferiority, and the Politics of Whiteness* (Chapel Hill: University of North Carolina Press, 2014), 144–65.

30. Allen Tate, "The Man of Letters in the Modern World," in *Essays of Four Decades* (Chicago, IL: The Swallow Press, 1968), 6.

31. Tate, "The Man of Letters," 4.

32. John Fekete, *The Critical Twilight: Explorations in the Ideology of Anglo-American Literary Theory from Eliot to McLuhan* (London: Routledge & K. Paul, 1977), 45.

33. Qtd. in Luther H. Martin, Huck Gutman, and Patrick H. Hutton (eds.), *Technologies of the Self: A Seminar with Michel Foucault* (London: Tavistock, 1988), 3.

34. Michel Foucault, "Technologies of the Self," in Martin, Gutman, and Hutton (eds.), *Technologies of the Self*, 16–50.

35. Foucault, "Technologies of the Self," 18.

36. As Mark E. Kelly observes, "Subjectivity . . . is not for Foucault merely the passive product of impersonal process. . . . Rather, he insists that the subject constitutes itself . . . under the techniques available to it historically, and doubtless under the influence of myriad factors outside its control," "Foucault, Subjectivity,

and Technologies of the Self," in *A Companion to Foucault*, eds. Christopher Falzon, Timothy O'Leary, and Jana Sawicki (Hoboken, NJ: Blackwell Publishing 2013), 513.

37. Kelly, "Foucault, Subjectivity, and Technologies, 515.

38. Christopher Lehman and Kate Roberts, *Falling in Love with Close Reading: Lessons for Analyzing Texts and Life* (Portsmouth, NH: Heinemann, 2013), 15. Similarly, *Writing Analytically* guarantees that its two basic heuristics will "retrain your focus and your attention from the global (general) to the local," David Rosenwasser and Jill Stephen, *Writing Analytically*, 6th ed. (Boston, MA: Wadsworth Publishing, 2011), 23.

39. Paul de Man, *Blindness and Insight: Essays in the Rhetoric of Contemporary Criticism* (Minneapolis: University of Minnesota Press), 1986, 27; Jane Gallop, "The Ethics of Close Reading: Close Encounters," *Journal of Curriculum Theorizing* 16, no. 3 (2000): 8; Eagleton, *Literary Theory*, 41.

40. Andrew DuBois, "Close Reading: An Introduction," in *Close Reading: The Reader*, eds. Frank Lentricchia and Andrew DuBois (Durham, NC: Duke University Press, 2003), 4.

41. Wimsatt and Beardsley, "The Intentional Fallacy," 469.

42. Wimsatt and Beardsley, "The Intentional Fallacy," 480.

43. René Wellek and Austin Warren, *Theory of Literature*, 3rd ed. (New York: Harcourt Brace Jovanovich, 1977), 251.

44. Allen Tate, "Is Literary Criticism Possible?," in *Essays of Four Decades* (Chicago, IL: Swallow Press, 1968), 35.

45. Tate, "Is Literary Criticism Possible?," 42.

46. Tate, "Is Literary Criticism Possible?," 42. Tate's call for self-abnegation might seem to have a Christian undertone to it, especially if we recall that Tate's contribution to the infamous *I'll Take My Stand* was titled "Remarks on the Southern Religion." But, in principle, Tate was more concerned with form than with religion, as Bruce Bawer notes, which reconciles his explicit political conservatism with his admiration of experimental modernism, ("Religious Atheist: The Case of Allen Tate," *Hudson Review* 55, no. 1 [2002], 167–75). This is true of the New Critics more generally. Indeed, as David Marno's work on John Donne points out, the New Critics' interest in Donne's devotional understanding of "attention" was not fueled by theological preoccupations but with an interest with literary form. Though Marno does not specify what "attention" meant for the New Critics, he makes clear that their view was different from Donne's, who designed his poems to provoke "holy attention" in the reader as a "preparation for prayer" (*Death Be Not Proud: The Art of Holy Attention* [Chicago, IL: University of Chicago Press, 2017], 28, 2). To continue in Marno's line of thought, my sense is that the New Critics understood attention not as a theological praxis but in terms of cognitive self-control.

47. Tate, "Is Literary Criticism Possible?," 35.

48. Brooks writes to Tate in 1973, "From a very early period you were my special hero as man of letters," in *Cleanth Brooks and Allen Tate: Collected Letters, 1933–1976*, ed. Alphonse Vinh (Columbia: University of Missouri Press, 1998), 254.

49. Cleanth Brooks, "The Formalist Critics," *Kenyon Review* 13, no. 1 (1951): 76–77.

50. Brooks, "Formalist Critics," 77.

51. Decades later, at the peak of the New Critics' rejection by the North American intellectual milieu, Frank Lentricchia points out the imperative of self-depletion recorded in the New Critical creed without relating it to attention or mental education. Lentricchia argues that Georges Poulet's phenomenology was so positively received in the US because it coincided with the New Critical image of "the critical reader becoming a transparency who presents the thought of others without distortion," an "objective, nonideological reader" who is engaged in "self-effacement, and perfect openness to the Other." Not only do I agree with Lentricchia about the New Critics' view of the (educated) reader as a "transparency," I also share his view that it resonates with later poststructuralist theories. However, I take issue with his negative value judgment of this ideal attentive reader, *After the New Criticism* (Chicago, IL: University of Chicago Press, 1980), 70.

52. I owe much of my understanding of Derrida's ethics to Michal Ben-Naftali's work and instruction. For example, see Michal Ben-Naftali, "Deconstruction: Derrida," in *The Edinburgh Encyclopedia of Continental Philosophy*, ed. Simon Glendinning (Edinburgh, UK: Edinburgh University Press, 1999), 653–64. Derrida's works that most guided my thinking include: *Specters of Marx: The State of the Debt, the Work of Mourning, & the New International*, trans. Peggy Kaufman (London: Routledge, 1994); "Fors: The Anglish Words of Nicolas Abraham and Maria Torok," in *The Wolf Man's Magic Word: A Cryptonomy*, by Nicholas Abraham and Maria Torok, ed. Barbara Johnson, trans. Nicholas Rand (Minneapolis: Minnesota University Press, 1986); and *Mémoires for Paul de Man*, eds. Avital Ronell and Eduardo Cadava, trans. Cecile Lindsay, Jonathan Culler, and Peggy Kamuf (New York: Columbia University Press, 1989).

53. A similar stance arises from John Crowe Ransom's "Poetry: A Note on Ontology," where he presents attention as the ability to entertain the object in its "remarkability" without trying to "possess" it, in *Close Reading: The Reader*, ed. Frank Lentricchia and Andrew DuBois (Durham, NC: Duke University Press, 2003), 60.

54. For more humanistic understandings of close reading, see Love, "Close but Not Deep," 372; Ian Hunter, "The History of Theory," *Critical Inquiry* 33 (2006): 78–112.

55. For example, Annette Federico begins *Engagements with Close Reading* by depicting close reading as formulated in a specific time and place, but ends up favoring close reading, since she believes it "supersedes" any specific theory or literary form (New York: Routledge, 2015), 6. Catherine Gallagher adds that this neutraliza-

tion permitted "what came to be thought of simply as techniques of 'close reading' or 'practical criticism'" to be used uncritically in literary interpretations guided by "Freudian and Jungian Psychoanalysis, existentialism, archetypal analysis, Marxism, and structuralism" ("The History of Literary Criticism," *Daedalus* 126, no. 1 [1997]: 140).

56. Chana Kronfeld, *On the Margins of Modernism: Decentering Literary Dynamics* (Berkeley: University of California Press, 1996), 125; James, *Modernism and Close Reading*, 1–19.

57. Ransom, "Poetry: A Note on Ontology," 44.

58. John Guillory, "The Ideology of Canon-Formation: T. S. Eliot and Cleanth Brooks," *Critical Inquiry* 10, no. 1 (1983): 173.

59. Guillory, "Ideology of Canon-Formation," 174.

60. My understanding of nonattentive reading modes was informed by various scholarly and philosophical investigations into nonattention per se. See Walter Benjamin, "Theory of Distraction," in *Walter Benjamin: Selected Writings, Vol. 3: 1935–1938*, eds. Howard Eiland and Michael W. Jennings (Cambridge, MA: Harvard University Press, 2006), 141–42; Sigmund Freud, "Recommendations to Physicians Practicing Psycho-Analysis," in *The Standard Edition of the Complete Psychological Works of Sigmund Freud*, trans. James Strachey, vol. 12 (London: Hogarth Press, 1953), 111–20; Siegfried Kracauer, "Cult of Distraction: On Berlin's Picture Palaces," trans. Thomas Y. Levin, *New German Critique*, no. 40 (1987): 91–96; Paul North, *The Problem of Distraction* (Stanford, CA: Stanford University Press, 2011); Natalie M. Phillips, *Distraction: Problems of Attention in Eighteenth-Century Literature* (Baltimore, MD: Johns Hopkins University Press, 2016). Exciting attempts have also been made to understand readerly attention in a context other than that of the New Criticism. See, Lily Gurton-Wachter, *Watchwords: Romanticism and the Poetics of Attention* (Redwood City, CA: Stanford University Press, 2016); Lucy Alford, *Forms of Poetic Attention* (New York: Columbia University Press, 2020).

61. For that reason, R. P. Blackmur feels the need in 1949 to make a plea for rethinking close reading in relation to the novel. See "For a Second Look," *Kenyon Review* 11, no. 1 (1949): 9. In following what indeed happened to the New Critical concept of "attention" as it was applied to prose-fiction generally, and the novelistic form specifically, I respond to Nicholas Dames's question: "What . . . is the precise quality of the attention a novel asks of us?" "Reverie, Sensation, Effect: Novelistic Attention and Stendhal's 'De l'Amour,'" *Narrative* 10, no. 1 (2002): 47.

62. Ransom, "Criticism, Inc."

63. John Crowe Ransom, *The New Criticism* (Norfolk, VA: New Directions, 1941), 271–72.

64. Ransom writes, "[The purpose of suspense is] to obtain the closer attention upon the items of context, knowing that as long as we do not yet know the values of the items for the final structure we shall look at them harder in order to have the right values ready when they can be used," Ransom, *New Criticism*, 272–74.

65. Ransom, *New Criticism*, 274.
66. Wellek and Warren, *Theory of Literature*, 261.
67. Ben-Porat and Hrushovski, *Structuralist Poetics in Israel*.
68. Ben-Porat and Hrushovski, *Structuralist Poetics in Israel*, 5.
69. Daniel Boyarin, "Placing Reading: Ancient Israel and Medieval Europe," in *The Ethnography of Reading*, ed. Jonathan Boyarin (Berkeley, CA: University of California Press, 1993), 10–38.
70. Boyarin, "Placing Reading: Ancient Israel," 14.
71. Boyarin, "Placing Reading: Ancient Israel," 18.
72. Harold Fisch, "Reading and Carnival: On the Semiotics of Purim," *Poetics Today* 15, no. 1 (1994): 59.
73. Isidore Epstein, trans., Tractate "Megillah," Order "Mo'ed," in *The Babylonian Talmud* (London: Soncino Press, 1935), 103.
74. José Martiniano de Alencar, *Iracema: lenda do Ceará* (São Paulo, Brazil: Ed Cultrix, 1968). As in this case, all unattributed translations in this chapter and the following are mine.
75. Clarice Lispector, "Felicidade clandestina," in *Felicidade clandestina*, 4th ed. (Rio de Janeiro, Brazil: Editora Nova Fronteira, 1981), 7–11; "Covert Joy," in *The Complete Stories*, ed. Benjamin Moser, trans. Katrina Dodson (New York: New Directions, 2015), 369–72.
76. Lispector, "Covert Joy," 37.
77. Hélène Cixous, *Reading with Clarice Lispector*, ed. and trans. Verena Andermatt Conley (Minneapolis: University of Minnesota Press, 1990), 131.
78. Cixous, *Reading with Clarice Lispector*, 128.
79. This is the case in the 4th and 5th editions of the book by Editora Nova Fronteira.
80. Steven Connor, "Postmodernism and Literature," in *The Cambridge Companion to Postmodernism*, ed. Steven Connor (Cambridge, UK: Cambridge University Press, 2006), 77.

Chapter One

1. Allen Tate, "Miss Emily and the Bibliographer," *The American Scholar* 9, no. 4 (1940): 449–60.
2. Tate, "Miss Emily and the Bibliographer," 455, 456.
3. Tate, "Miss Emily and the Bibliographer," 450.
4. Tate, "Miss Emily and the Bibliographer," 450.
5. Tate, "Miss Emily and the Bibliographer," 450.
6. Tate, "Miss Emily and the Bibliographer," 458, 459.
7. Tate, "Miss Emily and the Bibliographer," 459, 460.

8. In that vein, Joseph North insists that while the British predecessors, Richards and Empson, designed their reading practice to "intervene in the context of reception . . . the minds of actual, living readers," their North American disciples took "'aesthetic value' . . . as residing, not in anything the text could be used to achieve in the mind of the reader, but somehow solely in the text itself," since "what is really being rejected [by the New Critics] is the *reader*," *Literary Criticism*, 154, 40 (emphasis in original).

9. John Paul Russo, "The Tranquilized Poem: The Crisis of New Criticism in the 1950s," *Texas Studies in Literature and Language* 30, no. 2 (1988): 205. As early as 1963, Richard Foster associates the "impersonal, uninvolved, and 'technical'" tone with the New Criticism ("Recent American Criticism," *Critical Survey* 1, no. 3 [1963]: 160); later, Ernest Kaiser writes, "the creative writing called for by the New Critics" was "unemotional, uncommitted and uninvolved in the people's problems" ("A Critical Look at Ellison's Fiction and at Social and Literary Criticism by and about the Author," *Black World*, December issue, 1970: 57); Gerald Graff demonstrates how the New Critics have been consistently criticized for their "aloof intellectuality" (*Professing Literature: An Institutional History* [Chicago, IL: University of Chicago Press, 1987], 248); and William V. Spanos claims that "autotelic New Critical frame called for an 'objective' or 'disinterested' reader," "Against Distant Reading: Retrieving Close Reading in the Interregnum," *symplokē* 25, no. 1–2 (2017): 248.

10. Instances of this association are too numerous to count. Paradigmatically, the *Cambridge History of Literary Criticism* states that "the New Critics' definition of literary study conforms to what Bourdieu refers to as 'the aesthetic disposition' or 'the pure gaze.' This mode of perception is preoccupied with form over function, and privileges disinterested contemplation over use or utility," eds. Walton Litz, Louis Menand, Lawrence Rainey, *Vol. 7: Modernism and the New Criticism* (Cambridge, UK: Cambridge University Press, 2000), 214–15. At the end of the chapter, I return to the topic via Joseph North's critique of the New Critics' ostensible overreliance on Kant's disinterestedness.

11. Ransom, "Criticism, Inc."

12. Cleanth Brooks, *The Well Wrought Urn: Studies in the Structure of Poetry* (Orlando, FL: Harcourt, 1947); *William Faulkner: The Yoknapatawpha Country* (New Haven, CT: Yale University Press, 1966); *William Faulkner: Toward Yoknapatawpha and Beyond* (Baton Rouge: Louisiana State University Press, 1990). One of the reasons that Brooks's reading of Faulkner is rarely examined alongside the New Critical creed (Florence Dore's recent work is an exciting exception to this rule) is that close reading was first conceptualized with regard to poetry.

13. Douglas Mao, "The New Critics and the Text-Object," *ELH* 63, no. 1 (1996): 228. Discussing the political implications of this aesthetic view, John Guillory writes: "[T]hat the poem is a 'well-wrought urn,' is not just the proposition

that the poem is an artifact.... It is rather that the urn belongs to the world of value and not to the world of power. It is a celebration of its own purity, its escape from ... the assertion of power over other human beings" ("The Ideology of Canon-Formation," 192). The urn also came to stand for the New Criticism via its appearance in John Donne's celebrated "Canonization," which itself represents the early-modern tradition of metaphysical poetry the New Critics strove to revive within the Anglo-American canon. In addition, the urn is affiliated with the work of Faulkner, as will be discussed in chapter 2.

14. Brooks, *The Urn*, 14.

15. Jonathan Culler expresses the traditional view of Deconstruction as the mirror-image of the New Criticism when he writes that "[Derrida's] work appealed to students and teachers of literature, who found in it close reading that ... was not subservient to the ideological notion of organic form that underlay the most widespread practice of close reading, that of the New Criticism," *On Deconstruction: Theory and Criticism after Structuralism* (Ithaca, NY: Cornell University Press, 2007), preface to the twenty-fifth anniversary edition. By contrast, Gerald Graff and Frank Lentricchia condemn Deconstruction for continuing the ostensibly ahistorical and apolitical New Critical trend (*Literature against Itself: Literary Ideas in Modern Society* [Chicago, IL: University of Chicago Press, 1979)] *After the New Criticism*), and Timothy Aubry claims that Deconstruction continues the New Critical interest in aesthetic judgment, "Appetite for Deconstruction," in *Guilty aesthetic pleasures* (Cambridge, MA: Harvard University Press, 2018), 64–104.

16. On Derrida's philosophy as outlining an "ethics of alterity," see Penelope Deutscher, "Mourning the Other, Cultural Cannibalism, and the Politics of Friendship (Jacques Derrida and Luce Irigaray)," *Differences: A Journal of Feminist Cultural Studies* 10, no. 3 (1998): 159–84; François Raffoul, "Derrida and the Ethics of the Im-possible," *Research in Phenomenology* 38, no. 2 (2008): 270–90; and Shane Weller, *Beckett, Literature and the Ethics of Alterity* (Basingstoke, UK: Palgrave Macmillan, 2006).

17. Derrida, "Fors," xvi.

18. Derrida, *Mémoires*, 6.

19. Derrida, "Fors," xvi.

20. In discussing the ethics of close reading, I follow in the footsteps of both Heather Love and Ian Hunter, see Introduction.

21. Brooks refers to himself as a "typical New Critic" in "The New Criticism," *Sewanee Review* 87, no. 4 (1979): 592; Guillory, "The Ideology of Canon-Formation," 174.

22. Heilman, "Cleanth Brooks and 'The Well Wrought Urn,'" 323.

23. Peter Parolin and Phyllis Rackin, "Close Reading Shakespeare: An Introduction," *Early Modern Culture* 12, no. 1 (2017): 4.

24. Green, "Literature Itself," 64.

25. Heilman, "Cleanth Brooks and 'The Well Wrought Urn,'" 322.

26. Cleanth Brooks and Robert Penn Warren, *Understanding Fiction* (Englewood Cliffs, NJ: Pearson, 1979), 510; Brooks, *The Urn*, 195.
27. Brooks, *The Urn*, 32, 73, 153.
28. Brooks, *The Urn*, 81.
29. Brooks, *The Urn*, 67.
30. Brooks, *The Urn*, 7.
31. Brooks, *The Urn*, 7.
32. Brooks, *The Urn*, 8.
33. Brooks, *The Urn*, 28.
34. In his work on John Donne, David Marno perceptively points out this paragraph to demonstrate that the New Critics noticed "the significance of attention in Donne's poetry," a state of mind Marno argues held devotional purposes for Donne, acting as a "preparation for prayer" (*Death Be Not Proud*, 28, 2). He notes, however, that the New Critics turned more often to Donne's secular poetry. The reason, I believe, is that the New Critics developed a different understanding of attention, one oriented toward cognitive self-control rather than toward a potential interaction with the divine.
35. Brooks, *The Urn*, 10.
36. Brooks, *The Urn*, 6.
37. Brooks, *The Urn*, 6.
38. The paradox of death in life and life in death governs *The Urn*, despite Brooks's explicit definition of paradox as *any* tension "set up . . . by propositions, metaphors, symbols," which is then resolved via "an equilibrium of forces" (*The Urn*, 207). To name a few examples out of many, in Donne's "The Canonization," "[T]he lovers in rejecting life actually win to the most intense life" (*The Urn*, 15); in Tennyson's "Tears, Ideal Tears," "The dying man, soon to sleep the lasting sleep, is more fully awake than the 'half-awaken'd birds' whose earliest pipings come to his dying ears" (*The Urn*, 171); In Keats's "Ode on a Grecian Urn," "[T]he beauty portrayed is deathless because it is lifeless" (*The Urn*, 157); in Pope's "The Rape of the Lock," "[I]n some cases, little more is implied than a teasing of the popular clichés about bearing a 'living Death'" (*The Urn*, 101); and in Shakespeare's *Macbeth* it is "the clothed daggers and the naked babe . . . death and birth" that "are facets of two of the great symbols which run throughout the play" (*The Urn*, 49). It is not by mere accident that the paradox found at the center of the New Critics' conceptualization of the close reader echoes Yeats's famous line in "Byzantium," "I call it death-in-life and life-in-death." The New Critics were highly invested in Yeats's poetry more generally, and in "Byzantium" specifically. See, for example, Cleanth Brooks, "A Vision and the Byzantium Poems," in *Yeats: Poems, 1919–1935: A Casebook*, ed. Elizabeth Butler Cullingford (London: Macmillan, 1984), 63–74; and Cleanth Brooks and Robert Penn Warren, *Understanding Poetry* (Boston, MA: Wadsworth, 1976), 353–55.
39. Brooks, *The Urn*, 151.

40. Brooks, *The Urn*; emphasis in original.
41. Brooks, *The Urn*, 122.
42. Brooks, *The Urn*, 69.
43. Brooks, *The Urn*, 165.
44. Brooks, *The Urn*, 190.
45. Brooks, *The Urn*, 190.
46. Brooks, *The Urn*, 16–20.
47. Brooks, *The Urn*, 110.
48. "The Best Southern Novels of All Time," *Oxford American*, August 27, 2009, https://www.oxfordamerican.org/magazine/iten/470-the-best-southern-novels-of-all-time; William Faulkner, *Absalom, Absalom!* (New York: Vintage, 1990).
49. Max Miller, "*Absalom, Absalom!*" in *William Faulkner: The Contemporary Reviews* (Cambridge, UK: Cambridge University Press, 1995), 152; Bernard De Voto, "Witchcraft in Mississippi," in *William Faulkner: The Contemporary Reviews* (Cambridge, UK: Cambridge University Press, 1995), 149; Wallace Stegner, "Review," in *William Faulkner: Critical Assessments*, ed. Henry Claridge, vol. 3 (Robertsbridge, UK: Helm Information, 1999), 275.
50. Malcolm Cowley, "Poe in Mississippi," in *William Faulkner: Critical Assessments*, ed. Henry Claridge, vol. 3 (Robertsbridge, UK: Helm Information, 1999), 32.
51. See Lawrence H. Schwartz, *Creating Faulkner's Reputation: The Politics of Modern Literary Criticism* (Knoxville: University of Tennessee Press, 1988), 32.
52. Brooks, *Yoknapatawpha Country*, 295.
53. Brooks, *Yoknapatawpha Country*, 323.
54. Sheldon Brivic, *Tears of Rage: The Racial Interface of Modern American Fiction: Faulkner, Wright, Pynchon, Morrison* (Baton Rouge: Louisiana State University Press, 2008), 31; Faulkner, *Absalom*, 190.
55. George Marrion O'Donnell, "Mr. Faulkner Flirts with Failure," in *William Faulkner: The Contemporary Reviews*, ed. M. Thomas Inge (Cambridge, UK: Cambridge University Press, 1995), 144.
56. Faulkner, *Absalom*, 11. It could be justifiably claimed that at times Quentin is not "a Special Listener" at all. During the scene at Mrs. Rosa's house, for instance, the narrator informs us that "Quentin was not listening" (Faulkner, *Absalom*, 172). However, it is my sense that Quentin is listening at that moment, not to Rosa but to his internal Others. As Brooks writes: "Quentin was not listening because his imagination remained gripped by the confrontation between Henry and Judith when Henry bursts into her room to tell her he has killed her fiancé. This is a scene which Miss Rosa could not have personally witnessed" (*Yoknapatawpha and Beyond*, 306). The precision with which Quentin recounts that encounter, without, here again, treating it as his own imaginative invention, suggests that it emanates from an alterity within him.
57. Faulkner, *Absalom*, 7.

58. Panthea Reid Broughton writes in this regard, "Quentin Compson . . . would choose to live in the past. He faces backward in time . . . Becoming himself a 'stubborn back-looking ghost.' Quentin denies his involvement in both present and future. He consciously sets out to destroy the interconnectedness of time, to forestall progression," *William Faulkner: The Abstract and the Actual* (Baton Rouge: Louisiana State University Press, 1974), 113.

59. Derrida, "Fors," xvi.
60. Faulkner, *Absalom*, 80.
61. Faulkner, *Absalom*, 75.
62. Faulkner, *Absalom*, 100.
63. Faulkner, *Absalom*, 101.
64. Brooks, *The Urn*, 151, 165.
65. Faulkner, *Absalom*, 80.
66. Faulkner, *Absalom*, 102.
67. See, for example, Owen Robinson, *Creating Yoknapatawpha: Readers and Writers in Faulkner's Fiction* (New York: Routledge, 2006), 99; and John T. Irwin, *Doubling and Incest/Repetition and Revenge* (Baltimore, MD: Johns Hopkins University Press, 1975), 119. The location of this boundary between the first and second sections of the novel varies among critics.

68. Richard Godden, *Fictions of Labor: William Faulkner and the South's Long Revolution* (Cambridge, MA: Cambridge University Press, 1997), 168.

69. A central voice in this tradition is Peter Brooks, who claims that Quentin begins *Absalom, Absalom!* in the passive position associated with Roland Barthes's "readerly" text and transforms into a reader in the Barthian "writerly" sense, one that takes on the "authority of narrative" (*Reading for the Plot: Design and Intention in Narrative* [Cambridge, MA: Harvard University Press, 1992], 304–5).

70. Brooks, *Yoknapatawpha Country*, 327.
71. Brooks, *Yoknapatawpha Country*, 310.
72. Faulkner, *Absalom*, 243; Brooks, *Yoknapatawpha Country*, 314.
73. Faulkner, *Absalom*, 280, 208.
74. As Doreen Fowler points out, Quentin presents many of his own discoveries, such as Charles Bon being Sutpen's son, as if they were his father's or grandfather's, *Faulkner: The Return of the Repressed* (Charlottesville: Virginia University Press, 1997), 110.

75. For example, Quentin transitions without any apparent change in tone or language from recounting Sutpen's abandonment of Molly's baby-girl (a detail he knows from his father) to the conversation between Judith and Sutpen after the war, which he clearly makes up (Faulkner, *Absalom*, 300).

76. Faulkner, *Absalom*, 172.
77. Brooks, *Yoknapatawpha Country*, 318.
78. Quentin and Henry are also excessive in their "attachment" to each other. As Brooks prods us to recall, the readers forcefully witness Quentin's

"peculiar" susceptibility to Henry's story when the protagonist recounts to Shreve his meeting with Henry at Sutpen Hundred. While describing Henry's "wasted yellow face ... as if he were already a corpse," Quentin becomes a Henry of sorts and approaches death: "preparing for the dead moment before dawn ... he lay still and rigid on his back" (Faulkner, *Absalom*, 298).

79. Faulkner, *Absalom*, 5.
80. Brooks, *Yoknapawtapha Country*, 13.
81. Brooks, *Yoknapawtapha Country*, 311.
82. Brooks, *Yoknapawtapha Country*, 313.
83. North, *Literary Criticism*, 27.
84. North, *Literary Criticism*, 27, 43.
85. Brooks, *The Urn*, 108, 14, 30, 14, 100, 50.

Chapter Two

1. James B. Meriwether and Michael Millgate, ed., *Lion in the Garden: Interviews with William Faulkner* (New York: Random House, 1968), 239; Meta Carpenter Wilde and Orin Borsten, *A Loving Gentleman: The Love Story of William Faulkner and Meta Carpenter* (New York: Simon and Schuster, 1976), 76–77.

2. André Bleikasten, *The Ink of Melancholy: Faulkner's Novels from* The Sound and the Fury *to* Light in August (Bloomington: Indiana University Press, 1990), x.

3. Fredric Jameson, *The Antinomies of Realism* (London: Verso, 2013), 176, 210.

4. Godden, *Fictions of Labor*, 4.

5. Godden, *Fictions of Labor*, 4.

6. William Faulkner, *Faulkner in the University: Class Conferences at the University of Virginia, 1957–1958* (New York: Vintage, 1965), 61. In reading the novel's style from the vantage point of an ethics of alterity, I join such scholars as Paula M. L. Moya ("Reading as a Realist: Expanded Literacy in Helena María Viramontes's *Under the Feet of Jesus*," in *Learning from Experience: Minority Identities, Multicultural Struggles* [Berkeley: University of California Press, 2002], 175–214), and Dorothy J. Hale ("Zadie Smith's *On Beauty*: An Ethical Aesthetic as the Problem of Perspectivalism, in *The Novel and the New Ethics* [Redwood City, CA: Stanford University Press, 2020], 96–135).

7. William Faulkner, "An Introduction to *The Sound and the Fury*," ed. James B. Meriwether, *Mississippi Quarterly* 26 (1973): 415. Faulkner produced various drafts for his introductions to *The Sound and the Fury* during 1933 in anticipation of a limited edition that did not finally materialize. I quote from the two drafts published by James B. Meriwether in 1972 and 1973. For more about the genealogy of this introduction, see Philip Cohen and Doreen Fowler,

"Faulkner's Introduction to *The Sound and the Fury*," *American Literature* 62, no. 2 (1990): 262–83.

8. R. Murray Schafer also identifies in Faulkner a sonic sensitivity ("ear-witnessing") to the dead: "William Faulkner . . . knew the noise of corpses, which he described as 'little trickling bursts of secret murmurous bubbling,'" *The Soundscape: Our Sonic Environment and the Tuning of the World* (Rochester, NY: Destiny Books, 1994), 9. Yet, Murray focuses on the positive depiction of death, that is, actual vocalities generated by corpse, while I am interested the ways in which Faulkner's texts conjure "dead" or "ghostly" sounds in the reader's mind without their material presence in the text.

9. Faulkner, *Absalom*, 7.

10. My argument follows in the footsteps of Florence Dore, who has demonstrated that Faulkner's work conforms with what she terms the New Critical "protocols of reading" only if we change our understanding of what New Critical close reading means ("The New Criticism and the Nashville Sound: William Faulkner's *The Town* and Tock and Roll," *Contemporary Literature* 55, no. 1 [2014]: 32–57; *Novel Sounds: Southern Fiction in the Age of Rock and Roll* [New York: Columbia University Press, 2018]). Dore, however, finds this new dimension of close reading in later works such as *The Town*, and claims that the earlier novels, like *The Sound and the Fury*, fall in line quite easily with conventional understandings of New Critical close reading. In contrast, I believe that *The Sound and the Fury* proves the close reader to be, for both Faulkner and Brooks, not the detached contemplator of an autonomous urn-text, as even Dore assumes, but an active participant in the creation of the work, a participant whose function is, however narrowly specified, to occupy a hauntological subject position, to function as the text's echo-chamber and thus give it life. In addition, my argument is inspired by Marilia Librandi's work on the role of aurality in the oeuvre of Clarice Lispector (to be discussed in chapter 4). See, *Writing by Ear: Clarice Lispector and the Aural Novel* (Toronto, ON: University of Toronto Press, 2018).

11. Garrett Stewart, *Reading Voices: Literature and the Phonotext* (Berkeley: University of California Press, 1990), 192–232.

12. Sarah Gleeson-White, "Auditory Exposures: Faulkner, Eisenstein, and Film Sound," *PMLA* 128, no. 1 (2013): 87. In the last decade, Faulkner's soundscapes have been studied in relation to racialized power structures (Kristin Fujie, "'Through a Piece of Colored Glass': Faulkner, Race, and Mediation," *Modern Fiction Studies* 65, no. 3 [2019]: 411–38; Julie Beth Napolin, *The Fact of Resonance: Modernist Acoustics and Narrative Form* [New York: Fordham University Press, 2020]); to the early-twentieth century media revolution (Julian Murphet, *Faulkner's Media Romance* [Oxford, UK: Oxford University Press, 2017]; Julian Murphet and Stefan Solomon, eds., *William Faulkner in the Media Ecology* [Baton Rouge: Louisiana State University Press], 2015); to the rise of cinematic sound

technologies (Stefan Solomon, *William Faulkner in Hollywood: Screenwriting for the Studios* [Athens: University of Georgia Press, 2017]; Jay Watson, "The Unsynchable William Faulkner: Faulknerian Voice and Early Sound Film," in *William Faulkner and the Faces of Modernity* [Oxford, UK: Oxford University Press, 2019], 148–72.); to listening as a mode of storytelling (Julie Beth Napolin, "The Fact of Resonance: An Acoustics of Determination in Faulkner and Benjamin," *symplokē* 24, no. 1–2 [2016]: 171–86); and to popular music, ranging from blues and country to rock and roll (Tim A. Ryan, "'A Little Music Aint about the Nicest Thing a Fellow Can Have': Faulkner's *As I Lay Dying* and Country Songs," *Mississippi Quarterly* 67, no. 3 [2014]: 347–74; Tim A. Ryan, *Yoknapatawpha Blues: Faulkner's Fiction and Southern Roots Music* [Baton Rouge: Louisiana State University Press, 2015]; Florence Dore, "New Critical Noise in Music City: Thomas Pynchon's William Faulkner," in *Novel Sounds: Southern Fiction in the Age of Rock and Roll* [New York: Columbia University Press, 2018], 57–75; Dore, "The New Criticism and the Nashville Sound," 32–57). What has been left outside these conversations is the acoustic activity Faulkner carefully designs for his reader.

13. Napolin, *Modernist Acoustics*, 6.

14. William Faulkner, *As I Lay Dying* (New York: Vintage, 1991), 5.

15. William Faulkner, *Light in August*, 1st Vintage International edition (New York: Vintage, 1990), 8.

16. William Faulkner, *Novels 1942–1954: Go Down, Moses / Intruder in the Dust / Requiem for a Nun / A Fable* (New York: Library of America, 1994), 144–45.

17. Karl F. Zender, "The Power of Sound," in *The Crossing of the Ways: William Faulkner, the South, and the Modern World* (New Brunswick, NJ: Rutgers University Press, 1989), 6.

18. Zender, *Crossing of the Ways*, 10.

19. Napolin, "Acoustics of Determination," 174.

20. Jacques Derrida, "Ulysses Gramophone: Hear Say Yes in Joyce," in *Derrida and Joyce: Texts and Contexts*, ed. Andrew J. Mitchell and Sam Slote (Albany: SUNY Press, 2013), 41–86.

21. Derrida, "Ulysses Gramophone," 67–68.

22. Derrida, "Ulysses Gramophone," 80.

23. Anca Parvulescu, "To Yes-Laugh Derrida's Molly," *Parallax* 16, no. 3 (2010): 18.

24. Laura R. Davis, *Sensory Coding in William Faulkner's Novels: Investigating Class, Gender, Queerness, and Race through a Non-Visual Paradigm* (PhD diss., Georgia State University, 2011), 1.

25. William Faulkner, *The Sound and the Fury: The Corrected Text* (New York: Vintage, 1990), 34–35.

26. Cf. Imane Bouchakour, "Disabled or Idiosyncratic? Rethinking Mind and Language in Faulkner's Benjy," in *Poetics and Linguistics Association (PALA) 2019 Conference Proceedings*, Liverpool University, UK, 2019, 7, https://www.pala.ac.uk/2019.html.

27. Though unable to express himself vocally via language, Benjy does feel the desire to do so: "I was trying to say," he narrates when approaching a girl on the road who reminds him of Caddy, "and I caught her, trying to say, and she screamed and I was trying to say and trying and the bright shapes began to stop and I tried to get out" (*The Sound and the Fury*, 53).

28. Faulkner, *The Sound and the Fury*, 39. For more on the centrality of Benjy's cry to *The Sound and the Fury*, see Maurice Ebileeni, *Conrad, Faulkner, and the Problem of Nonsense* (London & New York: Bloomsbury Academic, 2015), 95–110, and Napolin, *Modernist Acoustics*, 103–14.

29. Philip M. Weinstein, *Faulkner's Subject: A Cosmos No One Owns* (Cambridge, UK: Cambridge University Press, 1992), 115.

30. Faulkner, *Sound and Fury*, 285, 316.

31. Ted Roggenbuck, "'The Way He Looked Said Hush': Benjy's Mental Atrophy in *The Sound and the Fury*," *Mississippi Quarterly* 58, no. 3 (2005): 583.

32. Faulkner, *Sound and Fury*, 81–82.

33. Jacques Lacan, *The Seminar of Jacques Lacan: The Four Fundamental Concepts of Psychoanalysis*, ed. Jacques-Alain Miller, trans. Alan Sheridan, rev. ed. (New York: W. W. Norton, 1998), 195.

34. The invasive quality of sound is true for smell as well, which might explain why these two sensations are key to Benjy's experience, as his senses are especially keen. On Benjy and olfactory sensory experience, see Laura Davis, "The Smeller's (Almost Always) a Feller: A Sensory Studies Approach to Examining Gender and Sexuality across Nine Faulkner Texts," *Faulkner Journal* 28, no. 2 (2014): 53–77.

35. Faulkner, *Sound and Fury*, 172.

36. Faulkner, *Sound and Fury*, 76–77.

37. Justin Skirry, "Sartre on William Faulkner's Metaphysics of Time in *The Sound and the Fury*," *Sartre Studies International* 7, no. 2 (2001): 15.

38. Faulkner, *Sound and Fury*, 76.

39. See, for example, Jonathan B. Fritz et al., "Auditory Attention: Focusing the Searchlight on Sound," *Current Opinion in Neurobiology* 17, no. 4 (2007): 437–55; István Winkler, Susan L. Denham, and Israel Nelken, "Modeling the Auditory Scene: Predictive Regularity Representations and Perceptual Objects," *Trends in Cognitive Sciences* 13, no. 12 (2009): 532–40.

40. In *Absalom, Absalom!* as well, Faulkner describes Quentin as perceptually receptive to sounds unheard by others: "Then hearing would reconcile and he would seem to listen to two separate Quentins . . . talking to one another in the long silence of notpeople in notlanguage," *Absalom*, 4.

41. Faulkner, *Sound and Fury*, 80, 83, 88, 96, 100.

42. Faulkner, *Sound and Fury*, 83–85.

43. Warwick Wadlington, in the context of his analysis of the novel as a tragedy, similarly suggests that Benjy's and Quentin's sections are unique in their activation of the readers, referring specifically to a mode of ethical listening yet

with a focus on narrative voice rather than on sound or negative audition, *Reading Faulknerian Tragedy* (Ithaca, NY: Cornell University Press, 1987), 88–91.

44. Weinstein, *Faulkner's Subject*, 120.

45. Faulkner, "An Introduction to *The Sound and the Fury*," 412–13.

46. Faulkner's portrayal of silence as conducive to creative labor follows a long American literary tradition, see Milette Shamir, *Inexpressible Privacy: The Interior Life of Antebellum American Literature* (Philadelphia: University of Pennsylvania Press, 2006).

47. Faulkner, "An Introduction for *The Sound and the Fury*," 708.

48. Faulkner, "An Introduction for *The Sound and the Fury*," 708.

49. It is worth noting that among the writers Faulkner attests to internally "hear" while writing *The Sound and the Fury* is Conrad, whose *The Nigger of the "Narcissus*," Julie Napolin proposes, echoes via Benjy's cry, *Modernist Acoustics*, 103–14.

50. Qtd. in Meriwether and Millgate, *Lion in the Garden*, 248.

51. John Keats, "Ode on a Grecian Urn," in *John Keats, the Complete Poems*, ed. John Barnard (New York: Penguin, 1988), 344.

52. Hilayne Cavanaugh similarly claims that Faulkner's fascination with the ode is related to "the Urn piper's silently piped ditties," which also resonates, she suggests, with Faulkner's comment upon seeing the Cathedral in the Piazza del Duomo in Milan: "Can you imagine stone lace? Or frozen music?" But for her, Faulkner's interest in "unheard music" is limited to his investment in art as stasis, in line with the view of Faulkner as a perfect formalist, which I am working to challenge, *Faulkner, Stasis, and Keats' "Ode on a Grecian Urn"* (PhD diss., University of Nebraska, 1977), 3–4.

53. See, Gail L. Mortimer, *Faulkner's Rhetoric of Loss: A Study of Perception and Meaning* (Austin: University of Texas Press, 1983), 71–91; Deborah Clarke, "Erasing and Inventing Motherhood: The Sound and the Fury and As I Lay Dying," in *Robbing the Mother: Women in Faulkner* (Jackson: University Press of Mississippi, 1994), 19–51; Fowler, *Faulkner: The Return of the Repressed*, 32–47; Bleikasten, *Ink of Melancholy*, 47–55.

54. Joanna Davis-McElligatt, "On Thingification: Faulkner and Afropessimism," in *The New William Faulkner Studies*, ed. Sarah Gleeson-White and Pardis Dabashi (Cambridge, UK: Cambridge University Press, 2022), 168.

55. Davis-McElligatt, "On Thingification," 168.

56. Davis-McElligatt, "On Thingification," 168.

57. Susanna Hempstead, "'Once a Bitch, Always a Bitch': Rereading Caddy in *The Sound and the Fury*," *Faulkner Journal* 31, no. 1 (2017): 23–42; Hale, *The Novel and the New Ethics*, 103.

58. Kristin Fujie, "'Through a Piece of Colored Glass,'" 413.

59. Aliyyah I. Abdur-Rahman, "'What Moves at the Margin': William Faulkner and Race," in *The New Cambridge Companion to William Faulkner*, ed. John

T. Matthews (Cambridge, UK: Cambridge University Press, 2015), 44–58. Abdur-Rahman reads Jim Bond's howl, which brings to a closure *Absalom, Absalom*, not as a sign of degeneracy and failure as it is commonly read, and perhaps lends itself to be interpreted, but as a moment of utopian potentiality.

60. Davis-McElligatt, "On Thingification," 168.

61. Davis-McElligatt, "On Thingification," 168.

62. Fred Moten, *In the Break: The Aesthetics of the Black Radical Tradition* (Minneapolis: University of Minnesota Press, 2003), 5. On race and the sonic, see Tricia Rose, *Black Noise: Rap Music and Black Culture in Contemporary America* (Middletown, CT: Wesleyan University Press, 1994); Nicole Brittingham Furlonge, *Race Sounds: The Art of Listening in African American Literature* (Iowa City: University of Iowa Press, 2018); Nina Sun Eidsheim, *The Race of Sound: Listening, Timbre, and Vocality in African American Music* (Durham, NC: Duke University Press, 2019).

63. Faulkner, *Sound and Fury*, 293.

64. Faulkner, *Sound and Fury*, 292.

65. Faulkner, *Sound and Fury*, 293.

66. William Dahill-Baue writes in this context that "Faulkner characterizes the preacher in racist terms, animalizing him based on racial features," but he quickly adds that "a closer examination of Faulkner's language suggests another, quite opposite possibility," which he believes is rooted in the African-American folk hero, the Signifying Monkey: "[I]t is precisely Shegog's initial insignificance, his ability to conceal his power beneath the mask of his physical weakness, that establishes him as a trickster figure in his act of Signifyin(g)," "Insignificant Monkeys: Preaching Black English in Faulkner's *The Sound and the Fury* and Morrison's *The Bluest Eye* and *Beloved*," *Mississippi Quarterly* 49, no. 3 (1996): 465–66. I too agree that Shegog's scene, in its complexity, lends itself to be read via the lens of resistance.

67. Faulkner, *Sound and Fury*, 293.

68. Faulkner, *Sound and Fury*, 293–94.

69. Stephen M. Ross, *Fiction's Inexhaustible Voice: Speech and Writing in Faulkner* (Athens: University of Georgia Press, 1989), 41.

70. Stephen M. Ross, "Rev. Shegog's Powerful Voice," *Faulkner Journal* 1, no. 1 (1985): 8–9.

71. André Bleikasten, *The Most Splendid Failure: Faulkner's* The Sound and the Fury (Bloomington: Indiana University Press, 1976), 201.

72. Akira Mizuta Lippit, "In the Break: The Aesthetics of the Black Radical Tradition (Review)," *Modern Language Notes (MLN)* 118, no. 5 (2003): 1336–37. Moten, *In the Break*, 1.

73. Moten, *In the Break*, 1.

74. Faulkner, *Sound and Fury*, 294–95.

75. Qtd. in Malcolm Cowley, ed., *The Faulkner-Cowley File: Letters and Memories 1944–1962* (New York: Viking Press, 1966), 114.

76. Erik Steinskog, *Afrofuturism and Black Sound Studies: Culture, Technology, and Things to Come* (London: Palgrave Macmillan, 2017), 13.

77. Faulkner, *Absalom*, 4.

78. Hortense J. Spillers, "Faulkner Adds Up: Reading *Absalom, Absalom!* And *The Sound and the Fury*," in *Black, White, and in Color: Essays on American Literature and Culture* (Chicago, IL: University of Chicago Press, 2003), 338.

79. Faulkner, *The Sound and the Fury*, 3.

Chapter Three

1. On the history of early print in Brazil, see Valéria Gauz, "Early printing in Brazil," *Bulletin du bibliophile* 1 (2013): 23–47.

2. On the link between colonial oppression of local languages and illiteracy, see Stella Maris Bortoni-Ricardo et al., "The Sociolinguistic Roots of Illiteracy in Brazil," *Cultivating Literacy in Portuguese-Speaking Countries* 1, no. 4 (2012), http://www.acoalfaplp.net/en_index.html; on the Jesuits' role in circulating books and promoting local literacy, see Mark L. Grover, "The Book and the Conquest: Jesuit Libraries in Colonial Brazil," *Libraries & Culture* 28, no. 3 (1993): 266–83.

3. On the role print prohibition played in the con/destruction of the Brazilian reader, see Marisa Lajolo and Regina Zilberman, *A formaçao da leitura no Brasil* (São Paulo, Brazil: Editora Unesp, 1996), 170–79.

4. Alencar, *Iracema: lenda do Ceará*.

5. There exist three translations into English of Alencar's *Iracema*: *Iraçéma, The Honey-Lips: A Legend of Brazil*, trans. Isabel Burton (London: Bickers and Son, 1886); *Iracema: A Legend of Ceará*, trans. D. N. Bidell (Rio de Janeiro, Brazil: Impresa Ingela, 1921); and *Iracema*, trans. Clifford E. Landers (New York: Oxford University Press, 2000). Since Alencar's prologue does not appear in these versions, quotes from this section are mine. Other quotes from *Iracema* are taken from Landers's translation.

6. Alencar, *Iracema*, 111.

7. Naomi Lindstrom, foreword to *Iracema: A Novel* (New York: Oxford University Press, 2000), xix.

8. Marisa Lajolo, "José de Alencar, um criador de autores e de leitores," *Revista de Letras* 29, no. 2 (2009): 89–91.

9. Scholarship had established that Alencar had in mind his cousin (Domingos Jaguaribe) when writing this letter-like prologue, but since the interlocutor remains unnamed in this text, he functions as the marker of *any* (white and male as Lejolo points out) Brazilian reader.

10. As Lajolo explains, Alencar had to educate his readers since he assumed they are approaching his novel with an oral rather than written textual tradition

in mind. That is, given the low rate of literacy in Brazil of the mid-nineteenth century, authors like Alencar "had to 'seduce' their readers into becoming a 'reading public' . . . by evoking traces of *residual orality* as a narrative strategy," "The Role of Orality in the Seduction of the Brazilian Reader," *Poetics Today* 15, no. 4 (1994): 553; emphasis in original.

11. Alencar, *Iracema: lenda do Ceará*. Translation mine.

12. Luís C. Cascudo, *Rêde De Dormir: Uma Pesquisa Etnográfica* (Rio de Janeiro, Brazil: Ministério da Educação e Cultura, Serviço de Documentação, 1959), 81–87.

13. João Cezar de Castro Rocha, *Crítica literária: Em busca do tempo perdido?* (Chapecó, Brazil: Argos Editora da Unochapecó, 2011), 11.

14. On the history of the Brazilian *nordeste*, along with the history of this concept's invention, see Durval Muniz de Albuquerque Jr., *The Invention of the Brazilian Northeast*, trans. Jerry Dennis Metz (Durham, NC: Duke University Press, 2014).

15. Cunha e Silva Filho, "Afrânio Coutinho e as mudanças de rumos na crítica literária, na história literária e no ensino de literatura no Brasil," *Entretextos*, August 2, 2013, https://www.portalentretextos.com.br/post/afranio-coutinho-e-as-mudancas-de-rumos-na-critica-literaria-na-historia-literaria-e-no-ensino-de-literatura-no-brasil.

16. Coutinho is listed as a visiting scholar in Columbia University's 1943–1944 student directory. For more on Coutinho's biography and intelectual history see, Odilon Belém, *Afrânio Coutinho: Uma filosofia da literatura* (Rio de Janeiro, Brazil: Pallas, Didática e Científica, 1987); Inês Cardin Bressan, "Afrânio Coutinho, crítico e historiador da literatura Brasileira: Uma leitura" (PhD diss., Universidade Estadual Paulista, 2007), https://repositorio.unesp.br/handle/11449/94135.

17. The first edition of *A literatura no Brasil* (1955–1959) included three volumes. It was enlarged to six volumes in its second edition (1968–1971).

18. Coutinho later collects and publishes his columns in book form. See, Coutinho, *Correntes cruzadas*.

19. A letter by Holanda dated July 24, 1948, quoted in Vagner Camilo, "O aerólito e o zelo dos neófitos: Sérgio Buarque, crítico de poesia," *Revista USP* 80 (2009): 112; Antonio Arnoni Prado, Introduction to *O espírito e a letra: Estudos de crítica Literária (1948-1959)*, by Sérgio Buarque de Holanda, vol. 2 (São Paulo, Brazil: Companhia das Letras, 1996), 29.

20. Roberto Schwarz, "Roberto Schwarz: Um crítico na periferia do capitalismo [A critic on the periphery of capitalism]," interview by Luiz Henrique Lopes dos Santos and Mariluce Moura, *PESQUISA FAPESP*, 2004, http://revistapesquisa.fapesp.br/2004/04/01/um-critico-na-periferia-do-capitalismo.

21. Castro Rocha, *Crítica literária*, 11.

22. Denis Heyck qualifies this claim when she adds, "It was the New Criticism and its leading practitioners that had by far the greatest influence on Coutinho

personally," "Coutinho's Controversy: The Debate Over the *Nova Crítica*," *Latin American Research Review* 14, no. 1 (1979), 112–13.

23. Álvaro Lins, *Teoria literária: Poesia, romance, teatro, biografia, crítica* (Rio de Janeiro, Brazil: Editora de Ouro, 1967), 195. For more on the criticism mounted against the nova crítica for being a mere imitation, see Marcelo Jose Silva, "Percurso e percalços de Afrânio Coutinho na crítica literária brasileira," *Terra Roxa e Outras Terras* 16 (2016): 64.

24. The Brazilian reception of the New Criticism is primarily studied in three contexts: (1) the influence of the Anglo-American movement on the establishment of autonomous departments of literary studies in Brazil (see Vagner Camilo, *Drummond: da Rosa do povo à rosa das trevas* [São Paulo, Brazil: Ateliê Editorial, 2001], and Silva, "Percurso e percalços de Afrânio Coutinho," 63–71); (2) the impact the New Criticism had on curricula and methodology development in Brazilian literary studies (see, for example, Roberto Corrêa dos Santos, "A crítica literária no Brasil: Últimos quinze anos," *Revista de Crítica Literária Latinoamericana* 16, no. 31/32 [1990]: 85–97); and (3) the role the New Criticism played in the abovementioned cultural battle between the traditional *rodapé* literary critics and the "new" literary thinkers, who aimed at specialization (see Flora Süssekind, "Rodapés, tratados e ensaios: A formação da crítica brasileira moderna," in *Papéis Colados* [Rio de Janeiro, Brazil: Editora da UFRJ, 1993], 13–33; and Cláudia Nina, *Literatura nos jornais: a crítica literária dos rodapés às resenhas* [São Paulo, Brazil: Summus Editorial, 2007]). This chapter wishes to add a yet uninvestigated fourth context to this list: the influence of the Anglo-American New Critical ideas on the construction of a new Brazilian readerly subjectivity.

25. See, for example, Isobel Armstrong, "Textual Harassment: The Ideology of Close Reading, or How Close Is Close?" *Textual Practice* 9, no. 3 (1995): 401–20.

26. W. E. B. Du Bois, *The Souls of Black Folk* (Oxford, UK and New York: Oxford University Press, 2007), 8.

27. Rocha, *Crítica Literária*, 168.

28. Coutinho, *Correntes*, 75.

29. Coutinho, *Correntes*, 122.

30. Coutinho, *Correntes*, 122, 148, 55, 144.

31. For more on Coutinho's attitude toward Portuguese colonialism, see Denis Lynn Heyck "Coutinho, The Nova Crítica and Portugal," *Hispania* 64, no. 4 (1981): 564–69.

32. Coutinho, *Correntes*, 55.

33. Coutinho, *Correntes*, 172.

34. Coutinho, *Correntes*, 122, 119.

35. Heyck, "The Nova Crítica and Portugal," 564.

36. Coutinho, *Correntes*, 75.

37. For a detailed presentation of the strife between the *rodapé* and the academic (*catédra*) critics, see Rocha, *Crítica literária*.

38. Heyck, "Coutinho's Controversy," 100.
39. Coutinho, *Correntes*, 119.
40. Coutinho, *Correntes*, 83.
41. Quoted in Rocha, *Crítica literária*, 191; Afrânio Coutinho, *Da crítica e da nova crítica* (Rio de Janeiro, Brazil: Editora Civilizacão Brasileira, 1957), 168.
42. I thank Ramsey McGlazer for this insight.
43. Afrânio Coutinho, *Na hospital das letras* (Rio de Janeiro, Brazil: Editora Tempo Brasileiro, 1963). "Letras" signifies in Portuguese both alphabetical characters and the world of literature and its teachings, as in *belles lettres*.
44. Coutinho, *Na hospital das letras*, 25.
45. Coutinho, *Correntes*, 44, 144.
46. Coutinho, *Correntes*, 77.
47. As an illustration, in Jorge Alcázar's introductory article "La nueva critica norteamericana," he uses no local term for close reading, instead reverting to English, defining the practice as a "método de explicacién detallada de textos (close reading)," *Acta poetica* 8,(1987): 135–63. Similarly, the Spanish Wikipedia page on New Criticism leaves the English "close reading" untouched (https://es.wikipedia.org/wiki/New_criticism).
48. Coutinho, *Correntes*, 206.
49. Coutinho, *Correntes*, 131.
50. Both Sérgio Buarque de Holanda and Terry Eagleton similarly suggest that the Anglo-American New Critics were in fact very much aligned with positivist thought over and above their explicit repudiation of it. See Terry Eagleton, *The Event of Literature* (New Haven, CT: Yale University Press, 2012), 35; Sérgio Buarque de Holanda, *O espírito e a letra: Estudos de crítica Literária (1948–1959)*, vol. 2 (São Paulo, Brazil: Companhia das Letras, 1996), 412.
51. Eduardo Portella, "Crítica literária: Brasileira e totalizante," *Tempo Brasileiro*, no. 1 (1962): 67–69.
52. Coutinho, *A literatura*, 640.
53. Jonathan Crary extensively outlines the historical tradition of conceptualizing "attention" in terms of "light," *Suspensions of Perception*, 237–81.
54. Coutinho, *Correntes*, 131.
55. Coutinho, *Correntes*, 99.
56. Heyck, "Coutinho's Controversy," 104.
57. Coutinho, *No Hospital*, 18.
58. Afrânio Coutinho, *A literatura no Brasil* (Rio de Janeiro/Niterói, Brazil: José Olympio/Universidade Federal Fluminense, 1968), 634.
59. Coutinho, *Correntes*, 224.
60. Thaventhiran, *Radical Empiricists*, 1.
61. Coutinho, *Correntes*, 10.
62. Thavanthiran, *Radical Empiricists*, 90.
63. Coutinho, *Correntes*, 13.

64. Coutinho, *Correntes*, v.
65. Coutinho, *A literatura*, 647.
66. Coutinho, *Correntes*, 84.
67. Foucault, "Technologies of the Self," 18.
68. James Baldwin, *Notes of a Native Son* (Boston, MA: Beacon Press, 2012), 167.
69. Coutinho, *Correntes*, 145–48.
70. Coutinho, *Da crítica*, 168.
71. Coutinho, *Correntes*, 145–48.
72. The superimposition of Alencar and Coutinho's scenes might appear to sketch a sentimental and politically problematic transition from a once harmonious Brazilian past, where absent-mindedness and intellectual rigor were imagined to reside in one reader, to a modern disjointed present, where these characteristics can no longer be seen as complimentary. However, the interrelationship between these two scenes is far more complex. First, Alencar's imagined reader, though to later become a Brazilian "commonplace," is not at all typical of his time, as Lajolo points out. And Alencar's view of the Brazilian subject, like Coutinho's, is fraught with colonial stereotypes, imagining the native's "wild" and "natural" tendencies to be acculturated by the arrival of the Portuguese, to quote Lindstrom. Lindstrom writes: "In the vision projected in *Iracema*, native communities appear to have lived in the wild, enjoying a timeless unity with the natural world. The arrival of the Portuguese brings changes in this hitherto unblemished society, sets national history in motion, and marks the beginning of the Brazilian people" (Forward to *Iracema*, xix).
73. Coutinho, *Correntes*, 48, iv, 144.
74. Antonio Candido, Introduction to *Roots of Brazil* by Sérgio Buarque de Holanda, trans. G. Harvey Summ (Notre Dame, IN: University of Notre Dame Press, 2012), xxiv–vi.
75. Sérgio Buarque de Holanda, *Roots of Brazil*, trans. G. Harvey Summ (Notre Dame, IN: University of Notre Dame Press, 2012), 9.
76. For another instance of affiliation between "sloth" and Brazilian interiority, see Coutinho, *Correntes*, 131.
77. For a recent reconsideration of this descriptor, see James R. Krause, David P. Wiseman, and Faith Blackhurst, "The Boom Novel that Never Was: *Grande sertão: Veredas*, by João Guimarães Rosa," *Hispania* 103, no. 4 (2020): 603–19.
78. On Rosa and Faulkner, see Luiz Fernando Valente, "Marriages of Speaking and Hearing: Mediation and Response in *Absalom, Absalom!* and *Grande Sertão: Veredas*," *Faulkner Journal* 11, no. 1/2 (1996): 149–64; Paulo da-Luz-Moreira, "Regionalism and Modernism in the Short Stories of William Faulkner, João Guimarães Rosa, and Juan Rulfo" (PhD diss., University of California, Santa Barbara, 2007); M. Thomas Inge and Donária Romeiro Carvalho Inge, "William Faulkner and Guimarães Rosa: A Brazilian Connection," in *Faulkner and His*

Contemporaries, eds. Joseph R. Urgo and Ann J. Abadie (Jackson: University Press of Mississippi, 2004): 173–88.

79. Rosa's "O espelho" enters into clear intertextual dialogue with Machado de Assis's 1882 short story, carrying the same title. My analysis, however, will not engage Machado's work and instead focuses on Rosa's story's dialogue with its contemporary moment. For a comparison between Machado's and Rosa's stories, see Audemaro Taranto Goulart, "Machado e Rosa nos vêem no espelho," *ASAS DA PALAVRA* 11, no. 1 (2019): 52–69; Edna Maria F.S. Nascimento and Maria Célia Leonel, "Frente a 'O espelho' de Machado e de Guimarães Rosa," *Revista da Anpoll* 2, no. 24 (2008), https://doi.org/10.18309/anp.v2i24.44; Luiz Cláudio Vieira de Oliveira, "Guimarães Rosa, leitor de Machado," *O Eixo e a Roda: Revista de Literatura Brasileira* 7, no. 1 (2001): 79–91.

80. João Guimarães Rosa, *Primeiras estórias*, segunda edição (Rio de Janeiro, Brazil: José Olympio, 1969).

81. Heyck, "Coutinho's Controversy," 110; Rocha, *Crítica literária*.

82. Gabriel Giorgi, "La alianza salvaje: 'Meu tio o Iauaretê' de Guimarães Rosa," in *Formas comunes: animalidad, cultura, biopolítica* (Buenos Aires, Brazil: Eterna Cadencia, 2014), 47–52.

83. Oswald de Andrade, "Manifesto antropófago," in *Vanguardas Latino-Americanas: Polêmicas, Manifestos e Textos Críticos*, ed. Jorge Schwartz (São Paulo, Brazil: Editora da Universidade de São Paulo, 2008), 142–47; Oswald de Andrade, "Cannibalist Manifesto," trans. Leslie Bary, *Latin American Literary Review* 19, no. 38 (1991): 38–47.

84. Susan Basnett, *Translation (The New Critical Idiom)* (London: Routledge, Taylor & Francis, 2014), 53.

85. Andrade, "Cannibalist Manifesto," 43.

86. Coutinho, *Correntes*, 83.

87. Rosa, *Primeiras estórias*, 117; João Guimarães Rosa, *The Third Bank of The River, and Other Stories*, trans. Barbara Shelby (New York: Knopf, 1968), 140. From this point onward I will refer to the English translation only.

88. Ana Paula Pacheco, *Lugar do mito: narrativa e processo social nas Primeiras estórias de Guimarães Rosa* (São Paulo, Brazil: Nankin, 2006), 228.

89. Yudith Rosenbaum, "Notas sobre o conto 'O espelho' de Guimarães Rosa," *Ide: psicanálise e cultura* 31, no. 47 (2008), http://pepsic.bvsalud.org/scielo.php?script=sci_arttext&pid=S0101-31062008000200015.

90. Rosa, *Third Bank*, 135.

91. Rosa, *Third Bank*, 139.

92. Rosa, *Third Bank*, 140.

93. Rosa, *Third Bank*, 138.

94. Rosa, *Third Bank*, 138; trans. modified.

95. Rosa, *Third Bank*, 139; trans. modified.

96. Coutinho, *Correntes*, 81.

97. Rosa, *Third Bank*, 141; trans. modified.
98. Rosa, *Third Bank*, 139; trans. modified (Shelby renders "*preconceito afetivo*" as "affectionate partiality"). Wimsatt and Beardsley's articles, along with Wimsatt's *Verbal Icon*, were never translated into Portuguese, so that a few possible translations of the "affective fallacy" are found in circulation, among them also "falácia afetiva."
99. Rosa, *Third Bank*, 141.
100. João Guimarães Rosa, "Meu tio o Iauaretê," *Senhor* 25, March 19, 1961, 65–90.
101. See Giorgi, *Formas comunes*, 47–52.
102. Rosa, *Third Bank*, 142.
103. Rosa, *Third Bank*, 142.
104. Rosa, *Third Bank*, 140.
105. Rosa, *Third Bank*, 143; trans. modified.
106. Rosa, *Third Bank*, 143; trans. modified.
107. Among Rosa's well-known works to depict the outcast as the locus of truth are "Sorôco, sua mãe, sua filha," "Recado do Morro," and "A terceira margem do rio."
108. João Guimarães Rosa, "Guimarães Rosa fala aos jovens," *O Cruzeiro*, December 23, 1967.
109. Rosa, *Third Bank*, 145; trans. modified.
110. Rosa, *Third Bank*, 138.
111. Rosa, *Third Bank*, 146; trans. modified.
112. James Joyce, *Ulysses* (London: Penguin Books, 2000), 933.

Chapter Four

1. Clarice Lispector, *Perto do coração selvagem* (Rio de Janeiro, Brazil: Rocco, 1998).
2. Clarice Lispector, *Near to the Wild Heart*, trans. Alison Entrekin (New York: New Directions, 2012), 83.
3. Lispector, *Near to the Wild Heart*, 84.
4. James Joyce, *A Portrait of the Artist as a Young Man* (Oxford, UK: Oxford University Press, 2000), 144.
5. Hélène Cixous also links Lispector's work with the "savage": "What does it mean to work on texts that are 'near to the wild heart'? Reading Clarice's text, I was struck by its extraordinary power. . . . At the same time, it gives the impression of being poorly written, it does not display a mastery of form and language and does not raise the question of art. . . . One has to have a touch of something savage, uncultured, in order to let it happen," "Writing and the Law: Blanchot, Joyce, Kafka, and Lispector," in *Readings: The Poetics of Blanchot,*

Joyce, Kakfa, Kleist, Lispector, and Tsvetayeva, trans. Conley Verena Andermatt (Minneapolis: University of Minnesota Press, 1991), 1.

6. Coutinho, *Correntes,* iv, 83.

7. Emília Amaral, "O pacto com o leitor e o misticismo da escrita em *A Paixão Segunado G.H.*, de Clarice Lispector," in *Leitores e leituras de Clarice Lispector,* ed. Regina Pontieri (São Paulo, Brazil: Hedra, 2004), 13–16.

8. Clarice Lispector, *A maçã no escuro* (Rio de Janeiro, Brazil: Rocco, 1998); *The Apple in the Dark,* trans. Gregory Rabassa (London: Haus Publishing, 2009).

9. Echoing the same terminology, Italo Moriconi convincingly demonstrates that Lispector's books to follow *The Apple in the Dark* "stage the limit, the exhaustion of a project of progressive radicalization of self-reflective writing," "*The Hour of the Star* or Clarice Lispector's Trash Hour," trans. Paulo Henriques Britto, *Portuguese Literary and Cultural Studies* 4/5 (2000): 215; emphasis mine. *The Apple's* "exhausting" thrust, it seems, impacts not only the reader, but Lispector's body of work as well.

10. Amaral, Nunes, and Fronckowiak focus on another of Lispector's novels (*The Passion According to G.H.; A paixão segundo G.H.* [1964]). Amaral, "O pacto com o leitor," 11–20; Benedito Nunes, "Os destroços da intersecção," in *Clarice Lispector: A Narração do Indizível,* ed. Regina Zilberman (Porto Alegre, Brazil: Artes e Ofícios, EDIPUC/Instituto Cultural Judaico Marc Chagall, 1998), 35–48; Ângela Fronckowiak, "A ato de narrar em A paixão segundo G.H.," in *Clarice Lispector: A Narração do Indizível,* ed. Regina Zilberman (Porto Alegre, Brazil: Artes e Ofícios, EDIPUC/Instituto Cultural Judaico Marc Chagall, 1998), 65–74.

11. Amaral, "O pacto com o leitor," 14. In this citation, Amaral is quoting Joaquim Brasil Fontes Júnior from his work "Poesias de Isidore Ducasse: O Argumento pela Metamorfose," published in *Letras,* vol. 2, no. 1 (April 1983), 40.

12. The *crônica* is a Brazilian genre, mostly journalist, which exists at the intersection between autofiction, short story, and essay. The *crônicas* mentioned here were first published in the second half of Lispector's *A legião estrangeira,* titled "Fundo de gaveta" (1964).

13. Clarice Lispector, *A legião estrangeira* (São Paulo, Brazil: Editora Ática, 1983), 143.

14. Coutinho, *A literatura,* 640.

15. Clarice Lispector, *A paixão segundo G.H* (Rio de Janeiro, Brazil: Rocco, 2009).

16. For more on *A literatura's* innovations and form, see Bressan, "Afrânio Coutinho."

17. José Guilherme Merquior, *Razão do Poema: Ensaios de Crítica e de Estética* (Rio de Janeiro, Brazil: Topbooks, 1996), 51. Already in 1948, Sergio Buarque de Holanda writes in his review of the Geração de '45 that "The opinion according to which a word is only an aesthetically significant element, a colorless and neutral thing, is making its way amongst us and leaves its devastating marks

on our literary criticism and, above all, on our poetry" (Holanda, *O espírito*, 576).

18. Coutinho, *A Literatura*, 197–98.
19. Coutinho, *Correntes*, 184.
20. Coutinho, *Correntes*, 206.
21. Coutinho, *A literatura*, 451, 461.
22. Jefferson Mello, "Os estudos literários brasileiros nos anos 1970 e o lugar da teoria no trabalho de Luiz Costa Lima," *Remate de Males* 40, no. 2 (2020): 697–722.
23. For that reason, as Jefferson Mello demonstrates, when an article titled "O estruturalismo dos pobres" ("The Structuralism of the Poor") seeks to condemn the local structuralists, it refers to them as part of the nova crítica, qtd. in Mello, "Costa Lima," 700.
24. Lima, *A literatura*, 461.
25. Lima, *A literatura*, 453.
26. Lima, *A literatura*, 452.
27. Quoted in Rocha, *Crítica literária*, 191.
28. Coutinho, *Correntes*, 77, 206.
29. Coutinho, *Correntes*, 75, xi.
30. Luís Costa Lima, "Clarice Lispector," in *A literatura no Brasil*, vol. 5, ed. Afrânio Coutinho (Rio de Janeiro, Brazil: Sul Americana, 1968), 526–53.
31. Cixous, *Reading with Clarice Lispector*, 66.
32. Vilma Arêas and Berta Waldman, "Eppur, se muove," *Remate de males* 9 (1989): 162.
33. Moser, Introduction to *The Apple in the Dark*, vii.
34. On the novel's challenging writing and publishing process, see Benjamin Moser, *Why This World: A Biography of Clarice Lispector* (Oxford, UK: Oxford University Press, 2009), 230–32.
35. Lispector, *The Apple*, 27, 26.
36. Lispector, *The Apple*, 166.
37. Lispector, *The Apple*, 32, 33, 44, 166, 423.
38. Lispector, *The Apple*, 3.
39. Lispector, *The Apple*, 4.
40. Lispector, *The Apple*, 4.
41. Lispector, *The Apple*, 6.
42. Lispector, *The Apple*, 6.
43. Lispector, *The Apple*, 8.
44. Lispector, *The Apple*, 9.
45. Lispector, *The Apple*, 9–10.
46. Lispector, *The Apple*, 31.
47. Lispector, *The Apple*, 32.

48. Lispector, *The Apple*, 50, 60.
49. Lispector, *The Apple*, 32, 227.
50. Lispector, *The Apple*, 40, 46.
51. Arêas and Weldman, "Eppur," 164–67.
52. The primacy effect is a cognitive bias to better remember the first piece of information one encounters than the information received later on. Menakhem Perry, who will play a central role in chapter 5 of this book, intriguingly examined this tendency's effect on the reading process. See, for example, "'O Rose Thou Art Sick': Al tachbulot bniyat ha-mashma'ut be-'Vered le-Emily' le-William Faulkner ve-haflagot le-te'orya shel ha-retorika ba-siporet," *Siman Kri'a* 3/4 (1974): 423–59.
53. Lispector, *The Apple*, 286, 389, 34, 25, 34, 291, 292.
54. Lispector, *The Apple*, 20.
55. Lispector, *The Apple*, 31.
56. Lispector, *The Apple*, 32.
57. Lispector, *The Apple*, 37.
58. Lispector, *The Apple*, 40.
59. Kristin E. Pitt, "Discovery and Conquest through a Poststructural and Postcolonial Lens: Clarice Lispector's *A maçã no escuro*," *Luso-Brazilian Review* 50, no. 1 (2013): 184–200.
60. Kristin E. Pitt, "Discovery and Conquest," 198.
61. Beatriz de Castro Amorim, "Between Heaven and Hell: A (Re)evaluation of Generic Problems in Lispector's *A maçã no escuro* and 'Perdoando Deus,'" *Brasil/Brazil* 5, no. 8 (1992): 29–51; Mara Negrón-Marrero, *Une genése au 'féminin': Étude de* La pomme dans le noir *de Clarice Lispector* (Amsterdam, the Netherlands: Rodopi, 1997).
62. Maria José Somerlate, *Clarice Lispector: Des/fiando as teias da paixão* (Porto Alegre, Brazil: EDIPUCRS, 2001).
63. Rebecca E. Biron, "Crime and Punishment Reconsidered: Lispector's *A maçã no escuro*," in *Murder and Masculinity: Violent Fictions of Twentieth-Century Latin America* (Nashville, TN: Vanderbilt University Press, 2000), 67–89.
64. Cixous, *Reading with Clarice Lispector*, 62. Antonio Ladeira, for his part, agrees with Cixous that Martin is a feminized man but also believes that the novel retells the story of patriarchal masculinity in Brazil, "Patriarchal Violence and Brazilian Masculinities in Clarice Lispector's *A maçã no escuro*," *Bulletin of Hispanic Studies* 86, no. 5 (2009): 690–705.
65. Moser, Introduction to *The Apple in the Dark*, viii. In this book, for lack of space, I do not explore the inspiration Lispector might have received from Jewish sources in devising her reader's experience. However, I do so elsewhere. See, Yael Segalovitz, "'My Error Is My Mirror': Clarice Lispector's Jewish Rhetoric of Mistakes," in *After Clarice: Reading Lispector's Legacy in the Twenty-First Century*, eds. Adriana X. Jacobs and Claire Williams (Oxford, UK: Legenda, 2023), 139–55.

66. Júlio César Vieira and Osmar Oliva, "Crime e libertação–um estudo de *A maçã no escuro* de Clarice Lispector," *Revista de Letras* 51, no. 2 (2011): 171. In a similar manner, Sônia Maria Machado writes, "The work of Clarice Lispector is considered difficult to understand by a great many readers: 'I don't see where she's going,' 'what she wants to say' . . . if learning means being able to linger in between the right and wrong, then learning means confronting the challenge of reading *The Apple in the Dark* ("Uma Tentativa de Entender *A maçã no escuro*," *Travessia* 3 [1981]: 20).

67. Machado, "Uma Tentativa de Entender," 165.

68. Machado, "Uma Tentativa de Entender," 47.

69. Georges Elgozy, "Le bluff du futur," *La revue administrative* 166 (1975): 385.

70. Both Bruno Carvalho and Gabriel Giorgi have presented exciting ideas about Lispector's treatment of the future from a different angle. See, Gabriel Giorgi, "The Form of the Improper: Clarice Lispector and the Rhetoric of Precarity," *Frame* 30, no. 2 (2017): 123–38; Bruno Carvalho, "The Future as a Necessity: Reading Clarice Lispector in the Anthropocene," in *Literature Beyond the Human: Post-Anthropocentric Brazil*, ed. Luca Bacchini and Victoria Saramago (New York: Routledge, 2022), 181–94.

71. Clarice Lispector, *Para não esquecer* (São Paulo, Brazil: Editora Ática, 1979), 21.

72. Lispector, *The Apple*, 332.

73. Leo Gilson Ribeiro, "Tentativa de explicação," *Correio da manhã*, March 21, 1965; qtd. in Moser, *Why This World*, 236. For Lispector's ample correspondences during her time abroad, see *Correspondências* (Rio de Janeiro, Brazil: Rocco, 2002).

74. For a detailed description of Lispector's years outside Brazil, see Nádia Batella Gotlib, *Clarice: uma vida que se conta* (São Paulo, Brazil: Editora Ática, 1995), 188–313; and Moser, *Why This World*, 200–40.

75. Being so true to Brazilian culture, *Family Ties* was considered right upon publication "the most important story collection published in this country since Machado de Assis," letter from Erico Verissimo (1961), qtd. in Moser, *Why This World*, 231.

76. Lispector, *Wild Heart*, 112, 110.

77. Lispector, *Wild Heart*, 115.

78. Lispector, *Wild Heart*, 116.

79. Lispector, *Wild Heart*, 115.

80. Lispector, *Wild Heart*, 127.

81. Lispector, *Wild Heart*, 109.

82. Lispector, *Wild Heart*, 112.

83. Lispector, *Wild Heart*, 111.

84. Lispector, *Wild Heart*, 112.

85. For a detailed study of Lispector's affinity with Spinoza's philosophy, see Adam Morris, "The Uses of Nonsense: Antimodernism in Latin American Fiction 1920–1977" (PhD diss., Stanford University, 2015), https://www.proquest.com/docview/2510259377?pq-origsite=gscholar&fromopenview=true.

86. Clarice Lispector, *The Passion According to G.H.*, trans. Idra Novey (New York: New Directions, 2012), xi.

87. D. A. Miller, *Hidden Hitchcock* (Chicago, IL: University of Chicago Press, 2016), 2–5.

Chapter Five

1. Orit Meital, *Lisno gam et asher ahavnu: mishpacha ve-le'umiyut be-shirat Uri Zvi Greenberg* (Tel Aviv, Israel: Ha-Kibbutz ha-Me'uchad, 2018).

2. Benjamin Harshav, "Ritmus ha-rachavut: halakha u-ma'ase be-shirato ha-ekspresionistit shel Uri Zvi Greenberg," *Ha-Sifrut* 1 (1968): 176–205. As mentioned in earlier chapters, all unattributed translations are mine.

3. Harshav, "Ritmus ha-rachavut," 176, emphasis in the original.

4. My argument is in line with that of Hamutal Tsamir, who claims that the universalization of the subject in the Israeli discourse of the fifties and sixties had a national import, *Be-shem ha-nof: le'umiyut, migdar ve-subyektiviyut ba-shira ha-yisra'elit bi-shnot ha-chamishim ve-ha-shishim* (Jerusalem/Be'er Sheva, Israel: Keter/Heksherim, 2006).

5. Two more pivotal figures in the importation of the New Criticism into Israel are Shlomo Tzemach and Aryeh Ludwig Strauss. The first was responsible for the translation of key New Critical articles in his journal, *Bekhinot* (*Investigations*, 1952–1957), such as T. S. Eliot's "Experiment in Criticism" (1929), John Crowe Ransom's "Criticism as Pure Speculation" (1941), and Allen Tate's "Is Literary Criticism Possible" (1952), even though his own critical practice was far from theirs (for more, see chapter 6). Strauss, who published in *Investigations* (see "*Al mizmor 124 mi-sefer Tehilim*," *Bekhinot* 1 [1952]: 26–32), was a practitioner rather than a theoretician of close reading, and was considered a precursor of the TA School by its members.

6. The term *Yishuv* indicates Jewish residency in Palestine prior to the establishment of the State of Israel in 1948.

7. On Halkin, see, for example, Shmuel Werses, "The Portrait of Shimon Halkin as a Young Poet," *Jerusalem Studies in Hebrew Literature* (1990): 19–38.

8. Ariel Hirschfeld, "Toldot ha-chug," https://hebliterature.huji.ac.il/about/history.

9. Natan Zach, "Ani ezrach ha-olam," in *Shirim shonim* (Tel Aviv, Israel: Alef, 1967), 66–67.

10. Michael Gluzman, *Shirat ha-tvu'im: ha-melankolya shel ha-ribonut ba-shira ha-ivrit bi-shnot ha-chamishim ve-ha-shishim* (Tel Aviv, Israel: University of Haifa Press and Yedi'ot Acharonot Books, 2018).

11. Moshe Dor, "Paytanim le-atid lavo," *Siman kri'a* 9 (1979), 342.

12. Alan Mintz, "On the Tel Aviv School of Poetics," *Prooftexts* 4, no. 3 (1984): 215.

13. Tel Aviv University as a whole understood itself as a reaction against and an alternative for the more conservative Hebrew University; see Uri Cohen, *Academia be-Tel Aviv: tzmichata shel universita* (Tel Aviv, Israel: Magnes Publishing House, 2014).

14. For discussions of the TA School's interaction with various theoretical movements, see Mintz, "On the Tel Aviv School," and Yael S. Feldman, "Poetics and Politics: Israeli Literary Criticism between East and West," *Proceedings of the American Academy for Jewish Research* 52 (1985): 9–35.

15. As Harshav explicates in the by now legendary diagram and article that opens the first issue of *Ha-Sifrut*, there are three main intertwined objects of study to the "science of literature": (1) the single text, whose field of study is "interpretation"; (2) the essence of literature, studied as "poetics"; and (3) "literature generally, in its historical existence," "al tchumey mada ha-sifrut," *Ha-Sifrut* 1, no. 1 (1968): 1.

16. Brian McHale and Eyal Segal, "Small World: The Tel Aviv School of Poetics and Semiotics," in *Theoretical Schools and Circles in the Twentieth-Century Humanities: Literary Theory, History, Philosophy*, eds. Marina Grishakova and Silvi Salupere (New York: Routledge, 2015). Other scholars that briefly mention the New Critical imprint on the Tel Aviv School include Esther Fuchs, who describes the Israeli critical discourse of the 1960s and 1970s as a "New Critical rebellion against the socialist realist platforms of the Palmah Generation," *Israeli Mythogynies: Women in Contemporary Hebrew Fiction* (Albany: State University of New York Press, 1987), 3; and Ariel Hirschfeld, who claims that "this shift [towards the New Criticism] . . . developed via Halkin's students (Harsahv, Ha-Ephrati, Perry) into the Department of General Literary Theory at Tel Aviv University, which saw itself as spearheading Israeli literary theory," "Toldot ha-chug."

17. The early 1980s witnessed different radical shifts in Israeli political and military reality, marked by the First Lebanon War (1982); the dramatic rise of neoliberalism; and a significant aesthetic transformation in Hebrew literature generally, and prose-fiction specifically, events that help delineate a tentative finish line for the period I am describing in this chapter. See, for example, Dror Mishani, *Be-khol ha-inyan ha-mizrachi yesh eyze absurd* (Tel Aviv, Israel: Am Oved, 2006); Ariel Hirschfeld, "Nigmeret zehut u-matchila acheret," in *Yofyam shel ha-menutzachim: bikoret u-mechkar al yetzirato shel Yehoshua Kenaz*, eds. Keren Dotan and Chen Strauss (Tel Aviv/Be'er Sheva, Israel: Am Oved/Heksherim, 2016), 441–60; Hanan Hever, *Sifrut she-nikhtevet mi-kan* (Tel Aviv, Israel: Yedi'ot Achar-

onot Books, 1999). For the rise of neoliberalism in Israel, see Ronen Mandelkern, "Kitzur toldot ha-neʾo-liberalizem be-Israel," in *Kitzur toldot ha-neʾo-liberalizem*, by David Harvey, trans. Guy Herling (Tel Aviv, Israel: Molad, 2015), 271–91.

18. Gershon Shaked, *Gal chadash ba-siporet ha-ivrit* (Tel Aviv, Israel: Poʾalim Publishing, 1971).

19. Eliot, "Tradition and the Individual Talent," 42.

20. Jewel Spears Brooker, *T. S. Eliot's Dialectical Imagination* (Baltimore, MD: Johns Hopkins University Press, 2018). On modernism and impersonality see, for example, Maud Ellmann, *The Poetics of Impersonality: T. S. Eliot and Ezra Pound* (Cambridge, MA: Harvard University Press, 1988); Walter, *Optical Impersonality*; and Rochelle Rives, *Modernist Impersonalities: Affect, Authority, and the Subject* (London: Palgrave Macmillan, 2012).

21. Oren Yiftachel, "'Ethnocracy' and Its Discontents: Minorities, Protests, and the Israeli Polity," *Critical Inquiry* 26, no. 4 (2000): 745.

22. Hirschfeld, "Nigmeret zehut u-matchila acheret," 444.

23. Nissim Calderon, *Pluralistim be-al korcham: al ribuy ha-terbuyot shel ha-yisraʾelim* (Haifa, Israel: University of Haifa Press, 2000), 11.

24. Gershon Shaked, *Gal achar gal ba-sifrut ha-ivrit* (Jerusalem, Israel: Keter, 1985), 179.

25. Amos Oz, *Be-or ha-tkhelet ha-aza* (Tel Aviv, Israel: Poʾalim Publishing, 1979), 130.

26. Hanna Soker-Schwager, *Mekhashef ha-shevet mi-mʾonot ovdim: Yaakov Shabtai ba-tarbut ha-yisraʾelit* (Tel Aviv, Israel: Ha-Kibbutz ha-Meʾuchad, 2007), 172, 175.

27. Hever, *Sifrut she-nikhtevet mi-kan*, 98.

28. For more about the Israeli integration policy in the education system, see Nura Resh and Yechezkel Dar, "The Rise and Fall of School Integration in Israel: Research and Policy Analysis," *British Educational Research Journal* 38, no. 6 (2012): 929–51.

29. Harshav uses the Hebraized "integration" (*integratzya*) as early as 1972 in *Sade u-misgeret: masot be-teʾorya shel sifrut u-mashmaʾut* (Jerusalem, Israel: Porter Institute for Poetics and Semiotics, Tel Aviv University, 1972), 14. He continues to employ the term in English throughout the 1970s, discussing, for example, his "theory of the process of semantic integration in understanding language," in his and Ben-Porat's *Structuralist Poetics in Israel* (Tel Aviv, Israel: Department of Poetics and Comparative Literature at Tel Aviv University, 1974), 1. Harshav then adopts it as the official title of his theory in the 1980s.

30. McHale and Segal, "Small World," 200.

31. Ben-Porat and Hrushovski, *Structuralist Poetics in Israel*, 4; Harshav borrows this definition from Wellek and Warren who write: "[A]s we have envisaged a rationale for the study of literature, we must conclude the possibility of a systematic and integrated study of literature" (*Theory of Literature*, 38).

32. Editorial Board, *Riv'on le-mada ha-sifrut*, Opening Manifesto, *Ha-Sifrut* 1 (1968): 1.

33. In the journal *Ha-Sifrut*, Yosef Sadan and Sasson Somekh regularly published articles on Arabic literature; Benjamin Harshav, Menakhem Perry, and Uriel Weinreich were central voices in the discussion of Yiddish literature; and Joseph Yahalom, Israel Levin, and Zvi Malachi dedicated much of their articles to the tradition of the *Piyyut*, associated with *Mizrahi* culture. Editorial Board, Opening Manifesto, 1.

34. Ben-Porat and Hrushovski lament that "literature became a tool of indoctrination in the Israeli school system" and "criticism was interested primarily in literature as a vehicle of ideology" (*Structuralist Poetics in Israel*, 4).

35. Menakhem Perry, interviewed by the author, July 6, 2016.

36. Perry, "'O Rose Thou Art Sick,'" 428. A version of this article in English was later published as "Literary Dynamics: How the Order of a Text Creates Its Meanings (With an Analysis of Faulkner's 'A Rose for Emily')," *Poetics Today* 1, no. 1/2 (1979): 35–64; 311–61.

37. As mentioned in the Introduction, I see the American reader-response theories as an expansion of rather than a backlash against the New Critical creed. See, Beck and Rhoades, "'Stanley Fish Was My Reader,'" 211–27.

38. Ben-Porat and Hrushovski, *Structuralist Poetics in Israel*, 13.

39. Ben-Porat and Hrushovski, *Structuralist Poetics in Israel*, 15.

40. Benjamin Harshav, "An Outline of Integrational Semantics," in *Explorations in Poetics* (Stanford, CA: Stanford University Press, 2007), 100.

41. Ben-Porat and Hrushovski, *Structuralist Poetics in Israel*, 15.

42. See Benjamin Harshav, "The Meaning of Sound Patterns in Poetry: An Interaction Theory," *Poetics Today* 2, no. 1 (1980): 39–56.

43. Naomi Tamir, "I. A. Richards ke-te'oretikan shel sifrut," *Ha-Sifrut* 4, no. 3 (1973): 442.

44. Tamir, "I. A. Richards ke-te'oretikan," 441.

45. Tamir, "I. A. Richards ke-te'oretikan," 442, 472.

46. Mintz, "On the Tel Aviv School," 227.

47. Menakhem Perry, "Counter-Stories in the Bible: Rebekah and her Bridegroom, Abraham's Servant," *Prooftexts* 27, no. 2 (2007): 278–79.

48. Perry is referring here to the very specific Freud-as-reader whom one encounters in the interpretations of Jensen's *Gradiva*, Sophocles's *Oedipus Rex*, or Shakespeare's *Hamlet*. These literary analyses earned Freud his reputation as a hyperobservant (Eve Sedgwick would claim, paranoid) archeologist or detective: a reader whom no detail escapes, who ties all elements of the text together with perfection, and who is able to demonstrate how the most trivial of features is in fact crucial. However, I believe that there is an alternative Freudian reader who emphasizes a dreamlike state of "evenly suspended attention," which is beneficial for valuable interpretation. See Yael Segalovitz, "A Leap of Faith into *Moses*: Freud's

Invitation to Evenly Suspended Attention," in *Freud and Monotheism: Moses and the Violent Origins of Religion*, eds. Karen Feldman and Gilad Sharvit (New York: Fordham University Press, 2018), 108–37.

49. Menakhem Perry, "Shirat ha-pratim: lama katavti et *Shev alay ve-hitchamem*," *Moznayim* 91 (2017): 59.

50. McHale and Segal, "Small World," 202.

51. See, for example, Perry's interpretation of the judges' verdict in the case of the former Israeli justice minister, Haim Ramon, "Ha-neshika: sipur be-shalosh varyatzyot," *Ha'aretz*, March 5, 2007. www.haaretz.co.il/literature/1.1391540.

52. Laura Heffernan and Rachel Sagner Buurma beautifully demonstrate how following the pedagogical practice of various thinkers complicates their written and usually more categorical conceptualizations (see *The Teaching Archive*).

53. Shlomo Grodzensky, "William Faulkner," *Davar*, July 3, 1962, 7.

54. There is a peak in Israeli newspaper publications on Faulkner in the decade of 1960 to 1970. See, Historical Jewish Press Collection, The National Library of Israel, "Search Results for 'Faulkner' in Hebrew language newspapers published in the Middle East (primarily in Israel) between 1950–1990. Results by decade: 1950–1959 (119 appearances), 1960–1969 (487 appearances), 1970–1979 (352 appearances), 1980–1989 (32 appearances)." Available at https://www.nli.org.il/en. Accessed February 22, 2024.

55. Translations until 1980 by chronological order: *The Town* and *The Mansion*, translated by Arnon Ben-Nahum, published in 1962; *The Reivers*, translated by Aliza Netzer, published in 1963; *The Unvanquished*, translated by Vira Israelit, published in 1968; *Light in August*, translated by Rina Litwin, published in 1968; "A Rose for Emily" and "Barn Burning," translated by Yael Renan, published in 1972; "The Bear" and "Was," translated by Amazia Porat, published in 1973; *Sanctuary*, translated by Amazia Porat, published in 1976; *As I Lay Dying*, translated by Rina Litwin, published in 1980.

56. Yehoshua explains: "In the 1970s a whole lot of Israeli literature began to use the Faulknerian method of multiple voices in the novels. . . . This technique was used in [my works] *The Lover*, in *A Late Divorce*, in Amos Oz's *The Black Box*, in *The Smile of the Lamb* by David Grossman, in some books by Binyamin Tammuz, and in many others," Bernard Horn, *Facing the Fires: Conversations with A. B. Yehoshua* (Syracuse, NY: Syracuse University Press, 1997), 52.

57. Kronfeld, *Margins of Modernism*, 125.

58. Rina Litwin, "*Or be-ogust* le-William Faulkner: im hofa'at ha-tirgum ha-ivrit," *Ha-Sifrut* 1, no. 3–4 (1968–1969): 590–98; Meir Sternberg, "Al ekronot ha-kompozitzya shel *Or be-ogust* le-Faulkner: al ha-po'etica shel ha-roman ha-moderni," *Ha-Sifrut* 3, no. 2 (1970): 498–538; Tzefira Porat, "Bubot shel nesoret: goral tragi ve-cherut komit be-Or le-ogust le-William Faulkner," *Ha-Sifrut* 2, no. 4 (1971): 767–82.

59. Menakhem Perry and Meir Sternberg, "Ha-melekh be-mabat ironi: al tachbulot ha-mesaper be-sipur David ve-Bat Sheva u-shtey haflagot le-te'orya

shel ha-proza," *Ha-Sifrut* 1 (1968–1969): 283. A later version of the article was published in English as "The King through Ironic Eyes: Biblical Narrative and the Literary Reading Process," *Poetics Today* 7, no. 2 (1986): 275–322. For Perry and Sternberg's theory of Literary Dynamics, see Perry, "Literary Dynamics," 35–64, 311–61. This article was simultaneously published in Hebrew: "Ha-dinamika shel ha-tekst ha-sifruti: eykh kove'a seder ha-tekst et mashma'uyotav," *Ha-Sifrut* 28 (1979): 6–46. Yael Renan, "Li-shmo'a et rachash ha-galim: ha-hazara, hachya'ata shel klitat ha-metzi'ut ba-yetzira ha-sifrutit," *Siman Kri'a* 2 (1973): 343–61; later published in English as "Disautomatization and Comic Deviations from Models of Organizing Experience," *Style* 18, no. 2 (1984): 160–76.

60. Faulkner's "A Rose for Emily" and "Barn Burning" are still today part of the small group of translated short stories included in the Israeli literature high school matriculation exam.

61. Perry, "'O Rose Thou Art Sick.'"

62. The Israeli reception of Faulkner complicates Pascale Casanova's analysis of Faulkner's global reception. According to Casanova, in the "centers" of the "World Republic of Letters" Faulkner's "technical innovations" were understood and valued only as formalist devices," while "in the outlaying countries of the literary world they were welcomed as tools of liberation," *The World Republic of Letters* (Cambridge, MA: Harvard University Press, 2004): 336. On the one hand, the reception of Faulkner in Israel (which can be considered one of the "outlaying countries") is aligned with the "center" due to its emphasis on Faulkner as a formalist; on the other hand, as I demonstrate in this and the following chapters, the ostensibly apolitical Israeli interpretations of Faulkner carried an implicit political valence. Moreover, the Israeli literary rewritings of Faulkner, such as those by A. B. Yehoshua, explicitly viewed Faulkner's work as political in nature.

63. According to Nili Levi, Sternberg found in Faulkner a specific "organizing compositional principle" in which several different plotlines are presented simultaneously as if unlinked, *Me-rechov ha-even el ha-chatulim: iyunim ba-sifrut shel Yehoshua Kenaz* (Tel-Aviv, Israel: Ha-Kibbutz ha-Me'uchad, 1997), 86–87.

64. Jameson, *The Antinomies of Realism*, 176.

65. As Dorothy Hale puts it, Jameson, from a Marxist point of view, "believes that the modern novel narrative time is overwhelmed by the expansion of anti-narrative time—thus eliminating the genre's dialectical projection of the realm of freedom and possibility," a failure that is expressed in Faulkner's oeuvre through the infliction of the reader with an unnecessary sense of suspense, "Faulkner's *Light in August* and New Theories of Novelistic Time," in *A Question of Time: American Literature from Colonial Encounter to Contemporary Fiction*, ed. Cindy Weinstein (Cambridge, UK: Cambridge University Press, 2018), 269.

66. Perry and Sternberg, "Ironic Eyes," 304.

67. McHale and Segal, "Small World," 199.

68. Sternberg, "Al ekronot ha-kompozitzia," 510.

69. Sternberg, "Al ekronot ha-kompozitzia," 504.
70. Sternberg, "Al ekronot ha-kompozitzia," 498.
71. Sternberg relies in his argument on Harshav's differentiation between reality-like and purely literary patterns, in the spirit of Jakobson's poetic function. According to Sternberg, the language of Faulkner's novel, as an extreme example of the modernist novel, grants dominance to the purely literary patterns, very much as in the case of poetry.
72. Sternberg, "Al ekronot ha-kompozitzia," 526.
73. Sternberg, "Al ekronot ha-kompozitzia," 514.
74. Sternberg, "Al ekronot ha-kompozitzia," 515.
75. Sternberg, "Al ekronot ha-kompozitzia," 515.
76. Sternberg, "Al ekronot ha-kompozitzia," 508.
77. Sternberg, "Al ekronot ha-kompozitzia," 518.
78. Sternberg, "Al ekronot ha-kompozitzia," 526.
79. Sternberg, "Al ekronot ha-kompozitzia," 529, 530.
80. Sternberg, "Al ekronot ha-kompozitzia," 530.
81. Sternberg, "Al ekronot ha-kompozitzia," 516.
82. Perry, "'O Rose Thou Art Sick,'" 424.
83. Perry, "'O Rose Thou Art Sick,'" 423–25.
84. Perry, "'O Rose Thou Art Sick,'" 425.
85. A. B. Yehoshua, *Ha-me'ahev* (Jerusalem, Israel: Schocken, 1977); A. B. Yehoshua, *Gerushim me'ucharim* (Tel Aviv, Israel: Ha-kibbutz ha-Me'uchad, 1982); A. B. Yehoshua, *A Late Divorce*, trans. Hillel Halkin (New York: Doubleday, 1984). All quotes from the novel are taken from Halkin's translation into English, apart from those related to the tenth chapter, "Ha-layla ha-acharon" ("The Final Night"), which was not included in the American publication of the novel. Hence, quotes from it will rely on the 2010 reedited edition, and will be translated by me. The American translation follows the 1982 Hebrew edition of *A Late Divorce*.
86. A. B. Yehoshua, "Kama he'arot al ha-retzenzya ha-yisra'elit betzeruf retzenzya," *Siman Kri'a* 7 (1977): 422–25; "Li-khtov proza: sicha im A. B. Yehoshua," interview by Menakhem Perry and Nissim Calderon, *Siman Kri'a* 5 (1976): 280.
87. Dror Mishani, "A. B. Yehoshua ve-aviv mevakrim etzel S. Y. Agnon," *Ot* 7 (2017): 215–26. Ranen Omer-Sherman suggests that Yehoshua takes a much more radical stance in relation to the Israeli occupation and the status of Arab-Israeli citizens in his 2001 novel, *Ha-kala ha-meshachreret* (*The Liberated Bride*), "The Guests and Hosts in A. B. Yehoshua's *The Liberated Bride*," *Shofar* 31, no. 3 (2013): 25–63.
88. Shmuel Huppert, "Ha-merkaz she-ibed et kocho ha-melaked: iyun ba-roman ha-chadash shel A. B. Yehoshua, *Gerushim me'ucharim*," *Zehut* 3 (1983): 190, 194.
89. Yosef Oren, "Toldot ha-medina ke-sipur nisu'im," *Yedi'ot Acharonot*, July 16, 1982; Chaim Chertok, "A. B. Yehoshua: Dismantler," in *We Are All Close:*

Conversations with Israeli Writers (New York: Fordham University Press, 1989), 45. Hillel Barzel advance a similar argument in "*Gerushim me'ucharim* le-A. B. Yehoshua: makbilot ve-to'amuyot," *Alei si'ach* 19–20 (1983–1984): 86–103.

Joseph Cohen, *Voices of Israel: Essays on and Interviews with Yehuda Amichai, A. B. Yehoshua, T. Carmi, Aharon Appelfeld, and Amos Oz* (Albany: State University of New York Press, 1990), 59.

90. Exceptional in that sense is Joseph Cohen, who, perhaps since he himself is an American, points to the similarity between the social world depicted by Yehoshua and Faulkner: "Yehoshua views the shredding fabric of Israel in much the same way that Faulkner described the disintegration of the post-bellum American South." However, Cohen does not discuss the two authors' engagement with (dis)integration on the level of form and their similar affinity to the New Criticism (*Voices of Israel*, 59).

91. Cohen, *Voices of Israel*, 51–52.

92. Cohen, *Voices of Israel*, 60.

93. Cohen, *Voices of Israel*, 72–75.

94. Eric J. Sundquist, *Faulkner: A House Divided* (Baltimore, MD: Johns Hopkins University Press, 1985), 32–33, ix.

95. J. F. Desmond, "Faulkner: The House Divided/Faulkner's MGM Screenplays," *World Literature Today* 58, no. 4 (1984): 610.

96. Horn, *Facing the Fires*, 51.

97. As Bernard Horn puts it, "Both Yehoshua and Faulkner ground their novels in a realistic depiction of the disintegration of the family. But while Faulkner uses the Freudian material as a psychological allegory to illuminate the inner life of the family, Yehoshua uses his Freudian material as a psychohistorical allegory to move from the family to history" (*Facing the Fires*, 63).

98. Paradigmatically, Alan Mintz claims that "the publication of A. B. Yehoshua's first novel, *The Lover*, in 1977 marked a turning point in the representation of the Arab . . . when he [Na'im] first speaks a third of the way through the novel, it has the force of a stunning debut. It is the first time in Hebrew literature that an Arab character is given his or her own voice and allowed to articulate an inner life that is not largely a projection of a Jewish fantasy or dilemma," "Fracturing the Zionist Narrative," *Judaism* 48, no. 4 (1999): 408. However, the ideology behind Na'im's "social discourse" has been greatly criticized ever since; a particularly forceful critique was that of the Israeli-Arab author Anton Shammas in his novel *Arabesques*, where Yehoshua's stance toward Israeli-Arabs is mocked through the character of Yosh (Yehoshua) Bar. For more, see Hannan Hever and Orin D. Gensler, "Hebrew in an Israeli Arab Hand: Six Miniatures on Anton Shammas's *Arabesques*," *Cultural Critique* 7 (1987): 57–59.

99. Joseph Cohen writes: "Yehoshua's six characters in *The Lover*, as real and believable as they are, function simultaneously as symbols for the author's political and social concerns," *Voices of Israel*, 57.

100. According to Nehama Aschkenasy, the characters of *A Late Divorce* fit quite neatly with those of *The Sound and the Fury*, "Yehoshua's *Sound and Fury*: *A Late Divorce* and its Faulknerian Model," *Modern Language Studies* 21, no. 2 (1991): 92–94.

101. Aschkenasy, "Yehoshua's *Sound and Fury*," 103–4.

102. Aschkenasy, "Yehoshua's *Sound and Fury*," 31.

103. Aschkenasy, "Yehoshua's *Sound and Fury*," 298. Huppert similarly claims that these two quotes form the scaffolding of the novel ("Ha-merkaz she-ibed et kocho ha-melaked," 190).

104. Yehoshua, *A Late Divorce*, 234, 235.

105. Yehoshua, *A Late Divorce*, 234, 264, 247.

106. Yehoshua, *A Late Divorce*, 234–36, 241.

107. Yehoshua, *A Late Divorce*, 297. In his interview with Bernard Horn, Yehoshua discloses his sense of identification with Yael: "'I [Horn] felt that the voice that was strongly yours was the voice of Yael.' 'Yael's,' he [Yehoshua] said. 'Yes . . . she is the more normal one, with a certain patience. And compassion. And not so aggressive'" (*Facing the Fires*, 59).

108. Yehoshua, *A Late Divorce*, 254–55. Interestingly, the reedited version of the novel published in 2010 mitigates the fractured style of this and other paragraphs. In the revised version the sentences are full, and the ellipses, italics, and exclamation marks disappear, thus that Yael's process of solving the riddle appears almost effortless. In that spirit, Avraham Balban describes the new edition as more "readable," for better or worse ("*Gerushim me'ucharim* me'et A. B. Yehoshua: le-ha'ir klavim mi-shnatam," *Ha'aretz*, March 24, 2010, https://www.haaretz.co.il/literature/1.1194521).

109. Yehoshua, *A Late Divorce*, 264.

110. Menakhem Perry, "Beyn nevicha li-nshikha: al ha-siyum ha-acher shel *Gerushim me'ucharim*," *Siman Kri'a* 21 (1990): 58.

111. Perry, "Beyn nevicha li-nshikha," 58.

112. Perry, "Beyn nevicha li-nshikha," 58.

113. Perry, "Counter-Stories," 278–79.

114. Perry, "Beyn nevicha li-nshikha," 9. Yehoshua also clearly alludes here to S. Y. Agnon's famous and insane dog character, Balak, in *Tmol shilshom* (Only Yesterday), who, like Horace, stands for the disillusion of the Zionist dream of Jewish integration and unification in the state of Israel.

115. A. B. Yehoshua, *Gerushim me'ucharim* (Tel Aviv, Israel: Ha-kibbutz ha-Me'uchad, 2010), 421.

116. Yehoshua, *Gerushim me'ucharim*, 422.

117. Yehoshua, *Gerushim me'ucharim*, 422.

118. The current discussion offers a possible explanation for Yehoshua's specific reception history. In his insightful editorial introduction to a critical collection on Yehoshua's work, Amir Banjabi divides the interpretations of Yehoshua roughly

into two groups. The canonical one, he claims, is born out of "the TA School and Science of Literature approach of the 1970s and 1980s," and holds that Yehoshua's work "notif[ies] us" of the Israeli "political paradox" and "internal conflict," only to then use "literature . . . to transcend the political-social discrepancy." The critical perspective that remained marginal, according to Banjabi, viewed Yehoshua's work as emphasizing "contradicting forces." Indeed, if Yehoshua was read against the backdrop of the TA School's readings of Faulkner, it is to be expected that the "integrating" view of Yehoshua's oeuvre would be canonized; what is telling, however, is that the process of integration reemerges in the context of Yehoshua's oeuvre not only as the ability to "transcend" formal "discrepancy," but to overcome "political paradox" as well, "Yehoshua be-re'i bikoret ha-sifrut ha-ivrit" in *Mabatim mitztalvim: iyunim bi-ytzirat A. B. Yehoshua*, eds. Amir Banjabi, Nitza Ben-Dov, and Ziva Shamir (Tel Aviv, Israel: Ha-kibbutz ha-Me'uchad, 2010), 19, 14, 17.

119. Cohen, *Voices of Israel*, 72–75.

Chapter Six

1. Yehuda Amichai, "Ba-eretz ha-lohetet ha-zot, milim tzrikhot li-hiyot tzel," Interview by Dan Omer, *Proza* 25 (1978): 5–11.

2. Amichai, "Ba-eretz ha-lohetet ha-zot," 6. Though the "soil" and "plant" (namely, prose fiction and poetry) are no doubt interlinked for Amichai, his work undoes linear progression from prose to poetry and from literal to figurative. This is typically articulated not in metapoetic terms but as a reflection on the thoughts and dreams of ordinary lovers. As in his poem "Re'i, machshavot va-chalomot" ("Look: Thoughts and Dreams"): "Look, we too are going / in the reverse-flower-way: / to begin with a calyx exulting toward the light, / to descend with the stem growing more and more solemn, / to arrive at the closed earth and to wait there for a while, / and to end as a root, in the darkness, in the deep womb" (*The Selected Poetry of Yehuda Amichai*, trans. Chana Bloch and Stephen Mitchell [Berkeley: University of California Press, 2013], 7).

3. Following Chana Kronfeld's extensive discussion of Amichai's figural language, I use *metaphor* in this chapter as a superordinate category that encompasses not only metaphor proper but also simile and analogy (*The Full Severity of Compassion*, 349).

4. Yehuda Amichai, "Avi," in *Shirim 1948–1962* (Jerusalem and Tel-Aviv, Israel: Schocken, 1977), 27, © Schocken Publishing House, Tel Aviv, Israel; Yehuda Amichai, "My Father," in *The Poetry of Yehuda Amichai*, ed. Robert Alter, trans. Stephen Mitchell (New York: Farrar, Straus and Giroux, 2015), 35.

5. Yehuda Amichai, "Mitot avi," in *Ba-ru'ach ha-nora'a ha-zot* (Jerusalem and Tel-Aviv, Israel: Schocken, 1961), 132; Yehuda Amichai, "The Times My

Father Died," in *The World Is a Room and Other Stories*, trans. Yosef Schachter (Philadelphia, PA: Jewish Publication Society of America, 1984), 185–86.

6. Amichai, "The Times My Father Died," 191, 187.

7. Michael Gluzman, " 'Moto shel Dicky': ha-tekst ha-tra'umati shel Yehuda Amichai," *Mechkarey Yerushalayim be-sifrut ivrit* 31 (2020), 453–88.

8. Donald Winnicott, "Ego Integration and Child Development," in *The Maturational Processes and the Facilitating Environment: Studies in the Theory of Emotional Development* (New York: Routledge, 2018), 56–63.

9. Dan Miron astutely identifies in Amichai's poetry a departure from "succinctness." However, he still disregards his prose fiction. Even in his article comparing Amichai with S. Yizhar, "the founding father of Israeli prose fiction," Miron does not as much as mention Amichai's short stories and novels, "Zman-merchav bi-yetzirot S. Yizhar vi-Yehuda Amichai: shney modelim kognitiviyim ba-sifrut ha-yisra'elit ha-mukdemet," in *Tarbut, zikaron ve-historiya: be-hokara le-Anita Shapira* (Tel Aviv, Israel: Tel Aviv University Press, 2012), 383–419.

10. Amichai, "Ba-eretz ha-lohetet ha-zot," 6. Prior to Harshav, Amichai sent his poems to Leah Goldberg, the predominant woman writer of the previous literary generation (the *moderna*). For more, see chapter 3 of Kronfeld, *The Full Severity of Compassion*.

11. Shlomo Tzemach, "Matzevet ve-shalakhta," *Davar*, July 5, 1957, 6. In the previous chapter, I noted that Tzemach played an important role in the introduction of the New Criticism into Israeli culture through his publication of translated New Critical articles in his journal, *Behinot*. Here, we see that his New Critical orientation did not prevent him from continually rejecting Israeli modernism, even when it was aligned with the American modernists the New Critics advanced.

12. B. Y. Michali, "Be-eyn chush mida," *Davar*, June 3, 1955, 25.

13. Yehuda Amichai, *Yehuda Amichai: A Life of Poetry (1948–1994)*, trans. Benjamin Harshav and Barbara Harshav (New York: Harper Collins, 1994).

14. Benjamin Harshav, "Hirhurim ishiyim al Amichai: ha-shira ve-ha-mdina," *Alpayim* 33 (2008): 126, 132.

15. Brooks and Warren, *Understanding Fiction*, 510. For more on this, see chapter 1.

16. Tzemach, "Matzevet ve-shalakhta," 5.

17. Benjamin Harshav, "Poetic Metaphor and Frames of Reference: With Examples from Eliot, Rilke, Mayakovsky, Mandelshtam, Pound, Creeley, Amichai, and the *New York Times*," *Poetics Today* 5, no. 1 (1984): 19.

18. Harshav, "Poetic Metaphor and Frames of Reference," 41.

19. Natan Zach, "Shirey Yehuda Amichai," *Al Ha-Mishmar*, July 29, 1955. Republished in *Ha-shira she-me'ever la-milim: Te'orya u-vikoret 1954–1973* (Tel Aviv, Israel: Ha-Kibbutz Ha-Me'uchad, 2011), 325.

20. Zach, "Shirey Yehuda Amichai." Zach quotes R. P. Blackmur from *Language as Gesture* (London: G. Allen & Unwin, 1954), 6, 13. For Blackmur as a New Critic, see Russell Fraser, "R. P. Blackmur: The Politics of a New Critic," *Sewanee Review* 87, no. 4 (1979): 557–72.

21. Natan Zach, "Sipurav ha-shiriyim shel Yehuda Amichai," *Yokhani* 2 (1962): 26; republished in *Ha-shira she-me'ever la-milim*, 331.

22. This paragraph is another example of Zach's ambivalence toward Amichai's figurative language. After his imperative that a poet must "resist the use of the poetic figure if . . . it is not 'toned down' by humor, irony, or self-directed humor," Zach adds in parentheses, "[A]s in the poetry of Amichai, who is gifted with an exceptional figurative creativity," thus exempting Amichai by presenting him as an exemplar of "toning town." However, a sentence later Zach uses the exact same terminology to urge poets to "restrain figurative creativity." Once again, then, we witness the degree to which Amichai's metaphors posed a challenge for Zach, and were acceptable for him only in their "restrained" poetry form, "Le-akliman ha-signoni shel shnot ha chamishim ve-ha-shishim be-shiratenu," *Ha'aretz*, July 29, 1966, 12.

23. Zach, "Sipurav ha-shiriyim shel Yehuda Amichai," 27, 29.

24. Menakhem Perry, "Nokhach ha-metim: ha-po'etika ha-chadasha shel Yehuda Amichai ha-tza'ir," in *Ha-ne'eman: minchat hokara vi-ydidut le-Uzi Shavit Il Pastor Fido: Papers and Literary Works Dedicated to Uzi Shavit*, eds. Ziva Shamir and Menakhem Perry (Tel Aviv, Israel: Ha-Kibbutz Ha-Me'uchad, 2016), 193.

25. It is interesting that one of the contributors to the debate over whether or not Trumpeldor uttered the famous words before his death was Shlomo Grodzensky, himself invested in the New Criticism, as noted in the previous chapter. For Grodzensky on Trumpeldor, see "Tov la-mut," *Davar*, March 29, 1960, 3.

26. Yehuda Amichai, "Geshem bi-sde krav," in *Shirim 1948–1962* (Jerusalem and Tel-Aviv, Israel: Schocken, 1977), 21, © Schocken Publishing House, Tel Aviv, Israel; Yehuda Amichai, "Rain Falls on the Faces of My Friends," in *The Poetry of Yehuda Amichai*, ed. and trans. Robert Alter (New York: Farrar, Straus and Giroux, 2015), 28.

27. Zach wrote his dissertation on Ezra Pound and Imagism, and later published its précis in the entry "Imagism and Vorticism," in the prestigious *Modernism: A Guide to European Literature 1890–1930*, Penguin Literary Criticism Series, eds. Malcolm Bradbury and James McFarlane (London: Penguin Books, 1978), 228–43.

28. On Zach's purported editing of Amichai, see Harshav, "Hirhurim ishiyim al Amichai," 129; and Perry, "Nokhach ha-metim," 196.

29. Perry, "Nokhach ha-metim," 196.

30. Naama Lanski, "Shir mecha'a," *Israel Ha-Yom*, April 8, 2011, https://www.israelhayom.co.il/article/35847; Hana Amichai, "Shalosh bdayot al Likrat ve-

Amichai," *Ha'aretz*, July 9, 2015, https://www.haaretz.co.il/literature/letters-to-editor/.premium-1.2680679.

31. Harshav, "Hirhurim ishiyim al Amichai," 129.
32. Ben-Porat and Hrushovski, *Structuralist Poetics in Israel*, 15.
33. Perry, "Nokhach ha-metim," 195.
34. Perry, "Nokhach ha-metim," 193.
35. Perry, "Nokhach ha-metim," 198.
36. Perry, "Nokhach ha-metim," 199–200.
37. In the same spirit, when Harshav recalls his invitation of Amichai to the Hebrew University in 1962 to discuss his *Poems 1948–1962*, he neglects to say a single word about *In This Terrible Wind*, published just a few months earlier, "Hirhurim ishiyim al Amichai," 123.
38. Boaz Arpali, "Ha-alegia al ha-yeled she-avad: mavo le-shirat Yehuda Amichai," *Siman Kri'a* 2 (1973): 63–95; *Ha-prachim ve-ha-agartal; shirat Amichai: mivne, mashmau't, po'etika* (Tel Aviv, Israel: Ha-Kibbutz Ha-Me'uchad, 1986). On the figure of the urn in the New Criticism, see chapters 1 and 2.
39. Arpali, "Ha-alegia al ha-yeled she-avad," 66.
40. Arpali, "Ha-alegia al ha-yeled she-avad," 66.
41. Arpali, "Ha-alegia al ha-yeled she-avad," 67.
42. Arpali, *Ha-prachim ve-ha-agartal*, 67–85.
43. Arpali, "Ha-alegia al ha-yeled she-avad," 68–69.
44. Amichai, *Selected Poetry*, 1.
45. Arpali, "Ha-alegia al ha-yeled she-avad," 78–79.
46. A similar idea of Amichai as dangerously playing around with metaphors that might run wild is communicated in Shimon Sandbank's article published in *Ha-Sifrut* in 1971. There, Sandbank compares Amichai's poetry with that of Rilke and Auden. Yet in contrast with them, Sandbank writes, "Amichai . . . does not take seriously either the interiorization of the world or the physical exteriorization of the internal world. The transformation of the human in the inanimate is an expression of an overflowing spirit that plays in a game of analogy with the world," "Rilke, Auden, Amichai," *Ha-Sifrut* 2, no. 4 (1971): 714.
47. Yehuda Amichai, "Pgishat ha-kita," in *Ba-ru'ach ha-nora'a ha-zot*, 7–48.
48. The narrator recalls that upon graduation, during the Second World War, he volunteered to serve in the British army: "When they built the central [bus] station in Tel Aviv, about ten or twenty years ago, I was in the British army, guarding the [Israeli] shores from submarine warfare" ("Pgishat ha-kita," 24). The central station was built in 1938, which means that the narration takes place during the mid-1950s.
49. Amichai, "Pgishat ha-kita," 8.
50. Amichai, "Pgishat ha-kita," 40–45 (plotline at the border); 9, 37, 39 (soldiers and the War of Independence); 13 (eucalyptus trees); 11, 12 (Generali Building and Salameh Square).

51. Amichai, "Pgishat ha-kita," 8, 18.
52. Amichai, "Pgishat ha-kita," 46.
53. Amichai, "Pgishat ha-kita," 27. As Chana Kronfeld notes, Amichai frequently utilizes the third person plural "they" (as in "they always cover up") in order to refer to "institutional powers" such as the state and organized religion (*The Full Severity of Compassion*, 30).
54. Eyal Bassan's insightful recent study similarly explores the political valence of Amichai's prose fiction metaphors. Bassan puts into conversation Amichai's *In This Terrible Wind* and *Not of This Time, Not of This Place* with Louis Althusser's concept of interpellation to claim that Amichai's metaphors dramatize and complicate "the material functionality of ideology (the workings of its apparatuses, practices, and rituals) and the processes of interpellation in which, in the nascent Israeli society of the 1950s, individuals are constituted as subjects," "Interpellation, Metaphorization, and the Time of the Subject: The Politics of Yehuda Amichai's Fiction" (unpublished article).
55. Kronfeld, *The Full Severity of Compassion*, 225.
56. Amichai, "Pgishat ha-kita," 7.
57. Kronfeld, *The Full Severity of Compassion*, 117–75.
58. "Even as R. Zera, who, whenever he chanced upon scholars engaged thereon [i.e., in calculating the time of the Messiah's coming], would say to them: I beg of you, do not postpone it, for it has been taught: Three come unawares [literally, the messiah comes when the mind is diverted]: Messiah, a found article and a scorpion," Isidore Epstein, trans., *The Babylonian Talmud: Tractate Sanhedrin* (London: Sonico Press, 1935), 97a.
59. Winnicott, "Ego Integration," 61.
60. In psychodynamic terms, though "disintegration" is destructive, it can also be thought of as a defense mechanism: "[D]isintegration . . . is an active production of chaos in defense against unintegration in the absence of maternal ego-support. . . . The chaos of disintegration may be as 'bad' as the unreliability of the environment, but it has the advantage of being produced by the baby and therefore of being non-environmental," Winnicott, "Ego Integration," 61.
61. Winnicott, "Ego Integration," 61.
62. Donald Winnicott, *Playing and Reality* (London: Routledge, 1991), 64.
63. Amichai, "Pgishat ha-kita," 36.
64. Arpali, "Ha-alegia al ha-yeled she-avad," 79.
65. Harshav, "Hirhurim ishiyim al Amichai," 124.
66. Gershon Shaked contends that Amichai "not only expanded the traditional thematic borders" of Israeli prose fiction, but also "produced a novel style, compatible with that which characterizes his poetry," "Ve-akhsav achrey ha-kibushim le'an yachzeru?," in *Gal chadash ba-siporet ha-ivrit*, 89–125.
67. Shaked, *Gal chadash ba-siporet ha-ivrit*, 93, 100.
68. Shaked, *Gal chadash ba-siporet ha-ivrit*, 98.

69. Shaked, *Gal chadash ba-siporet ha-ivrit*, 99.
70. Shaked, *Gal chadash ba-siporet ha-ivrit*, 102.
71. Shaked, *Gal chadash ba-siporet ha-ivrit*, 102.

Epilogue

1. Maggie Nelson, *The Argonauts* (Minneapolis, MN: Graywolf Press, 2015), 90–91.
2. Wellek and Warren, *Theory of Literature*, 251.
3. Shoshana Felman writes, "The scene of the critical debate is thus a repetition of the scene dramatized in the text. The critical interpretation, in other words, not only elucidates the text but also reproduces it dramatically, unwittingly *participates in it*. Through its very reading, the text, so to speak, acts itself out," "Turning the Screw of Interpretation," *Yale French Studies* 55/56 (1977): 101; emphasis in original.
4. Kurnick, "A Few Lies."
5. Kurnick, "A Few Lies," 351, 353.
6. Best and Marcus, "Surface Reading"; Kurnick, "A Few Lies," 358.
7. Moretti, "Conjectures on World Literature," 57; Best and Marcus, "Surface Reading," 10.
8. Kurnick, "A Few Lies," 358.
9. Kurnick, "A Few Lies," 359.
10. Alencar, *Iracema*, translation mine.
11. Coutinho, *Correntes*, 145–48.
12. Quoted in Rocha, *Crítica literária*, 191.
13. Faulkner, *The Sound and the Fury*, 6, 51, 49.
14. Faulkner, "An Introduction to *The Sound and the Fury*," 414.

Bibliography

Abdur-Rahman, Aliyyah I. "'What Moves at the Margin': William Faulkner and Race." In *The New Cambridge Companion to William Faulkner*, edited by John T. Matthews, 44–58. Cambridge, UK: Cambridge University Press, 2015.

Albuquerque, Durval Muniz de, Jr. *The Invention of the Brazilian Northeast*. Translated by Jerry Dennis Metz. Durham, NC: Duke University Press, 2014.

Alcázar, Jorge. "La nueva critica norteamericana." *Acta poetica* 8 (1987): 135–63.

Alencar, José Martiniano de. *Iraçéma, the Honey Lips: A Legend of Brazil*. Translated by Isabel Burton. London: Bickers, 1886.

———. *Iracema: A Legend of Ceará*. Translated by D. N. Bidell. Rio de Janeiro, Brazil: Impresa Inglesa, 1921.

———. *Iracema: lenda do Ceará*. São Paulo, Brazil: Ed Cultrix, 1968.

———. *Iracema: A Novel*. Translated by Clifford E. Landers. New York: Oxford University Press, 2000.

Alford, Lucy. *Forms of Poetic Attention*. New York: Columbia University Press, 2020.

Amaral, Emília. "O pacto com o leitor e o misticismo da escrita em *A Paixão Segunado G.H.*, de Clarice Lispector." In *Leitores e leituras de Clarice Lispector*, edited by Regina Pontieri, 11–20. São Paulo, Brazil: Hedra, 2004.

Amichai, Hana. "Shalosh bdayot al Likrat ve-Amichai" ("Three fabrications on *Likrat* and Amichai"). *Ha'aretz*, July 9, 2015. https://www.haaretz.co.il/literature/letters-to-editor/.premium-1.2680679.

Amichai, Yehuda. *Ba-ru'ach ha-nora'a ha-zot* (In This Terrible Wind). Jerusalem and Tel Aviv, Israel: Schocken, 1961.

———. *Shirim 1948–1962* (Poems 1948–1962). Jerusalem and Tel Aviv, Israel: Schocken, 1977.

———. "Ba-eretz ha-lohetet ha-zot, milim tzrikhot li-hiyot tzel" (In This Hot Land Words Must Cast a Shadow). Interview by Dan Omer. *Proza* 25 (1978): 5–11.

———. *The World Is a Room and Other Stories*. Translated by Yosef Schachter. Philadelphia, PA: Jewish Publication Society of America, 1984.

———. *Yehuda Amichai: A Life of Poetry (1948–1994)*. Translated by Benjamin Harshav and Barbara Harshav. New York: HarperCollins, 1994.

---. *The Selected Poetry of Yehuda Amichai*. Translated by Chana Bloch and Stephen Mitchell. Berkeley: University of California Press, 2013.

---. *The Poetry of Yehuda Amichai*. Edited and translated by Robert Alter. New York: Farrar, Straus and Giroux, 2015.

Amorim, Beatriz de Castro. "Between Heaven and Hell: A (Re)evaluation of Genderic Problems in Lispector's *A maçã no escuro* and 'Perdoando Deus.'" *Brasil/Brazil* 5, no. 8 (1992): 29–51.

Andrade, Oswald de. "Cannibalist Manifesto." Translated by Leslie Bary. *Latin American Literary Review* 19, no. 38 (1991): 38–47.

---. "Manifesto antropófago." In *Vanguardas latino-americanas: polémicas, manifestos e textos críticos*, edited by Jorge Schwartz, 142–47. São Paulo, Brazil: Editora da Universidade de São Paulo, 2008.

Arêas, Vilma, and Berta Waldman. "Eppur, se muove." *Remate de males* 9 (1989): 161–68.

Armstrong, Isobel. "Textual Harassment: The Ideology of Close Reading, or How Close Is Close?" *Textual Practice* 9, no. 3 (1995): 401–20.

Arpali, Boaz. "Ha-alegia al ha-yeled she-avad: mavo le-shirat Yehuda Amichai" (The Elegy on the Lost Child: An Introduction to Yehuda Amichai's Poetry). *Siman Kri'a* 2 (1973): 63–101.

---. *Ha-prachim ve-ha-agartal; shirat Amichai: mivne, mashmau't, po'etika* (The Flowers and the Urn: Amichai's Poetry 1948–1968). Tel Aviv, Israel: Ha-Kibbutz Ha-Me'uchad, 1986.

Aschkenasy, Nehama. "Yehoshua's *Sound and Fury*: A Late Divorce and Its Faulknerian Model." *Modern Language Studies* 21, no. 2 (1991): 92–104.

Aubry, Timothy. *Guilty Aesthetic Pleasures*. Cambridge, MA: Harvard University Press, 2018.

Balban, Avraham. "*Gerushim me'ucharim* me'et A. B. Yehoshua: le-ha'ir klavim mi-shnatam" (*A Late Divorce* by A. B. Yehoshua: Don't Let Sleeping Dogs Lie). *Ha'aretz*, March 24, 2010. https://www.haaretz.co.il/literature/1.1194521.

Baldwin, James. *Notes of a Native Son*. Boston, MA: Beacon Press, 2012.

Banjabi, Amir. "Yehoshua be-re'i bikoret ha-sifrut ha-ivrit" (Yehoshua as Reflected in Hebrew Literary Criticism). In *Mabatim mitztalvim: iyunim bi-ytzirat A. B. Yehoshua* (Intersecting Perspectives: Essays on A. B. Yehoshua's Oeuvre), edited by Amir Banjabi, Nitza Ben-Dov, and Ziva Shamir, 14–29. Tel Aviv, Israel: Ha-kibbutz ha-Me'uchad, 2010.

Barzel, Hillel. "*Gerushim me'ucharim* le-A. B. Yehoshua: makbilot ve-to'amuyot" (*A Late Divorce* by A. B. Yehoshua: Parallels and Similarities). *Alei si'ach* 19–20 (1983–84): 86–103.

Basnett, Susan. *Translation (The New Critical Idiom)*. London: Routledge, 2014.

Bassan, Eyal. "Interpellation, Metaphorization, and the Time of the Subject: The Politics of Yehuda Amichai's Fiction." Unpublished Paper, 2024.

Bawer, Bruce. "Religious Atheist: The Case of Allen Tate." *Hudson Review* 55, no. 1 (2002): 167–75.

Beck, Charlotte H., and John P. Rhoades. "'Stanley Fish Was My Reader': Cleanth Brooks, the New Criticism, and Reader-Response Theory." In *The New Criticism and Contemporary Literary Theory: Connections and Continuities*, edited by William J. Spurlin and Michael Fischer, 211–27. New York: Garland, 1995.

Belém, Odilon. *Afrânio Coutinho: Uma filosofia da literatura*. Rio de Janeiro, Brazil: Pallas, Didática e Científica, 1987.

Ben-Porat, Ziva, and Benjamin Hrushovski. *Structuralist Poetics in Israel*. Tel Aviv, Israel: Department of Poetics and Comparative Literature at Tel Aviv University, 1974.

———. *Poética e estruturalismo em Israel*. Translated by Jacó Guinsburg. São Paulo, Brazil: Editora Perspectiva, 1978.

Benjamin, Walter. "Theory of Distraction." In *Walter Benjamin: Selected Writings, Vol. 3: 1935–1938*, edited by Howard Eiland and Michael W. Jennings, 141–42. Cambridge, MA: Harvard University Press, 2006.

Ben-Naftali, Michal. "Deconstruction: Derrida." In *The Edinburgh Encyclopedia of Continental Philosophy*, edited by Simon Glendinning, 653–64. Edinburgh, UK: Edinburgh University Press, 1999.

Best, Stephen, and Sharon Marcus. "Surface Reading: An Introduction." *Representations* 108, no. 1 (2009): 1–21.

"The Best Southern Novels of All Time." *Oxford American*, August 27, 2009. https://www.oxfordamerican.org/magazine/iten/470-the-best-southern-novels-of-all-time

Biron, Rebecca E. "Crime and Punishment Reconsidered: Lispector's *A maçã no escuro*." In *Murder and Masculinity: Violent Fictions of Twentieth-Century Latin America*, 67–89. Nashville, TN: Vanderbilt University Press, 2000.

Blackmur, R. P. "For a Second Look." *Kenyon Review* 11, no. 1 (1949): 7–10.

———. *Language as Gesture*. London: G. Allen & Unwin, 1954.

Bleikasten, André. *The Most Splendid Failure: Faulkner's The Sound and the Fury*. Bloomington: Indiana University Press, 1976.

———. *The Ink of Melancholy: Faulkner's Novels from The Sound and the Fury to Light in August*. Reprint, Bloomington: Indiana University Press (1990) 2016.

Bortoni-Ricardo, Stella Maris, Maria da Guia Taveiro Silva, Maria do Rosário Rocha Caxangá, and Marli Vieira Lins. "The Sociolinguistic Roots of Illiteracy in Brazil." *Cultivating Literacy in Portuguese-Speaking Countries* 1, no. 4 (2012). http://www.acoalfaplp.net/en_index.html.

Bouchakour, Imane. "Disabled or Idiosyncractic? Rethinking Mind and Language in Faulkner's Benjy." In *PALA 2019 Conference Proceedings, Liverpool University, UK*, 2019. https://www.pala.ac.uk/2019.html.

Boyarin, Daniel. "Placing Reading: Ancient Israel and Medieval Europe." In *The Ethnography of Reading*, edited by Jonathan Boyarin, 10–38. Berkeley: University of California Press, 1993.

Bressan, Inês Cardin. "Afrânio Coutinho, crítico e historiador da literatura Brasileira: Uma leitura." PhD diss., Universidade Estadual Paulista, 2007. https://repositorio.unesp.br/handle/11449/94135.

Brivic, Sheldon. *Tears of Rage: The Racial Interface of Modern American Fiction: Faulkner, Wright, Pynchon, Morrison*. Baton Rouge: Louisiana State University Press, 2008.

Brooker, Jewel Spears. *T. S. Eliot's Dialectical Imagination*. Baltimore, MD: Johns Hopkins University Press, 2018.

Brooks, Cleanth. *The Well Wrought Urn: Studies in the Structure of Poetry*. Orlando, FL: Harcourt, 1947.

———. *William Faulkner: The Yoknapatawpha Country*. New Haven, CT: Yale University Press, 1966.

———. "The New Criticism." *Sewanee Review* 87, no. 4 (1979): 592–607.

———. "A Vision and the Byzantium Poems." In *Yeats: Poems, 1919–1935: A Casebook*, edited by Elizabeth Butler Cullingford, 63–74. London: Macmillan, 1984.

———. *William Faulkner: Toward Yoknapatawpha and Beyond*. Baton Rouge: Louisiana State University Press, 1990.

Brooks, Cleanth, and Allen Tate. *Cleanth Brooks and Allen Tate: Collected Letters, 1933–1976*. Edited by Alphonse Vinh. Columbia: University of Missouri Press, 1998.

Brooks, Cleanth, and Robert Penn Warren. *Understanding Poetry*. Boston, MA: Wadsworth, 1976.

———. *Understanding Fiction*. Englewood Cliffs, NJ: Pearson, 1979.

Brooks, Peter. *Reading for the Plot: Design and Intention in Narrative*. Cambridge, MA: Harvard University Press, 1992.

Broughton, Panthea Reid. *William Faulkner: The Abstract and the Actual*. Baton Rouge: Louisiana State University Press, 1974.

Button, Peter. "The Aesthetic Critique of Modernity in Chinese Marxism, New Criticism, and Adorno." In *Configurations of the Real in Chinese Literary and Aesthetic Modernity*, 120–59. Leiden, the Netherlands; Boston, MA: Brill, 2009.

Buurma, Rachel Sagner, and Laura Heffernan. *The Teaching Archive: A New History for Literary Study*. Chicago, IL: University of Chicago Press, 2020.

Calderon, Nisim. *Pluralistim be-al korcham: al ribuy ha-terbuyot shel ha-yisra'elim* (Multiculturalism Versus Pluralism in Israel). Haifa, Israel: University of Haifa Press, 2000.

Camilo, Vagner. *Drummond: da Rosa do povo à rosa das trevas*. São Paulo, Brazil: Ateliê Editorial, 2001.

———. "O aerólito e o zelo dos neófitos: Sérgio Buarque, crítico de poesia." *Revista USP* 80 (2009): 111–24.

Candido, Antonio. Introduction to *Roots of Brazil*, by Sérgio Buarque de Holanda, xxi–xxxiv. Translated by G. Harvey Summ. Notre Dame, IN: University of Notre Dame Press, 2012.

Carvalho, Bruno. "The Future as a Necessity: Reading Clarice Lispector in the Anthropocene." In *Literature Beyond the Human: Post-Anthropocentric Brazil*, edited by Luca Bacchini and Victoria Saramago, 181–94. New York: Routledge, 2022.

Casanova, Pascale. *The World Republic of Letters*. Cambridge, MA: Harvard University Press, 2004.

Cascudo, Luís C. *Rêde de dormir: Uma pesquisa etnográfica*. Rio de Janeiro, Brazil: Ministério da Educação e Cultura, Serviço de Documentação, 1959.

Cavanaugh, Hilayne. "Faulkner, Stasis, and Keats' 'Ode on a Grecian Urn.'" PhD diss., University of Nebraska, 1977.

Chertok, Chaim. "A. B. Yehoshua: Dismantler." In *We Are All Close: Conversations with Israeli Writers*, 37–48. New York: Fordham University Press, 1989.

Christian, Barbara. "The Race for Theory." *Cultural Critique* 6 (1987): 51–64.

Cixous, Hélène. *Reading with Clarice Lispector*. Translated by Verena Andermatt Conley. Minneapolis: University of Minnesota Press, 1990.

———. "Writing and the Law: Blanchot, Joyce, Kafka, and Lispector." In *Readings: The Poetics of Blanchot, Joyce, Kakfa, Kleist, Lispector, and Tsvetayeva*, 1–28. Translated by Conley Verena Andermatt. Minneapolis: University of Minnesota Press, 1991.

Clarke, Deborah. "Erasing and Inventing Motherhood: *The Sound and the Fury* and *As I Lay Dying*." In *Robbing the Mother*, edited by Deborah Clarke, 19–51. Jackson: University Press of Mississippi, 1994.

Cohen, Joseph. *Voices of Israel: Essays on and Interviews with Yehuda Amichai, A. B. Yehoshua, T. Carmi, Aharon Appelfeld, and Amos Oz*. Albany: State University of New York Press, 1990.

Cohen, Philip, and Doreen Fowler. "Faulkner's Introduction to *The Sound and the Fury*." *American Literature* 62, no. 2 (1990): 262–83.

Cohen, Uri. *Academia be-Tel Aviv: tzmichata shel universita* (Academy in Tel Aviv: The Rise of a University). Tel Aviv, Israel: Magnes, 2014.

Connor, Steven. "Postmodernism and Literature." In *The Cambridge Companion to Postmodernism*, edited by Steven Connor, 62–81. Cambridge, UK: Cambridge University Press, 2006.

Coutinho, Afrânio. *Correntes cruzadas: questões de literatura*. Rio de Janeiro, Brazil: Editora A Noite, 1953.

———. *Da crítica e da nova crítica*. Rio de Janeiro, Brazil: Editora Civilizacão Brasileira, 1957.

———. *Na hospital das letras*. Rio de Janeiro, Brazil: Editora Tempo Brasileiro, 1963.

———, ed. *A literatura no Brasil*. Rio de Janeiro, Brazil: Sul Americana, 1968.
Cowley, Malcolm, ed. *The Faulkner-Cowley File: Letters and Memories 1944–1962*. New York: Viking Press, 1966.
———. "Poe in Mississippi." In *William Faulkner: Critical Assessments*, vol. 3, edited by Henry Claridge, 268–70. Robertsbridge, UK: Helm Information, 1999.
Crary, Jonathan. *Suspensions of Perception: Attention, Spectacle, and Modern Culture*. Cambridge, MA: MIT Press, 1999.
Culler, Jonathan. *On Deconstruction: Theory and Criticism after Structuralism*. Ithaca, NY: Cornell University Press, 2007.
Da-Luz-Moreira, Paulo. "Regionalism and Modernism in the Short Stories of William Faulkner, João Guimarães Rosa, and Juan Rulfo." PhD diss., University of California, Santa Barbara, 2007. https://www.proquest.com/docview/304880819?pqorigsite=gscholar&fromopenview=true.
Dalill-Baue, William. "Insignificant Monkeys: Preaching Black English in Faulkner's *The Sound and the Fury* and Morrison's *The Bluest Eye* and *Beloved*." *Mississippi Quarterly* 49, no. 3 (1996): 457–73.
Dames, Nicholas. "Reverie, Sensation, Effect: Novelistic Attention and Stendhal's 'De l'Amour.'" *Narrative* 10, no. 1 (2002): 47–68.
Damrosch, David. *What Is World Literature?* Princeton, NJ: Princeton University Press, 2003.
Davis, Laura R. "Sensory Coding in William Faulkner's Novels: Investigating Class, Gender, Queerness, and Race through a Non-Visual Paradigm." PhD diss., Georgia State University, 2011.
———. "The Smeller's (Almost Always) a Feller: A Sensory Studies Approach to Examining Gender and Sexuality across Nine Faulkner Texts." *Faulkner Journal* 28, no. 2 (2014): 53–77.
Davis-McElligatt, Joanna. "On Thingification: Faulkner and Afropessimism." In *The New William Faulkner Studies*, edited by Sarah Gleeson-White and Pardis Dabashi, 166–81. Cambridge, UK: Cambridge University Press, 2022.
de Man, Paul. *Blindness and Insight: Essays in the Rhetoric of Contemporary Criticism*. Minneapolis: University of Minnesota Press, 1986.
DeVoto, Bernard. "Witchcraft in Mississippi." In *William Faulkner: The Contemporary Reviews*, edited by M. Thomas Inge, 144–49. Cambridge, UK: Cambridge University Press, 1995.
Derrida, Jacques. "Fors: The Anglish Words of Nicolas Abraham and Maria Torok." Introduction to *The Wolf Man's Magic Word: A Cryptonomy*, by Nicholas Abraham and Maria Torok, xi–il. Edited by Barbara Johnson. Translated by Nicholas Rand. Minneapolis: Minnesota University Press, 1986.
———. *Memoires: For Paul de Man*. Edited by Avital Ronell and Eduardo Cadava. Translated by Cecile Lindsay, Jonathan Culler, and Peggy Kamuf. New York: Columbia University Press, 1990.
———. *Specters of Marx: The State of the Debt, the Work of Mourning, & the New International*. Translated by Peggy Kaufman. London: Routledge, 1994.

———. "Ulysses Gramophone: Hear Say Yes in Joyce." In *Derrida and Joyce: Texts and Contexts*, edited by Andrew J. Mitchell and Sam Slote, 41–86. Albany: State University of New York Press, 2013.

Desmond, J. F. "Faulkner: The House Divided/Faulkner's MGM Screenplays." *World Literature Today* 58, no. 4 (1984): 610.

Deutscher, Penelope. "Mourning the Other, Cultural Cannibalism, and the Politics of Friendship (Jacques Derrida and Luce Irigaray)." *Differences: A Journal of Feminist Cultural Studies* 10, no. 3 (1998): 159–84.

Dor, Moshe. "Paytanim le-atid lavo" (Forthcoming Poets). *Siman Kri'a* 9 (1979): 341–49.

Dore, Florence. "The New Criticism and the Nashville Sound: William Faulkner's *The Town* and Rock and Roll." *Contemporary Literature* 55, no. 1 (2014): 32–57.

———. *Novel Sounds: Southern Fiction in the Age of Rock and Roll*. New York: Columbia University Press, 2018.

Du Bois, W. E. B. *The Souls of Black Folk*. Oxford, UK: Oxford University Press, 2007.

DuBois, Andrew. "Close Reading: An Introduction." In *Close Reading: The Reader*, edited by Frank Lentricchia and Andrew DuBois, 1–40. Durham, NC: Duke University Press, 2003.

Eagleton, Terry. *Literary Theory: An Introduction*. 2nd ed. Minneapolis: Minnesota University Press, 1996.

———. *The Event of Literature*. New Haven, CT: Yale University Press, 2012.

Ebileeni, Maurice. *Conrad, Faulkner, and the Problem of Nonsense*. London and New York: Bloomsbury Academic, 2015.

Editorial Board. Opening Manifesto. *Ha-Sifrut: Riv'on le-mada ha-sifrut* 1 (1968): 5–7.

Eidsheim, Nina Sun. *The Race of Sound: Listening, Timbre, and Vocality in African American Music*. Durham, NC: Duke University Press, 2019.

Elgozy, Georges. "Le bluff du futur." *La revue administrative* 166 (1975): 385–89.

Eliot, T. S. "Tradition and the Individual Talent." *Perspecta* 19 (1982): 36–42.

Ellmann, Maud. *The Poetics of Impersonality: T. S. Eliot and Ezra Pound*. Cambridge, MA: Harvard University Press, 1988.

Epstein, Isidore, trans. *The Babylonian Talmud: Tractate Sanhedrin*. London: Sonico Press, 1935.

Faulkner, William. *Faulkner in the University: Class Conferences at the University of Virginia, 1957–1958*. Edited by Frederick L. Gwynn and Joseph L. Blotner. New York: Vintage, 1965.

———. "An Introduction to *The Sound and the Fury*." Edited by James B. Meriwether, *Mississippi Quarterly* 26 (1973): 410–15.

———. *Absalom, Absalom!* New York: Vintage, 1990.

———. *Light in August*. New York: Vintage, 1990.

———. *The Sound and the Fury: The Corrected Text*. New York: Vintage, 1990.

———. *As I Lay Dying*. Reissue edition. New York: Vintage, 1991.

———. *Novels 1942–1954: Go Down, Moses / Intruder in the Dust / Requiem for a Nun / A Fable*. New York: Library of America, 1994.

Federico, Annette. *Engagements with Close Reading*. New York: Routledge, 2015.

Fekete, John. *The Critical Twilight: Explorations in the Ideology of Anglo-American Literary Theory from Eliot to McLuhan*. London: Routledge & K. Paul, 1977.

Feldman, Yael S. "Poetics and Politics: Israeli Literary Criticism between East and West." *Proceedings of the American Academy for Jewish Research* 52 (1985): 9–35.

Felman, Shoshana. "Turning the Screw of Interpretation." *Yale French Studies*, no. 55/56 (1977): 94–207.

Filho, Cunha e Silva. "Afrânio Coutinho e as mudanças de rumos na crítica literária, na história literária e no ensino de literatura no Brasil." *Entretextos*, August 2, 2013. https://www.portalentretextos.com.br/post/afranio-coutinho-e-as-mudancas-de-rumos-na-critica-literaria-na-historia-literaria-e-no-ensino-de-literatura-no-brasil.

Fisch, Harold. "Reading and Carnival: On the Semiotics of Purim." *Poetics Today* 15, no. 1 (1994): 55–74.

Foster, Richard. "Recent American Criticism." *Critical Survey* 1, no. 3 (1963): 158–63.

Foucault, Michel. "Technologies of the Self." In *Technologies of the Self: A Seminar with Michel Foucault*, edited by Luther H. Martin, Huck Gutman, and Patrick H. Hutton, 16–50. London: Tavistock, 1988.

Fowler, Doreen. *Faulkner: The Return of the Repressed*. Charlottesville: Virginia University Press, 1997.

Fraser, Russell. "R. P. Blackmur: The Politics of a New Critic." *Sewanee Review* 87, no. 4 (1979): 557–72.

Freud, Sigmund. "Recommendations to Physicians Practicing Psycho-Analysis." In *The Standard Edition of the Complete Psychological Works of Sigmund Freud*, vol. 12, 111–20. Translated by James Strachey. London: Hogarth Press, 1953.

Fritz, Jonathan B., Mounya Elhilali, Stephen V. David, and Shihab A. Shamma. "Auditory Attention—focusing the Searchlight on Sound." *Current Opinion in Neurobiology* 17, no. 4 (2007): 437–55.

Fronckowiak, Ângela. "O ato de narrar em *A paixão segundo G.H.*" In *Clarice Lispector: A narração do indizível*, edited by Regina Zilberman, 65–74. Porto Alegre: Artes e Ofícios, EDIPUC/Instituto Cultural Judaico Marc Chagall, 1998.

Fuchs, Esther. *Israeli Mythogynies: Women in Contemporary Hebrew Fiction*. Albany: State University of New York Press, 1987.

Fujie, Kristin. "'Through a Piece of Colored Glass': Faulkner, Race, and Mediation." *Modern Fiction Studies* 65, no. 3 (2019): 411–38.

Furlonge, Nicole Brittingham. *Race Sounds: The Art of Listening in African American Literature*. Iowa City: University of Iowa Press, 2018.

Gallagher, Catherine. "The History of Literary Criticism." *Daedalus* 126, no. 1 (1997): 133–53.

Gallop, Jane. "The Ethics of Close Reading: Close Encounters." *Journal of Curriculum Theorizing* 16, no. 3 (2000): 7–17.

———. "The Historicization of Literary Studies and the Fate of Close Reading." *Profession* (2007): 181–86.

Gang, Joshua. "Behaviorism and the Beginnings of Close Reading." *ELH* 78, no. 1 (2011): 1–25.

Gaskill, Nicholas. "The Close and the Concrete: Aesthetic Formalism in Context." *New Literary History* 47, no. 4 (2016): 505–24.

Gauz, Valéria. "Early printing in Brazil." *Bulletin du bibliophile* 1 (2013): 23–47.

Geertz, Clifford. *The Interpretation of Cultures: Selected Essays*. New York: Basic Books, 1973.

Giorgi, Gabriel. "La alianza salvaje: 'Meu tio o Iauaretê de Guimarães Rosa." In *Formas comunes: animalidad, cultura, biopolítica*, 47–52. Buenos Aires, Brazil: Eterna Cadencia, 2014.

———. "The Form of the Improper: Clarice Lispector and the Rhetoric of Precarity." *Frame* 30, no. 2 (2017): 123–38.

Gleeson-White, Sarah. "Auditory Exposures: Faulkner, Eisenstein, and Film Sound." *PMLA* 128, no. 1 (2013): 87–100.

Gluzman, Michael. *Shirat ha-tvu'im: ha-melankolya shel ha-ribonut ba-shira ha-ivrit bi-shnot ha-chamishim ve-ha-shishim* (The Poetry of the Drowned: Melancholy and Sovereignty in Hebrew Poetry after 1948). Tel Aviv, Israel: University of Haifa Press and Yedi'ot Acharonot Books, 2018.

———. " 'Moto shel Dicky': ha-tekst ha-tra'umati shel Yehuda Amichai" (Dicky's Death: Yehuda Amichai's Traumatic Text). *Mechkarey Yerushalayim be-sifrut ivrit* 31 (2020): 453–88.

Godden, Richard. *Fictions of Labor: William Faulkner and the South's Long Revolution*. Cambridge, UK: Cambridge University Press, 1997.

Gotlib, Nádia Batella. *Clarice: uma vida que se conta*. São Paulo, Brazil: Editora Ática, 1995.

Goulart, Audemaro Taranto. "Machado e Rosa nos vêem n'o espelho." *ASAS DA PALAVRA* 11, no. 1 (2019): 52–69.

Graff, Gerald. *Professing Literature: An Institutional History. Literature against Itself: Literary Ideas in Modern Society*. Chicago, IL: University of Chicago Press, 1979.

———. *Professing Literature: An Institutional History*. Chicago, IL: University of Chicago Press, 1987.

Green, Daniel. "Literature Itself: The New Criticism and Aesthetic Experience." *Philosophy and Literature* 27, no. 1 (2003): 62–79.

Greenblatt, Stephen. "The Touch of the Real." *Representations* no. 59 (1997): 14–29.

Grodzensky, Shlomo. "Tov la-mut" (It Is Good to Die). *Davar*, March 29, 1960.

———. "William Faulkner." *Davar*, July 3, 1962.
Grover, Mark L. "The Book and the Conquest: Jesuit Libraries in Colonial Brazil." *Libraries & Culture* 28, no. 3 (1993): 266–83.
Guillory, John. "The Ideology of Canon-Formation: T. S. Eliot and Cleanth Brooks." *Critical Inquiry* 10, no. 1 (1983): 173–98.
Gurton-Wachter, Lily. *Watchwords: Romanticism and the Poetics of Attention*. Redwood City, CA: Stanford University Press, 2016.
Hale, Dorothy J. "Faulkner's *Light in August* and New Theories of Novelistic Time." In *A Question of Time: American Literature from Colonial Encounter to Contemporary Fiction*, edited by Cindy Weinstein, 266–92. Cambridge, UK: Cambridge University Press, 2018.
———. *The Novel and the New Ethics*. Redwood City, CA: Stanford University Press, 2020.
Harshav, Benjamin. "Al tchumey mada ha-sifrut" (On the Fields in the Science of Literature). *Ha-Sifrut* 1, no. 1 (1968): 1–10.
———. "Ritmus ha-rachavut: halakha u-ma'ase be-shirato ha-ekspresionistit shel Uri Zvi Greenberg" (The Rhythm of Open Spaces: The Theory and Practice of Rhythm in the Expressionist Poetry of Uri Zvi Greenberg). *Ha-Sifrut* 1, no. 1 (1968): 176–205.
———. *Sade u-misgeret: masot be-te'orya shel sifrut u-mashma'ut* (Fields and Frames: Essays on Theory of Literature and Meaning). Jerusalem, Israel: Tel Aviv University, 1972.
———. "The Meaning of Sound Patterns in Poetry: An Interaction Theory." *Poetics Today* 2, no. 1 (1980): 39–56.
———. "Poetic Metaphor and Frames of Reference: With Examples from Eliot, Rilke, Mayakovsky, Mandelshtam, Pound, Creeley, Amichai, and *The New York Times*." *Poetics Today* 5, no. 1 (1984): 5–43.
———. "An Outline of Integrational Semantics." In *Explorations in Poetics*, 76–112. Stanford, CA: Stanford University Press, 2007.
———. "Hirhurim ishiyim al Amichai: ha-shira ve-ha-mdina" (Personal Reflections on Amichai: The Poetry and the State). *Alpayim* 33 (2008): 121–38.
Heffernan, James. "Ekphrasis and Representation." *New Literary History* 22, no. 2 (1991): 297–316.
Heilman, Robert B. "Cleanth Brooks and 'The Well Wrought Urn.'" *Sewanee Review* 91, no. 2 (1983): 322–34.
Hempstead, Susanna. "'Once a Bitch, Always a Bitch': Rereading Caddy in *The Sound and the Fury*." *Faulkner Journal* 31, no. 1 (2017): 23–42.
Hever, Hannan. *Sifrut she-nikhtevet mi-kan* (Literature Written Here). Tel Aviv, Israel: Yedi'ot Acharonot Books, 1999.
Hever, Hannan, and Orin D. Gensler, "Hebrew in an Israeli Arab Hand: Six Miniatures on Anton Shammas's *Arabesques*." *Cultural Critique* 7 (1987): 47–76.

Heyck, Denis Lynn. "Coutinho's Controversy: The Debate Over the *Nova Crítica*." *Latin American Research Review* 14, no. 1 (1979): 99–115.

———. "Coutinho, the Nova Crítica and Portugal." *Hispania* 64, no. 4 (1981): 564–69.

Hines, Andy. *Outside Literary Studies: Black Criticism and the University*. Chicago, IL: University of Chicago Press, 2022.

Hirschfeld, Ariel. "Nigmeret zehut u-matchila acheret" (One Identity Ends and the Other Begins). In *Yofyam shel ha-menutzachim: bikoret u-mechkar al yetzirato shel Yehoshua Kenaz* (The Beauty of the Defeated: Critical Essays on Yehoshua Kenaz), edited by Keren Dotan and Chen Strauss, 441–60. Tel Aviv/Be'er Sheva, Israel: Am Oved/Heksherim, 2016.

———. "Toldot ha-chug" (The History of the Department of Hebrew Literature). Hebrew University. Accessed February 22, 2024. https://hebliterature.huji.ac.il/about/history.

Holanda, Sérgio Buarque de. *O Espírito e a Letra: Estudos de Crítica Literária (1948–1959)*. São Paulo, Brazil: Companhia das Letras, 1996.

———. *Roots of Brazil*. Translated by G. Harvey Summ. Notre Dame, IN: University of Notre Dame Press, 2012.

Horn, Bernard. *Facing the Fires: Conversations with A. B. Yehoshua*. Syracuse, NY: Syracuse University Press, 1997.

Howarth, Peter. "Close Reading as Performance." In *Modernism and Close Reading*, edited by David James, 45–68. Oxford, UK: Oxford University Press, 2020.

Hunter, Ian. "The History of Theory." *Critical Inquiry* 33, no. 1 (2006): 78–112.

Huppert, Shmuel. "Ha-merkaz she-ibed et kocho ha-melaked: iyun ba-roman ha-chadash shel A. B. Yehoshua, *Gerushim me'ucharim*" (The Centre Cannot Hold: An Exploration of A. B. Yehoshua's New Novel, *A Late Divorce*). *Zehut* 3 (1983): 190–95.

Inge, M. Thomas, and Donária Romeiro Carvalho Inge. "William Faulkner and Guimarães Rosa: A Brazilian Connection." In *Faulkner and His Contemporaries*, edited by Joseph R. Urgo and Ann J. Abadie, 173–88. Jackson: University Press of Mississippi, 2004.

Inoue, Kazuki. "Ghost Psychology in T. S. Eliot and W. B. Yeats." PhD diss., University of York, 2020. https://etheses.whiterose.ac.uk/29519/.

Irwin, John T. *Doubling and Incest/Repetition and Revenge*. Baltimore, MD: Johns Hopkins University Press, 1975.

Jameson, Fredric. *The Antinomies of Realism*. London: Verso Books, 2013.

Jancovich, Mark. *The Cultural Politics of the New Criticism*. Cambridge, UK: Cambridge University Press, 1993.

Joyce, James. *A Portrait of the Artist as a Young Man*. Oxford, UK: Oxford University Press, 2000.

———. *Ulysses*. London: Penguin Books, 2000.

Kaiser, Ernest. "A Critical Look at Ellison's Fiction and at Social and Literary Criticism by and about the Author." *Black World* 20, no. 2 (1970): 53–97.

Keats, John. "Ode on a Grecian Urn." In *John Keats, the Complete Poems*, edited by John Barnard, 344–46. New York: Penguin, 1988.

Kelly, Mark E. "Foucault, Subjectivity, and Technologies of the Self." In *A Companion to Foucault*, edited by Christopher Falzon, Timothy O'Leary, and Jana Sawicki, 510–25. Hoboken, NJ: Blackwell, 2013.

Kopec, Andrew. "The Digital Humanities, Inc.: Literary Criticism and the Fate of a Profession." *PMLA* 131, no. 2 (2016): 324–39.

Kracauer, Siegfried. "Cult of Distraction: On Berlin's Picture Palaces." Translated by Thomas Y. Levin. *New German Critique*, no. 40 (1987): 91–96.

Krause, James R., David P. Wiseman, and Faith Blackhurst. "The Boom Novel that Never Was: *Grande sertão: Veredas*, by João Guimarães Rosa." *Hispania* 103, no. 4 (2020): 603–19.

Kronfeld, Chana. *On the Margins of Modernism: Decentering Literary Dynamics*. Berkeley: University of California Press, 1996.

———. *The Full Severity of Compassion: The Poetry of Yehuda Amichai*. Redwood City, CA: Stanford University Press, 2016.

Kurnick, David. "A Few Lies: Queer Theory and Our Method Melodramas." *ELH* 87, no. 2 (2020): 349–74.

Lacan, Jacques. *The Seminar of Jacques Lacan: The Four Fundamental Concepts of Psychoanalysis*. Edited by Jacques-Alain Miller. Translated by Alan Sheridan. New York: W. W. Norton, 1998.

Ladeira, Antonio. "Patriarchal Violence and Brazilian Masculinities in Clarice Lispector's *A maçã no escuro*." *Bulletin of Hispanic Studies* 86, no. 5 (2009): 690–705.

Lajolo, Marisa. "José de Alencar, um criador de autores e de leitores." *Revista de Letras* 29, no. 2 (2009): 89–91.

———. "The Role of Orality in the Seduction of the Brazilian Reader." *Poetics Today* 15, no. 4 (1994): 553–67.

Lajolo, Marisa, and Regina Zilberman. *A formaçao da leitura no Brasil*. São Paulo, Brazil: Editora Unesp, 1996.

Lanski, Naama. "Shir mecha'a" (A Protest Poem). *Israel Ha-Yom*. April 8, 2011, https://www.israelhayom.co.il/article/35847.

Lehman, Christopher, and Kate Roberts. *Falling in Love with Close Reading: Lessons for Analyzing Texts and Life*. Portsmouth, NH: Heinemann, 2013.

Lentricchia, Frank. *After the New Criticism*. Chicago, IL: University of Chicago Press, 1980.

Levi, Nili. *Me-rechov ha-even el ha-chatulim: iyunim ba-sifrut shel Yehoshua Kenaz* (From Stone Street to the Cats: The Narrative Art of Joshua Kenaz). Tel Aviv, Israel: Ha-Kibbutz ha-Me'uchad, 1997.

Librandi, Marília. *Writing by Ear: Clarice Lispector and the Aural Novel*. Toronto, ON: University of Toronto Press, 2018.
Lima, Luís Costa. "Clarice Lispector." In *A literatura no Brasil*, vol. 5, edited by Afrânio Coutinho, 526–53. Rio de Janeiro, Brazil: Sul Americana, 1968.
Lindstrom, Naomi. Foreword to *Iracema: A Novel*, by José Martiniano de Alencar, xi–xxiv. Translated by Clifford E. Landers. New York: Oxford University Press, 2000.
Lins, Álvaro. *Teoria literária: Poesia, romance, teatro, biografia, crítica*. Rio de Janeiro, Brazil: Editora de Ouro, 1967.
Lippit, Akira Mizuta. "In the Break: The Aesthetics of the Black Radical Tradition (Review)." *MLN* 118, no. 5 (2003): 1336–37.
Lispector, Clarice. *Para não esquecer*. São Paulo, Brazil: Editora Ática, 1979.
———. "Felicidade clandestina." In *Felicidade clandestina*. 4th edition, 7–11. Rio de Janeiro, Brazil: Editora Nova Fronteira, 1981.
———. *A legião estrangeira*. São Paulo, Brazil: Editora Ática, 1983.
———. *A maçã no escuro*. Rio de Janeiro, Brazil: Rocco, 1998.
———. *Perto do coração selvagem*. Rio de Janeiro, Brazil: Rocco, 1998.
———. *Correspondências*. Rio de Janeiro, Brazil: Rocco, 2002.
———. *A paixão segundo G.H.* Rio de Janeiro, Brazil: Rocco, 2009.
———. *The Apple in the Dark*. Translated by Gregory Rabassa. London: Haus Publishing, 2009.
———. *Near to the Wild Heart*. Translated by Alison Entrekin. New York: New Directions, 2012.
———. *The Passion According to G.H.* Translated by Idra Novey. New York: New Directions, 2012.
———. "Covert Joy." In *The Complete Stories*, 369–72. Edited by Benjamin Moser. Translated by Katrina Dodson. New York: New Directions, 2015.
Litwin, Rina. "*Or be-ogust* le-William Faulkner: im hofa'at ha-tirgum ha-ivri" (William Faulkner's *Light in August*: Following the Appearance of the Hebrew Translation). *Ha-Sifrut* 1, no. 3–4 (1968–1969): 590–98.
Litz, Walton, Louis Menand, and Lawrence Rainey, eds. *Modernism and the New Criticism*. Vol. 7, *The Cambridge History of Literary Criticism*. Cambridge, UK: Cambridge University Press, 2000.
Love, Heather. "Close but Not Deep: Literary Ethics and the Descriptive Turn." *New Literary History* 41, no. 2 (2010): 371–91.
Machado, Sônia Maria. "Uma Tentativa de Entender *A maçã no escuro*." *Travessia* 3 (1981): 20–24.
Mandelkern, Ronen. "Kitzur toldot ha-ne'o-liberalizem be-Israel" (The Concise History of Neoliberalism in Israel). Preface to the Hebrew Edition of *Kitzur toldot ha-ne'o-liberalizem* (A Brief History of Neoliberalism) by David Harvey, translated by Guy Herling, 271–312. Tel Aviv, Israel: Molad, 2015.

Mao, Douglas. "The New Critics and the Text-Object." *ELH* 63, no. 1 (1996): 227–54.
Marno, David. *Death Be Not Proud: The Art of Holy Attention*. Chicago, IL: University of Chicago Press, 2017.
Martin, Luther H., Huck Gutman, and Patrick H. Hutton (eds.). *Technologies of the Self: A Seminar with Michel Foucault*. London: Tavistock, 1988.
Maxwell, Angie. *The Indicted South: Public Criticism, Southern Inferiority, and the Politics of Whiteness*. Chapel Hill: University of North Carolina Press, 2014.
McHale, Brian, and Eyal Segal. "Small World: The Tel Aviv School of Poetics and Semiotics." In *Theoretical Schools and Circles in the Twentieth-Century Humanities: Literary Theory, History, Philosophy*, edited by Marina Grishakova and Silvi Salupere, 96–215. New York: Routledge, 2015.
Meital, Orit. *Lisno gam et asher ahavnu: mishpacha ve-le'umiyut be-shirat Uri Zvi Greenberg* (To Hate What We Loved: Family and Nationality in the Poetry of Uri Zvi Greenberg). Tel Aviv, Israel: Ha-Kibbutz ha-Me'uchad, 2018.
Mello, Jefferson. "Os estudos literários brasileiros nos anos 1970 e o lugar da teoria no trabalho de Luiz Costa Lima." *Remate de Males* 40, no. 2 (2020): 697–722.
Meriwether, James B., and Michael Millgate, eds. *Lion in the Garden: Interviews with William Faulkner*. New York: Random House, 1968.
Merquior, José Guilherme. *Razão do Poema: Ensaios de Crítica e de Estética*. Rio de Janeiro, Brazil: Topbooks, 1996.
Michali, B. Y. "Be-eyn chush mida" (When Proportion Is Lacking). *Davar*, June 3, 1955.
Miller, D. A. *Hidden Hitchcock*. Chicago, IL: University of Chicago Press, 2016.
Miller, Max. "*Absalom, Absalom!*" In *William Faulkner: The Contemporary Reviews*, edited by M. Thomas Inge, 139–66. Cambridge, UK: Cambridge University Press, 1995.
Mintz, Alan. "On the Tel Aviv School of Poetics." *Prooftexts* 4, no. 3 (1984): 215–35.
———. "Fracturing the Zionist Narrative." *Judaism* 48, no. 4 (1999): 407–15.
Miron, Dan. "Zman-merchav bi-yetzirot S. Yizhar vi-Yehuda Amichai: shney modelim kognitiviyim ba-sifrut ha-yisra'elit ha-mukdemet" (Timespace in S. Yizhar and Yehuda Amichai: Two Cognitive Models in Early Israeli Literature). In *Tarbut, zikaron ve-historiya: be-hokara le-Anita Shapira* (Culture, Memory, and History: In Appreciation of Anita Shapira), 383–419. Tel Aviv, Israel: Tel Aviv University Press, 2012.
Mishani, Dror. *Be-khol ha-inyan ha-mizrachi yesh eyze absurd* (There Is Some Kind of Absurdity in This Mizrahi Matter). Tel Aviv, Israel: Am Oved, 2006.
———. "A. B. Yehoshua ve-aviv mevakrim etzel S. Y. Agnon" (A. B. Yehoshua and His Father Jacob Visit S. Y. Agnon). *Ot* 7 (2017): 215–26.
Moretti, Franco. "Conjectures on World Literature." *New Left Review* 1 (2000): 54–69.
———. *Distant Reading*. London: Verso Books, 2013.

———. "Franco Moretti: A Response." *PMLA* 132, no. 3 (2017): 686–89.
Moriconi, Italo. "*The Hour of the Star* or Clarice Lispector's Trash Hour." Translated by Paulo Henriques Britto. *Portuguese Literary and Cultural Studies* 4/5 (2000): 213–21.
Morris, Adam. "The Uses of Nonsense: Antimodernism in Latin American Fiction 1920–1977." PhD diss., Stanford University, 2015. https://www.proquest.com/docview/2510259377?pq-origsite=gscholar&fromopenview=true.
Mortimer, Gail L. *Faulkner's Rhetoric of Loss: A Study of Perception and Meaning*. Austin: University of Texas Press, 1983.
Moser, Benjamin. *Why This World: A Biography of Clarice Lispector*. Oxford, UK: Oxford University Press, 2009.
Moten, Fred. *In the Break: The Aesthetics of the Black Radical Tradition*. Minneapolis: University of Minnesota Press, 2003.
Moya, Paula M. L. "Reading as a Realist: Expanded Literacy in Helena María Viramontes's *Under the Feet of Jesus*." In *Learning from Experience: Minority Identities, Multicultural Struggles*, 175–214. Berkeley: University of California Press, 2002.
Murphet, Julian, and Stefan Solomon, eds. *William Faulkner in the Media Ecology*. Baton Rouge: Louisiana State University Press, 2015.
Nadal, Paul. "Cold War Remittance Economy: US Creative Writing and the Importation of New Criticism into the Philippines." *American Quarterly* 73, no. 3 (2021): 557–95.
Napolin, Julie. "The Fact of Resonance: An Acoustics of Determination in Faulkner and Benjamin." *symplokē* 24, no. 1 (2016): 171–86.
———. *The Fact of Resonance: Modernist Acoustics and Narrative Form*. New York: Fordham University Press, 2020.
Nascimento, Edna Maria F.S., and Maria Célia Leonel. "Frente a 'O espelho' de Machado e de Guimarães Rosa." *Revista da Anpoll* 2, no. 24 (2008). https://doi.org/10.18309/anp.v2i24.44.
National Library of Israel. Historical Jewish Press Collection. "Search Results for 'Faulkner' in Hebrew Language Newspapers Published in the Middle East (Primarily in Israel) between 1950–1990." Accessed February 22, 2024. https://www.nli.org.il/en.
Negrón-Marrero, Mara. *Une genése au féminin: Étude de La pomme dans le noir de Clarice Lispector*. Amsterdam, the Netherlands: Rodopi, 1997.
Nelson, Maggie. *The Argonauts*. Minneapolis, MN: Graywolf Press, 2015.
Nina, Cláudia. *Literatura nos jornais: a crítica literária dos rodapés às resenhas*. São Paulo, Brazil: Summus Editorial, 2007.
North, Joseph. "What's 'New Critical' about 'Close Reading': I. A. Richards and His New Critical Reception." *New Literary History* 44, no. 1 (2013): 141–57.
———. *Literary Criticism: A Concise Political History*. Cambridge, MA: Harvard University Press, 2017.

North, Paul. *The Problem of Distraction*. Stanford, CA: Stanford University Press, 2011.

Nunes, Benedito. "Os destroços da introspecção." In *Clarice Lispector: A Narração do Indizível*, edited by Regina Zilberman, 35–48. Porto Alegre, Brazil: Artes e Ofícios, EDIPUC/Instituto Cultural Judaico Marc Chagall, 1998.

O'Donnell, George Marrion. "Mr. Faulkner Flirts with Failure." In *William Faulkner: The Contemporary Reviews*, edited by M. Thomas Inge, 142–44. Cambridge, UK: Cambridge University Press, 1995.

O'Kane, Karen. "Before the New Criticism: Modernism and the Nashville Group." *Mississippi Quarterly* 51, no. 4 (1998): 683–97.

Oliveira, Luiz Cláudio Vieira de. "Guimarães Rosa, leitor de Machado." *O Eixo e a Roda: Revista de Literatura Brasileira* 7, no. 1 (2001): 79–91.

Omer-Sherman, Ranen. "The Guests and Hosts in A. B. Yehoshua's *The Liberated Bride*." *Shofar* 31, no. 3 (2013): 25–63.

Oren, Yosef. "Toldot ha-medina ke-sipur nisu'im" (The State's History as a Marriage Plot). *Yedi'ot Acharonot*, July 16, 1982.

Oz, Amos. *Be-or ha-tkhelet ha-aza* (Under This Blazing Light). Tel Aviv, Israel: Po'alim, 1979.

Pacheco, Ana Paula. *Lugar do mito: narrativa e processo social nas* Primeiras estórias *de Guimarães Rosa*. São Paulo, Brazil: Nankin, 2006.

Parolin, Peter, and Phyllis Rackin. "Close Reading Shakespeare: An Introduction." *Early Modern Culture* 12, no. 1 (2017): 1–4.

Parvulescu, Anca. "To Yes-Laugh Derrida's Molly." *Parallax* 16, no. 3 (2010): 16–27.

Perry, Menakhem. "'O Rose Thou Art Sick': Al tachbulot bniyat ha-mashma'ut be-'Vered le-Emily' le-William Faulkner ve-haflagot le-te'orya shel ha-retorika ba-siporet" ("O Rose Thou Art Sick": On the Devices of Meaning Construction in William Faulkner's "A Rose for Emily," and Reflections on a Theory of Rhetoric in Literature). *Siman Kri'a* 3/4 (1974): 423–59.

———. "Ha-dinamika shel ha-tekst ha-sifruti: eykh kove'a seder ha-tekst et mashma'uyotav" (Literary Dynamics: How the Order of a Text Creates Its Meanings). *Ha-Sifrut* 28 (1979): 6–46.

———. "Literary Dynamics: How the Order of a Text Creates Its Meanings (With an Analysis of Faulkner's 'A Rose for Emily')." *Poetics Today* 1, no. 1/2 (1979): 35–64, 311–61.

———. "Beyn nevicha li-nshikha: al ha-siyum ha-acher shel *Gerushim me'ucharim*" (From Bark to Bite: On the Different Ending of a *Late Divorce*). *Siman Kri'a* 21 (1990): 58–60.

———. "Counter-Stories in the Bible: Rebekah and her Bridegroom, Abraham's Servant." *Prooftexts* 27, no. 2 (2007): 275–323.

———. "Ha-neshika: sipur be-shalosh varyatzyot" (The Kiss: A Story in Three Variations). *Ha'aretz*, March 5, 2007. https://www.haaretz.co.il/literature/2007-03-05/ty-article/0000017f-e736-da9b-a1ff-ef7f17b20000.

———. Interview by the author. July 6, 2016.

———. "Nokhach ha-metim: ha-po'etika ha-chadasha shel Yehuda Amichai ha-tza'ir" (Facing the Dead: The Poetics of the Young Amichai). In *Ha-ne'eman: minchat hokara vi-ydidut le- Uzi Shavit* (Il Pastor Fido: Papers and Literary Works Dedicated to Uzi Shavit), edited by Ziva Shamir and Menakhem Perry, 193–231. Tel Aviv, Israel: Ha-Kibbutz ha-Me'uchad, 2016.

———. "Shirat ha-pratim: lama katavti et *Shev alay ve-hitchamem*" (The Poetry of Details: Why I Wrote *The Homoerotic Dialogue Between Brenner and Gnessin*). *Moznayim* 91 (2017): 54–60.

Perry, Menakhem, and Meir Sternberg. "Ha-melekh be-mabat ironi: al tachbulot ha-mesaper be-sipur David ve-Bat Sheva u-shtey haflagot le-te'orya shel ha-proza (The King through Ironic Eyes: The Narrator's Devices in the Story of David and Bathsheba and Two Excursuses on the Theory of the Narrative Text). *Ha-Sifrut* 1 (1968–1969): 263–92.

———. "The King through Ironic Eyes: Biblical Narrative and the Literary Reading Process." *Poetics Today* 7, no. 2 (1986): 275–322.

Phillips, Natalie M. *Distraction: Problems of Attention in Eighteenth-Century Literature*. Baltimore, MD: Johns Hopkins University Press, 2016.

Pickering, Edward D. "The Roots of New Criticism." *Southern Literary Journal* 41, no. 1 (2008): 93–108.

Pitt, Kristin E. "Discovery and Conquest through a Poststructural and Postcolonial Lens: Clarice Lispector's *A maçã no escuro*." *Luso-Brazilian Review* 50, no. 1 (2013): 184–200.

Porat, Tzefira. "Bubot shel nesoret: goral tragi ve-cherut komit be-*Or le-ogust* le-William Faulkner (Dolls Stuffed with Sawdust: Tragic Fate and Comic Freedom in William Faulkner's *Light in August*). *Ha-Sifrut* 2, no. 4 (1971): 767–82.

Portella, Eduardo. "Crítica literária: Brasileira e totalizante." *Tempo Brasileiro*, no. 1 (1962): 67–69.

Prado, Antonio Arnoni. Introduction to vol. 1 of *O Espírito e a Letra: Estudos de Crítica Literária (1948–1959)*, by Sérgio Buarque de Holanda, 1–35. São Paulo, Brazil: Companhia das Letras, 1996.

Puxan-Oliva, Marta and Annalisa Mirizio. "Rethinking World Literature Studies in Latin American and Spanish Contexts." *Journal of World Literature* 2, no. 1 (2017): 1–9.

Raffoul, François. "Derrida and the Ethics of the Im-possible." *Research in Phenomenology* 38, no. 2 (2008): 270–90.

Ransom, John Crowe. "Criticism, Inc." *VQR* 13, no. 4 (1937). https://www.vqr online.org/essay/criticism-inc-0.

———. *The New Criticism*. Norfolk, CT: New Directions, 1941.

———. "Poetry: A Note on Ontology." In *Close Reading: The Reader*, edited by Frank Lentricchia and Andrew DuBois, 43–60. Durham, NC: Duke University Press, 2003.

Renan, Yael. "Li-shmo'a et rachash ha-galim: ha-hazara, hachya'ata shel klitat ha-metzi'ut ba-yetzira ha-sifrutit" (To Hear the Waves' Whisper: Defamiliarization and the Revivification of Perception in the Literary Work). *Siman Kri'a* 2 (1973): 343–61.

———. "Disautomatization and Comic Deviations from Models of Organizing Experience." *Style* 18, no. 2 (1984): 160–76.

Resh, Nura, and Yechezkel Dar, "The Rise and Fall of School Integration in Israel: Research and Policy Analysis." *British Educational Research Journal* 38, no. 6 (2012): 929–51.

Richards, I. A. *Practical Criticism: A Study of Literary Judgment.* San Diego, CA: Harcourt Brace, 1950.

———. *How to Read a Page: A Course in Effective Reading.* 2nd ed. London: Routledge & K. Paul, 1961.

Rives, Rochelle. *Modernist Impersonalities: Affect, Authority, and the Subject.* London: Palgrave Macmillan, 2012.

Robinson, Owen. *Creating Yoknapatawpha: Readers and Writers in Faulkner's Fiction.* New York: Routledge, 2006.

Rocha, João Cezar de Castro. *Crítica literária: Em busca do tempo perdido?* Chapecó, Brazil: Argos Editora da Unochapecó, 2011.

Roggenbuck, Ted. "'The Way He Looked Said Hush': Benjy's Mental Atrophy in *The Sound and the Fury*." *Mississippi Quarterly* 58, no. 3 (2005): 581–93.

Rosa, João Guimarães. "Meu tio o Iauaretê." *Senhor* 25, March 19, 1961, 65–90.

———. "Guimarães Rosa fala aos jovens." *O Cruzeiro*, December 23, 1967.

———. *The Third Bank of The River, and Other Stories.* Translated by Barbara Shelby. New York: Knopf, 1968.

———. *Primeiras estórias.* 2nd ed. Rio de Janeiro, Brazil: José Olympio, 1969.

Rose, Tricia. *Black Noise: Rap Music and Black Culture in Contemporary America.* Middletown, CT: Wesleyan University Press, 1994.

Rosenbaum, Yudith. "Notas sobre o conto 'O espelho' de Guimarães Rosa." *Ide: psicanálise e cultura* 31, no. 47 (2008). http://pepsic.bvsalud.org/scielo.php?script=sci_arttext&pid=S0101-31062008000200015.

Rosenwasser, David, and Jill Stephen. *Writing Analytically.* 6th ed. Boston, MA: Wadsworth, 2011.

Ross, Stephen M. "Rev. Shegog's Powerful Voice." *Faulkner Journal* 1, no. 1 (1985): 8–16.

———. *Fiction's Inexhaustible Voice: Speech and Writing in Faulkner.* Athens: University of Georgia Press, 1989.

Russo, John Paul. "The Tranquilized Poem: The Crisis of New Criticism in the 1950s." *Texas Studies in Literature and Language* 30, no. 2 (1988): 198–229.

———. *The Future without a Past: The Humanities in a Technological Society.* Columbia: University of Missouri Press, 2005.

Ryan, Tim A. "'A Little Music Aint about the Nicest Thing a Fellow Can Have': Faulkner's *As I Lay Dying* and Country Songs." *Mississippi Quarterly* 67, no. 3 (2014): 347–74.

———. *Yoknapatawpha Blues: Faulkner's Fiction and Southern Roots Music*. Baton Rouge: Louisiana State University Press, 2015.

Said, Edward. "Traveling Theory." In *World Literature in Theory*, edited by David Damrosch, 114–33. Hoboken, NJ: John Wiley, 2014.

Sandbank, Shimon. "Rilke, Auden, Amichai." *Ha-Sifrut* 2, no. 4 (1971): 697–714.

Santos, Roberto Corrêa dos. "A crítica literária no Brasil: Últimos quinze anos." *Revista de Crítica Literária Latinoamericana* 16, no. 31/32 (1990): 85–97.

Schafer, R. Murray. *The Soundscape: Our Sonic Environment and the Tuning of the World*. Rochester, NY: Destiny Books, 1994.

Schwartz, Lawrence H. *Creating Faulkner's Reputation: The Politics of Modern Literary Criticism*. Knoxville: University of Tennessee Press, 1988.

Schwarz, Roberto. "Roberto Schwarz: Um crítico na periferia do capitalismo." Interview by Luis Henrique Lopes dos Santos and Mariluce Moura. *Pesquisa FAPESP* 98 (2004). http://revistapesquisa.fapesp.br/en/2004/04/01/a-critic-on-the-periphery-of-capitalism/.

Sedgwick, Eve Kosofsky. "Paranoid Reading and Reparative Reading, or, You're So Paranoid, You Probably Think This Introduction Is About You." In *Novel Gazing: Queer Readings in Fiction*, edited by Eve Kosofsky Sedgwick, 1–41. Durham, NC: Duke University Press, 1997.

Segalovitz, Yael. "A Leap of Faith into *Moses*: Freud's Invitation to Evenly Suspended Attention." In *Freud and Monotheism: Moses and the Violent Origins of Religion*, edited by Karen Feldman and Gilad Sharvit, 108–37. New York: Fordham University Press, 2018.

———. "'My Error Is My Mirror': Clarice Lispector's Jewish Rhetoric of Mistakes." In *After Clarice: Reading Lispector's Legacy in the Twenty-First Century*, edited by Adriana X. Jacobs and Claire Williams, 139–55. Oxford, UK: Legenda, 2023.

Shaked, Gershon. *Gal chadash ba-siporet ha-ivrit* (A New Wave in Hebrew Literature). Tel Aviv, Israel: Po'alim, 1971.

———. *Gal achar gal ba-sifrut ha-ivrit* (Wave after Wave in Hebrew Literature). Jerusalem, Israel: Keter, 1985.

Shamir, Milette. *Inexpressible Privacy: The Interior Life of Antebellum American Literature*. Philadelphia: University of Pennsylvania Press, 2006.

Silva, Marcelo Jose. "Percurso e percalços de Afrânio Coutinho na crítica literária brasileira." *Terra Roxa e Outras Terras* 16 (2009): 63–71.

Skirry, Justin. "Sartre on William Faulkner's Metaphysics of Time in *The Sound and the Fury*." *Sartre Studies International* 7, no. 2 (2001):15–43.

Soker-Schwager, Hanna. *Mekhashef ha-shevet mi-m'onot ovdim: Yaakov Shabtai ba-tarbut ha-yisra'elit* (The Wizard of the Tribe from the Worker's Quarters: Yaakov Shabtai in Israeli Culture). Tel Aviv, Israel: Ha-Kibbutz ha-Me'uchad, 2007.

Solomon, Stefan. *William Faulkner in Hollywood: Screenwriting for the Studios*. Athens: University of Georgia Press, 2017.

Somerlate, Maria José. *Clarice Lispector: Des/fiando as teias da paixão*. Porto Alegre, Brazil: EDIPUCRS, 2001.

Spanos, William V. "Against Distant Reading: Retrieving Close Reading in the Interregnum." *symplokē* 25, no. 1–2 (2017): 247–60.

Spillers, Hortense J. "Faulkner Adds Up: Reading *Absalom, Absalom!* and *The Sound and the Fury*." In *Black, White, and in Color: Essays on American Literature and Culture*, 336–79. Chicago, IL: University of Chicago Press, 2003.

Steinskog, Erik. *Afrofuturism and Black Sound Studies: Culture, Technology, and Things to Come*. London: Palgrave Macmillan, 2017.

Stegner, Wallace. "Review." In *William Faulkner: Critical Assessments*, vol. 3, edited by Henry Claridge, 274–76. Robertsbridge, UK: Helm Information, 1999.

Sternberg, Meir. "Al ekronot ha-kompozitzya shel *Or be-ogust* le-Faulkner: al ha-po'etica shel ha-roman ha-moderni" (Composition in Faulkner's *Light in August*: On the Poetics of the Modern Novel). *Ha-Sifrut* 2, no. 3 (1970): 498–537.

Stewart, David M. "New Criticism and Value in Taiwanese College English." *American Literature* 89, no. 2 (2017): 397–423.

Stewart, Garrett. *Reading Voices: Literature and the Phonotext*. Berkeley: University of California Press, 1990.

Strauss, Aryeh Ludwig. "Al mizmor 124 mi-sefer Tehilim" (On Hymn 124, Psalms). *Bekhinot* 1 (1952): 26–32.

Sundquist, Eric J. *Faulkner: A House Divided*. Baltimore, MD: Johns Hopkins University Press, 1985.

Süssekind, Flora. "Rodapés, tratados e ensaios: a formação da crítica brasileira moderna." In *Papéis Colados*, 13–33. Rio de Janeiro, Brazil: Editora da Universidade Federal do Rio de Janeiro, 1993.

Tamir, Naomi. "I. A. Richards ke-te'oretikan shel sifrut" (I. A. Richards as a Theoretician of Literature). *Ha-Sifrut* 4, no. 3 (1973): 441–74.

Tate, Allen. "Miss Emily and the Bibliographer." *American Scholar* 9, no. 4 (1940): 449–60.

———. *Essays of Four Decades*. Chicago, IL: Swallow Press, 1968.

Thaventhiran, Helen. *Radical Empiricists: Five Modernist Close Readers*. Oxford, UK: Oxford University Press, 2015.

Tsamir, Hamutal. *Be-shem ha-nof: le'umiyut, migdar ve-subyektiviyut ba-shira ha-yisra'elit bi-shnot ha-chamishim ve-ha-shishim* (In the Name of the Land:

Nationalism, Subjectivity and Gender in the Israeli Poetry of the Statehood Generation). Jerusalem/Be'er Sheva, Israel: Keter/Heksherim, 2006.

Tzemach, Shlomo. "Matzevet ve-shalakhta" (an untranslatable reference to Isa. 6:13). *Davar*, July 5, 1957.

Valente, Luiz Fernando. "Marriages of Speaking and Hearing: Mediation and Response in *Absalom, Absalom!* and *Grande Sertão: Veredas*." *Faulkner Journal* 11, no. 1/2 (1996): 149–64.

Vieira, Júlio César, and Osmar Oliva. "Crime e libertação - um estudo de *A maçã no escuro* de Clarice Lispector." *Revista de Letras* 51, no. 2 (2011): 171–90.

Wadlington, Warwick. *Reading Faulknerian Tragedy*. Ithaca, NY: Cornell University Press, 1987.

Walter, Christina. *Optical Impersonality: Science, Images, and Literary Modernism*. Baltimore, MD: Johns Hopkins University Press, 2014.

Watkins, Evan. *The Critical Act: Criticism and Community*. New Haven, CT: Yale University Press, 1978.

Watson, Jay. "The Unsynchable William Faulkner: Faulknerian Voice and Early Sound Film." In *William Faulkner and the Faces of Modernity*, 148–72. Oxford, UK: Oxford University Press, 2019.

Weinstein, Philip M. *Faulkner's Subject: A Cosmos No One Owns*. Cambridge, UK: Cambridge University Press, 1992.

Welleck, René, and Austin Warren. *Theory of Literature*. 3rd ed. New York: Harcourt Brace Jovanovich, 1977.

Weller, Shane. *Beckett, Literature and the Ethics of Alterity*. Basingstoke, UK: Palgrave Macmillan, 2006.

Werses, Shmuel. "The Portrait of Shimon Halkin as a Young Poet." *Jerusalem Studies in Hebrew Literature* (1990): 19–38.

Wilde, Meta Carpenter, and Orin Bornsten. *A Loving Gentleman: The Love Story of William Faulkner and Meta Carpenter*. New York: Simon and Schuster, 1976.

Wimsatt, William K., and Monroe C. Beardsley. "The Intentional Fallacy." *Sewanee Review* 54, no. 3 (1946): 468–88.

Winkler, István, Susan L. Denham, and Israel Nelken. "Modeling the Auditory Scene: Predictive Regularity Representations and Perceptual Objects." *Trends in Cognitive Sciences* 13, no. 12 (2009): 532–40.

Winnicott, Donald. *Playing and Reality*. London: Routledge, 1991.

———. "Ego Integration and Child Development." In *The Maturational Processes and the Facilitating Environment: Studies in the Theory of Emotional Development*, 56–63. New York: Routledge, 2018.

Yehoshua, A. B. "Li-khtov proza: sicha im A. B. Yehoshua" (Writing Prose: A Conversation with A. B. Yehoshua). Interview by Menakhem Perry and Nissim Calderon. *Siman Kri'a* 5 (1976): 276–88.

———. *Ha-me'ahev* (The Lover). Jerusalem, Israel: Schocken, 1977.

———. "Kama he'arot al ha-retzenzya ha-yisra'elit betzeruf retzenzya" (Some Notes on the Israeli Literary Review with a Review Enclosed). *Siman Kri'a* 7 (1977): 422–25.

———. *Gerushim me'ucharim* (A Late Divorce). Tel Aviv, Israel: Ha-Kibbutz ha-Me'uchad, 1982.

———. *A Late Divorce*. Translated by Hillel Halkin. New York: Doubleday, 1984.

———. *Gerushim me'ucharim* (A Late Divorce). Tel Aviv, Israel: Ha-Kibbutz ha-Me'uchad, 2010.

Yiftachel, Oren. "'Ethnocracy' and Its Discontents: Minorities, Protests, and the Israeli Polity." *Critical Inquiry* 26, no. 4 (2000): 725–56.

Zach, Natan. "Le-akliman ha-signoni shel shnot ha-chamishim ve-ha-shishim be-shiratenu" (On the Stylistic Climate of the 1950s and 1960s in Our Poetry). *Ha'aretz*, July 29, 1966.

———. "Ani ezrach ha-olam" (I'm a Citizen of the World). In *Shirim shonim* (Various Poems), 66–67. Tel Aviv, Israel: Alef, 1967.

———. "Imagism and Vorticism." In *Modernism: A Guide to European Literature 1890–1930*, edited by Malcolm Bradbury and James McFarlane, 228–43. Penguin Literary Criticism Series. London: Penguin Books, 1978.

———. "Shirey Yehuda Amichai" (The Poems of Yehuda Amichai). In *Ha-shira she-me'ever la-milim: Te'orya u-vikoret 1954–1973* (Poetry Beyond Words: Theory and Criticism 1954–1973), 325–30. Tel Aviv, Israel: Ha-Kibbutz ha-Me'uchad, 2011.

———. "Sipurav ha-shiriyim shel Yehuda Amichai" (The Poetic Stories of Yehuda Amichai). In *Ha-shira she-me'ever la-milim: Te'orya u-vikoret 1954–1973* (Poetry Beyond Words: Theory and Criticism 1954–1973), 331–36. Tel Aviv, Israel: Ha-Kibbutz ha-Me'uchad, 2011.

Zender, Karl F. *The Crossing of the Ways: William Faulkner, the South, and the Modern World*. New Brunswick, NJ: Rutgers University Press, 1989.

Index

Absalom, Absalom! (Faulkner), 40–51, 79, 184–185, 187
acoustics: absent-presence sonorities 59, 65, 69, 72-74, 80-81; acoustic sensitivity, 56; counter-, 74; evocalization, 59, 75; in Faulkner's work, 58–59, 61–62, 65–66, 67, 69–70, 72, 77; "inward ear," 201; in Lispector's work, 243n10; as resistance, 75
aesthetics: attention and, 16–20, 166; in Coutinho's work, 94, 112; disinterestedness and, 52; *Geração de '45* and, 129–130; minimalist aesthetics, 197, 199–207; modernist aesthetics, 2, 7, 16–20; transcendentalism and, 52, 58; the urn (figure of) and, 31
Afropessimism, 74
Agrarianism, 6, 8–9, 232n29
Akhshav u-va-yamim ha-acherim (Now and in Other Days) (Amichai), 200, 203
Alencar, José de, 22, 89–91, 107, 226, 248n10, 252n72; *Iracema: A Legend of Ceará (Iracema: lenda do Ceará),* 22, 23, 87–91, 106–10, 140
A literatura no Brasil (ed. Coutinho), 128–29, 130–31, 133

alterity: ethics of (Derrida), 16, 31–32, 33, 42, 61, 238n16, 242n6; literary texts and, 11, 14–16, 51–52, 55–56; reader's subjectivity and, 118, 133. *See also* ethics; otherness
Amichai, Yehuda: difference (poetics of), 209; distraction in work of, 212–13; integration and, 192, 207, 215; language and metaphor in work of, 194, 196–97, 200, 201, 204, 206–7, 210, 211, 212, 215–16, 219–20, 226, 268n3, 270n22, 272n54; life, 199; poetry vs. prose fiction and, 193, 197, 198, 268n2; reception of work, 18, 193, 197, 199, 201–5, 206–7, 209, 212–13, 217, 218–20, 269n9, 272n66; on the sun, 226; theory of reading, 213, 226–27; unintegrated reading, 17, 198, 223; writing career, 157; "Along the Deserted Boulevard," 201; "And My Parents Migration," 201; "Class Reunion," 207–12, 213, 215–16; *In This Terrible Wind*, 193, 194, 196–197, 201–202, 207–212, 214; "My Father" (*Poems 1948–1962*), 194–95; *Now and in Other Days*, 203; "Rain on a Battlefield," 202–6

Index

"Among School Children" (Yeats), 37
animality, 106, 109, 114–15, 116, 117, 118–19; Jaguar, 10, 115–16, 119
anthropophagic movement (Brazil), 111–12, 116, 129; *Manifesto antropófago* (de Andrade), 111
A pesca milagrosa ("The Miraculous Catch of Fish") (Lispector), 127
Arab-Israelis, 161–162
Araripe Júnior, Tristão de Alencar, 107–8, 226
"A Rose for Emily" (Faulkner), 28, 173, 174, 178–179, 183
Ashkenazi and Mizrahi Jews, 161, 162, 181, 186, 262n33
As I Lay Dying (Faulkner), 60, 172
attention: as term, 6, 13–16; aesthetics and, 16–20; criticism on, 18; defining, 13; distraction and, 132–33; ghostly readerly attention, 118; integration and, 165, 179, 180, 192, 200; intensity and, 142; labor of, 13, 167, 170; as loving, 14; mastery and, 125; metaphor as intensifying, 200; modernism and, 16–20; modernity and, 34; noise and, 68; paradox and, 35–36; performativity and, 231n19; as self-deadening, 9, 43; the sun and, 226–27; as unselfing, 5–12, 85; as ventriloquizing voices, 59; the wild and, 144; in *The Sound and the Fury*, 68–69
audition, 60–70, 71; negative audition, 60–62, 69, 70, 72–73, 75, 77–79, 227
"Avi" ("My Father") (Amichai), 194–95

Baldwin, James, 106
Ba-ru'ach ha-nora'a ha-zot (*In This Terrible Wind*) (Amichai), 193, 194, 196–97, 196–197, 201–2, 201–202, 207–12, 207–212, 214
Beardsley, M. C., 6, 13–14, 168, 254n98
Ben-Porat, Ziva, 20–21, 153, 164, 165–66, 261n31, 262n34
Bible (Hebrew), 21, 175–76
Blackmur, R. P., 201, 235n61
Black Panthers movement (Israel), 161
Black Studies, 73, 74, 75, 78
Brazil: history of colonization, 88–89, 92, 98, 106, 252n72; exact reading and (*see* exact reading); history, 106; indigeneity and, 89, 92, 96, 109, 112, 124; intellectual history, 85, 88, 92, 93, 95–96, 97, 103, 108, 112–13, 126; landscape, 137; modernism, 111–12; New Criticism's history in, 4, 8, 10, 92–93, 250n24; the sun in, 226
Brazilian reader (as figure): characteristics of, 89; colonialism and, 105–6; as "degenerate," 96–98, 99, 106, 108–10; disciplining of, 86–87; instructions to, 22; as "savage," 17, 86, 109, 112, 124
Brazilian Structuralism, 130–31
Brooks, Cleanth, 15; life, 33–34; on paradox, 34–35; on poems, 27, 31, 36–38; reception of work, 33–34; theory of reading, 30–31, 33, 34, 35, 37–38, 39, 43, 48–49, 50–51, 86; as typical New Critic, 29–30; on urns, 27, 31, 38, 43; *The Well Wrought Urn: Studies in the Structure of Poetry* (see *The Well Wrought Urn: Studies in the Structure of Poetry*); *William Faulkner: The Yoknapatawpha Country*, 31, 39–40, 41, 46–47, 52

Campos, Haroldo de, 230n9

Canabrava, Euríalo, 102
Cândido, Antônio, 93, 109
canonization and New Criticism, 17, 111, 173
Cixous, Hélène: on Lispector, 123, 134, 140, 254n5, 257n64; on reading, 22
close, as term, 11–12, 167
cognition as political space, 9
Coleridge, Samuel Taylor, 35
colonialism: civilized vs. uncivilized trope, 124; distraction and, 87, 106; exact reading and, 107; gaze of, 119; history in Brazil, 88–89; mental pathology and, 96–97; perceptions of Brazilians and, 10; reading process and, 86; tropes, 109
"Composed upon Westminster Bridge" (Wordsworth), 34–35
"Corinna's Gone a-Maying" (Herrick), 37
Coutinho, Afrânio, 4, 10; as editor, 128–29; on education, 99, 103, 104, 105; influences on, 94; on intellectualism in Brazil, 85; life, 92–93, 110, 111, 249n16; literary career, 92–93; modernism and, 112; reception of work, 103–4; rewriting of Alencar, 91–92, 108–9; on Richards, 7; theory of reader, 96–99, 106, 112–13, 133; theory of reading, 93–95, 99–106, 108, 120, 125, 226; unselfing, 95, 106
Cowley, Malcolm, 40, 78, 176–77, 178
creativity, 214, 221
crime novels, 134–35
Czech Structuralism, 155, 168

David (biblical figure), 175–76
death: afterlife, 141; in *The Apple in the Dark* (*A maçã no escuro*) (Lispector), 135, 138–39; in *A Late Divorce* (Yehoshua), 187; in life and life in death, 239n38; as living, 28, 33, 38, 42; mourning, 16, 32, 42; nationalism and, 203; ontology of, 42; in poetry, 28; proximity to paradox, 36; in "Rain on a Battlefield" (Amichai), 202–3, 205; of reader, 33–40; the self and, 30, 31, 32; smell of, 65; sound and, 243n8; by suicide, 66, 68; through reading, 30; tombstones, 36–37; in *The Well-Wrought Urn* (Brooks), 239n38; in *The Sound and the Fury*, 65, 66, 68
Deconstruction vs. New Criticism, 238n15
Derrida, Jacques: on absent sound, 61; on the crypt, 27; ethics of alterity, 16, 31–32, 33, 42, 61, 238n16, 242n6; hauntology, 16, 33, 38; melancholia and, 32–33, 42; on mourning, 32; the Other and, 16, 221; link to New Criticism, 238n15; on refusal, 42; on the self, 27
difference, erasure of, 209
difficulty of reading, 57, 118, 141
disintegration: in the Bible, 176; as defense mechanism, 272n60; Harshav and, 163; integration and, 161–62, 163, 209; Israel and, 155, 161–62, 182; self-, 37, 51; social disintegration, 150, 172, 180, 182, 185, 192
disinterestedness, 29, 52, 115, 137n10
distraction: in Amichai's work, 212–13; attention and, 132–33; Brazilian New Criticism and, 86, 91, 97–100; colonialism and, 87; hammock and, 108; light as metaphor for, 101, 109; metaphor and, 197; reader (figure of) and, 91, 97–100; as weakness, 91

Donne, John, 31, 35–36, 38, 39, 233n46, 239n34

"Elegy Written in a Country Churchyard" (Gray), 37, 38
Eliot, T. S., 7, 8, 18–19, 129, 157, 160, 232n23; juxtaposition in work of, 201
"Escrever, humildade, técnica" ("Writing, Humility, Technique") (Lispector), 143
ethics: of alterity (Derrida), 16, 31–32, 33, 42, 61, 238n16, 242n6; approaches in this book, 16; ethical listening, 61, 67, 72; ghostly ethics, 73; *The Sound and the Fury* and, 73, 74, 75. See also alterity; otherness; Derrida
Even-Zohar, Itamar, 206
exact, as term, 100–101, 102
exact reading, 86, 137, 197–98; vs. American New Criticism, 5; colonialism and, 107, 108–9, 120, 226; descriptions of, 100–106, 132–34; exhausted reading and, 141–44; Lispector as challenging, 19, 125–26, 128, 137, 145; Rosa and, 112, 115, 119, 120; unselfing and, 121
excess, 205, 213, 241n77
exhausted reading, 17, 125, 128, 141–44, 150, 167, 223

family, 182, 184, 185–86, 194–96, 266n97
Faulkner, William: as aesthetic model, 172; attention in work of, 18, 49; Brooks on, 39–40; family in work of, 185–86; on hearing voices, 72, 78; (dis)integration and, 180, 182–83, 185; Israeli reception, 171–80, 264n62; literary career, 71; models of reading, 44–45; New Critics' interest in, 29, 56; on "Ode on a Grecian Urn" (Keats), 56, 73; race in work of, 40–41, 45–46, 61, 73–78, 185, 247n66; readerly listening, 58–59, 72; reception of work, 40, 56–57, 86, 159, 171–75, 176, 180–81, 182–84, 185–86, 187, 190, 192, 264n63, 268n118; on *The Sound and the Fury*, 57–58, 71–72; the sun in work of, 227; translation into Hebrew, 171–72, 173, 180; urns in work of, 55–58, 72; on writing, 78; *Absalom, Absalom!*, 40–51, 79, 185, 187; "A Rose for Emily," 28, 173, 174, 178–79, 183; *As I Lay Dying*, 60; *Light in August*, 60, 173, 174, 176–78, 180, 183; *Sartoris*, 71. See also *The Sound and the Fury* (Faulkner)
feelings, objectification of, 15
formalism, 4, 57, 155, 165. See also Russian Formalism
Foucault, Michel, 1, 10–11, 105, 232n36
Freud, Sigmund, 32, 169, 262n48

gender and reading, 89, 90, 146–47
Geração de '45, 129, 130, 255n17
"Geshem bi-sde krav" ("Rain on a Battlefield") (Amichai), 202–6
ghosts: ghostly ethics, 73; ghostly readerly attention, 118; ghostly sounds, 60–70; gothic imaginary, 29, 39, 60; hauntology, 16, 33, 38
Gray, Thomas: "Elegy Written in a Country Churchyard," 37, 38
Greenberg, Uri Zvi, 153, 154–55
Grodzensky, Shimon, 171–72, 270n25
Guimarães Rosa, João: on attention, 118; reception of work, 110; theory of reader, 110, 114, 115–16, 120.

See also *O espelho* ("The Mirror") (Rosa)

ha-Ephrati Yosef, 206
Halkin, Shimon, 157, 158–59
hammock, 22; distraction and, 108; reader as on, 91, 226
Harshav, Benjamin, 4, 261n31, 262n34; on Amichai's work, 193, 203–4, 209, 212, 217, 218–19; on gaps in text, 153, 165–66; on integration, 261n29; Jewish hermeneutics and, 20–21; legacy of work, 158; life, 157, 158–59, 163, 168, 199–200; theory of reading, 153, 154–55, 164, 166, 167–68, 260n15; *Ha-Sifrut* (*Literature*), 154; *Now and in Other Days*, 200
Ha-Sifrut (journal), 154, 163, 168, 173, 206, 260n15, 262n33
hauntology, 16, 33, 38
hearing, 61, 62–64, 68, 71
Herrick, Robert: "Corinna's Gone a-Maying," 37
Heyck, Denis, 94, 97, 102, 103, 111, 249n22
Hidden Hitchcock (Miller), 148–50
Hirschfeld, Ariel, 157, 161–62
history: as term, 202; historical reading, 27, 28, 39–40, 43–44, 49–51, 79, 80, 87; imagination and, 49–50, 51; sonic counter- 78
Holanda, Sérgio Buarque de (SBH), 93, 109

imagination: history and, 49–50, 51; play of, 47–48
impersonality: as term, 7, 8, 160; modernism and, 7–8, 160. See also disinterestedness
integration: as term, 261n29; Amichai's work and, 192, 207, 215; attention and, 165, 179, 180, 192, 200; close reading and, 10, 155–56, 198; difficult integration, 207; disintegration and, 161–62, 163, 209; Faulkner and, 174; as fragmentation, 174; Harshav and, 163; poetry and, 169; political policies and, 162; Tel Aviv School and, 165, 168–69, 181; unintegration, 197, 207–17, 223
intensity, 101, 102. See also light as metaphor
intertextuality, 213
Iracema: lenda do Ceará (*Iracema: A Legend of Ceará*) (Alencar), 22, 23, 87–91, 106–10, 140
Iser, Wolfgang, 165
Israeli context: difference within society, 198, 208–9, 217, 268n118; history of, 157, 161–62; (dis)integration and, 182, 185, 208–9; intellectual history, 153, 161; maximalist reading in, 155–56; New Criticism's history in, 4, 8, 10, 156, 158, 269n11; reader (figure of), 150, 192; the sun in, 226–27

Jameson, Fredrick, 57, 175, 264n65
Joyce, James, 61–62, 110, 121, 124, 125
Judaism: Amichai and, 194–96; history, 161, 162; Lispector and, 257n65; reading methods, 20–21; textual sources, 213

Keats, John: "Ode on a Grecian Urn," 36, 37, 56, 72–73, 239n38, 246n52
Kenaz, Yehoshua, 174
Kronfeld, Chana, 5, 16, 173, 209, 213, 268n3, 272n53
Kurnick, David, 2, 224–25

Lacan, Jacques: on listening, 66
Laços de família (*Family Ties*) (Lispector), 145, 258n75
language: allegory, 134–35, 139, 154, 177; alliteration, 60; gesture in, 201; "I," 157; intelligibility of, 57, 137–38; in Lispector's work, 132, 142–43; metaphor, 18, 57–58, 91, 138, 142, 194; nonlinguistic vocalities, 60; onomatopoeia, 60, 63; similes, 196; "yes," 121, 138
laughter, 61, 71
Leavis, F. R., 102
"Le-orekh ha-sdera she-eyn ba ish" ("Along the Deserted Boulevard") (Amichai), 201
letters, love, 43–45
light as metaphor, 101, 109
Light in August (Faulkner), 60, 173, 174, 176–178, 180, 183
Likrat Statehood Generation poetry (Israel), 157–158, 160, 173, 197–212
Lima, Luiz Costa, 130–34, 139, 144
Lins, Álvaro, 94
Lispector, Clarice: exhausted reading, 17, 128, 141–44; genre in work of, 19, 134–36; on her own work, 134; opacity in work of, 131–32, 133; reception of work, 22, 111, 123, 124, 130–34, 255n9, 258n66; temporality in work of, 142; theory of reader, 122, 125–28; theory of reading, 123, 144, 145, 147–48, 149–50; as translator, 142; on writing, 127, 143; *A pesca milagrosa* ("The Miraculous Catch of Fish"), 127; *Escrever, humildade, técnica* ("Writing, Humility, Technique"), 143; *Laços de família* (*Family Ties*), 145, 258n75; *Perto do coração selvagem* (*Near to the Wild Heart*), 123–24, 145; *The Passion According to G.H.*, 147–48. See also *Perto do coração selvagem* (*Near to the Wild Heart*) (Lispector); *The Apple in the Dark* (*A maçã no escuro*) (Lispector)
listening: in *Absalom, Absalom!* (Faulkner), 240n55; ethical listening, 58, 245n43; Faulkner on, 72, 78; hearing, 61, 62–64, 68, 71; to music, 146; narration and, 73; to one's self, 210–11, 226; otherwise, 70; for the past, 47–48, 79; readerly listening, 56, 59; in *The Sound and the Fury* (Faulkner), 74–75, 76–78; to voices, 48, 67–68; witnessing, 78. See also acoustics; hearing; audition; sound
literacy, 88
(un)localization, 155, 160–61, 216–17

A maçã no escuro (*The Apple in the Dark*) (Lispector): excess and exhaustion in reading, 205; exhausted reading, 125–26, 141–44; genre and, 19, 134; plot details, 135, 136–41, 145–47; reading in, 146–47; reception of work, 133, 134, 139–41; symbolism, 140; temporality and, 142–43
maximalist reading: generally, 159, 164, 177, 188, 189–90; close reading vs., 166–67, 170–71; minimalist aesthetics and, 199–207; New Criticism and, 197; Tel Aviv School and, 197, 212
McHale, Brian, 159, 163, 170–71, 176
melancholia, mourning and, 32–33, 42–43
memory, 30, 32, 61, 187, 188, 194–95; aural memory, 61
metaphor, 18, 57–58, 91, 138, 142, 194; in Amichai's work, 194, 196,

200, 201, 202, 207, 210, 211, 212, 215–16, 219, 226, 268n3, 271n46, 272n54; attention intensified by, 200; concatenated metaphors, 194; distraction and, 197
method wars, 2, 224
Miller, D. A.: *Hidden Hitchcock*, 148–50
mind, theory of, 9–10
minimalist aesthetics and maximalist reading, 199–207
mirrors, 113–14, 117, 118–19
modernism: aesthetics of attention, 16–20; Amichai and, 200–201; Brazilian *Instrumentalismo* ("Instrumentalism") and, 130; Coutinho and, 112; Faulkner and, 29, 40, 52; impersonality and, 7–8, 160; Lispector and, 124, 129; New Criticism and, 17, 59, 160, 223; Yehoshua and, 181–182; Rosa and, 110–113; Sound and, 243–244n12. See also Geração de '45, anthropophagic movement, Likrat Statehood Generation Poetry
modernity and attention, 34
Moten, Fred, 75, 77
mourning, 32–33, 42–43

naturalist materialism, 107
North, Joseph, 51–52, 222, 237n8
Nova crítica, 86, 87–88, 91, 95–101

"Ode on a Grecian Urn" (Keats), 36, 37, 56, 72–73, 239n38, 246n52
O espelho ("The Mirror") (Rosa): narration in, 113, 115, 116–17, 118–19, 120–22; as parody of unsavaged reader, 17, 88, 126; plot details, 111, 113–14, 119; unsavaging and, 17, 88, 113
opacity, 131–32, 133

orthography vs. sound, 119
Other, the: acoustic sensibility towards, 56; alterity of, 33, 42; erasure of, 33; hauntology and, 16; openness to, 16; self and, 50, 60, 221; space and, 221; text as, 31. See also alterity; ethics
Oz, Amos, 162

paradox, 34, 35–36, 38–39, 200, 239n38
parody, 111–21, 190
A paixao segundo G.H. (*The Passion According to G.H.*) (Lispector), 147–48
Perry, Menakhem, 159; on Amichai's work, 202, 203, 204–5, 212; on Faulkner, 173, 175, 178–80; on Freudian reader, 262n48; legacy of work, 169; life, 157, 173; teaching, 191; on "The Final Night" (*A Late Divorce*, Yehoshua), 189–90; Theory of Gap Filling, 190; theory of reading, 155, 169–70, 175–76, 179–80, 183
Perto do coração selvagem (*Near to the Wild Heart*) (Lispector), 123–24, 145
"Pgishat ha-kita" ("Class Reunion") (Amichai), 207–12, 213, 215–16
Poetics Today (journal), 159
poetry: as alterity, 52; formal aspects, 130; historical context and, 27, 39–40; integration and, 169; in Israel, 156–58; line breaks, 205; modernist poetry, 129; as national allegories, 154; new critical approaches, 13–14; as object, 6, 222; ontology of, 37; paradox and, 38–39; vs. prose fiction, 193, 197; subjectivity and, 7; as tombstone, 31, 38, 44

Pope, Alexander: "The Rape of the Lock," 36–37
Portela, Eduardo, 102
Portugal (as colonizer), 2, 3, 88–89, 140, 248n1, 250n31, 252n72
positivism, 4, 101–2, 113
possession, 189
posthumanism, 111
Pound, Ezra, 157, 201–2, 270n27
pregnancy, 221
projection, 49–51
psychoanalysis, 214; Freud and, 32, 169, 262n48; Lacan and, 66
PTL: Poetics and Theory of Literature (journal), 159

race: distraction and, 91; racialized histories, 40–41, 45–46, 51, 86, 171–72, 185; readerly listening and, 59; *The Sound and the Fury* and, 73–78; stereotypes, 75, 76. See also Brazilian reader (as figure)
Ransom, John Crowe, 16, 17, 18–19, 20, 33, 235n64
"The Rape of the Lock" (Pope), 36–37
reader: agency of, 18, 29, 36, 50, 165–66; as alive, 37; as dead, 33–40, 58; distraction and, 91; gender of, 89, 90, 231n12; instructions to, 22, 30, 52, 79, 89–91, 104–5, 123, 147–48, 149–50, 165; instructions to (lack of), 49; as listener, 47; in New Criticism, 5, 6, 8, 29, 46; as (a)political, 87; sonic imagination of, 58, 67, 69; as urn, 55, 56, 79, 85
Reader Response theory, 7, 164–65, 180, 231n15
relationality, 216
Richards, I. A., 7, 104, 105, 168–69
Rocha, João Cezar de Castro, 93, 95, 98–99, 111
rodapé criticism, 95–96, 97
romanticism, 18–19

Russian Formalism, 155, 165

Sartoris (Faulkner), 71
savage: Brazilian reader as, 17, 86, 109, 112, 124; extracting from within, 126–27
self, the: boundaries of, 42, 137; the Other and, 50, 60, 221; selflessness, 15; technologies of, 1, 5, 10–12, 51, 95, 105
self-: abnegation, 233n46; annihilation, 117; censorship, 103; civilization, 100; comportment, 108; deadening, 30, 31, 39, 43; dehumanization, 135; depletion, 39, 110, 234n51; discipline, 100, 130, 147; disintegration, 37, 51; draining, 30; emancipation, 87; extraction, 51, 86; formation, 147, 160; formulation, 10; loss, 40; mastery, 125; negation, 10; parody, 190; recuperation, 32; reflection, 115; sufficiency, 52; surveillance, 103; suspension, 155; undoing, 37; unsavaging, 127; vigilance, 103, 117
senses, 62–64, 68, 187, 188, 245n34
Shabtai, Yaakov, 162
Shaked, Gershon, 159, 162, 218–20, 272n66
silence, 63–64, 65, 70, 71, 72, 74
Siman Kri'a (journal), 173, 181, 206
singing, 75–76
smell: as invasive, 245n34
social disintegration, 150, 172, 180, 182, 185, 192
sonic imagination, 58–59, 67
sound: absent sound, 61; as collective experience, 66–67; of cries, 64–65, 70, 79; death and, 243n8; distortions, 75–76; emerging from text, 61–62; ghostly sounds, 59, 60–70; as invasive, 245n34; vs. orthography, 119;

reader auditioning, 69; sonic counterhistory, 78

The Sound and the Fury (Faulkner), 52; attention and, 68–69; ethics and, 74; family in, 185–86; Faulkner on, 57–58; race and, 73–78; readerly audition and, 59, 67; reception of work, 57, 70, 173, 187; senses in, 62–63, 187; soundscape in, 60–61, 62, 65–66, 68–70, 74, 78, 79–80, 243n12; the sun in, 227

Sternberg, Meir, 174, 175; on Faulkner, 173, 180, 264n63, 265n71; Theory of Gap Filling, 190; theory of reading, 155, 159, 175–78

structuralism, 4, 130–31, 155, 159, 168

subjectivity: definitions, 30; as active, 232n36; for American New Criticism, 94; as life force, 155; reading and, 12, 14, 15, 145–48; suspension while reading, 6–7, 15, 52, 155

sun, 225–27

surface reading, 223, 224

suspense as aesthetic quality, 19

Tate, Allen, 9, 15, 16, 27–28, 233n46

Tel Aviv School, 4, 7, 260n13, 260n16; Amichai and, 197, 206; as constructivist, 170–71; criticisms of, 191–92; as genre, 191–92; history of, 163; influences, 155; integration and, 165, 168–69, 181; maximalist reading and, 197, 212; reading methods, 20–21, 164, 197; theory of reading, 156, 165, 187; Yehoshua and, 183–84

temporality, 142, 211–12

Tzemach, Shlomo, 199, 200, 215, 259n5, 269n11

tzmuda (Hebrew, "close"), 167

Ulysses (Joyce), 61–62

unification, 188, 210

unintegration, 197, 207–17, 223

unintengrated reading, 17, 198

universalization, 160, 171

unlocalization, 155, 160–61, 216–17

unsavaging: generally, 87; *O espelho* (Rosa) and, 17, 88, 113; self-, 127; as self-extraction, 86; as self-mastery, 125

unselfing: defined, 1; attention as, 5–12, 85; Coutinho's use of, 95, 106; *experiência* and, 115–16; vs. impersonality, 160; liveliness and, 37; as praxis, 30, 51; reader's responsibility for, 103; reading (encounter of) and, 110; related terms, 7, 8; for Rosa, 115–16; selfless reading, 15, 16; vs. unlocalizing, 160; US context, 86. *See also* unsavaging

urn, the: Brooks on, 27, 31, 38, 43; in Faulkner's work, 55–58, 72, 73; as ghostly, 58; literary work as, 55, 72; in New Criticism, 55; "Ode on a Grecian Urn" (Keats), 36, 37, 56, 72–73; reader as, 55, 56, 79, 85

"Va-hagirat horai" ("And My Parents Migration") (Amichai), 201

Vanderbilt New Critics, 9

Vargas, Getúlio, 106

vase, as metaphor, 57–58, 72

vulnerability, 221

Warren, Austin, 14–15, 16, 20, 224, 261n31

Warren, Robert Penn, 33

wars: Civil War (US), 30, 40–41, 172, 185; Lebanon War (first, 1982), 260n17; Six Days War, 159, 161, 162; War of Independence (Israel),

wars *(continued)*
  157, 197, 202, 208; World War II, 106, 271n48; Yom Kippur War, 161
Wellek, René, 4, 14–15, 16, 20, 129, 158, 164, 223–24, 261n31
The Well Wrought Urn: Studies in the Structure of Poetry (Brooks): generally, 30; canonization in, 38; death and, 36–37, 44, 52; history and, 50; paradox in, 35; reception of work, 33; theory of reading, 34, 40, 49
wildness, 219
William Faulkner: The Yoknapatawpha Country (Brooks), 31, 39–40, 41, 46–47, 52
Wimsatt, W. K., 6, 13–14, 33
Winnicott, Donald, 197, 214, 216
wonder, 35
Wordsworth, William: "Composed upon Westminster Bridge," 34–35; death and aliveness in, 37
world, 184–85, 196
world literature (academic discipline), 3, 163, 184
writing: handwriting, 146; as technology of self, 11; words and non-words, 127–28, 142–43

Yeats, William Butler, 38, 186; "Among School Children," 37
Yehoshua, A. B.: aesthetics of attention in work of, 18; on comprehension of order, 153; Faulkner and, 159, 180–81, 182–84, 185–86, 190, 192, 263n56; genre in work of, 180–81; integration in work of, 181; reception of work, 267n118; Tel Aviv School and, 183–84; theory of reading, 187, 190–91; "world" for, 184–85; writing career, 180; *A Late Divorce*, 182, 183, 186–91, 267n108; *The Lover*, 180, 182, 186, 266n98

Zach, Natan, 157, 158, 193, 201–2, 203–4, 212, 270n22, 270n27
Zender, Karl F., 60
Zionist teleology, 154, 155, 157; criticism of 161–163, 186, 216

www.ingramcontent.com/pod-product-compliance
Lightning Source LLC
Chambersburg PA
CBHW070752230426
43665CB00017B/2332